What's on the CD?

The CD included with the *MCSE: TCP/IP Study Guide* contains several valuable tools to help you prepare for your MCSE exams. The contents of the folders you'll find on the CD and the steps for installing the various programs are de⬚⬚⬚⬚⬚⬚⬚⬚⬚⬚⬚⬚⬚⬚⬚⬚⬚ ⬚ADME file located in the root directory of the CD for further i⬚⬚

Microsoft's Roadmap to Education

⬚⬚⬚⬚⬚⬚⬚⬚⬚⬚⬚⬚ xam preparation guide that pro-⬚⬚⬚⬚⬚⬚⬚⬚⬚⬚⬚⬚coming an MCSE. To install the *Roadmap to Education and Certification* program to your computer, run the SETUP.EXE program located in the ROADMAP folder.

Microsoft's Personal Exam Prep

An evaluation copy of Microsoft's official exam preparation software for testing your knowledge of TCP/IP. To install this program, run the GOPEPTCP.EXE file located in the EXAMPREP folder. Please see the accompanying Readme file located in the EXAMPREP folder for more information about this product.

Microsoft TechNet Technical Information Network

An evaluation copy of a vast database of information related to Microsoft products and technologics. It includes more than 100,000 pages of articles, technical notes, service packs, and Knowledge Bases. To install the *TechNet Technical Information Network* program to your computer, run the SETUP.EXE file located in the TECHNET folder. For further installation instructions, please read the MANSETUP text file located in the TECHNET folder. This text file also contains the user license agreement for this product.

Transcender Corporation's Certification Sampler

Provides sample exam questions to give you a clear idea of the types of questions you'll encounter when you take your MCSE exams. To install the program, simply run the SETUP.EXE file located in the TRANSCEN folder. Please read the accompanying Readme file in the TRANSCEN folder for more information about both the programs and Transcender Corporation.

MCSE: TCP/IP
Study Guide

October 9, 1996

Dear SYBEX Inc. Customer:

Microsoft is pleased to inform you SYBEX Inc. is a participant in the Microsoft®
Independent Courseware Vendor (ICV) program. Microsoft ICVs design,
develop, and market self-paced courseware, books, and other products that
support Microsoft software and the Microsoft Certified Professional (MCP)
program.

To be accepted into the Microsoft ICV program, an ICV must meet set criteria. In
addition, Microsoft reviews and approves each ICV training product before
permission is granted to use the Microsoft Certified Professional Approved Study
Guide logo on that product. This logo assures the consumer that the product has
passed the following Microsoft standards:

- The course contains accurate product information.
- The course includes labs and activities during which the student can
  apply knowledge and skills learned from the course.
- The course teaches skills that help prepare the student to take
  corresponding MCP exams.

Microsoft ICVs continually develop and release new MCP Approved Study
Guides. To prepare for a particular Microsoft certification exam, a student may
choose one or more single, self-paced training courses or a series of training
courses.

You will be pleased with the quality and effectiveness of the MCP Approved
Study Guides available from SYBEX Inc..

Sincerely,

Holly Heath
ICV/OCV Account Manager
Microsoft Channel Programs, Education & Certification

MICROSOFT INDEPENDENT COURSEWARE VENDOR PROGRAM

MCSE: TCP/IP
Study Guide

Todd Lammle with
Monica Lammle
and
James Chellis

San Francisco ▪ Paris ▪ Düsseldorf ▪ Soest

Associate Publisher: Steven Sayre
Acquisitions Manager: Kristine Plachy
Developmental Editors: Guy Hart-Davis, Neil Edde
Editor: Kris Vanberg-Wolff
Project Editor: Ben Miller
Technical Editor: David Kearns
Book Designer: Catalin Dulfu
Graphic Illustrator: Patrick Dintino
Electronic Publishing Specialists: Deborah Bevilacqua, Bill Gibson
Production Coordinator: Grey B. Magauran
Indexer: Nancy Guenther
Cover Designer: Anchor Design
Cover Illustrator/Photographer: John Gadja

Screen reproductions produced with Collage Plus.
Collage Plus is a trademark of Inner Media Inc.

Library of Congress Card Number: 96-71018
ISBN: 0-7821-1969-7

Manufactured in the United States of America

10 9 8 7 6 5 4

After the 90-day period, you can obtain replacement media of identical format by sending us the defective disk, proof of purchase, and a check or money order for $10, payable to SYBEX.

Disclaimer

SYBEX makes no warranty or representation, either expressed or implied, with respect to this media or its contents, its quality, performance, merchantability, or fitness for a particular purpose. In no event will SYBEX, its distributors, or dealers be liable to you or any other party for direct, indirect, special, incidental, consequential, or other damages arising out of the use of or inability to use the media or its contents even if advised of the possibility of such damage.

The exclusion of implied warranties is not permitted by some states. Therefore, the above exclusion may not apply to you. This warranty provides you with specific legal rights; there may be other rights that you may have that vary from state to state. The pricing of the book with the Software by SYBEX reflects the allocation of risk and limitations on liability contained in this agreement of Terms and Conditions.

Shareware Distribution

This Software media may contain various programs that are distributed as shareware. Copyright laws apply to both shareware and ordinary commercial software, and the copyright Owner(s) retains all rights. If you try a shareware program and continue using it, you are expected to register it. Individual programs differ on details of trial periods, registration, and payment. Please observe the requirements stated in appropriate files.

Copy Protection

None of the files on the disk is copy-protected. However, in all cases, reselling or redistributing these files without authorization is expressly forbidden except as specifically provided for by the Owner(s) therein.

This book could only be dedicated to our son Joshua, whose patience with his parents during this project reached far beyond his years.

Acknowledgments

THE AUTHORS WOULD like to recognize with much appreciation our friend and colleague Erik Rozell, whose brilliant technical contribution to several chapters in this volume has served to ensure its quality and integrity. Erik is an experienced networking professional who directs his own consulting firm, Net Pro Computer Services, in Southern California's San Fernando Valley. This project owes a great debt to Erik's exacting mind and technical expertise.

Also crucial to the success of this book were the keen insights and guidance extended generously by Craig Russell, a seasoned Microsoft instructor and integration specialist who owns and operates Craig Russell Connectivity Consulting Inc. Craig's astute eye tirelessly examined and edited our pages, while freely offering important advice throughout this work. Craig can be reached at: craigr@mindspring.com

Many thanks are due to our editors, Neil Edde and Kris Vanberg-Wolff. Neil's sharp intellect, wry wit, and positive attitude, combined with his limitless patience, guided the development and evolution of this project. Without Kris's profound ability to direct, organize, and problem-solve, this book would not have been possible. Thanks also to Sybex's Grey Magauran, production coordinator; Deborah Bevilacqua and Bill Gibson, electronic publishing specialists; and Ben Miller, project editor; for all their work to make this book a reality.

Contents at a Glance

Table of Contents

Table of Exercises

Introduction

WHETHER YOU ARE just getting started or are ready to move ahead in the computer industry, the knowledge and skills you have are your most valuable assets. Microsoft, recognizing this, has developed its Microsoft Certified Professional (MCP) program to give you credentials that verify your ability to work with Microsoft products effectively and professionally. The Microsoft Certified Systems Engineer (MCSE) certification is the premier MCP credential designed for professionals who support Microsoft networks.

This book has been certified by Microsoft to help you prepare for the Internetworking Microsoft TCP/IP on Microsoft Windows NT exam. Here you will find the information you need to acquire a solid foundation in the field of Microsoft TCP/IP internetworking, to prepare for the Windows NT TCP/IP exam, and to take a big step toward MCSE certification.

Is This Book for You?

If you want to learn the basics of how Microsoft Windows NT TCP/IP works, this book is for you. You'll find clear explanations of the fundamental concepts you need to grasp.

If you want to become certified as a Microsoft Certified Systems Engineer (MCSE), this book is also for you. The MCSE is *the* hot ticket in the field of professional computer networking. Microsoft is putting its weight behind the program, so now is the time to act. This book will start you off on the right foot.

What Does This Book Cover?

Think of this book as your guide to Microsoft Windows NT TCP/IP. It begins by covering the most basic of TCP/IP concepts, such as:

- What is TCP/IP?
- IP addressing

- Subnet addressing

- How do you install TCP/IP?

Next it covers more advanced topics, including:

- IP routing

- IP address resolution

- NetBIOS name resolution

- Windows Internet Name Service

- Dynamic Host Configuration Protocol

- Internetwork browsing

- Host name resolution

- Connectivity in heterogeneous environments

- Simple Network Management Protocol

- Performance tuning

- Troubleshooting

- The new NT 4.0 with Microsoft TCP/IP

How Do You Become an MCSE?

Attaining Microsoft Certified Systems Engineer (MCSE) status is a serious challenge. The exams cover a wide range of topics and require dedicated study and expertise. Many who have achieved other computer industry credentials have had troubles with the MCSE. This is, however, why the MCSE certificate is so valuable. If achieving MCSE status was easy, the market would be quickly flooded by MCSEs and the certification would quickly become meaningless. Microsoft, keenly aware of this fact, has taken steps to ensure that the certification means its holder is truly knowledgeable and skilled.

To become an MCSE, you must pass four core requirements and two electives. Most people select the following exam combination for the MCSE core requirements for the 4.0 track, which is the most current track:

CLIENT REQUIREMENT

70-73: Implementing and Supporting Windows NT Workstation 4.0

NETWORKING REQUIREMENT

70-58: Networking Essentials

WINDOWS NT SERVER 4.0 REQUIREMENT

70-67: Implementing and Supporting Windows NT Server 4.0

WINDOWS NT SERVER 4.0 IN THE ENTERPRISE REQUIREMENT

70-68: Implementing and Supporting Windows NT Server 4.0 in the Enterprise

For the electives, you have about ten choices. Two of the most popular electives are:

70-53: Internetworking Microsoft TCP/IP on Microsoft Windows NT 3.5x/4.0

70-75: Implementing and Supporting Microsoft Exchange Server 4.0

For a complete description of all the MCSE options, see the Microsoft Roadmap to Education and Certification on the CD that comes with this book.

This book is a part of a series of MCSE study guides, published by Network Press (Sybex), that covers four core requirements and two electives—the entire MCSE track.

Where Do You Take the Exams?

You may take the exams at any of more than 800 Authorized Prometric Testing Centers (APTCs) around the world. For the location of an APTC near you, call (800) 755-EXAM (755-3926). Outside the United States and Canada, contact your local Sylvan Prometric Registration Center.

To register for a Microsoft Certified Professional exam:

1. Determine the number of the exam you want to take.

2. Register with the Sylvan Prometric Registration Center that is nearest to you. At this point you will be asked for advance payment for the exam. At this writing, the exams are $100 each. Exams must be taken within one year of payment. You can schedule exams up to six weeks in advance or as late as one working day prior to the date of the exam. You can cancel or reschedule your exam if you contact Sylvan Prometric at least two working days prior to the exam. Same-day registration is available in some locations, although this is subject to space availability. Where same-day registration is available, you must register a minimum of two hours before test time.

3. After you receive a registration and payment confirmation letter from Sylvan Prometric, call a nearby Authorized Prometric Testing Center (APTC) to schedule your exam.

When you schedule the exam, you'll be provided with instructions regarding appointment and cancellation procedures, ID requirements, and information about the testing center location.

What the Microsoft NT TCP/IP Exam Measures

The Windows NT TCP/IP exam covers concepts and skills required for the support of Windows NT computers running the TCP/IP protocol. It emphasizes the following areas of TCP/IP support:

- Standards and terminology

- Planning

- Implementation

- Troubleshooting

The exam focuses on fundamental concepts relating to Windows NT TCP/IP operation. It can also be quite specific regarding Windows NT requirements and operational settings, in particular about how administrative tasks are performed in the operating system. Careful study of this book, along with hands-on experience with the operating system, will be especially helpful in preparing you for the exam.

Tips for Taking the Microsoft NT TCP/IP Exam

Here are some general tips for taking the exams successfully:

- Arrive early at the exam center so you can relax and review your study materials, particularly tables and lists of exam-related information.

- Read the questions carefully. Don't be tempted to jump to an early conclusion. Make sure you know *exactly* what the question is asking.

- Don't leave any unanswered questions. They count against you.

- When answering multiple-choice questions you're not sure about, use a process of elimination to get rid of the obviously incorrect questions first. This will improve your odds if you need to make an educated guess.

- Because the hard questions will eat up the most time, save them for last. You can move forward and backward through the exam.

- This test has many exhibits (pictures). It can be difficult, if not impossible, to view both the questions and the exhibit simulation on 14- and 15-inch screens usually found at the testing centers. Call around to each center and see if they have 17" monitors available. If they don't, perhaps you can arrrange to bring in your own. Failing this, some have found it useful to quickly draw the diagram on the scratch paper provided by the testing center and use the monitor to view just the question.

- This test is often perceived as the most difficult of the Microsoft Certified Professional tests. Many participants run out of time before they are able to complete the test. If you are unsure of the answer to a question, you may want to choose one of the answers, mark the question, and go on—an unanswered question does not help you. Once your time is up, you cannot go on to another question. However, you can remain on the question you are on indefinitely when the time runs out. Therefore, when you are almost out of time, go to a question you feel you can figure out—given enough time—and work until you feel you have got it (or the night security guard boots you out!).

- Many of the Multiple Rating Items (MRI) questions that ask you "How well does this solution address the problem?" seem to have the same answer: E) Does not meet the requirements and does not work. Although it is not recommended that you answer "E" to every MRI question, if you are stuck, you may wish to answer "E" first, and then go back to them if or when you have time.

- This is not simply a test of your knowledge of TCP/IP, but of how TCP/IP is implemented in Windows NT. You will need to know about Windows NT, NetBIOS, WINS, and DHCP.

- You are allowed to use the Windows calculator during your test. However, it may be better to memorize a table of the subnet addresses and to write it down on the scratch paper supplied by the testing center before you start the test.

How to Use This Book

This book can provide a solid foundation for the serious effort of preparing for the Internetworking Microsoft TCP/IP on Microsoft Windows NT exam. To best benefit from this book, you might want to use the following study method:

1. Study a chapter carefully, making sure you fully understand the information.

2. Complete all hands-on exercises in the chapter, referring to the chapter so that you understand each step you take.

3. Answer the exercise questions related to that chapter. (You will find the answers to these questions in Appendix A.)

4. Note which questions you did not understand, and study those sections of the book again.

5. Study each chapter in the same manner.

6. Before taking the exam, try the practice exams included on the CD that comes with this book. They will give you a good idea of what you can expect to see on the real thing.

If you prefer to use this book in conjunction with classroom or online training, you have many options. Both Microsoft-authorized training and independent training are widely available. Free network training referral services, such as Keeler Education, at (800) 800-1638, can help you locate available resources.

To learn all the material covered in this book, you will need to study regularly and with discipline. Try to set aside the same time every day to study, and select a comfortable and quiet place in which to do it. If you work hard, you will be surprised at how quickly you learn this material. Good luck.

What's on the CD?

The CD contains several valuable tools to help you study for your MCSE exams:

- Microsoft's Roadmap to Education and Certification is a good place to start, if you want to gain an overview of Microsoft education and the process of becoming an MCSE.

- Microsoft's TechNet Technical Information Network demonstration copy is a vast database of technical information relating to Microsoft products. It can also be a very helpful study aid.

- Transcender Corporation's TCP/IP-Cert 1.0 Sampler provides excellent simulations of the real exam questions.

- Self-Test Software's Personal Exam Prep TCP/IP product (demonstration version) can help further test your knowledge of TCP/IP.

How to Contact the Authors

You can e-mail Todd and Monica at their training and consulting company, Globalnet System Solutions:

globalnetsys@earthlink.net

An Introduction to TCP/IP

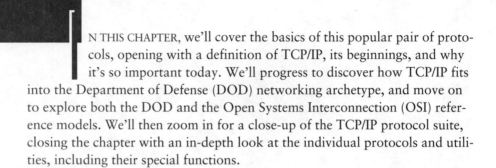

N THIS CHAPTER, we'll cover the basics of this popular pair of protocols, opening with a definition of TCP/IP, its beginnings, and why it's so important today. We'll progress to discover how TCP/IP fits into the Department of Defense (DOD) networking archetype, and move on to explore both the DOD and the Open Systems Interconnection (OSI) reference models. We'll then zoom in for a close-up of the TCP/IP protocol suite, closing the chapter with an in-depth look at the individual protocols and utilities, including their special functions.

Objectives

F YOU ARE unfamiliar with TCP/IP, or are planning to take the certification test, keep these important objectives in mind as you work through this chapter. They are target issues of the chapter, and it's your goal to be thoroughly familiar with them when you've completed it. The exercise and review section at the end of the chapter will also help you achieve these goals. You should be able to:

- Define TCP/IP

- Describe its advantages on Windows NT

- Explain the Request for Comments (RFCs) document

- Describe how the TCP/IP protocol suite maps to a four-layer model

- Identify and describe the protocols and utilities in the Microsoft TCP/IP protocol suite

What Is TCP/IP?

TCP/IP STANDS FOR *Transmission Control Protocol/Internet Protocol*. Essentially, it is a set of two communication protocols that an application can use to package its information for sending across a network or networks. For readers familiar with traditional NetWare protocols, TCP is roughly comparable to SPX (Sequenced Packet Exchange), and IP approximates IPX (Internetwork Packet Exchange).

TCP/IP also refers to an entire collection of protocols, called a *protocol suite*. This collection includes application protocols for performing tasks such as e-mail, file transfers, and terminal emulation. Additional supporting protocols take an application's data and package it for transmission. Two examples of this sort would be the TCP and IP protocols. Still others exist for the physical transmission of data, such as Ethernet and Token Ring. All of these are related, and part of the TCP/IP protocol suite.

Whether we realize it or not, many of us use the *SMTP—Simple Mail Transport Protocol*. SMTP is an application protocol that enables us to communicate by e-mail. E-mail programs running on personal computers, minicomputers, UNIX workstations, and even mainframes can use the SMTP protocol to exchange e-mail between applications.

A Brief History of TCP/IP

The period of computer history spanning the 1950s and 1960s was not a good time for networking. During this Dark Age of Computerdom, almost all computer systems were "technocentric," operating autonomously—they weren't designed to connect to other systems. In that politically incorrect period of computer prejudice, hardware, operating systems, file formats, program interfaces, and other components were all designed to work only with a particular type of computer system, excluding all others.

The Interest in Packet-Switched WANs

In the late 1960s, the United States Department of Defense (DOD) became interested in some academic research concerning a *packet-switched wide-area network*, or *WAN*. The basic idea was to connect multiple, geographically dispersed networks, and allow for data, in the form of *packets*, to be sent to the various locations within the WAN.

The concept of packets can be explained like this: Imagine you have a really long letter to send—so long, it's impossible to fit it into one measly little #10 envelope. You've been given explicit instructions—you must use the #10s. So, you begin to break up the letter into smaller sections, fitting each into an individual envelope. As you address each envelope, you number them sequentially so the recipient at its destination can successfully reassemble your letter. The letter we're talking about is analogous to data that a user has created within an application and wishes to send to another user. The envelopes represent packets. In WANs, information is transported by electronically putting it into packets, which are addressed, sequenced, and then sent on their way.

The *switched* part of a packet-switched network refers to the routing of the packets to a destination. Because packets are addressed individually, they can be transmitted along different physical routes to their ultimate destination. This flexible transmission method is referred to as *packet-switching*. The original reason the DOD was interested in this research was because they wanted to create a fault-tolerant WAN that could carry, command, and control information in the event of a nuclear war. Because a network of this type would have multiple, geographically dispersed sites, and data would be sent in a packet-switched manner, there would be no single point of failure in the system.

The Initial Research Issues Behind the Internet

The research arm of the DOD was an agency called the Advanced Research Projects Agency (ARPA), now called the Defense Advanced Research Projects Agency (DARPA). The mission of this group was to fund basic research that could possibly contribute to the defense effort. It was this agency that funded and managed the project to create a packet-switched WAN. The scientists and engineers that were recruited for this project came from major universities and the private firm of Bolt, Beranek, and Newman (BBN) in Cambridge, Massachusetts. The challenge they faced related to two main areas: *interconnectivity* and *interoperability*.

Interconnectivity deals with transporting information. A software protocol was needed that could package and route information between multiple sites. Out of the concept of the packet-switched WAN evolved the protocol that eventually rose to meet this need: the *Internet Protocol (IP)*.

With the problem of transmission resolved, the team moved on to tackle the next issue—communication. What good was transporting information from an application on a computer *here* if the system's applications on the receiving end *there* couldn't understand it? This would be about as effective as arguing with Bavarian airport staff about your shredded luggage in Swahili—you'd be hearing each other loud and clear, but failing to communicate because you spoke different languages. As you're sure to be guessing, interoperability has to do with application-to-application communication—the interpreter rushed to the scene. Achieving interoperability was a real challenge. Applications would be running on vastly disparate hardware platforms, with equally different operating systems, file formats, terminal types, and so on. For interoperability to be a reality, a way to bridge all these differences was required.

The solution was to develop a series of standard application protocols that would enable application-to-application communication and be independent of the extensive array of computer platforms. For instance, if a mainframe-based e-mail program and a PC-based e-mail program were both using the same standard e-mail protocol, they could exchange e-mail. This would be possible despite the use of two totally different systems. This same principle was used to create standard protocols for file transfers, terminal emulation, printing, network management, and other applications.

From the ARPANET to the Internet

When the original team of researchers decided to conduct their first test of these ideas, they chose four universities for sites: the University of California at Los Angeles (UCLA), the Stanford Research Institute (SRI), the University of California at Santa Barbara (UCSB), and the University of Utah. In September of 1969, these four sites were connected using 50Kbps (kilobits per second) leased voice lines, and the resulting network was called the *Advanced Research Projects Agency Network*, or *ARPANET*.

Although the original aim of this research was military, it was soon used for other purposes. Researchers at the different sites utilized the ARPANET to log into distant sites and communicate with each other by sending files and electronic mail.

Because the funding for this research was obtained from the U.S. government, and therefore from U.S. taxpayers, the subsequent technology was considered owned by the U.S. public. Since the government hadn't classified the technology as top secret, it was considered to be in the public domain. This meant that any individual, organization, or company could receive documentation of the protocols and write programs based on them. That's exactly what happened. Other universities and research and commercial organizations soon began to use this technology to create their own networks. Some of these networks were then connected to the ARPANET.

Another factor in the rapid growth of this technology was the inclusion of the TCP/IP protocols in the Berkeley version of UNIX. The DOD folks funded two projects that lead to this. First, they had the company Bolt, Beranek, and Newman (BBN) modify the TCP/IP protocols to work with the UNIX operating system. Then they had the University of California at Berkeley include them in their version of UNIX, called Berkeley UNIX or Berkeley Software Distribution UNIX (BSD UNIX). Things from Berkeley get around. Because 90 percent of all university science departments were using this version of UNIX, the TCP/IP protocols quickly gained wide usage, and more and more networks were created with them.

Mainframes, minicomputers, and microcomputers all became hardware platforms for TCP/IP protocols. Likewise, software environments from Digital Equipment Corporation (DEC), International Business Machines (IBM), Microsoft, and many others developed products that supported them. Over time, these networks began to connect to each other. Where there was originally only one, the ARPANET, soon there were many separate networks. Eventually, all these individual, interconnected TCP/IP networks were collectively referred to as the Internet, or more simply, The Net.

The Internet Today

Though the numbers increase with each day, the Internet connects about 40 million users worldwide. The following is a very short list of some of the networks on the Internet:

- NSFNet (National Science Foundation Network)

- SPAN (Space Physics Analysis Network)

- CARL (Colorado Alliance of Research Libraries)

- LawNet: Columbia Law School Public Information Service

- The WELL (Whole Earth 'Lectronic Link)

- E.T.Net: The National Library of Medicine

- USEnet: A very large bulletin board system made up of thousands of different conferences

We commonly use the Internet for sending e-mail. The TCP/IP protocol that relates to this function is SMTP. As mentioned earlier, this protocol allows people from all over the world, using disparate hardware and software platforms, to communicate with one another.

Another common application of the Internet is to transfer files. Someone on a Macintosh computer in Iowa can download a file from a minicomputer in Norway. This type of file transfer is accomplished, in part, by the File Transfer Protocol (FTP) running on both machines.

A third frequently used application is *terminal emulation*, sometimes called *remote login*. TCP/IP's *Telnet* protocol allows a user to log in to a remote computer. The computer logging in acts as, or emulates, a terminal off the remote system; hence, the term terminal emulation.

Locating Information on the Internet

Surfing "The Net" has become so popular that it may soon be added to the Olympics like snowboarding. A reason for this is that whether you garden to Mozart, or bungee-jump to Pearl Jam, there's something for you there. Yes, a great feature of the Internet is its astounding amount of information and other resources, like shareware and freeware. However, as answers often lead to more questions, this enormous expanse of information does often raise a few concerns for you and me staring into the screen.

Let's explore this a bit. Imagine this: There you are—just you and your computer and your mind racing with all the amazing stuff you've heard can be found on The Net. You fire up Ol' Bessie—your computer may, of course, have a different name—and the screen crackles to life. With heady anticipation, you click on the Internet icon, listen for that squeal/collision, modem noise, and...there it is! THE INTERNET. The Information superhighway that, full of promise, can lead nowhere fast, like a bad relationship, if you don't know what to do with it.

Has this been you? You know the information you are looking for. You know it's out there...but where? And what's the easiest way to get there? Fortunately, TCP/IP has application protocols that address these issues. The following are four methods of finding information on the Internet, known as *information retrieval services.*

- WAIS
- Archie
- Gopher
- World Wide Web (WWW)

WAIS

Wide Area Information Servers allow you to search for a specific document inside a database. You can Telnet to DS.INTERNIC.NET to access a *WAIS* client. Log in as wais, without a password. WAIS searches may also be done in the WWW.

Archie

A program called *Archie* was created to help users find files. Archie works by indexing a large number of files. Periodically, participating Internet host computers will download a listing of their files to a few specified computers called *Archie servers*. The Archie server then indexes all these files.

When you are looking for a specific file, you can run the Archie client software and *query* (search through) the Archie server. The Archie server will examine its indexes and send back a description and location of the files that match your query. You can then use FTP to transfer the file or files. Archie is essentially an indexing and search tool.

Gopher

Another great Internet tool is *Gopher*. Created at the University of Minnesota, where the school mascot is a gopher, it organizes topics into a menu system and allows you to access the information on each topic listed. Through its menu system, you can see at a glance what information is available there. This menu system includes many levels of submenus, allowing you to burrow down to the exact type of information you're looking for. When you choose an item, Gopher transparently transfers you to another system on the Internet where your choice resides.

Gopher actually uses the Telnet protocol to log you into the other system. This action is hidden from users, who just see the Gopher menu interface. This means that Gopher doesn't merely tell you where your information is located, as Archie does, but also transparently takes you to it. Gopher could be characterized as a menuing tool, a search tool, and a navigation tool that sends you places.

World Wide Web

The *World Wide Web (WWW)* is a type of data service running on many computers on the Internet. These computers utilize a type of software that allows for text and graphics to have cross-links to other information. You can access a WWW server, and a particular Web page, to see a great—depending on its creator's talent—graphic display of text, pictures, icons, colors, and other elements.

To access the Web server, you use client software called a *browser program*. With a browser, you can choose an element on the Web page, which can then cross-link you to a computer animation, or play sounds, or display another Web page. Browsers can even contact another Web server located across the world. All the Web servers on the Internet are collectively referred to as the World Wide Web (WWW) and can be thought of as Jungian consciousness for computers.

The most popular World Wide Web browsers are Netscape's Navigator and Microsoft's Internet Explorer.

Request for Comments (RFCs)

In Life, if it's there long enough, politics will find it. Sometimes this is good. Sometimes its absolutely necessary, as is the case when the goal is setting *standards* for TCP/IP. These standards are published in a series of documents called *Request for Comments*, or *RFCs*, and they describe the internal workings of the Internet.

RFC's and standards are not one and the same. Though many are actual standards, some RFC's are there for informational purposes or to describe a work in progress. Still others exist as a sort of forum, providing a place for industry input relevant to the process of updating IP standards.

The Internet's standardization process resembles that of a bill becoming a law. Similarities include the fact that there exists more than one governing body and interested parties watching closely and making decisions about it. Another resemblance is that an RFC document goes through several stages, each subjecting it to examination, analysis, debate, critique, and testing on its way to becoming a standard.

First, an individual, company, or organization proposing a new protocol, improvement to an existing protocol, or even simply making comments on the state of the Internet, creates an RFC. If it deems it worthy, after at least a six-month wait, the *IESG (Internet Engineering Steering Group)* promotes the RFC to the status of *Draft Standard*, where it reenters the arena of review before finally becoming a bonafide *Internet Standard*. It is then published and assigned a permanent RFC number.

If the standard is changed or updated in any way, it gets a whole new number, so rest assured—you've got the latest model. Also handy to note: If what you're looking at *is* a revised edition, the dated version or versions are referenced on its title page. Also noteworthy, a letter that follows an RFC's number indicates the status of that RFC (for example, RFC 1390H). The following is a list of status designations for Internet protocols:

- Historic: Protocols that have either been outmoded or are no longer undergoing consideration for standardization

- Experimental: Protocols being experimented with

- Informational: Exactly what you might think

- Proposed Standard: Being analyzed for future standardization

- Draft Standard: In home stretch—the final review period prior to becoming a standard

- Standard: An Internet protocol which has arrived, and is fully official

There are also instructions for the treatment of Internet protocols. They are:

- Limited: Of possible use to some computer systems. Highly specialized or experimental protocols are sometimes given this designation. Historic protocols can be given this status as well.

- Elective: These protocols may possibly be implemented.

- Recommended: These should be implemented.

- Required: Protocols considered a "must." They are required to be implemented on the Internet.

Important to note is the fact that not every protocol enjoying wide usage on the Net is an Internet standard. TCP/IP's *NFS (Network File System)* is a stellar example. Developed by Sun Microsystems, the NFS is a critical TCP/IP protocol, and is therefore inextricably entwined with the Internet. This protocol, though indispensable, has not received approval from the IAG, and so cannot be given the status of Standard.

Internet Activities Board (IAB)

The *IAB* is a committee responsible for setting Internet standards and for managing the process of publishing RFCs. The IAB is in charge of two task forces: the *Internet Research Task Force (IRTF)* and the *Internet Engineering Task Force (IETF)*. The IRTF is responsible for coordinating all TCP/IP-related research projects. The IETF focuses on problems on the Internet.

For more information on the Internet, try (you guessed it) the Internet. There's a memo called Internet Official Protocol Standards, and the last time I checked, its publishing number was RFC 1800. It describes the above process much more thoroughly than space allows us here.

InterNIC Directory and Database Services

The *InterNIC Directory and Database*, provided by AT&T, is a service that furnishes us with sources of information about the Internet, including RFCs. A WHOIS server provides a white page directory of Internet users and a Gopher database provides access to Internet documents. InterNIC is a primary depository that offers many options for retrieval. Have fun!

One of the best ways to check out RFCs, and to get up-to-date information about their sources, is to send electronic mail to: rfc-info@ISI.EDU, including the message: help: ways_to_get_rfcs. If you aren't looking for a specific RFC, download a file named rfc—inde.txt, which offers the complete banquet of all the RFCs in the whole-wide-world. RFCs may be obtained via FTP from these servers:

- `DS.INTERNIC.NET` (InterNIC Directory and Database Services)

- `NIS.NSF.NET`

- `NISC.JVNC.NET`

- `FTP.ISI.EDU`

- `WUARCHIVE.WUSTL.EDU`

- `SRC.DOC.IC.AC.UK`

- `FTP.NCREN.NET`

- `FTP.SESQUI.NET`

- `NIS.GARR.IT`

First Section Summary

Y OU BEGAN YOUR foray into the TCP/IP Jungle with an introduction, during which you learned that TCP/IP is a pair of popular communication protocols an application can use to transmit its data across a network or networks. You found that TCP/IP also refers to a protocol suite: a collection of protocols that perform tasks like e-mail, file transfers, and terminal emulation, and that these protocols enjoy dutiful support from others that package their data for transmission.

Shovels in hand, you moved on to dig into TCP/IP's history, unearthing the research on packet-switched WANs, finding out that the switched part of this type of network refers to the routing of the packets to a destination. Because packets are addressed individually, they can be transmitted along different physical routes to their ultimate destination. Hence, the term packet-switched. You found that our taxpayer dollars do actually fund important things, like the military project initiated by the DOD that started it all, resulting in the first network, ARPANET, and you unearthed the important role U.C. Berkeley played in the expansion and dispersal of TCP/IP through BSD UNIX.

Upon emerging from our romp in the archives, you found yourself caught in The Net and helpless—until being rescued by your guides: WAIS, Archie, Gopher, and a very famous one known as the World Wide Web, or WWW. While Archie is there to help users find files, WAIS allows you to search for a specific document inside a database by indexing a large number of them. Gopher doesn't merely tell you where your information is located, but also transparently takes you to it. WWW uses client software called a browser program, and can put on quite a show complete with graphic displays of text, pictures, icons, colors, and sounds.

These brave guides masterfully macheted a path through the dense forest of Request for Comments. You learned that Request for Comments, or RFCs, are a published series of documents of protocol standards for the Internet, and that they describe the internal workings of it. You also learned about the careful process undergone by a proposal becoming a standard, as well as the different classifications of RFC documents: historic, experimental, informational, proposed, draft, and finally, full-blown standard. We also discussed the requirements for how standards enjoying differing status were to be treated: limited, elective, recommended, and required. You then discovered some handy ways to locate RFCs on the Net.

The TCP/IP Protocol Suite and the DOD Networking Model

COMPUTERS, LIKE PEOPLE, become confused and offended when protocols for proper communication aren't followed. Give one an offending command once too often, and the screen just might go dark on you—complete rejection! Try that on a person, and lo an' behold... same thing happens. The TCP/IP protocol suite is essentially an integration of various communications functions governed by strict, required, and agreed-upon rules for how they are performed, implemented, and so on. The required, agreed-upon rules part refers to the standard class of protocols we talked about in our discussion of RFCs. The DOD's networking model conforms to the *International Standards Organization's (ISO) model*, which is similar in concept to the *Open Systems Interconnection (OSI)* reference model. Before we see how they all compare, let's take a look at the general concept of reference models.

Reference Models: An Overview

A *reference model* is a conceptual blueprint of how communications should take place. It addresses all the processes that are required for effective communication. These processes are divided into logical groupings called *layers*.

When a communication system is designed in this manner, it's known as *layered architecture*.

Think of it like this: Imagine you and some friends want to start a company. One of the first things you'd do is sit down and think through the things that must be done, who will do them, in what order, and how they relate to each other. Ultimately, you might group these tasks into departments. Let's say you decide on having an order-taking department, an inventory department, and a shipping department. Each of your departments have their own unique tasks keeping them very busy, requiring them to focus on only their own duties.

In this scenario, departments are a metaphor for the layers in a communication system. For things to run smoothly, each department will have to trust and rely heavily on the others to do their jobs and handle their special responsibilities. In your planning sessions, you'll probably take notes to document the meeting. The entire process will then be recorded for you to discuss later, agreeing upon standards of operation that will serve as your business blueprint, or reference model, if you will.

Once your business is launched, your department heads, armed with the part of the blueprint relating to their department, will need to develop practical methods to implement the tasks assigned to them. These practical methods, or protocols, will need to be classified into a Standard Operating Procedures manual, and followed closely. The various procedures in your manual will have different reasons for having been included, as well as varying degrees of importance and implementation. If you form a partnership, or acquire another company, it will be imperative for their business protocols—their business blueprint—to match yours.

Software developers can use a reference model to understand computer communication processes, and to see what types of functions need to be accomplished on any one layer. If they are developing a protocol for a certain layer, all they need to concern themselves with is their chosen layer's functions, not those of any other layer. The other functions will be handled by some other layer and protocol. The technical term for this idea is *binding*. The communication processes that are related to each other are bound, or grouped together, at a particular layer.

Advantages of Reference Models

The advantages of using a model are many. Remember, because developers know that functions they're not currently working on will be handled by another layer, they can confidently focus on just one layer's functions. This promotes specialization. Another benefit is that if changes are made to one layer, it doesn't necessarily change anything with the other layers.

Suppose an executive in your company, who's in the management layer, sends a letter. This person doesn't necessarily care if his or her company's shipping department, a different layer, changes from UPS to Federal Express, or vice-versa. All they're concerned with is the letter, and the recipient of the letter. It is someone else's job to see to its delivery. The technical phrase for this idea is *loose coupling*. Phrases you've probably heard more often go like: "It's not *my* fault—its not my department!" Or: "So-'n-So's group always messes up stuff like this—we never do!" Loose coupling provides for a *stable* protocol suite. Passing the buck doesn't.

Another big advantage is *compatibility*. If software developers adhere to the specifications outlined in the reference model, all the protocols written to conform to that model will work together. This is very good. Compatibility creates the potential for a large number of protocols to be written and used.

Physical and Logical Data Movement

The two additional concepts that need to be addressed in a reference model are the *physical movement of data*, and the *logical movement of data*.

As illustrated in Figure 1.1, the physical movement of data begins by going down the model. For example, an application creates some information. It passes it down to a communication protocol that packages it and hands it down to a transmission protocol for its actual physical transmission. The data then moves across the model, which signifies it moving across some type of physical channel—like cable, fiber, or radio frequencies and microwaves.

When the data reaches the destination computer, it moves up the model. Each layer at the destination only sees and deals with the data that was packaged by its counterpart on the sending side. Referring back to our analogy about the executive and the letter, the shipping department at the destination only sees the shipping packaging and the information provided by the sending side's shipping department. The destination's shipping department does not see the actual letter because peeking into mail addressed to someone else is a federal offense. The destination company's executive is the party who will open and process the letter.

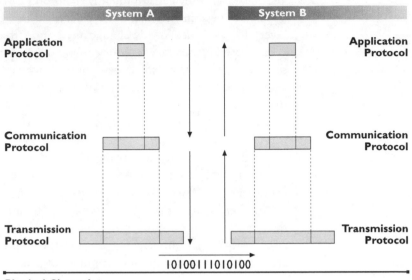

FIGURE 1.1

Physical data flow
through a model

The logical movement of data is another concept addressed in a reference model. From this perspective, each layer is only communicating with its counterpart layer on the other side (see Figure 1.2). Communication in the realm of humans flows best when it happens between peers—between people on the same level, or layer in life. The more we have in common, the more similarities in our personalities, experiences, and occupations, the easier it is for us to relate to one another—for us to connect. Again, its the same with computers. This type of logical communication is called *peer-to-peer communication*. When more than one protocol is needed to successfully complete a communication process, they are grouped into a team we call a *protocol stack*. Layers in a system's protocol stack only communicate with the corresponding layers in another system's protocol stack.

The OSI Reference Model and the DOD Model

The International Organization for Standardization is the Emily Post of the protocol world. Just like Ms. Post, who wrote the book setting the standards—or protocols—for human social interaction, the OSI developed the OSI reference model as the guide and precedent for an open protocol set.

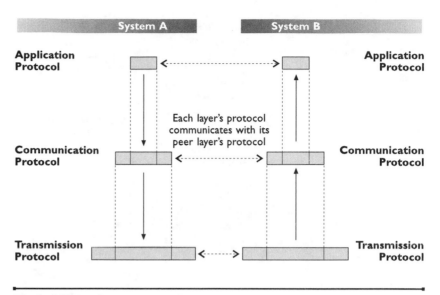

Physical Channel

Defining the etiquette of communication models, it remains today the most popular means of comparison for protocol suites. The OSI reference model has seven layers:

- Application

- Presentation

- Session

- Transport

- Network

- Data Link

- Physical

Figure 1.3 shows the way these "macro-layers" fit together.

The Application, Presentation, and Session Layers

The OSI model's top three layers—Application, Presentation, and Session—deal with functions that aid applications in communicating with other applications.

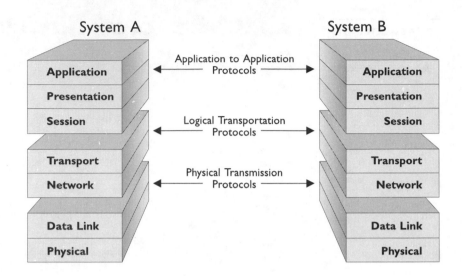

FIGURE 1.3

The macro-layers of the
OSI reference model

They specifically deal with tasks like filename formats, code sets, user interfaces, compression, encryption, and other functions relating to the exchange occurring between applications.

THE APPLICATION LAYER At the *Application layer* reside the many services and protocols that user applications require and employ to communicate with one another over a network. Commonly, these responsibilities include network management, remote job execution and file access, directory use, and e-mail functions, as well as user interfaces like Telnet and FTP.

An important thing to mention here is something called an *application program interface (API)*. Used jointly with Application layer services, it is often included by developers of protocols and programs in the package with their products. They are important because they make it possible for programmers to customize applications and reap the benefits of their wares. An API is essentially a set of guidelines for user-written applications to follow when accessing the services of a software system. It's a channel into the harbor. Remember BSD UNIX? It has an API called Berkeley Sockets. Microsoft changed it slightly and renamed it Windows Sockets. I told you things from Berkeley get around!

THE PRESENTATION LAYER The *Presentation layer* gets its name from its purpose: presenting data to the Application layer. It's essentially a translator. A successful data transfer technique is to adapt the data into a standard format before transmission. Computers are configured to receive this generically formatted data, then convert it back into their native format for reading. The OSI has protocol standards that define how standard data should be formatted.

The *Abstract Syntax Representation, Revision #1 (ASN.1)* is the standard data syntax used by the Presentation layer. An example of a situation where this kind of standardization is necessary would be when transmitting numerical data which happens to be represented very differently by various computer systems' architecture. Data compression and decompression, as well as encryption and decryption, are also tasks associated with this layer.

THE SESSION LAYER The *Session layer's* job can be likened to that of a mediator or referee. Its central concern is *dialog* control between devices, or *nodes*. It serves to organize their communication by offering three different modes—*simplex, half-duplex, and full-duplex*—and by splitting up a communication session into three different phases. These phases are: *connection establishment*, *data transfer*, and *connection release*. In simplex mode, communication is actually a monologue with one device transmitting and another receiving. To get a picture of this, think of the telegraph machine's form of communication: .....--..----...---..-...

When in half-duplex mode, nodes take turns transmitting and receiving—the computer equivalent of talking on a speaker phone. Some of us have experienced proper conversation etiquette being forced upon us by the unique speaker phone phenomenon of forbidden interruption. The speakerphone's mechanism dictates that you may indeed speak your mind, but you'll have to wait until the other end stops chattering first. This is how nodes communicate when in half-duplex mode.

Full-duplex's only conversational proviso is *flow control*. This mitigates the problem of possible differences in the operating speed of two nodes, where one may be transmitting faster than the other can receive. Other than that, communication between the two flows unregulated, with both sides transmitting and receiving simultaneously.

Formal communication sessions occur in three phases. In the first, the connection-establishment phase, contact is secured and devices agree upon communication parameters and the protocols they will use. Next, in the data transfer phase, these nodes engage in conversation, or dialog, and exchange information. Finally, when they're through communicating, nodes participate in a systematic release of their session.

A formal communications session is connection-oriented. In a situation where a large quantity of information is to be transmitted, rules are agreed upon by the involved nodes for the creation of checkpoints along their transfer process. These are highly necessary in the case of an error occurring along the way. Among other things, they afford us humans the luxury of preserving our dignity in the face of our closely watching computers. Let me explain... In the 44th minute of a 45-minute download, a loathsome error occurs...again! This is the third try, and the file-to-be-had is needed more than sunshine. Without your trusty checkpoints in place you'd have to start all over again. Potentially, this could cause the coolest of cucumbers to tantrum like a two-year-old, resulting in an extremely high degree of satisfaction on the part of his or her computer. Can't have that! Instead, we have checkpoints secured—something we call *activity management*—ensuring that the transmitting node only has to retransmit the data sent since the last checkpoint. Humans: 1; Computers: 0... And the crowd goes crazy!

It's important to note that in networking situations, devices send out simple, one-frame status reports that aren't sent in a formal session format. If they were, it would unnecessarily burden the network and result in lost economy. Instead, in these events, a *connectionless* approach is used, where the transmitting node simply sends off its data without establishing availability, and without acknowledgment from its intended receiver. Connectionless communication can be thought of like a message in a bottle—they're short, sweet, they go where the current takes them, and arrive at an unsecured destination.

The Transport and Network Layers

The Transport and Network layers deal with the logical transmission of data. They take care of the sizing of packets sent and received from each application, and then handle the routing of them. They also set the degree of reliability for packets reaching their destination, and the logical addressing of each machine.

At the *Transport layer*, the data created above it is divided up into the proper sized fragments specified by the kind of technology the network is running. Ethernet imposes a 1500-byte limit for each fragment. Remember our analogy about the really long letter? If your network is using Ethernet, each one of your envelopes could contain no more than that specified limit. One advantage of doing things this way is that no single long-winded machine can steal the show and monopolize the network.

It's also beneficial that errors can be corrected with the greatest of ease. During transmission, the tiniest of errors would require resending the whole message. This would be kind of like having to create a drawing in ink, perfectly, without error, and then making a mistake somewhere along the process. You'd have to get a whole new piece of paper, and start all over. If, on the other hand, you divided up the paper into little sections, each presenting only a small portion of the drawing, and made a mistake on one, you'd only have to redraw that little part with the mistake on it. Much better, right?

This error detection stuff is a big responsibility of the Transport layer, though it can happen at lower layers. The Transport layer has two ways it handles errors during its *reliable delivery* mode. In a way, reliable delivery is like certified mail—it doesn't guarantee the stuff that's sent is perfect, but it does imply the stuff is important. If it weren't, you wouldn't bother with the added time and expense of sending it certified. The certified mail packet's importance also guarantees that someone will check it for damage at the receiving end. Sometimes, the Transport layer handles errors simply by informing the upper layers of their existence. Other times, it will request a retransmission of the fouled packet. Alternately, during *unreliable delivery*, the Transport layer doesn't check for errors. Unreliable delivery is not at all bad. Sending things off on a network with the added requirement of reliable delivery is burdensome to it, costing extra time and reducing the network's performance. So when a network is known to be highly reliable, or when an individual packet contains a complete message, unreliable is the mode of choice. When a packet is individually a message in itself like this, it's known as a *datagram*.

The *Network layer* is where software addressing occurs. There's a distinct difference between the Network layer's software addressing and the lower, data link layer's hardware addressing. Going back to our postal service analogy…software addresses will get you as far as the right street, while hardware addresses designate the full home address—getting the goods all the way to the right mailbox. When messages reach this layer from the ones above it, the Network layer attaches a directive to it that includes both the message's source and it's destination's address, forming a packet ready for delivery. Next, the best route for the packet to take across the network to its destination must be chosen. This is known as *routing*, and is handled by *routers*. Because routing is such a complicated task, routers are nearly always *dedicated* Network layer machines; that is, they have no other responsibilities.

Data Link and Physical Layers

These bottom layers handle the physical transmission of data. They take what is passed down to them and put it into a format that can be sent over a variety of physical transmission media like cable, fiber optics, microwave, and radio. They encode data into different media signals to match the specific media over which they'll be transmitted.

The *Data Link layer* provides the service of ensuring that messages are delivered to the proper device, and translates messages from up above into bits for the Physical layer to transmit. It formats the message into *data frames* and adds to them a customized header containing the hardware destination and source address. All of this added information surrounding the original message forms a sort of capsule around it much like the way various engines, navigational devices, and other necessary tools were attached to the lunar modules of the Apollo project. These various pieces of equipment were only useful during certain stages of space flight, and were stripped off the module and discarded when their designated stage was complete. Data traveling through networks is much the same. A data frame that's all packaged up and ready to go follows this format:

- The *start indicator* is made up of a special bit pattern that alerts devices to the beginning of a data frame.

- The *source address* is the address of the sending device and exists to facilitate replies to the messages.

- The *destination address* is there for obvious reasons. Each Data Link layer of every device on the network examines this to see if there's a match to its own address.

- The *control* portion is included when there's additional information required by individual protocols. These controls are like special handling instructions.

- The *data* is the actual message, plus all the information sent down to the sending device's data link layer from the layers above it.

- Finally, there's the *error control* segment. Its purpose corresponds to its name, and it houses something called a *CRC (Cyclic Redundancy Checksum)*. CRCs work like this: The device sending the data determines a value summary for it and stashes it in with the frame. The device on the receiving end performs the same procedure, then checks to see if its value matches the total, or sum, of the sending node. Hence the term *checksum*.

Checksum works a bit like counting all of the jellybeans in your bag, then passing the bag to someone else to give to your friend. To make sure none of the jellybeans get pilfered along the way, you send a message along with them advising your friend of the total number of jellybeans in the bag, and a bid to recount them. If your friend arrives at the same total, you both can safely assume none were snagged en route—that your jellybeans were successfully transmitted without error.

The *Physical layer* focuses on two responsibilities. It sends bits and receives bits. Bits only come in values of 1 or 0—a Morse code with numerical value. The Physical layer is that which communicates directly with the various types of actual communication media. Different kinds of media represent these bit values of 1 and 0 in different ways. Some use audio tones, while others employ *state transitions*—changes in voltage from high to low and low to high. Specific protocols are needed for each type of media that describe the proper bit patterns to be used, how data is encoded into media signals, and the various qualities of the physical media's attachment interface.

The DOD Reference Model

The DOD model is a condensed version of the OSI model. It is comprised of four instead of seven layers:

- Process/Application
- Host-to-Host
- Internet
- Network Access

Figure 1.4 shows a comparison of the four-layer DOD model and the seven-layer OSI reference model. As you can see, the two are similar in concept, but have a different number of layers with different names.

The DOD model's corresponding layer to the OSI's top three is known as the *Process/Application layer*. A whole lot of work gets done at this layer, and in it is found a vast array of protocols that combine to integrate the various activities and duties spanning the focus of the OSI's Session, Presentation, and Application layers. We'll be looking closely at those protocols in the next part of this lesson. The Process/Application layer defines protocols for host-to-host application communication. It also controls user interface specifications.

FIGURE 1.4

The DOD model and the
OSI model

DOD Model

OSI Reference Model

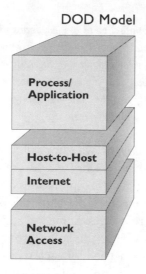

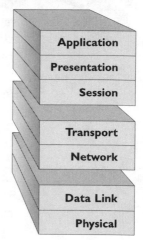

The *Host-to-Host layer* parallels the functions of OSI's Transport layer, defining protocols for setting up the level of transmission service for applications. It tackles issues like creating reliable end-to-end communication and ensuring the error-free delivery of data. It handles packet sequencing, and maintains data integrity.

The *Internet layer* corresponds to the Network layer, designating the protocols relating to the logical transmission of packets over the entire network. It takes care of the addressing of hosts by giving them an *IP address,* and handles the routing of packets among multiple networks. It also controls the communication flow between two applications.

At the bottom, the *Network Access layer* monitors the data exchange between the host and the network. The equivalent of the data link and physical layers of the OSI model, it oversees hardware addressing and defines protocols for the physical transmission of data.

Second Section Summary

N THIS SECTION, we focused on how interdependent and specialized TCP/IP's different layers are, as well as how complex networking actually is. In design, though infinitely more intricate than TCP/IP, our nervous systems can be looked upon as living protocol stacks. Different parts of the system govern different functions with different levels of sophistication. Some parts exist solely to support others, shielding them from the whopping amount of mundane data and menial tasks that life support requires. Would you be able to concentrate on reading this book if, while doing so, you had to remember to breathe in, breathe out, blink, swallow, and digest your dinner? The resulting massive data jam would surely cause our quick demise—and that's only the short list! Like your forebrain layer (the part engaged in reading this book—not digesting dinner), the Process/Application layer is where networking's higher functions get done. As with the forebrain, which the other parts of the brain and body exist to support, the lower layers exist for the support of the Process/Application layer—shielding it from matters of mundane functioning.

We also took a look at reference models—those conceptual blueprints that define the processes of effective computer communication, and describe the logical grouping of these processes into layers. We defined this design to be layered architecture, an organized system without which both human and computer systems would cease to function. Reference models exist because it's not efficient to reinvent the wheel, and for two other very important reasons: specialization and compatibility. This makes product and protocol development much easier—even possible, for software developers.

From there, you followed both the physical and logical movement of data through the communications model. We also explained another way in which humans and computers are similar—in their methods of communication. Communication is easier between peers, or those on the same layer in life. Between computers, this is known as peer-to-peer communication.

Getting into the thick of things, you examined the OSI reference model's seven layers: Application, Presentation, Session, Transport, Network, Data Link, and last, but not in the least bit unimportant, the Physical layer. (NOTE: If you didn't get the pun in that sentence, review the section on the Physical layer immediately!)

You learned that at the Application layer reside the many services and protocols that user applications require and employ to communicate with one another over a network, and that its responsibilities include network management, remote job execution and file access, directory use, e-mail functions, and user interfaces.

The Presentation layer is essentially a translator—a presenter that gets its name from its purpose of presenting data to the Application layer. Also, it was noted that Abstract Syntax Representation, Revision #1 (ASN.1) is the standard data syntax used by the Presentation layer for this task.

Moving on to the Session layer, the mediator or referee concerned with dialog control between devices, you explored three different types of communication modes a communication session can run in: simplex, half-duplex, and full-duplex. We described how this layer can further organize a session by splitting it up into three different phases: connection establishment, data transfer, and connection release.

Progressing down the protocol suite, you encountered the Transport and Network layers, which deal with the logical transmission of data. These layers handle the sizing of packets, and manage the routing of them. They also decide on reliability issues for the transmission of packets and the logical addressing of each machine on the network. A discussion on the Transport layer followed, in which you found that the data created above it is divided up into the proper sized fragments, or packets, and that these proportions are specified by the kind of technology the network is running. We also covered guidelines for choosing between reliable or unreliable delivery. When a network is known to be highly reliable, or when an individual packet or datagram contains a complete message, unreliable is the mode of choice.

Traveling on, you ran into the Network layer, where software addressing occurs. When messages reach this layer from the ones above it, this layer attaches encoded directions which include both the message's source and its destination's address.

Moving further down the model, you reached The Data Link layer, which provides the service of ensuring that messages are delivered to the proper device, and translates information from up above into bits for the Physical layer to transmit. It formats messages into data frames and adds to it a customized, five-part header comprised of the source and destination address, the control, the actual data, and finally, the error control segment.

Hitting bottom, you ended up at the Physical layer that has only a bit part in the show—it sends and receives bits, which come in only two values: 1 or 0. It's the Physical layer that communicates directly with the various types of actual communication media: fiber optics, cable, radio, and microwaves. These different media represent bits differently with some using audio tones and others, called state transitions, using changes from high to low, and low to high voltage.

We then compared the four-layer DOD model to the seven-layer OSI reference model, and found that sometimes less is more. The DOD model has four layers that map to the OSI model's seven in the following manner:

- DOD's Process/Application layer is equal in function to the Application, Presentation, and Session layers of the OSI model.

- It's Host-to-Host layer parallels the functions of OSI's Transport layer.

- The Internet layer corresponds to the Network layer.

- The Network Access layer at the bottom is the equivalent of the Data Link and Physical layers of the OSI model.

The DOD Protocols

WHILE THE DOD model and the OSI model are truly alike in design and concept, with similar things happening in similar places, the specifications on *how* those things happen are different. This leads to a much different suite of protocols for the DOD model than those existing for the OSI model. Figure 1.5 shows the TCP/IP protocol suite, and how its protocols relate to the DOD model layers.

FIGURE 1.5

The TCP/IP protocol suite

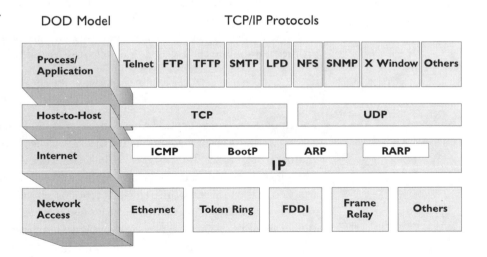

DOD Model   **TCP/IP Protocols**

| Process/Application | Telnet | FTP | TFTP | SMTP | LPD | NFS | SNMP | X Window | Others |

| Host-to-Host | TCP | UDP |

| Internet | ICMP | BootP | ARP | RARP | IP |

| Network Access | Ethernet | Token Ring | FDDI | Frame Relay | Others |

Process/Application Layer Protocols

As we explored earlier, one of the design goals of the original creators of the Internet was to have applications that could run on different computer platforms and yet, somehow, still communicate. The cavalry arrived in the form of Process/Application layer protocols, which address the ability of one application to communicate with another, regardless of hardware platform, operating system, and other features of the two hosts.

Most applications written with TCP/IP protocols can be characterized as *client/server* applications. This means that there are two major parts to the software involved, and that it's probably running on two different machines.

The server part of this software duo usually runs on the machine where the data is actually residing. This machine is the Big Dog. It tends to be powerful because much of the data processing, as well as storage, is done on it. It works like this: The client software sends requests to the server software for it to fulfill. Some typical requests include searches for information, printing, e-mail stuff, application services, and file transfers.

The server software is sometimes called a *daemon program*. Most daemon programs are usually running in what could be called *sleep* or *background* mode, which means that, like beer-bellied sofa surfers on a holiday weekend, they're loaded, but not actively doing anything. However, unlike the human variety, when someone beckons (or certain events take place, such as a request from a client program), daemons zing to life, and carry out whatever task is commissioned of them. Another function of *client software* is to provide an interface for the user. It also allows you to mess around with the data you've managed to coax from the server.

These matters in hand, we'll move along and investigate just what sort of protocols populate the DOD model's Process/Application layer.

Telnet

The chameleon of protocols, *Telnet*'s specialty is terminal emulation. It allows a user on a remote client machine, called the *Telnet client,* to access the resources of another machine, the *Telnet server.* Telnet achieves this by pulling a fast one on the Telnet server, dressing up the client machine to appear like a terminal directly attached to the local network. This projection is actually a software image, a virtual terminal that can interact with the chosen remote host. These emulated terminals are of the text-mode type and can execute refined procedures like displaying menus that give users the opportunity to choose options from them, accessing the applications on the duped server. Users begin a Telnet session by running the Telnet client software, then logging on to the Telnet server.

Telnet's capabilities are limited to running applications or peeking into what's on the server. It's a "just looking" protocol. It can't be used for file sharing functions like downloading stuff. For the actual snatching of goodies, one must employ the next protocol on the list: FTP.

FTP (File Transfer Protocol)

This is the "grab it—give it" protocol that affords us the luxury of transferring files. *FTP* can facilitate this between any two machines that are using it. But FTP is not just a protocol—it's also a program. Operating as a protocol, FTP is used by applications. As a program, it's employed by users to perform file tasks by hand. FTP also allows for access to both directories and files, and can also accomplish certain types of directory operations, like relocating into different ones. FTP teams up with Telnet to transparently log you in to the FTP server, and then provides for the transfer of files.

Wow! Obviously, a tool this powerful would need to be secure—and FTP is! Accessing a host through FTP is only the first step. Users must then be subjected to an authentication login that's probably secured with passwords and usernames placed there by system administrators to restrict access. (And you thought this was going to be easy!) Not to fear, you can still get in by adopting the username "anonymous," but what you'll gain access to once in there will be limited.

Even when being employed by users manually as a program, FTP's functions are limited to listing and manipulating directories, typing file contents, and copying files between hosts. It can't execute remote files as programs.

At this point, a formal apology to all those UNIX wizards in the audience is due. WE ARE SORRY FOR CAPITALIZING FTP EVEN THOUGH IT'S A PROPER NOUN-CRONYM. We must note here that even if you're not a UNIX whiz, capitalizing FTP out there on The Net is not wise. Why are we mentioning UNIX? FTP has its origins in it, that's why—and many devices and networks out there use it as their operating system. Anybody familiar with UNIX, even remotely (pun intended), knows that it's very important not to offend UNIX. Capitalizing FTP as a command out there in Networkland could result in a black screen of death. This is because UNIX, even though it is capitalized, is case-sensitive. Most of its commands, directories, and filenames accept only the lowercase variety, and UNIX is much more likely to be gracious if you command things in the way IT prefers. Windows NT isn't case-sensitive, although it does recognize both upper and lowercase characters in its filenames. Operating Windows NT, you may type in a command any way you please. But remember, not everyone is running NT—instead, just be on the safe side and type in the command, `ftp`*.*

TFTP (Trivial File Transfer Protocol)

TFTP is the stripped-down, stock version of FTP, though it's the protocol of choice if you know exactly what you want, and where it is to be found. It doesn't spoil you with the luxury of functions that FTP does. TFTP has no directory browsing abilities; it can do nothing but give and receive files. This austere little protocol also skimps in the data department, sending much smaller blocks of data than FTP. Also noteworthy is that TFTP will only open boring, public files, thereby depriving you of both the rush of having gotten away with something *and* the feeling of being special and privileged.

NFS (Network File System)

Introducing...*NFS*! This is a jewel of a protocol specializing in file sharing. It allows two different types of file systems to interoperate. It's like this...Suppose the NFS server software is running on a NetWare server, and the NFS client software is running on a UNIX host. NFS allows for a portion of the RAM on the NetWare server to transparently store UNIX files, which can, in turn, be used by UNIX users. Even though the NetWare file system and the UNIX file system are unlike—they have different case sensitivity, filename lengths, security, and so on—both the UNIX users and the NetWare users can access that same file with their normal file systems, in their normal way.

Imagine yourself as an African back at the airport in Bavaria, heading toward the baggage claim area. With NFS in tow, you're equipped to actually retrieve your luggage, in a non-annihilated state, and get it through customs—all whilst chatting glibly in Swahili as you normally would! Additionally, the good news doesn't end there. Where Telnet, FTP, and TFTP are limited, NFS goes the extra mile. Remember that FTP cannot execute remote files as programs? NFS can! It can open a graphics application on your computer at work, and update the work you did on the one at home last night on the same program. NFS has the ability to import and export material—to manipulate applications remotely.

SMTP (Simple Mail Tranport Protocol)

Out of baggage-claim, and into the mail room.... *SMTP*, answering our ubiquitous call to e-mail, uses a *spooled, or queued,* method of mail delivery. Once a message has been sent to a destination, the message is spooled to a device—usually a disk. The server software at the destination posts a vigil, regularly checking this spool for messages, which upon finding, proceeds to deliver to their destination.

LPD (Line Printer Daemon)

This protocol is designed for printer sharing. The *LPD* daemon, along with the *LPR (Line Printer)* program, allows print jobs to be spooled and sent to the network's printers.

X Windows

Designed for client-server operations, *X Windows* defines a protocol for the writing of graphical user interface-based client/server applications. The idea is to allow a program, called a client, to run on one computer and allow it to display on another computer that is running a special program called a window server.

SNMP (Simple Network Management Protocol)

Just as doctors are better equipped to maintain the health of their patients when they have the patient's history in hand, network managers are at an advantage if they possess performance histories of the network in their care. These case histories contain valuable information that enables the manager to anticipate future needs and analyze trends. By comparing the network's present condition to its past functioning patterns, managers can more easily isolate and troubleshoot problems.

SNMP is the protocol that provides for the collection and manipulation of this valuable network information. It gathers data by *polling* the devices on the network from a management station at fixed intervals, requiring them to disclose certain information. When all is well, SNMP receives something called a *baseline*—a report delimiting the operational traits of a healthy network. This handy protocol can also stand as a watchman over the network, quickly notifying managers of any sudden turn of events. These network watchmen are called *agents,* and when aberrations occur, agents send an alert called a *trap* to the management station.

The sensitivity of the agent, or threshold, can be increased or decreased by the network manager. An agent's threshold is like a pain threshold; the more sensitive it is set to be, the sooner it screams an alert. Managers use baseline reports to aid them in deciding on agent threshold settings for their networks. The more sophisticated the management station's equipment is, the clearer the picture it can provide of the network's functioning. More powerful consoles have better record-keeping ability, as well as the added benefit of being able to provide enhanced graphic interfaces that can form logical portraits of network structure.

Host-to-Host Layer Protocols

As you learned earlier, the broad goal of the Host-to-Host layer is to shield the upper layer applications from the complexities of the network. This layer says to the upper layer, "Just give me your data, with any instructions, and I'll begin the process of getting your information ready for sending." The following sections describe the two main protocols at this layer.

TCP (Transmission Control Protocol)

TCP has been around since networking's early years when WANs weren't very reliable. It was created to mitigate that problem, and reliability is TCP's strong point. It tests for errors, resends data if necessary, and reports the occurrence of errors to the upper layers if it can't manage to solve the problem itself.

This protocol takes large blocks of information from an application and breaks them down into *segments*. It numbers and sequences each segment so that the destination's TCP protocol can put the segments back into the large block the application intended. After these segments have been sent, TCP waits for acknowledgment for each one from the receiving end's TCP, retransmitting the ones not acknowledged.

Before it starts to send segments down the model, the sender's TCP protocol contacts the destination's TCP protocol in order to establish a connection. What is created is known as a *virtual circuit*. This type of communication is called *connection-oriented*. During this initial handshake, the two TCP layers also agree on the amount of information that is to be sent before the recipient TCP sends back an acknowledgment. With everything agreed upon in advance, the stage is set for reliable Application layer communication to take place.

TCP is a full-duplex connection, reliable, accurate, jellybean-counting protocol, and establishing all these terms and conditions, in addition to following through on them to check for error, is no small task. It's very complicated, and very costly in terms of network overhead. Using TCP should be reserved for use only in situations when reliability is of utmost importance. For one thing, today's networks are much more reliable than those of yore, and therefore the added security is often a wasted effort. We'll discuss an alternative to TCP's high overhead method of transmission, UDP, next.

UDP (User Datagram Protocol)

This protocol is used in place of TCP. *UDP* is the scaled down economy model, and is considered a *thin protocol*. Like a thin person on a park bench, it doesn't take up a lot of room—in this case, on a network. It also doesn't offer all the bells and whistles of TCP, but it does do a fabulous job of transporting stuff that doesn't require reliable delivery—and it does it using far fewer network resources.

There are some situations where it would definitely be wise to opt for UDP instead of TCP. Remember that watchdog SNMP up there at the Process/ Application layer? SNMP monitors the network sending intermittent messages and a fairly steady flow of status updates and alerts, especially when running on a large network. The cost in overhead necessary to establish, maintain, and close a TCP connection for each one of those little messages would reduce a normally healthy, efficient network to a sticky, sluggish bog in no time. Another circumstance calling for the deployment of UDP over TCP is when the matter of reliability is seen to at the Process/Application layer. NFS handles its own reliability issues, making the use of TCP both impractical and redundant.

UDP receives upper-layer blocks of information instead of streams of data like its big brother, TCP, and breaks them into segments. Also like TCP, each segment is given a number for reassembly into the intended block at the destination. However, UDP does *not* sequence the segments, and does not care in which order the segments arrive at the destination. At least it numbers them. But after that, UDP sends them off and forgets about them. It doesn't follow through, check up on, or even allow for an acknowledgment of safe arrival— complete abandonment. Because of this, it's referred to as an *unreliable* protocol. This does not mean that UDP is ineffective—only that it doesn't handle issues of reliability.

There are more things UDP doesn't do. It doesn't create a virtual circuit, and it doesn't contact the destination before delivering stuff to it. It is therefore considered a *connectionless* protocol.

Key Concepts of Host-to-Host Protocols

The following list highlights some of the key concepts that you should keep in mind regarding these two protocols.

TCP	UDP
Virtual circuit	Unsequenced
Sequenced	Unreliable
Acknowledgments	Connectionless
Reliable	Low overhead

Instructors commonly use a telephone analogy to help people understand how TCP works. Most of us understand that before you talk with someone on a phone, you must first establish a connection with that other person—wherever they may be. This is like a virtual circuit with the TCP protocol. If you were giving someone important information during your conversation, you might say, "Did you get that?" A query like that is like a TCP acknowledgment. From time to time, for various reasons, people also say, "Are you still there?" They end their conversations with a "goodbye" of some sort, putting closure on the phone call. These types of functions are done by TCP.

Alternately, using UDP is like sending a postcard. To do that, you don't need to contact the other party first. You simply write your message, address it, and mail it. This is analogous to UDP's connectionless orientation. Since the message on the postcard is probably not a matter of life or death, you don't need an acknowledgment of its receipt. Similarly, UDP does not involve acknowledgments.

Internet Layer Protocols

There are two main reasons for the Internet layer: routing, and providing a single network interface to the upper layers. None of the upper-layer protocols, and none of the ones on the lower layer, have any functions relating to routing. Routing is complex and important, and it's the job of the Internet layer to carry it out. The protocol *IP* is so integral to this layer, the very name of it is the name of the layer itself. So far, in discussing the upper layers, we've begun with a brief introduction, and left any specific treatise on their resident protocols to supporting sections. However here, IP, though only a protocol, is essentially the Internet layer. We've therefore included it in our introductory talk on the layer. The other protocols found here merely exist to support it. IP contains the Big Picture, and could be said to "see all," in that it is aware of all the interconnected networks. It can do this because all the machines on the network have a software address called an IP address, which we promise to cover more thoroughly later, in Chapter 3.

IP looks at each packet's IP address. Then, using a routing protocol, it decides where this packet is to be sent next, choosing the best path. The Network Access layer protocols at the bottom of the model don't possess IP's enlightened scope of the entire network; they deal only with point-to-point physical links.

A second main reason for the Internet layer is to provide a single network interface to the upper-layer protocols. Without this layer, application programmers would need to write "hooks" into every one of their applications for each different Network Access protocol. This would not only be a pain in the neck, it would lead to different versions of each application—one for Ethernet, another one for Token Ring, and so on. To prevent this, IP, lord of the Internet layer, provides one single network interface for the upper-layer protocols. That accomplished, it's then the job of IP and the various Network Access protocols to get along and work together.

All network roads don't lead to Rome—they lead to IP, and all the other protocols at this layer, as well as all the upper-layer protocols, use it. Never forget that. All paths through the model go through IP. The following sections describe the protocols at the Internet layer.

IP (Internet Protocol)

Identifying devices on networks requires having the answers to these two questions: Which network is it on, and what is it's ID on that network? The first is the *software address* (the right street); the second, the *hardware address* (the right mailbox). All hosts on a network have a logical ID called an IP address. This is the software address, and it contains valuable encoded information greatly simplifying the complex task of routing.

IP takes segments from the Host-to-Host layer and fragments them into *datagrams* (packets). IP also reassembles datagrams back into segments on the receiving side. Each datagram is assigned the IP address of the sender and the IP address of the recipient. Each machine that receives a datagram makes routing decisions based upon the packet's destination IP address.

ARP (Address Resolution Protocol)

When IP has a datagram to send, it has already been informed by upper-layer protocols of the destination's IP address. However, IP must also inform a Network Access protocol, such as Ethernet, of the destination's hardware address. If IP does not know the hardware address, it uses the *ARP* protocol to find this information. As IP's detective, ARP interrogates the network by sending out a broadcast asking the machine with the specified IP address to reply with its hardware address. ARP is able to translate a software address, the IP address, into a hardware address—for example, the destination machine's Ethernet board address—thereby deducing its whereabouts. This hardware address is technically referred to as the *media access control (MAC) address*.

RARP (Reverse Address Resolution Protocol)

When an IP machine happens to be a diskless machine, it has no way of initially knowing its IP address. But it does know its MAC address. The *RARP* protocol is the psychoanalyst for these lost souls. It sends out a packet that includes its MAC address, and a request to be informed of what IP address is assigned to its MAC address. A designated machine, called a *RARP server*, responds with the answer, and the identity crisis is over. Like a good analyst, RARP uses the information it does know about it, the machine's MAC address, to learn its IP address and complete the machines ID portrait.

BootP

BootP stands for *Boot Program*. When a diskless workstation is powered on, it broadcasts a BootP request on the network. A BootP server hears the request, and looks up the client's MAC address in its BootP file. If it finds an appropriate entry, it responds by telling the machine its IP address, and the file—usually via the TFTP protocol—that it should boot from.

BootP is used by a diskless machine to learn the following:

- Its IP address

- The IP address of a server machine

- The name of a file that is to be loaded into memory and executed at boot up

ICMP (Internet Control Message Protocol)

ICMP is a management protocol and messaging service provider for IP. Its messages are carried as IP datagrams. *RFC 1256, ICMP Router Discovery Messages* is an annex to ICMP, affording hosts extended capability in discovering routes to gateways. Periodically, router advertisements are announced over the network reporting IP addresses for its network interfaces. Hosts listen for these network infomercials to acquire route information. A *router solicitation* is a request for immediate advertisements, and may be sent by a host when it starts up. The following are some common events and messages that ICMP relates to:

Destination unreachable. If a router cannot send an IP datagram any further, it uses ICMP to send a message back to the sender advising it of the situation.

Buffer full. If a router's memory buffer for receiving incoming datagrams is full, it will use ICMP to send out this message.

Hops. Each IP datagram is allotted a certain number of routers that it may go through, called *hops*. If it reaches its limit of hops before arriving at its destination, the last router to receive that datagram throws it away. The executioner router then uses ICMP to send an obituary message informing the sending machine of the demise of its datagram. This is network population control.

Network Access Layer Protocols

Programmers for the DOD model didn't define protocols for this layer; instead, their focus began at the Internet layer. In fact, this is exactly the quality that makes this model able to be implemented on almost any hardware platform. Obviously, this is one of the reasons why the Internet protocol suite is so popular. Every protocol listed here relates to the physical transmission of data. The following are the Network Access layer's main duties:

- Receiving an IP datagram and *framing* it into a stream of bits—ones and zeros—for physical transmission. (The information at this layer is called a *frame*.) An example of a protocol that works at this level is *CSMA/CD*, or *Carrier Sense, Multiple Access with Collision Detect*. Again, purpose equals name. It checks the cable to see if there's already another PC transmitting (Carrier Sense), allows all computers to share the same bandwidth (Multiple Access), and detects and retransmits collisions. Essentially, it's Network Access layer highway patrol.

- Specifying the *MAC address*. Even though the Internet layer determines the destination MAC address (the hardware address), the Network Access protocols actually place that MAC address in the MAC frame.

- Ensuring that the stream of bits making up the frame have been accurately received by calculating a CRC (Cyclic Redundancy Checksum) jellybean count.

- Specifying the access methods to the physical network, such as *Contention-based for Ethernet* (first come, first served), *Token-passing* (wait for token before transmitting) for Token Ring, *FDDI*, and *Polling* (wait to be asked) for IBM mainframes.

- Specifying the physical media, the connectors, electrical signaling, and timing rules.

Some of the technologies used to implement the Network Access layer are:

- LAN-oriented protocols:

  - Ethernet (thick coaxial cable, thin coaxial cable, twisted-pair cable)

  - Token Ring

  - ARCnet

- WAN-oriented protocols:

  - Point-to-Point Protocol (PPP)

  - X.25

  - Frame Relay

Third Section Summary

TIME FOR THE recap. We've covered a lot of ground in this lesson. Important ground. These are the basics of networking from which all relative technology springs. A solid understanding of it is absolutely necessary, or all the heavy-duty technical stuff that comes later will only serve to confuse you worse than a bat without sonar.

PROTOCOLS...and...protocols...and...ProToCols...and more protocols. Lots of 'em—all different kinds! That's what we discussed. Hopefully, during that discussion, you began to get a picture of how their specialized functions fit into the grand TCP/IP scheme of things—how each one performs a task, or part of a task, and that without its proper execution, the whole system would crash or just plain run amuck. A military-like, chain-of-command-honoring, predictable order is provided by them, satisfying today's growing networking demands.

Order is kept in the Process/Application layer by a cavalry of protocols dealing with the ability of one application to communicate with another, regardless of hardware platform, operating system, and other features of the two hosts running it. The first protocol we discussed was the terminal emulation protocol, Telnet. Telnet allows a user on a remote client machine, called the *Telnet client,* to access the resources of another machine, the *Telnet server.* This is achieved by projecting a software image—a virtual terminal which appears to the Telnet server to be a terminal directly attached to the local network. With Telnet, image *is* everything!

From Telnet, we moved to FTP, the "grab it—give it" protocol that allowed us to touch as well as look. With it, we were given the luxury of transferring files. We found that FTP is more than just a protocol—it's also a program. When it's operating as a protocol, FTP is used by applications. As a program, it's employed by users to perform file tasks by hand. We also found that there's a catch to it all, and learned about built-in security provisos like passwords and usernames required of users during an authentication login process.

Next, we introduced TFTP, the smart shopper's choice. This thin, stripped-down, stock version of FTP works great if you know exactly what you want, and where it is to be found. Where Telnet, FTP, and TFTP are limited, NFS goes the extra mile. NFS can execute remote files as programs, and can import and export material to manipulate applications remotely.

We then discussed SMTP, LPD, and X Windows. SMTP dutifully answers the call to e-mail using a spooled, or queued, method of mail delivery. LPD is there so printers can be shared on the network, while X Windows provides us with a graphical user interface. We wrapped up this layer with the network manager's pal, SNMP, the protocol that allows us to collect and manipulate valuable network information. It gathers data by polling the devices on the network, requiring them to disclose certain information. SNMP sends out baseline reports providing a portrait of a healthy network, and acts as a watchman over the network, quickly notifying managers of any sudden turn of events.

The broad goal of the Host-to-Host layer is to shield the upper-layer applications from the functional complexities of the network. Its two main engines are TCP and UDP. Though both handle transmission issues, they deal with them in very different ways. TCP tests for errors, using CRC's, and resends data if necessary. It faithfully reports the occurrence of errors to the upper layers if it can't manage to solve the problem itself. It takes large blocks of information from above, and breaks them down into segments which it then numbers and sequences so that the destination's TCP protocol can put the segments back into the large block the application intended.

After these segments have been sent, TCP waits for acknowledgment for each one from the receiving end's TCP, retransmitting the ones not acknowledged. TCP is a full-duplex connection-oriented, reliable, accurate, jellybean-counting protocol that offers a lot and costs a lot in terms of network overhead. On the other hand, UDP doesn't offer all the bells and whistles of TCP, and so doesn't require all the network overhead of TCP. It's a thin protocol that's also referred to as an unreliable protocol, but it's an effective one all the same. UDP doesn't create a virtual circuit, as TCP does, and it doesn't contact the destination before delivering stuff to it. It's therefore considered a connectionless protocol.

Downwardly mobile, we traveled onward to Routing Rome—the Internet layer where you met an omniscient network god called IP. IP enjoys this position because of the existence of something called an IP address, which is a software address that all the machines on the network must have. IP, lord of the Internet layer, also provides one single network interface for the upper-layer protocols. Here you learned the network routing axiom: All roads lead through IP.

As do many important people, important protocols have a staff of others who work for them. IP, being no exception, has ARP. As IP's detective, ARP interrogates the network by sending out a broadcast asking the machine with the specified IP address to reply with its hardware address. ARP is able to translate a software address—the IP address—into a hardware address, solving the dilemma. You met another faithful IP employee, RARP, who uses the information it does know about a diskless machine, the machine's MAC address, to learn its IP address and complete the machine's ID portrait. A close associate, also dealing with the problems diskless machines encounter on networks, is BootP, which works by broadcasting a BootP request on the network. A BootP server hears the request, and looks up the client's MAC address in its BootP file.

The last member of the IP staff is ICMP, its managing and message service. Some examples of the kinds of messages ICMP deals with include: destination unreachable, if a router can't send an IP datagram any further; buffer full, if a router's memory buffer for receiving incoming datagrams is full; and time-to-live expired, sent when a datagram runs out of it's allotted hops and is rubbed out by the router at which this happens.

Coming in for a landing at the Network Access layer, we discussed one of the reasons TCP/IP is so popular—because developers didn't define protocols for the Network Access layer. Herein lies its adaptability to almost any hardware platform. Some of its main duties include:

- Receiving an IP datagram and framing it into a stream of bits

- Specifying the MAC address

- Calculating a CRC (Cyclic Redundancy Checksum)

- Specifying the access methods to the physical network

- Specifying the physical media

Lastly, we covered some of the different technologies used to implement the layer, such as Ethernet and Token Ring.

Exercise Questions

T O MAKE SURE you're getting all of this, take a moment to both read and work with the multiple choice and scenario-based questions offered below. Project yourself into the role of the employee facing these real-world challenges, coming up with solutions based on the material learned in Chapter 1. Oh, by the way, we knew that if we put answers here on this page, they would present an irresistible temptation. To keep you honest, we put them in Appendix A. If the urge to cheat is overwhelming, go ahead and peek. However, keep in mind that you'll remember this stuff better if you sweat over it a little first!

Multiple-Choice Questions

1. What is TCP/IP?

2. What are the layers in the four-layer model used by TCP/IP?

3. What core TCP/IP protocols are provided with Microsoft TCP/IP?

4. What parameters are required for a TCP/IP host to communicate in a wide-area network?

Scenario-Based Review

SCENARIO #1 It's Monday morning. Just as you arrive at your desk, your boss calls you into his office, and says he read about TCP/IP in a Microsoft magazine over the weekend. Because he now knows that all Microsoft products are fabulous, he's set on someone implementing MS TCP/IP at all twelve branch office sites. He says that because of your quality work over the past few months, you're his first choice. However, before he names you the project's leader, he wants you to give him a complete explanation of TCP/IP, and how it will meet his networking needs. Can you? Try it.

SCENARIO #2 To get a jump on the competition, you need to find some information on a new, highly efficient protocol being developed. Where would you find this information? How would you access it, and through which server? If you have access to the Internet, try this as an exercise on your computer.

SCENARIO #3 Your boss tells you she spent lunch at the gym, where she overheard a great way to look up information on the Internet. She tells you that it organizes subjects into a menu system, and allows you to access the information on each topic listed. She's frustrated because she can't remember what it's called—can you?

SCENARIO #4 You are the Senior Communication Technician for a small computer store. The sales staff is complaining that they cannot deliver or receive mail on their TCP/IP computers. All other applications on the network seem to work OK. The location of the problem is likely to be on *which layer* of the DOD model?

SCENARIO #5 The IS department is planning on implementing TCP/IP. Your manager, who knows and understands the OSI reference model, asks you "What are the layers in the four-layer model used by the DOD for TCP/IP and how does each layer relate to the OSI reference model?" What do you tell him?

SCENARIO #6 You are the network administrator for a large accounting office. They have seven offices, all connected. You get a complaint call from a remote office about how their workstations cannot connect to the network. After talking with them for a few minutes, it appears that network connectivity is down at all seven offices. What layer of the DOD model is likely at fault?

SCENARIO #7 The accounting department calls you about two problem workstations in their department, complaining that "they're taking turns like twins, with only one being able to log in to the network at a time." All the other workstations in the department are fine. What's the problem, and how do you fix it?

SCENARIO #8 You're the network manager for a large aircraft company. The reservationists have been griping for two weeks about the slow response of their computers. You've narrowed the problem down to noise on the thinnet coax cabling. Which layer of the DOD model is responsible?

SCENARIO #9 Your co-worker calls you because she is confused about the differences between the OSI reference model and the DOD model. She can't figure out where packets are framed with the hardware address and a cyclic redundancy check. What do you tell her?

SCENARIO #10 You're in an interview for an important position at a good company. You've studied hard, and know your TCP/IP. The interviewer asks you, "What is the connectionless protocol at the Internet layer of the DOD model, and what is its function?" Do you stare back blankly, with mouth agape, or answer confidently with....?

SCENARIO #11 After breezing through that last question in the interview, the interviewer then asks you, "At what layer are messages segmented and what protocol is used for segmenting them?" What's your answer?

SCENARIO #12 Your pal just landed a job as a Help Desk operator, and is brushing up on her TCP/IP protocols to prepare for her first day. She calls you with this question: "Ones and zeros are extracted from the cable and formed into logical groups called frames. The hardware destination is then checked, and a cyclic redundancy checksum is performed. If the hardware address is correct, and the CRC matches its original mathematical algorithm, the packet is then sent to which protocol at which layer?" What do you tell her?

SCENARIO #13 You're a software developer who enjoys writing video games to play on the Internet with TCP/IP. You want to use the fastest protocol at the Transport layer of the OSI model to ensure no delay when blowing up all the Morphofreaks. What protocol do you use? Also, at what corresponding layer of the DOD model would this protocol run?

SCENARIO #14 Your UNIX diskless workstations cannot logon to the host. After troubleshooting, you notice that when they boot up, the hardware address is sent to the host, but the host rejects them. Which protocol is asleep on the job?

SCENARIO #15 You need to install network management to keep track of network errors and to baseline for future growth. Which protocol do you use, and which layer of the DOD does it operate on?

Identifying Machines with IP Addressing

N THIS CHAPTER, we'll probe further into the basics of TCP/IP and examine the supremely important subject of how accurate communication is achieved between specific networks and host systems through proper IP addressing. We'll discuss how and why that communication happens, why it doesn't when it fails, and how to configure devices on both LANs and WANs to ensure solid performance for your network.

Objectives

THE FOLLOWING ITEMS are central to this chapter. As you look over the list, make a mental note of them to keep in mind as you read on. You should be able to define and/or perform them when you're finished with this section.

- Define IP address.

- What are the different classes of IP addresses?

- Identify both the network and host IDs in class A, B, and C addresses.

- Identify both valid and invalid class A, B, and C addresses.

- Assign appropriate host and network IDs.

- Understand which network components require IP addresses.

- Understand common IP addressing problems.

- What is a subnet?

- What is a subnet mask, and how does it work?

- What is a default subnet mask, and how does it work?

- Outline a range of valid host IDs for multiple subnets.

- Create an effective subnet mask for a WAN comprised of many subnets.

What Is Addressing?

ONE OF THE most important topics in any discussion of TCP/IP is *IP addressing*. An IP address is a numeric identifier assigned to each machine on an IP network. It designates the location of the device it's assigned to on the network. As mentioned earlier, this type of address is a software address, not a hardware address, which is hard-coded in the machine or network interface card.

The Hierarchical IP Addressing Scheme

An IP address is made up of 32 bits of information. These 32 bits are divided into four sections containing four bytes each. These sections are referred to as *octets*. There are three methods for depicting an IP address:

- Dotted-decimal, as in `130.57.30.56`

- Binary, as in `10000010.00111001.00011110.00111000`

- Hexidecimal, as in `82 39 1E 38`

All of these examples represent the same IP address.

The 32-bit IP address is a structured or hierarchical address, as opposed to a flat or nonhierarchical one. Although either type of addressing scheme could have been used, the hierarchical variety was chosen, and for a very good reason.

A good example of a flat addressing scheme is a social security number. There's no partitioning to it, meaning that each segment isn't allocated to numerically represent a certain area or characteristic of the individual it's assigned to. If this method had been used for IP addressing, every machine on the Internet would have needed a totally unique address, just as each social security number is unique. The good news about this scheme is that it can handle a large number of addresses, namely 4.2 billion (a 32-bit address space with two possible values for each position—either zero or one—giving you 2^{32}, which equals 4.2 billion). The bad news, and the reason for it being passed over, relates to routing. With every address totally unique, all routers on the Internet would need to store the address of each and every machine on the Internet. It would be fair to say that this would make efficient routing impossible even if a fraction of the possible addresses were used.

The solution to this dilemma is to use a two-level, hierarchical addressing scheme that's structured by class, rank, grade, and so on. An example of this type is a telephone number. The first section of a telephone number, the area code, designates a very large area, followed by the prefix, narrowing the scope to a local calling area. The final segment, the customer number, zooms in on the specific connection. It's similar with IP addresses. Rather than the entire 32 bits being treated as a unique identifier as in flat addressing, a part of the address is designated as the *network address*, and the other part as a *node address*, giving it a layered, hierarchical structure.

The network address uniquely identifies each network. Every machine on the same network shares that network address as part of its IP address. In the IP address 130.57.30.56, for example, the 130.57 is the network address.

The node address is assigned to, and uniquely identifies, each machine on a network. This part of the address must be unique because it identifies a particular machine—an individual, as opposed to a network, which is a group. This number can also be referred to as a *host address*. In the sample IP address 130.57.30.56, the .30.56 is the node address.

The designers of the Internet decided to create classes of networks based on network size. For the small number of networks possessing a very large number of nodes, they created the rank *Class A network*. At the other extreme is the *Class C network*, reserved for the numerous networks with a small number of nodes. The class distinction for networks in between very large and very small is predictably called a *Class B network*. How one would subdivide an IP address into a network and node address is determined by the class designation of one's network. Table 2.1 provides us with a summary on the three classes of networks, which will be described in more detail in the following sections.

TABLE 2.1

Summary of the Three Classes of Networks

CLASS	FORMAT	LEADING BIT PATTERN	DECIMAL RANGE OF FIRST BYTE OF NETWORK ADDRESS	MAXIMUM NETWORKS	MAXIMUM NODES PER NETWORK
A	Net.Node. Node.Node	0	1–127	127	16,777,216
B	Net.Net. Node.Node	10	128–191	16,384	65,534
C	Net.Net. Net.Node	110	192–223	2,097,152	254

To ensure efficient routing, Internet designers defined a mandate for the leading bits section of the address for each different network class. For example, since a router knows that a Class A network address always starts with a zero, it might be able to speed a packet on its way after reading only the first bit of its address. Figure 2.1 illustrates how the leading bits of a network address are defined.

Some IP addresses are reserved for special purposes, and shouldn't be assigned to nodes by network administrators. Table 2.2 lists the members of this exclusive little club, along with their reason for getting included in it.

TABLE 2.2

Reserved IP Addresses

ADDRESS	FUNCTION
Network address of all zeros	Interpreted to mean "this network"
Network address of all ones	Interpreted to mean "all networks"
Network 127	Reserved for loopback tests. Designates the local node and allows that node to send a test packet to itself without generating network traffic.
Node address of all zeros	Interpreted to mean "this node"
Node address of all ones	Interpreted to mean "all nodes" on the specified network; for example, 128.2.255.255 means "all nodes" on network 128.2 (Class B address)
Entire IP address set to all zeros	Used by the RIP protocol to designate the default route
Entire IP address set to all ones (same as 255.255.255.255)	Broadcast to all nodes on the current network; sometimes called an "all ones broadcast"

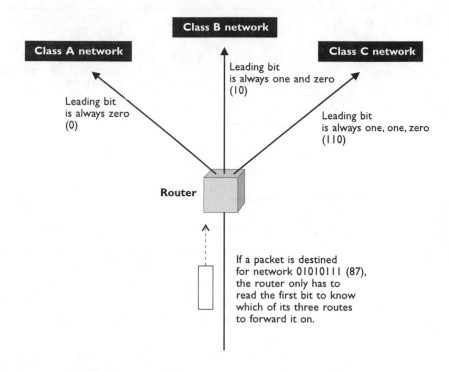

FIGURE 2.1

Leading bits of a network address

Class B network

Class A network

Class C network

Leading bit
is always one and zero
(10)

Leading bit
is always zero
(0)

Leading bit
is always one, one, zero
(110)

Router

If a packet is destined
for network 01010111 (87),
the router only has to
read the first bit to know
which of its three routes
to forward it on.

Class A Networks

In a Class A network, the first byte is assigned to the network address, and the three remaining bytes are used for the node addresses. The Class A format is

Network.Node.Node.Node

For example, in the IP address 49.22.102.70, 49 is the network address, and 22.102.70 is the node address. Every machine on this particular network would have the distinctive network address of 49.

With the length of a Class A network address being a byte, and with the first bit of that byte reserved, seven remain for manipulation. That means that the maximum number of Class A networks that could be created would be 128. Why? Because each of the seven bit positions can either be a zero or a one, thus 2^7 or 128. To complicate things further, it was also decided that the network address of all zeros (0000 0000) would be reserved (see Table 2.2). This means the actual number of usable Class A network addresses is 2^7 minus 1, or 127.

Take a peek and see this for yourself in the decimal-to-binary chart shown in Table 2.3. Start at binary 0 and view the first bit (the leftmost bit). Continue down through the chart until the first bit turns into the digit 1. See that? Sure enough, the decimal range of a Class A network is 0 through 127. Since the Much Ado About Nothing Address (all zeros) is one of those special, reserved-club members, the range of network addresses for a Class A network is 1 through 127. Eventually, we'll see that another Class A number is in that club—number 127. This little revelation technically brings the total down to 126. But for the exam, remember 127.

	DECIMAL	BINARY	DECIMAL	BINARY	DECIMAL	BINARY
TABLE 2.3 Decimal-To-Binary Chart	0	0000 0000	18	0001 0010	36	0010 0100
	1	0000 0001	19	0001 0011	37	0010 0101
	2	0000 0010	20	0001 0100	38	0010 0110
	3	0000 0011	21	0001 0101	39	0010 0111
	4	0000 0100	22	0001 0110	40	0010 1000
	5	0000 0101	23	0001 0111	41	0010 1001
	6	0000 0110	24	0001 1000	42	0010 1010
	7	0000 0111	25	0001 1001	43	0010 1011
	8	0000 1000	26	0001 1010	44	0010 1100
	9	0000 1001	27	0001 1011	45	0010 1101
	10	0000 1010	28	0001 1100	46	0010 1110
	11	0000 1011	29	0001 1101	47	0010 1111
	12	0000 1100	30	0001 1110	48	0011 0000
	13	0000 1101	31	0001 1111	49	0011 0001
	14	0000 1110	32	0010 0000	50	0011 0010
	15	0000 1111	33	0010 0001	51	0011 0011
	16	0001 0000	34	0010 0010	52	0011 0100
	17	0001 0001	35	0010 0011	53	0011 0101

	DECIMAL	BINARY	DECIMAL	BINARY	DECIMAL	BINARY
TABLE 2.3 Decimal-To-Binary Chart (continued)	54	0011 0110	78	0100 1110	102	0110 0110
	55	0011 0111	79	0100 1111	103	0110 0111
	56	0011 1000	80	0101 0000	104	0110 1000
	57	0011 1001	81	0101 0001	105	0110 1001
	58	0011 1010	82	0101 0010	106	0110 1010
	59	0011 1011	83	0101 0011	107	0110 1011
	60	0011 1100	84	0101 0100	108	0110 1100
	61	0011 1101	85	0101 0101	109	0110 1101
	62	0011 1110	86	0101 0110	110	0110 1110
	63	0011 1111	87	0101 0111	111	0110 1111
	64	0100 0000	88	0101 1000	112	0111 0000
	65	0100 0001	89	0101 1001	113	0111 0001
	66	0100 0010	90	0101 1010	114	0111 0010
	67	0100 0011	91	0101 1011	115	0111 0011
	68	0100 0100	92	0101 1100	116	0111 0100
	69	0100 0101	93	0101 1101	117	0111 0101
	70	0100 0110	94	0101 1110	118	0111 0110
	71	0100 0111	95	0101 1111	119	0111 0111
	72	0100 1000	96	0110 0000	120	0111 1000
	73	0100 1001	97	0110 0001	121	0111 1001
	74	0100 1010	98	0110 0010	122	0111 1010
	75	0100 1011	99	0110 0011	123	0111 1011
	76	0100 1100	100	0110 0100	124	0111 1100
	77	0100 1101	101	0110 0101	125	0111 1101

	DECIMAL	BINARY	DECIMAL	BINARY	DECIMAL	BINARY
TABLE 2.3 Decimal-To-Binary Chart (continued)	126	0111 1110	150	1001 0110	174	1010 1110
	127	0111 1111	151	1001 0111	175	1010 1111
	128	1000 0000	152	1001 1000	176	1011 0000
	129	1000 0001	153	1001 1001	177	1011 0001
	130	1000 0010	154	1001 1010	178	1011 0010
	131	1000 0011	155	1001 1011	179	1011 0011
	132	1000 0100	156	1001 1100	180	1011 0100
	133	1000 0101	157	1001 1101	181	1011 0101
	134	1000 0110	158	1001 1110	182	1011 0110
	135	1000 0111	159	1001 1111	183	1011 0111
	136	1000 1000	160	1010 0000	184	1011 1000
	137	1000 1001	161	1010 0001	185	1011 1001
	138	1000 1010	162	1010 0010	186	1011 1010
	139	1000 1011	163	1010 0011	187	1011 1011
	140	1000 1100	164	1010 0100	188	1011 1100
	141	1000 1101	165	1010 0101	189	1011 1101
	142	1000 1110	166	1010 0110	190	1011 1110
	143	1000 1111	167	1010 0111	191	1011 1111
	144	1001 0000	168	1010 1000	192	1100 0000
	145	1001 0001	169	1010 1001	193	1100 0001
	146	1001 0010	170	1010 1010	194	1100 0010
	147	1001 0011	171	1010 1011	195	1100 0011
	148	1001 0100	172	1010 1100	196	1100 0100
	149	1001 0101	173	1010 1101	197	1100 0101

	DECIMAL	BINARY	DECIMAL	BINARY	DECIMAL	BINARY
TABLE 2.3 Decimal-To-Binary Chart (continued)	198	1100 0110	217	1101 1001	237	1110 1101
	199	1100 0111	218	1101 1010	238	1110 1110
	200	1100 1000	219	1101 1011	239	1110 1111
	201	1100 1001	220	1101 1100	240	1111 0000
	202	1100 1010	221	1101 1101	241	1111 0001
	203	1100 1011	222	1101 1110	242	1111 0010
	204	1100 1100	223	1101 1111	243	1111 0011
	205	1100 1101	224	1110 0000	244	1111 0100
	206	1100 1110	225	1110 0001	245	1111 0101
	207	1100 1111	226	1110 0010	246	1111 0110
	208	1101 0000	227	1110 0011	247	1111 0111
	209	1101 0001	228	1110 0100	248	1111 1000
	210	1101 0010	229	1110 0101	249	1111 1001
	211	1101 0011	230	1110 0110	250	1111 1010
	212	1101 0100	231	1110 0111	251	1111 1011
	213	1101 0101	232	1110 1000	252	1111 1100
	214	1101 0110	233	1110 1001	253	1111 1101
	215	1101 0111	234	1110 1010	254	1111 1110
	216	1101 1000	235	1110 1011	255	1111 1111
	201	1100 1001	236	1110 1100		

Each Class A network has three bytes (24 bit positions) for the node address of a machine. That means there are 2^{24}—or 16,777,216—unique combinations, and therefore precisely that many unique node addresses possible for each Class A network. If math just isn't your thing, I'll explain—again, using the multifarious jellybean. Say you packed 24 of those tasty little critters in your briefcase for a snack. Considering you only have 24, and therefore no intention of sharing, you divide your beans (bits), into three equal mouthfuls (bytes), readying them for lightening quick consumption. While divvying them up, you notice how pretty they are, and get totally side-tracked—now absorbed instead in arranging them in various patterns and recording each grouping until you exhaust all possible unique combinations. Counting all your sequence entries, you make the important discovery that when one possesses 24 jellybeans, there are 16,777,214 possible unique combinations in which one can arrange them —or, 2^{24}. Try this next time you're bedridden, or just unspeakably bored.

Because addresses with the two patterns of all zeros and all ones are reserved, the actual maximum usable number of nodes per a Class A network is 2^{24} minus 2, which equals 16,777,214.

Class B Networks

In a Class B network, the first two bytes are assigned to the network address, and the remaining two bytes are used for node addresses. The format is:

Network.Network.Node.Node (sort of a Samba rhythm)

For example, in the IP address 130.57.30.56, the network address is 130.57, and the node address is 30.56.

With the network address being two bytes, there would be 2^{16} unique combinations. But the Internet designers decided that all Class B networks should start with the binary digits 1 and 0. This leaves 14 bit positions to manipulate, and therefore 2^{14} or 16,384 unique Class B networks. Consult jellybeans if confused.

If you take another peek at the decimal-to-binary chart in Table 2.3, you will see that the first two bits of the first byte are 1 0 from decimal 128 up to 191. Therefore, if you're still confused, even after a jellybean session, remember that you can always easily recognize a Class B network by looking at its first byte—even though there are 16,384 different Class B networks! All you have to do is look at that address. If the first byte is in the range of decimal 128 to 191, it is a Class B network.

A Class B network has two bytes to use for node addresses. This is 2^{16}, minus the two patterns in the reserved-exclusive club (all zeros and all ones), for a total of 65,534 possible node addresses for each Class B network.

Class C Networks

The first three bytes of a Class C network are dedicated to the network portion of the address, with only one measly byte remaining for the node address. The format is:

Network.Network.Network.Node

In the example IP address 198.21.74.102, the network address is 198.21.74, and the node address is 102.

In a Class C network, the first *three* bit positions are always the binary 110. The calculation is such: Three bytes, or 24 bits, minus three reserved positions, leaves 21 positions. There are therefore 2^{21} or 2,097,152 possible Class C networks.

Referring again to that decimal-to-binary chart in Table 2.3, you will see that the lead bit pattern of 110 starts at decimal 192 and runs through 223. Remembering our handy, non-calculatory, easy-recognition method, this means that although there are a total of 2,097,152 Class C networks possible, you can always spot a Class C address if the first byte is between 192 and 223.

Each unique Class C network has one byte to use for node addresses. This leads to 2^8 or 256, minus the two special club patterns of all zeros and all ones, for a total of 254 node addresses for each Class C network.

Additional Classes of Networks

Another class of network is Class D. This range of addresses is used for *multicast packets*. The range of numbers is from 224.0.0.0 to 239.255.255.255.

A *multicast transmission* is used when a host wants to broadcast to multiple destinations. Hosts do this when attempting to learn of all the routers on its network. Using the ICMP protocol, it sends out a *router discovery packet*. This packet is addressed to 224.0.0.2, fingering it as a multicast packet to all the routers on its network.

There is also a Class E range of numbers starting at 240.0.0.0 and running to 255.255.255.255. These numbers are reserved for future use.

Unless you revel in chaos, and desire to add stress to your life, both Class D and E addresses should not be assigned to nodes on your network.

Who Assigns Network Addresses?

If your network will be connected to the Internet, you must be proper and petition the official Internet authorities for the assignment of a network address. An official Internet organization called the Network Information Center (NIC) can assist you in this process. For further information, contact:

Network Solutions
InterNIC Registration Services
505 Huntmar Park Drive
Herndon, VA 22070

You may also obtain help by sending e-mail to:

hostmaster@internic.net

If your network will not be connected to the Internet, you are free to assign any network address you wish.

First Section Summary

Well, it would figure.... Even something that sounds as innocent and straightforward as one would think addressing would be is instead a complicated thing here in Networkland. After all, you wouldn't need to be reading a book about it if it weren't now, would you? However, if you think about it, it isn't really all that simple in our world either. If it were, the brothers Thomas would not be rich and famous, and tourists would never get lost. Also on an encouraging note, after you wrap your brain around the concepts and facts presented in this chapter, you will discover that unlike real world addresses and maps, Networkland's contain rhyme and reason.

In this last lesson, you determined an IP address to be a numeric identifier assigned to each machine on an IP network. You learned that it's a software address designating the location of the device it's assigned to on the network, and that it's made up of 32 bits of information. You found out about octets;

four divisions of the address containing eight bits each. You also learned about the two methods of describing an IP address—dotted decimal and binary. You then explored addressing schemes and came to understand that structured and partitioned hierarchical addressing, much like the scheme used to depict phone numbers, is the method of choice for creating network addresses. In this system, rather than the entire 32 bits being treated as a unique identifier as in flat addressing, a part of the address is designated as the network address, and the other part as a node address, giving it a layered, hierarchical structure.

Moving right along, you discovered there are three class distinctions of networks, and that these ranks are decided by the network's size. For the small number of networks possessing a very large number of nodes, the rank of Class A is awarded. There are 127 Class A network addresses, with the capability to contain 16,777,216 nodes each. The decimal range of the first byte of a Class A address is 1 to 127. Class B is for the medium gang. There are 16,384 possible, each with a 65,534 maximum node occupancy. The Class B first byte decimal range is 128 to 191. Lastly, we have Class C for the up to 2,097,152 networks with a potential of only 254 nodes each. The first byte decimal range for a Class C address is 192 to 223.

You then learned that the various types of networks are formatted thus:

- Class A = Network.Node.Node.Node, with a leading bit pattern of 0

- Class B = Network.Network.Node.Node, with a leading bit pattern of 10

- Class C = Network.Network.Network.Node, with a leading bit pattern of 110

We noted two additional grades of networks, Class D and E, and found that the Class D range of addresses, 224.0.0.0 to 239.255.255.255, is used when hosts attempt to learn of all the routers on their network when they broadcast to multiple destinations. You learned that this event is called a multicast transmission, and that the things it transmits are called multicast packets. There is also a Class E range of numbers starting at 240.0.0.0 running through 255.255.255.255, which are reserved for future use.

Also noteworthy are some special IP addresses, as follows:

- An IP address of 255.255.255.255 (all ones) is a broadcast.

- The IP address 127 is for loopback tests.

- All zeros in a network address denotes "this network."

- All ones in a network address denotes "all networks."

■ All zeros in a node address denotes "this node."

■ All ones in a node address denotes "all nodes."

Finally, we ended our introductory network addressing lesson with the revelation of how to go about acquiring one, and who to get it from. An Internet organization called the Network Information Center (NIC) can assist you if your network will be connected to the Internet. If it won't be connected, you're free to assign your own.

Subnetting a Network

F AN ORGANIZATION is large and has a whole bunch of computers, or if its computers are geographically dispersed, it makes good clean sense to divide its colossal network into smaller ones connected together by routers. The benefits to doings things this way include:

■ Reduced network traffic. We all appreciate less traffic of any kind! So do networks. Without trusty routers, packet traffic could grind the entire network down to near standstill. With them, most traffic will stay on the local network—only packets destined for other networks will pass through the router.

■ Optimized network performance, a bonus of reduced network traffic.

■ Simplified management. It's easier to identify and isolate network problems in a group of smaller networks connected together than within one gigantic one.

■ Facilitates spanning large geographical distances. Because WAN links are considerably slower and more expensive than LAN links, having a single large network spanning long distances can create problems in every arena listed above. Connecting multiple smaller networks makes the system more efficient.

All this is well and good, but if an organization with multiple networks has been assigned only one network address by the NIC, that organization has a problem. As the saying goes, "Where there is no vision, the people perish." The original designers of the IP protocol envisioned a teensy Internet with only mere tens of networks and hundreds of hosts. Their addressing scheme used a network address for each physical network.

As you can imagine, this scheme and the unforeseen growth of the Internet created a few problems. To name one, a single network address can be used to refer to multiple physical networks. An organization can request individual network addresses for each one of its physical networks. If these were granted, there wouldn't be enough to go around for everyone.

Another problem relates to routers. If each router on the Internet needed to know about each existing physical network, routing tables would be impossibly huge. There would be an overwhelming amount of administrative overhead to maintain those tables, and the resulting physical overhead on the routers would be massive (CPU cycles, memory, disk space, and so on).

An additional consequence is that because routers exchange routing information with each other, there would result a terrific overabundance of network traffic. Figure 2.2 illustrates some of these problems.

FIGURE 2.2

Liabilities to having individual network addresses for each physical network

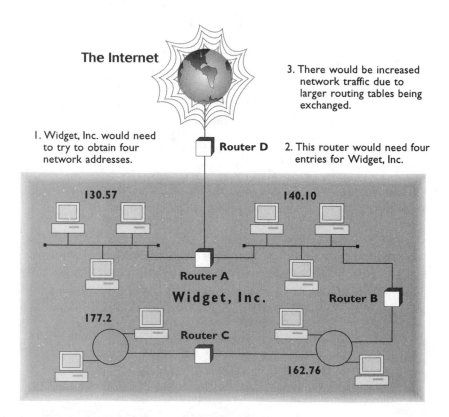

Although there's more than one way to approach this tangle, the principal solution is the one that we'll be covering in this book... subnetting.

What is subnetting? Subnetting is a dandy TCP/IP software feature that allows for dividing a single IP network into smaller, logical subnetworks. This trick is achieved by using the host portion of an IP address to create something called a subnet address.

Subnetting is network procreation. Its the act of creating little subnetworks from a single, large parent network. An organization with a single network address can have a subnet address for each individual physical network. Each subnet is still part of the shared network address, but it also has an additional identifier denoting its individual subnetwork number. This identifier is called a subnet address. Take a parent who has two kids. The children inherit the same last name as their parent. People make further distinctions when referring to someone's individual children like, "Kelly, the Jones's oldest, who moved into their guest house, and Jamie, the Jones's youngest, who now has Kelly's old room." (They may make other kinds of distinctions too, but we won't talk about those here.) Those further distinctions are like subnet addresses for people.

This practice solves several addressing problems. First, if an organization has several physical networks but only one IP network address, it can handle the situation by creating subnets. Next, because subnetting allows many physical networks to be grouped together, fewer entries in a routing table are required, notably reducing network overhead. Finally, these things combine to collectively yield greatly enhanced network efficiency.

Information Hiding

As an example, suppose that the Internet refers to Widget, Inc. only by its single network address, 130.57. Suppose as well that Widget Inc. has several divisions, each dealing with something different. Since Widget's network administrators have implemented subnetting, when packets come into its network, the Widget routers use the subnet addresses to route the packets to the correct internal subnet. Thus, the complexity of Widget, Inc.'s network can be hidden from the rest of the Internet. This is called *information hiding*.

Information hiding also benefits the routers inside the Widget network. Without subnets, each Widget router would need to know the address of each machine on the entire Widget network—a bleak situation creating additional overhead and poor routing performance. But alas, because of the subnet scheme, which alleviates the need for each router to know about every machine on the entire Widget network, their routers need only two types of information:

- The addresses of each machine on subnets to which it is attached

- The other subnet addresses

How to Implement Subnetting

Subnetting is implemented by assigning a subnet address to each machine on a given physical network. For example, in Figure 2.3, each machine on Subnet 1 has a subnet address of 1. Next, we'll take a look at how a subnet address is incorporated into the rest of the IP address.

FIGURE 2.3

The use of subnets

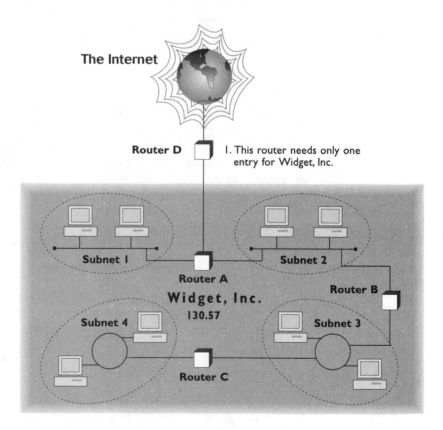

The network portion of an IP address can't be altered. Every machine on a particular network must share the same network address. In Figure 2.4, you can see that all of Widget, Inc.'s machines have a network address of 130.57. That principle is constant. In subnetting, it's the host address that's manipulated. The subnet address scheme takes a part of the host address and redesignates it as a subnet address. In essence, it's filching good jellybeans, and replacing them with fake ones. Bit positions are stolen from the host address to be used for the subnet identifier. Figure 2.4 shows how an IP address can be given a subnet address.

FIGURE 2.4

An IP address can be given a subnet address by manipulating the host address

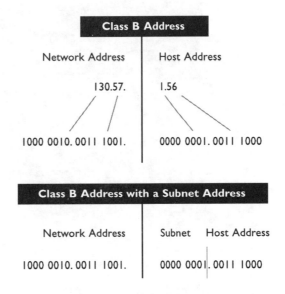

Since the Widget, Inc. network is the Class B variety, the first two bytes refer to the network address, and are shared by all machines on the network—regardless of their particular subnet. Here, every machine's address on the subnet must have its third byte read 0000 0001. The fourth byte, the host address, is the unique number—the portion we'd mess around with when subnetting. Figure 2.5 illustrates how a network address and a subnet address can be used. The same concepts and practices apply to each subnet created in the network.

FIGURE 2.5

A network address and a
subnet address

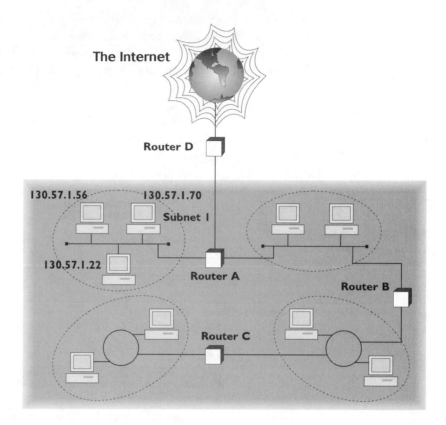

Subnet Masks

For the subnet address scheme to work, every machine on the network must know what part of the host address will be used as the subnet address. This is accomplished by assigning each machine a *subnet mask*.

The network administrator creates a 32-bit subnet mask comprised of ones and zeros. The ones in the subnet mask represent the positions that refer to the network or subnet addresses. The zeros represent the positions that refer to the host part of the address. These concepts are illustrated in Figure 2.6.

In our Widget, Inc. example, the first two bytes of the subnet mask are ones because Widget's network address is a Class B address formatted Net.Net .Node.Node (Samba rhythm). The third byte, normally assigned as part of the host address, is now used to represent the subnet address. Hence, those bit

FIGURE 2.6

A subnet mask

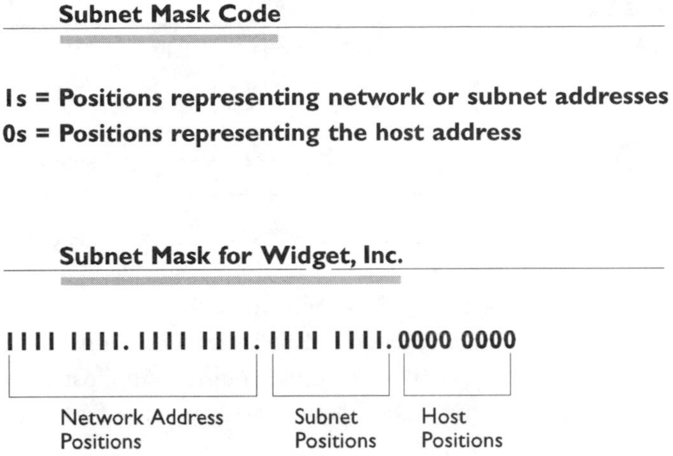

Subnet Mask Code

1s = Positions representing network or subnet addresses
0s = Positions representing the host address

Subnet Mask for Widget, Inc.

1111 1111. 1111 1111. 1111 1111. 0000 0000

Network Address   Subnet   Host
Positions   Positions   Positions

positions are represented with ones in the subnet mask. The fourth byte is the only part in our example that represents the unique host address.

The subnet mask can also be denoted using the decimal equivalents of the binary patterns. The binary pattern of 1111 1111 is the same as decimal 255 (see the decimal-to-binary chart in Table 2.3). Consequently, the subnet mask in our example can be denoted in two ways, as shown in Figure 2.7.

FIGURE 2.7

Subnet mask depiction

Subnet Mask in Binary: 1111 1111. 1111 1111. 1111 1111. 0000 0000

Subnet Mask in Decimal: 255 .   255 .   255 .   0

(The spaces in the above example are only for illustrative purposes.
The subnet mask in decimal would actually appear as 255.255.255.0.)

All networks don't need to have subnets, and therefore don't need to use subnet masks. In this event, they are said to have a default subnet mask. This is basically the same as saying they don't have a subnet address. The default subnet masks for the different classes of networks are shown in Table 2.4.

	CLASS	FORMAT	DEFAULT SUBNET MASK
TABLE 2.4 Default Subnet Masks	A	Net.Node.Node.Node	255.0.0.0
	B	Net.Net.Node.Node	255.255.0.0
	C	Net.Net.Net.Node	255.255.255.0

Once the network administrator has created the subnet mask and assigned it to each machine, the IP software views its IP address through the subnet mask to determine its subnet address. The word mask carries the implied meaning of a lens because the IP software looks at its IP address through the lens of its subnet mask to see its subnet address. An illustration of an IP address being viewed through a subnet mask is shown in Figure 2.8.

FIGURE 2.8

An IP address viewed through a subnet mask

Subnet Mask Code

1s = Positions representing network or subnet addresses
0s = Positions representing the host address

Positions relating to the subnet address

Subnet Mask: 1111 1111. 1111 1111. 1111 1111. 0000 0000

IP address of a machine on subnet 1: 1000 0010. 0011 1001. 0000 0001. 0011 1000
(**Decimal:** 130.57.1.56)

Bits relating to the subnet address

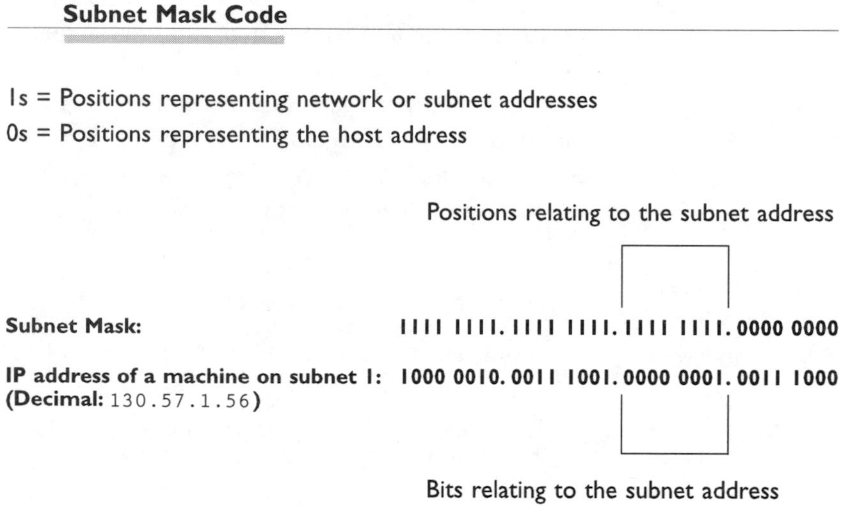

In this example, the IP software learns through the subnet mask that, instead of being part of the host address, the third byte of its IP address is now going to be used as a subnet address. IP then looks at the bit positions in its IP address that correspond to the mask, which are 0000 0001.

The final step is for the subnet bit values to be matched up with the binary numbering convention and converted to decimal. The binary numbering convention is shown in Figure 2.9.

FIGURE 2.9

Binary numbering convention

Binary Numbering Convention

Position / Value: ◄— (continued) 128 64 32 16 8 4 2 1

Binary Example: 0   0   0   1 0 0 1 0

Decimal Equivalent: 16 + 2 = 18

In the Widget, Inc. example, the binary-to-decimal conversion is simple, as illustrated in Figure 2.10.

FIGURE 2.10

Binary-to-decimal conversion

Binary Numbering Convention

Position / Value: ◄— (continued) 128 64 32 16 8 4 2 1

Widget third byte: 0   0   0   0 0 0 0 1

Decimal Equivalent: 0 + 1 = 1

Subnet Address: 1

By using the entire third byte of a Class B address as the subnet address, it is easy to set and determine the subnet address. For example, if Widget, Inc. wants to have a Subnet 6, the third byte of all machines on that subnet will be 0000 0110. The binary-to-decimal conversion for this subnet mask is shown in Figure 2.11.

Using the entire third byte of a Class B network address for the subnet allows for a fair number of available subnet addresses. One byte dedicated to

FIGURE 2.11

Setting a subnet

Binary Numbering Convention

Position / Value:	◄— (continued)	128	64	32	16	8	4	2	1

Binary Example:		0	0	0	0	0	1	1	0

Decimal Equivalent: 4 + 2 = 6

Subnet Address: 6

the subnet provides eight bit positions. Each position can be either a one or a zero, so the calculation is 2^8, or 256. But because you cannot use the two patterns of all zeros and all ones, you must subtract two, for a total of 254. Thus, our Widget, Inc. company can have up to 254 total subnetworks, each with 254 hosts.

Although the official IP specification limits the use of zero as a subnet address, some products do permit this usage. The Novell TCP/IP implementation for NetWare 4 and the Novell MultiProtocol Router (MPR) software are examples of products that do permit zero as a subnet address. This allows one additional subnet number. For example, if the subnet mask was 8 bits, rather than $2^8 = 256 - 2 = 254$, it would be $256 - 1 = 255$.

Allowing a subnet address of zero increases the number of subnet numbers by one. However, you should not use a subnet of zero (all zeros) unless all the software on your network recognizes this convention.

The formulas for calculating the maximum number of subnets and the maximum number of hosts per subnet are:

$2^{\text{(number of masked bits in subnet mask)}} - 2$ = maximum number of subnets

$2^{\text{(number of unmasked bits in subnet mask)}} - 2$ = maximum number of hosts per subnet

In the formulas, *masked* refers to bit positions of 1, and *unmasked* refers to positions of 0. Figure 2.12 shows an example of how these formulas can be applied.

FIGURE 2.12

Subnet and node formulas

Network Address: 161.11 (class B)

		Network	Subnet	
			Masked	Unmasked
Subnet Mask:		1111 1111. 1111 1111.	1110 0000.	0000 0000
Decimal:		255 . 255	. 224	. 0

The downside to using an entire byte of a node address as your subnet address is that you reduce the possible number of node addresses on each subnet. As explained earlier, without a subnet, a Class B address has 65,534 unique combinations of ones and zeros that can be used for node addresses. If you use an entire byte of the node address for a subnet, you then have only one byte for the host addresses, leaving only 254 possible host addresses. If any of your subnets will be populated with more than 254 machines, you have a problem on your hands. To solve it, you would then need to shorten the subnet mask, thereby lengthening the host address, which benefits you with more potential host addresses. A side-effect of this solution is that it causes the reduction of the number of possible subnets. Time to prioritize!

Figure 2.13 shows an example of using a smaller subnet address. A company called Acme, Inc. expects to need a maximum of 14 subnets. In this case, Acme does not need to take an entire byte from the host address for the subnet address. To get its 14 different subnet addresses, it only needs to snatch 4 bits from the host address ($2^4 - 2 = 14$). The host portion of the address has 12 usable bits remaining ($2^{12} - 2 = 4094$). Each of Acme's 14 subnets could then potentially have a total of 4094 host addresses, or 4094 machines on each subnet.

To complete this exercise, you'll need at least one computer with Microsoft Windows NT Workstation or Microsoft Windows NT Server installed on it.

In Exercises 2.1 and 2.2, you'll install and configure the TCP/IP transport.

FIGURE 2.13

Using four bits of the host address for a subnet address

Acme, Inc.

Network Address: 132.8 **(Class B; net.net.host.host)**

Example IP Address: 1000 0100. 0000 1000. 0001 0010. 0011 1100

Decimal: 132 . 8 . 18 . 60

Subnet Mask Code

1s = Positions representing network or subnet addresses

0s = Positions representing the host address

Subnet Mask:

Binary: 1111 1111. 1111 1111. 1111 0000. 0000 0000

Decimal: 255 . 255 . 240 . 0

(The decimal '240' is equal to the binary '1111 0000.'
Refer to Table 2.3: Decimal to Binary Chart.)

Positions relating to the subnet address

Subnet Mask: 1111 1111. 1111 1111. 1111 0000. 0000 0000

IP address of an Acme machine: 1000 0100. 0000 1000. 0001 0010. 0011 1100
(Decimal: 132.8.18.60)

Bits relating to the subnet address

Binary to Decimal Conversion for Subnet Address

Subnet Mask Positions:	1	1	1	1	0	0	0	0
Position / Value: ◄— (continue)	128	64	32	16	8	4	2	1
Third Byte of IP address:	0	0	0	1	0	0	1	0
Decimal Equivalent:				0 + 16 = 16				
Subnet Address for this IP address:				16				

To complete this exercise, you'll need at least one computer with Microsoft Windows NT Workstation or Microsoft Windows NT Server installed on it.

In Exercises 2.1 and 2.2, you'll install and configure the TCP/IP transport.

EXERCISE 2.1

Installing TCP/IP

Before installing and configuring the TCP/IP transport, you're going to remove the NetBEUI transport from your workstation configuration.

1. Log on as Administrator.

2. Select Control Panel ➢ Network.

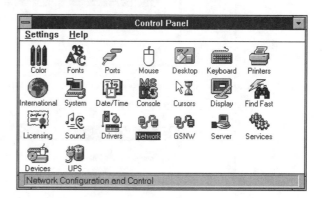

The Network Settings dialog box then appears.

EXERCISE 2.1 (CONTINUED FROM PREVIOUS PAGE)

3. Document what the default network software components are that are installed on your workstation. You're going to reference them later in the exercise.

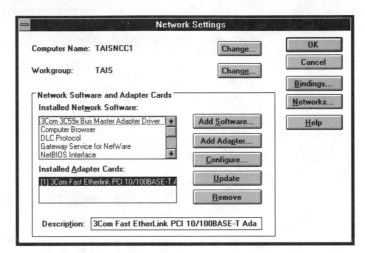

4. In the Installed Network Software box, select NetBEUI Protocol, and then choose Remove.

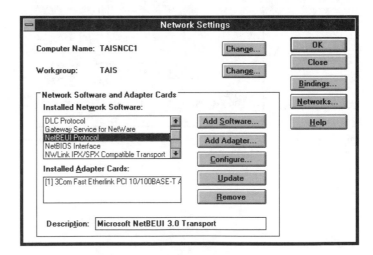

A Network Settings message confirms the operation.

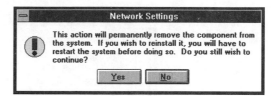

5. Choose Yes. The NetBEUI transport no longer appears.

6. Choose Add Software. The Add Network Software dialog box appears.

7. In the Network Software box, select TCP/IP Protocol and related components, then choose Continue.

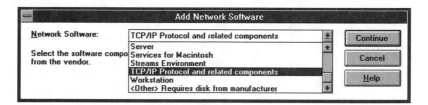

The Windows NT TCP/IP Installation Options dialog box appears, displaying the TCP/IP components available to be installed.

8. Verify that only Connectivity Utilities is selected, and then choose Continue.

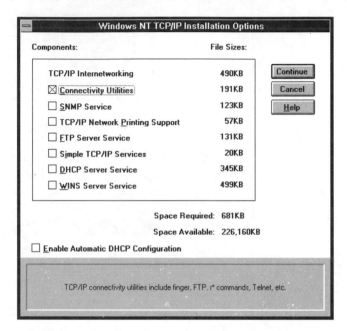

The Windows NT Setup box appears, prompting you for the full path of the Windows NT distribution files.

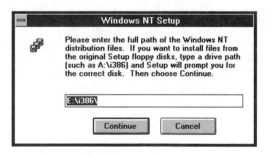

9. Type **\\rootdir** and then choose Continue. The appropriate files are copied to your workstation, and then the Network Settings dialog box appears.

10. Document the TCP/IP module(s) that were added to the Installed Network Software box. Compare this to the default components documented earlier.

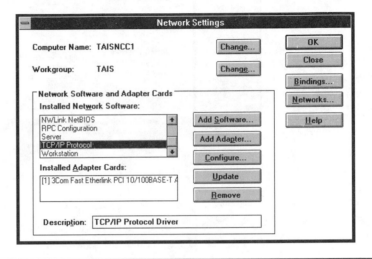

Configuring TCP/IP

1. From the Network Settings dialog box, choose OK. The TCPIP Configuration dialog box appears.

2. Type the following configuration information:

In this box	Type in:
IP Address	160.1.200.10
Subnet Mask	255.255.255.0
Default Gateway (if available)	your-default-gateway address

```
┌─────────────────────────────────────────────────────────┐
│ ─                    TCP/IP Configuration                │
├─────────────────────────────────────────────────────────┤
│ ┌Adapter: [1] 3Com Fast Etherlink PCI 10/100BA ±┐  ┌──OK──┐│
│ │                                                │  ├─Cancel─┤│
│ │ ┌─□ Enable Automatic DHCP Configuration ─────┐ │  ├─DNS...─┤│
│ │ │ IP Address:        160 .1   .200  .1       │ │  ├Advanced...┤│
│ │ │ Subnet Mask:       255 .255 .255  .0       │ │  ├──Help──┤│
│ │ └────────────────────────────────────────────┘ │          │
│ │ Default Gateway:    160 .1   .10   .10         │          │
│ │ Primary WINS Server:  [   .   .   ]            │          │
│ │ Secondary WINS Server:[   .   .   ]            │          │
│ └────────────────────────────────────────────────┘          │
│  ┌──────────────────────────────────────────────────────┐  │
│  │ Select the network adapter that you want to configure. │  │
│  │ This list contains the network adapters on this computer.│ │
│  └──────────────────────────────────────────────────────┘  │
└─────────────────────────────────────────────────────────┘
```

3. When you have finished, choose OK.

A Network Settings Change dialog box appears, indicating the computer needs to be restarted to initialize the new configuration.

4. Do not shut down your computer. When prompted, choose Don't Restart Now. If you shut down and restart your computer, the following exercise will not work.

In Exercises 2.3 and 2.4, you're going to use the IPCONFIG utility to look at IP configuration, as well as the ping utility to test your workstation configuration and connections to other TCP/IP hosts. You'll see ping work successfully, as well as fail miserably.

A portion of this lab requires having more than one available workstation.

EXERCISE 2.3

Testing the TCP/IP Configuration without Initializing TCP/IP

This procedure will enable you to see what happens when TCP/IP hasn't been initialized.

1. From a command prompt, use the IPCONFIG utility to view the TCP/IP configuration by typing **ipconfig** and then pressing ↵.

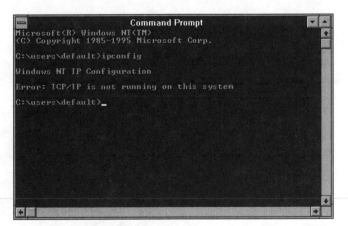

Notice the response is an empty table.

2. Now ping the loop back address. To do so, type: **Ping 127.0.0.1**.

3. Next, notice the error message.

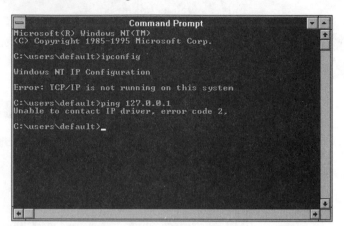

To return to Program Manager, type **exit** and then press ↵.

4. Next, shut down and then restart your computer.

EXERCISE 2.4

Testing the Configuration with TCP/IP Initialized

1. Log on to the computer as Administrator, and then go to a command prompt.

2. In order to view the TCP/IP configuration, remember to use the IPCONFIG utility.

```
                        Command Prompt
Microsoft(R) Windows NT(TM)
(C) Copyright 1985-1995 Microsoft Corp.

C:\users\default>ipconfig

Windows NT IP Configuration

Ethernet adapter E159x1:

        IP Address. . . . . . . . : 160.1.200.1
        Subnet Mask . . . . . . . : 255.255.255.0
        Default Gateway . . . . . : 160.1.10.10

C:\users\default>_
```

3. Be sure to document the information that's supplied by the IPCONFIG utility.

4. Now, ping the loopback IP address to verify that the bindings for TCPIP are correct. Type **Ping 127.0.0.1**.

```
                              Command Prompt
Microsoft(R) Windows NT(TM)
(C) Copyright 1985-1995 Microsoft Corp.

C:\users\default>ipconfig

Windows NT IP Configuration

Ethernet adapter E159x1:

        IP Address. . . . . . . . . : 160.1.200.1
        Subnet Mask . . . . . . . . : 255.255.255.0
        Default Gateway . . . . . . : 160.1.10.10

C:\users\default>ping 127.0.0.1

Pinging 127.0.0.1 with 32 bytes of data:

Reply from 127.0.0.1: bytes=32 time<10ms TTL=32
Reply from 127.0.0.1: bytes=32 time<10ms TTL=32
Reply from 127.0.0.1: bytes=32 time<10ms TTL=32
Reply from 127.0.0.1: bytes=32 time<10ms TTL=32

C:\users\default>_
```

5. Could you ping successfully? If not, why?

6. Ping the IP address of your workstation to ensure it was configured correctly. Type **Ping 160.1.y.z** (where y and z are your subnet and host numbers).

7. Could you ping successfully this time? If not, explain.

8. Ping the IP address of your default gateway to verify its configuration and connection. Type **Ping 160.1.y.1** (where y is your subnet number).

9. Now—could you ping successfully? If not, explain the result again.

10. Try to ping another IP address on another box. Type **Ping 160.1.y.z** (where y and z are the other box's assigned numbers).

11. Ping an IP address that is not configured on a workstation to see the error message. Type **Ping 160.1.200.200**.

12. Notice the error message.

In Exercises 2.5, 2.6, and 2.7, you will intentionally do something you should *never* do in real life—configure the local IP address to match the default gateway address. This will show you what happens when duplicate IP addresses exist on a network.

EXERCISE 2.5

Configuring a Duplicate Address

1. Select Control Panel ➢ Network. The Network Settings dialog box appears.

2. In the Installed Network Software box, select TCP/IP Protocol, and then choose Configure. The TCP/IP Configuration dialog box appears.

3. In the IP Address box, type the IP address of your default gateway.

4. When you are finished, choose OK. A Windows NT message box appears, indicating your network settings have changed.

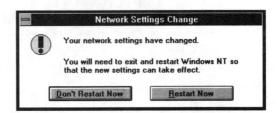

5. Choose Restart Now.

After rebooting, a system error message box appears, displaying the following message:

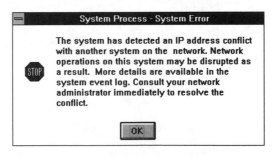

EXERCISE 2.6

Viewing the Error Message Caused by the Duplicate Address

1. Switch to Program Manager.

2. Select Administrative Tools ➢ Event Viewer.

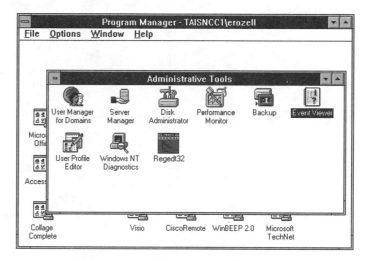

3. Select the System Log error with a source of TCPIP, and view the details.

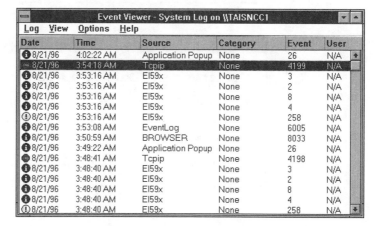

The Event Detail dialog box appears.

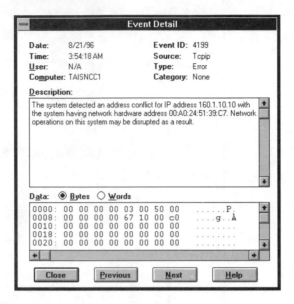

4. Document the contents of the error message.

5. Close Event Viewer and start a command prompt.

EXERCISE 2.7

Correcting the Duplicate Address Problem

1. View the TCP/IP configuration by typing **ipconfig** and then pressing ↵. The Windows NT IP Configuration box appears. Notice the IP address has been changed dynamically, and is now the same as the default gateway.

2. Exit the command prompt and switch to the Network Settings dialog box.

3. Select Installed Network Software ➤ TCP/IP Protocol, and then choose Configure. The TCP/IP Configuration dialog box appears.

4. In the IP Address box, type your original IP address.

5. When you are finished, choose OK. A Windows NT message box appears, indicating your Network Settings have changed.

6. Choose Restart Now.

7. After rebooting, switch to a command prompt, and then type **ipconfig** to verify that your address is correctly configured.

In Exercises 2.8 and 2.9, you will reconfigure your computer with an invalid subnet mask to see what happens when you try to communicate with a host on a local and remote network.

Modifying the Subnet Mask

1. Select Control Panel ➤ Network. The Network Settings dialog box appears.

2. In the Installed Network Software box, select the TCP/IP Protocol, then choose Configure. The TCP/IP Configuration dialog box appears.

3. In the Subnet Mask box, type **subnet_mask**, which is incorrect for your computer.

4. Choose OK. A Microsoft Windows NT message box appears, indicating that your Network settings have changed

5. Choose Restart Now.

EXERCISE 2.9

Testing the New Subnet Mask

1. Switch to a command prompt.

2. Use the IPCONFIG utility to view the configured parameters and verify that the change to the subnet mask has been implemented. The Windows NT IP configuration is displayed with the updated subnet mask parameter.

3. Ping the IP address of your default gateway, and then document the results.

4. Ping a host on your local network and document the results.

5. Convert your computer's IP address and the IP address of your default gateway (if available) to binary format, and then AND them to the subnet mask to determine why the subnet mask is invalid.

Your IP address	160.1.x.y
Subnet mask	*subnet_mask*
What is your Result?	
Destination IP address (gateway if available)	160.1.x.y

6. Did the result of ANDing indicate that the destination IP address and subnet mask were for a local or remote network?

7. What did you conclude about why you couldn't successfully ping your default gateway?

EXERCISE 2.10

Restoring the Subnet Mask to Its Correct Value

1. Restore your subnet mask to the original subnet mask for your workstation.

2. To verify the subnet mask update, use IPCONFIG.

3. Shut down and restart your computer.

4. Ping the IP address of your default gateway (if available) and a remote host to verify that the subnet mask is configured correctly.

5. Compare the error messages generated earlier in this exercise using incorrect subnet masks to see how differently TCP/IP responds when the subnet mask indicates a local versus remote network.

The subnet mask is used to determine whether an IP address is located on a local or remote network. If the destination IP address is on the local network, the datagram is sent directly to that host. If the destination IP address is on a remote network, the datagram is sent to the source host's default gateway.

Second Section Summary

WHO, WHAT, WHERE, when, why, and how? In regards to subnetting, this lesson explored the collective answers to that collective question, only not quite in that order. We began with when-oriented stuff, discussing a couple of conditions when subnetting a network is an extremely sensible thing to do. You found that when an organization is large and has a whole bunch of compu-ters, or if its computers are geographically dispersed, subnetting is a great idea. Reasons why this is a beneficial practice include:

- The reduction of network traffic

- Optimized network performance

- Simplified management

- Facilitates spanning large geographically distances

- Connecting multiple smaller networks makes the system more efficient

Next, we explored just what exactly subnetting is, showing it to be a TCP/IP software feature allowing for the division of a single IP network into smaller, logical subnetworks—network procreation. We jumped back from the "what" department into the "why" department with talk about the various addressing problems solved by subnetting. First, you learned that if an organization has several physical networks but only one IP network address, it can handle the situation by creating subnets. Next, you discovered that because subnetting allows many physical networks to be grouped together, fewer entries in a routing table are required, which notably reduces network overhead.

It all comes down to the sweeping goal of enhancing network efficiency. Another important reason for subnetting addresses is something called information hiding, which is important because it allows for the complexity of a given company's network to be hidden from the rest of the Internet.

We then jumped into the "how" issue with the very broad proclamation that subnetting is implemented by assigning a subnet address to each machine on a given physical network. You were warned that the network portion of an IP address can't be altered—that every machine on a particular network must share the same network address. In subnetting, it's the host address that's manipulated. This is achieved by taking a part of the host address and redesignating it as a subnet address. Bit positions are stolen from the host address to be used for the subnet identifier.

Delving deeper, we examined something called a subnet mask. These must be assigned to each machine on the network because every machine on the network must know what part of the host address will be used as the subnet address. If not, our addressing scheme becomes a scam—it won't work. The network administrator creates a 32-bit subnet mask comprised of ones and zeros. The ones in the subnet mask represent the positions that refer to the network or subnet addresses. The zeros represent the positions that refer to the host part of the address. Once the network administrator has created the subnet mask and assigned it to each machine, the IP software views its IP address through the subnet mask to determine its subnet address. You discovered that subnet masks can vary in the amount of bits they snag from the host address. If you shorten the subnet mask, you automatically lengthen the host address, which benefits you with more potential host addresses. Individual network needs must therefore be considered in deciding the size of a network's subnet masks.

Mapping Host Names to IP Addresses

MAPS ARE GOOD. They aid us in finding stuff we haven't even lost yet, and prevent us from becoming that way ourselves. We consult them for a rich variety of navigational issues, and it follows that there are many different species of maps. In the garden variety, Chamber of Commerce standard issue type, the only address you are likely to find of importance to Computerdom is Bill Gates'. Only, it won't be highlighted as his. On the other hand, in Networkland mapping, just as in addressing, logic abounds, and so it's much easier to find stuff—*if* you know how! Let's take a look.

Host Names

A *host name* is simply a name you can give to a computer. Machines on an IP network are given these to make it easier to access them. A reason for this is that people remember names better than they remember numbers. A host name is a symbolic name a network administrator assigns to a machine. Examples include SALES-AS400, ACCT-2, or OL-BESSIE-1. These names are considerably more readily recalled than digging into the ol' memory banks after numeric IP addresses. By mapping host names to IP addresses, the command and access procedure involving host machines is greatly simplified. Users don't even have to know a machine's IP address. Rather than having to grimace and enter the scornful command, TELNET 167.31.78.2, they can grin ear-to-ear while joyfully entering, TELNET ACCT-2. This sort of thing makes users very happy and causes them to revere and hold dear their network administrator instead of vengefully plotting his or her demise.

Domain Names

Host names can be further differentiated by *domain names,* which are descriptive categories created by Internet authorities to indicate generic types of organizations. Some examples of domain names and their meanings are:

com	Commerce
edu	Education
gov	U.S. government
mil	U.S. military
net	An administrative organization for a network
org	Organizations, usually private, that do not fit the above criteria

There are also domain names for countries. Some examples include:

de   Germany (Deutschland)

it   Italy

nz   New Zealand

The format of a host name with a domain name is:

HostName.DomainName

WARNING

Be advised... Never underestimate the power of little things... little things like punctuation. When holding conference with a computer, the stuff of petty human disputes like slashes, dots, spaces, and capitals are indescribably important. Notice, for instance, that the host name and the domain name are separated by a dot. This format is unalterably etched in stone. Here's an example designation: The host named SALES-AS400 in the com domain is right and proper when it looks like `sales-as400.com`. *Also indescribably noteworthy is the fact that there are no spaces afforded betwixt words and numbers and stuff. Do remember these LITTLE things.*

Subdomain Names

Domains can be further subdivided into *subdomains*. These are arbitrary names assigned by a network administrator to further differentiate a domain name. Think of them as network nicknames. The format of a host name with both subdomain and domain names is:

HostName.SubdomainName.DomainName

For example, if we add the subdomain name ACME to the example given in the previous section, the designation would look like:

`sales-as400.acme.com`

Both the domain and subdomain names serve as additional descriptors for a machine. Here are a few other examples of these names:

- `ftp.novell.de`
- `nic.ddn.mil`
- `internic.net`

There are three ways for host names to be mapped to IP addresses:

- Host tables
- Domain Name System (DNS)
- Network Information Services (NIS)

The following sections predictably explain techniques for mapping host names to their corresponding IP addresses. Let's move in now for a closer look at these three different name mapping methods.

Host Tables

A *host table* is an *ASCII file* that associates host names with their IP addresses. It's a map for Telnet. For example, if you entered the command TELNET ACCT-2, Telnet would reference a host table in order to find and connect that particular host name to its IP address.

On an NT server, the host table file is located in \systemroot\SYSTEM32\ DRIVERS\ETC. On a UNIX system, it is located in, and named, /etc/hosts. The format for the host table is:

IPAddress HostName Aliases Comments

Highly important computer syntax rules relevant to host tables include the following:

- Any number of blanks and/or tab characters can separate items.
- The # (pound) sign designates the beginning of a comment.
- Any software that references a host table will not read anything after the # symbol.

Here's an example of a host table:

```
167.31.78.2      ACCT-2
132.90.4.11      SALES-AS400 SALES
171.110.64.73    VAX-ADM VAX ADM
110.20.51.3      ACME #Located in Chicago
127.0.0.1        LOCALHOST #Loopback
```

Another file that is similar to a host table is the networks table. This file contains the names and addresses of networks that you want your software to know about. On a UNIX system, this file is located and named /etc/networks. As with the host table, anything that follows a # symbol is considered a comment.

The format for the networks table is:

NetworkName NetworkAddress Aliases

Here's an example of a networks table:

```
ACCT-2      167.31
SALES       132.90
VAX-ADM     171.110
ACME        110
ARPANET     46 ARPA
LOOPBACK    127
```

Since entries in a network table are fingering entire networks, they only depict the network portion of an IP address. Alternately, a host table depicts the entire IP address of a particular host.

Domain Name System (DNS)

The Domain Name System (DNS) is a mechanism that helps users locate the name of a machine and map that machine's name to an IP address.

Machines throughout the Internet, called *name servers*, keep a database containing large numbers of host names. These databases are arranged in a hierarchical manner, starting with the *root*, and moving down to the domain, subdomain, and finally coming to a stop at the host name. Their structure resembles an inverted tree, much like the directory structure on a DOS volume (see Figure 2.14).

FIGURE 2.14

Domain Name System (DNS) hierarchy

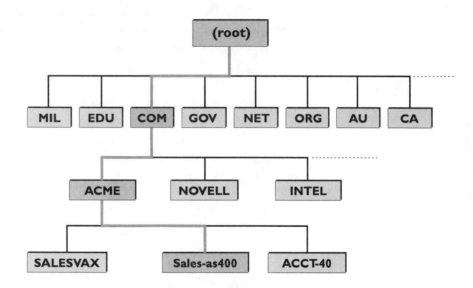

Sales-as400.ACME.com

Users can access a name server to find the exact name of a node. They can start at the top of the hierarchy and work their way down through it until they discover the full name of the desired node. This is called a *recursive query*.

The DNS protocol also provides the mapping of a host name to its IP address.

Network Information Services (NIS)

Another mechanism for mapping host names to IP addresses is Network Information Services (NIS). NIS servers can be created for a group of computers called a domain. These NIS servers contain databases called *maps*, which provide host name-to-IP address translation. Their databases can also contain user and group information. The major difference between NIS and DNS is that an NIS server covers a smaller area. NIS servers relate only to an internally contained group of computers, as in a private network—not to the entire Internet.

Third Section Summary

A HOST NAME IS a symbolic name a network administrator assigns to a machine to make it easier to access it. You learned that host names can be further differentiated by domain names, which are descriptive categories created by Internet authorities to indicate generic types of organizations. Subdomain names are further distinctions that can be given to a host name. Remember that it's a good idea to be picky and petty when communicating with a computer; to be ever vigilant of little things like choice of case and punctuation.

We then moved on to examine different ways of keeping track of all this, beginning with a discussion on host tables. Host tables are ASCII files that associate host names with their IP addresses—essentially, a map for Telnet. For example, if you entered the command TELNET ACCT-2, Telnet would reference a host table in order to find and connect that particular host name to its IP address. Next, you were introduced to DNS, or Domain Name System—a hierarchical database that starts with the root and moves down to the domain, subdomain, and finally comes to a stop at the host name. We wrapped up the section with a brief glimpse of the Network Information Service, learning that the major difference between NIS and DNS is that an NIS server covers a smaller area, relating only to a group of computers, not the entire Internet.

Shooting Trouble

A T THIS STAGE of the game, we thought it would be a great idea to introduce you to some of the realities of networking in the real world. Since this is, as we said, the real world, and not the sweet by-and-by, that reality necessarily involves a look into what can and does go wrong. The following section will give you a start in becoming prepared to deal with some commonly encountered network nightmares survived by many a network professional.

Bug Collections

Networks have special capabilities. One of them is turning molehills into mountains. Often, small network problems can turn into large network-outage catastrophes, but if a few prudent little precautions are taken, you can actually be found eating dinner with your family once in awhile instead of hunched over some console, working 36 hours straight chasing the cockroaches out of your system!

Here's an example. Because we humans are involved in the deed of sending electronic mail, error detection is built into the transmission process. This only serves to fabricate for you and I an exquisitely false sense of security. Why? Well, because even a horribly misconfigured server can present a terrifically realistic facade of working beautifully fine for weeks—even *months*. A positively heinous, but true fact. One morning you innocently walk into your office and your voice mail is already and unbelievably full by the wee hour of 8:00 am. This could most certainly mean that something significant has completely collapsed—something everyone depends on and wants—now! You check your messages, and find that, sure enough, no one can send or receive e-mail, and they are, of course, freaking out, and sending their stress your way. After checking out the network and finding everything in top form, you check the server. After two hours of sweaty investigation, you find the misconfigured setting, and reset it. The nightmare is finally over, and everyone now thinks you're Gandhi. Could this cataclysm have been prevented? Let's explore it a bit....

Pest Control

Employing that indispensable human faculty of hindsight, you remember that e-mail had been going more than a bit slow for weeks now, but, well, you had other problems. Since it was working—kind of—you ignored the phenomenon, hoping it would just go away, forgetting that this only happens with the good things in life that you ignore.

When planning a strategy to diagnose internetwork-related problems, it's important to reconsider the focus of the Internet layer we discussed in Chapter 1. Remember that its principle province is routing, with the desired result being successful connectivity between two hosts. Enlightened, we now know that inextricably associated with routing are the issues of addressing, subnet assignments, and masks. Because addresses are not always a known thing, protocols such as ARP (Address Resolution Protocol), RARP (Reverse Address Resolution Protocol), and BooTP may be used. As we learned, the DNS (Domain Name System) can be employed to this end. These things in mind, you are equipped with an ability to make an educated guess at where your network troubles likely originate.

For instance, if a problem occurs in the Internet, and the Network Interface Layer is happy and healthy, look for diagnostic clues at the Internet Layer. The Internet Protocol works at this layer, which you've now learned relates to datagram delivery, address assignment, and communication between routers.

Also, notification of router errors by ICMP, which gives messages to IP, may prove to be a fabulous source of information into why a problem has arisen in delivering datagrams.

Intelligent, CPU-operational devices known as routers use addresses to guide the datagram through the Internet. These routers communicate with each other using *RIP (Routing Information Protocol)* or *OSPF (Open Shortest Path First)* protocols. These protocols fall into a group known as *IGP's (Interior Gateway Protocols)*. ICMP (Internet Control Message Protocol), as you may recall, can help hosts determine if the packets weren't delivered correctly, and assist in discerning other malfunctions.

Ping, an ICMP Echo message, is used to verify connectivity between Internet devices. The Ping message can be used in a sequential manner to isolate a problem. For an exercise, first ping a device on your own subnet by going to a command prompt and typing **ping**, followed by the proper host name you desire to locate. If a response is received, existence is verified. Having this verification will further your cause because you are now certain it's there. Certainty is all-important in Networkland. By starting from a verified location and moving to the other side of the router, pinging each step of the way progressively until your ping-beckon is not returned, the source of your faulty connection trouble can be triumphantly isolated.

The following case studies will show examples of how the knowledge of these clues and what they mean will empower you in your role of network exterminator, physician, and sleuth.

Case Study #1: The Trouble with Clones

Or... double trouble. In our previous sections, we looked at the difference between physical hardware addresses and the logical software addresses related to Internet nodes. A chip on the network interface card, called a ROM (Read Only Memory), normally contains a six-byte physical address. Half of it (three bytes) is assigned by the IEEE, and the other three bytes by the manufacturer. The network administrator assigns the logical address. What would happen if two IP (Logical) addresses are assigned with the same number? Let's find out.

This is the story of two administrators, Jane and Bob, who wish to TELNET to a router in order to manage, or configure it. Jane TELNETs successfully, establishing a connection to the router. Her session appears to be first class until Bob starts to transmit. Then, poor Jane's connection fails. What happened?

When Jane connected to the router, she claimed that her source address was 131.195.116.42. The router responded with the following sequence number in the TCP header: seq=265153482.

Then, Bob began to transmit. When he did, his hosts sent an ARP broadcast looking for the hardware address of the router so he could TELNET. The router readily responded to the ARP request from Bob's workstation in the TCP header with a different sequence number then Jane's—let's say, seq=73138176. It was different because the router received the ARP request asking for a new connection.

Jane was communicating to the router using IP source address 131.195.116.42, which is the same as Bob's. Things began to sour when the router responded with a sequence number different from Jane's. That's why Jane's Telnet connection failed. Bob established a connection with the router using the same IP source address as Jane's, only Bob wasn't doing so from the same source. This happened because they had the same IP destination address but different sequence numbers related to the same source address.

Routers examine the IP source address, not the hardware address. As a result, it was unable to differentiate between the duplicate IP addresses with different sequence numbers.

THE MORAL OF THE STORY In Networkland, twins do not co-exist harmoniously, chatting happily in their own private languages. Give each thing its own private identity—or else! No duplicate IP addresses allowed!

Case Study #2: Hide and Seek

Introducing Scot, a network manager who's current desire is to check the status of a particular host on a different segment of his Class B network. The address of the host he has in mind is 132.163.129.15, and it's connected to his segment via a router. Scot hasn't implemented subnetting on his network, which means that only the datagrams meant for the local network will be delivered directly. All those destined for other networks should make a little trip through that router. Since Scot's network is the Class B variety without any subnetting, he'll be using a default subnet mask of 255.255.0.0, which corresponds with a network ID of 16 bits, and a host ID of 16 bits.

Introducing Kim, a network specialist whose workstation's software stores a number of parameters, including the above subnet mask. Kim happily logs on and uses the ICMP echo (Ping) command to check the status of her host. She experiences quite a delay in receiving the ICMP echo reply—and with some concern, wonders what's going on. After all, she knows that if all systems are functioning properly, an ICMP echo reply should follow the ICMP echo immediately.

Back to ol' Scot.

Scot's workstation first broadcasts an ARP message, looking for a router because it thinks the host Scot's after is not on the same segment as the source host. This is unexpected, since a router is not required for this transaction. Next, it attempts an ICMP echo request, and gets the ICMP redirect message in reply. This message indicates that datagrams are being redirected for the host, and gives the address of the correct router, 132.163.132.12, for the operation. Scot's workstation then sends another ARP request looking for the hardware address of 132.163.132.12, and the router responds. All this traffic is what caused the delay Kim experienced on her end.

The question remains, why did Scot's workstation access the router, causing the ICMP redirect message?

Scot's workstation and the router are both on the same network (132.163). Since this is a Class B network without subnetting, the subnet mask should be 255.255.0.0. When Scott examined the subnet mask in his workstation's parameters, he found that it had been set for a Class B network with an 8-bit subnet mask (255.255.255.0). Because the workstation found the source and destination devices had different subnet addresses, it incorrectly concluded that the two devices were on different subnets, requiring the assistance of the router. When Scott reconfigured his workstation's subnet address to 255.255.0.0, the ICMP Echo request proceeded without jumbling things up with a router-assisted search for a different segment it didn't actually need.

THE MORAL OF THE STORY In Networkland, looks are everything. Make sure your subnet masks fit properly before you go to the broadcast party.

Case Study #3: Do I Hear an Echo?

As we began to see in Case Study #2, using ICMP messages can answer many a question regarding the health of your network. The ICMP Echo and reply messages, commonly know as Ping, are some of the most frequently used.

You can invoke Ping from your local workstation to test the path to a particular host. If all is well, a message will return, verifying the existence of the path to the host or network. One caution is in order, however: Unpredictable results can occur if you ping an improper destination address. For example, pinging address 255.255.255.255 (broadcast) may cause excessive internetwork traffic. Let's take a look at an example.

At 3:30 a.m., one long night, Corrie, a network administrator, decides to test the paths to some of the hosts on the Internet. She can do this two ways: by sending an ICMP Echo message to each separately, or sending a directed broadcast to all the hosts on her network and subnetwork. Corrie's tired, so she decides on the latter, and enters the destination address 129.99.23.255. This will ping all of the hosts on Class B network 129.99, subnet 23.

Corrie's workstation receives an ICMP echo reply from all the hosts on her segment. The routers, however, did not respond to the ping because their design protects against such a transmission. Other hosts may be designed in a similar fashion. The originator's destination address is set for broadcast, causing echo replies to come back to the originating workstation. The first response is followed by 123 other host responses. The ICMP header contains an identifier that correlates echo and echo reply messages—in this case, pings to and from different hosts, which occur simultaneously. One needs only to pause fleetingly to imagine the epicly-proportioned, network-jamming ping-pong tournament Corrie caused from this well-intentioned, and normally appropriate little action.

THE MORAL OF THE STORY Look both ways before you ping. The ICMP Echo message can be a very valuable troubleshooting tool, but check your destination address before you initiate the command! A `ping` broadcast could have a great and terrible impact on the internetwork traffic.

Fourth Section Summary

Well, it seems everything's plagued by something, and as we now know, networks are no exception! Small network problems can turn into large ones, making them veritable bug collections. If a few prudent little precautions are taken, you can keep your network bug-free *and* keep your sanity, all at the same time! When planning a strategy to diagnose internetwork-related problems, it's important to consider the focus of the Internet layer and the role of routers. Protocols such as ARP (Address Resolution Protocol), RARP (Reverse Address Resolution Protocol), BooTP, and DNS (Domain Name System) can be employed to aid us in troubleshooting network ills.

We presented three case-study scenarios to help you get a taste of operating within the context of some real-world networking situations. At the end of each one you were given an important network precept by which to live. In the first one, you found that in Networkland individuality reigns supreme... No duplicate IP addresses allowed! Next, you learned to make sure your subnet masks are right and proper before transmitting. You were given one final admonition to look both ways before you ping, and were assured that the ICMP Echo message can be a very valuable troubleshooting tool. However, when using it, it's ultra-important to check your destination address before you initiate the command! A `ping` broadcast could have a great and terrible impact on network traffic.

One Final Note

We know that hindsight can prove an invaluable tool, but the tremendous benefits of vision and foresight cannot be ignored. It may have occurred to you that the blinding speed of progress in technology, coupled with the growing popularity of Internet communications, will impact current ways of doing things and require some changes in TCP/IP to meet present and future demands.

As we studied earlier, IP addresses are 32 bits in length, and they uniquely identify a device on one or both a TCP/IP-based internetwork, or the worldwide Internet itself. Due to the tremendous growth of the Internet, the number of available IP addresses—especially the Class B variety—is fast being depleted. As a result of this projected address shortage, the Internet Engineering Task Force (IETF) created a committee to study the problem and come up with a solution. They did. It's called *IPng* for Internet Protocol—Next Generation, or IP version 6 (IPv6), as the designated successor to IPv4, the current version.

A number of protocols were submitted to the IETF as proposed standards for IPv6. The Common Architecture for Next Generation Internet Protocol (CATNIP) has proposed to integrate ISO Connectionless Network Layer Protocol (CLNP), IP, and Novell's IPX. The TCP and UDP with Bigger Addresses (TUBA) protocol proposed to replace IPv4 with the OSI CLNP, which allows variable length addresses. The Simple Internet Protocol Plus (SIPP) proposal expanded the addressing and routing capabilities of IP, simplified the IP header, and added quality of service, authentication, and privacy (encryption) functions.

After much debate, the IETF incorporated elements from both TUBA and SIPP into IPng, which is defined in RFC 1752[7-33]. These features include a 16-octet address length, auto-configuration, encryption, flow control, and support for wireless networks. As TCP/IP internetworks migrate to IPv6, all devices utilizing IP will be affected in various ways. Changes could be direct, such as software upgrades, or possibly indirect, like the installation of gateway or proxy devices. As always, the future is yet to come, so we'll just have to wait and see. However, all those involved in network management should be aware of this, and keep it in mind before implementing any major reconfigurations in their networks.

Exercise Questions

1. In Class A, Class B, and Class C, which octets represent the network ID and which represents the host ID?

2. Which numbers are invalid as a network ID and why? Which numbers are invalid as a host ID and why?

3. When is a unique network ID required?

4. In a TCP/IP internetwork, which components require a host ID besides computers?

5. What are two common addressing problems and their effects?

6. What is the purpose of a subnet mask?

7. What requires a subnet mask?

8. When is a default subnet mask used?

9. When is it necessary to define a custom subnet mask?

Multiple-Choice Questions

1. **Problem:** Your company has offices in Los Angeles, San Francisco, and Sacramento. Each office currently has around 100 users and will be on its own subnet. Within the year, you expect to open offices in San Jose and San Diego. Each office will never have more than 350 users. You are assigned the network address 146.85.0.0, and you need to assign a subnet mask to the computers on your network so you can support this configuration.

   Solution: Specify the subnet mask 255.255.254.0

How well does this solution address the problem?

A. Meets the requirements and is an outstanding solution

B. Meets the requirements and is an adequate solution

C. Meets the requirements but is not a desirable solution

D. Does not meet the requirements, although it appears to work

E. Does not meet the requirements and does not work

2. **Problem:** Your company has offices in Los Angeles, San Francisco, and Sacramento. Each office currently has around 100 users and will be on its own subnet. With in the year, you expect to open offices in San Jose and San Diego. Each office will never have more than 350 users. You are assigned the network address 146.85.0.0, and you need to assign a subnet mask to the computers on your network so you can support this configuration.

Solution: Specify the subnet mask 255.192.0.0

How well does this solution address the problem?

A. Meets the requirements and is an outstanding solution

B. Meets the requirements and is an adequate solution

C. Meets the requirements but is not a desirable solution

D. Does not meet the requirements, although it appears to work

E. Does not meet the requirements and does not work

3. **Problem**: Your company has 25 offices in the United States. Each office currently has around 100 users and will be on its own subnet. Within the year, you expect these numbers to double. You are assigned the network address 146.85.0.0, and you need to assign a subnet mask to the computers on your network so you can support this configuration.

Solution: Specify the subnet mask 255.255.254.0

How well does this solution address the problem?

   A. Meets the requirements and is an outstanding solution

   B. Meets the requirements and is an adequate solution

   C. Meets the requirements but is not a desirable solution

   D. Does not meet the requirements, although it appears to work

   E. Does not meet the requirements and does not work

4. **Problem**: Your company has 25 offices in the United States. Each office currently has around 100 users and will be on its own subnet. Within the year, you expect these numbers to double. You are assigned the network address 146.85.0.0, and you need to assign a subnet mask to the computers on your network so you can support this configuration.

Solution: Specify the subnet mask 255.255.240.0

How well does this solution address the problem?

A. Meets the requirements and is an outstanding solution

B. Meets the requirements and is an adequate solution

C. Meets the requirements but is not a desirable solution

D. Does not meet the requirements, although it appears to work

E. Does not meet the requirements and does not work

5. **Problem:** Your company has been assigned a Class C address 196.43.201.0. There are currently four subnets on your network and you expect the number of subnets to increase. Each subnet must be able to support 60 hosts. You need to assign a subnet mask to the computers on your network so you can support this configuration.

Solution: Specify the subnet mask 255.255.255.224

How well does this solution address the problem?

A. Meets the requirements and is an outstanding solution

B. Meets the requirements and is an adequate solution

C. Meets the requirements but is not a desirable solution

D. Does not meet the requirements, although it appears to work

E. Does not meet the requirements and does not work

6. You are designing a network and have been assigned the address
   201.14.6.0. You want to have six subnets and must be able to support
   12 hosts. Which subnet masks meet your requirements?

   A. 255.255.255.240

   B. 255.255.255.128

   C. 255.255.255.224

   D. 255.255.255.248

7. You have been assigned a Class A address and intend to have eight subnets on your network. Which subnet mask would you use to maximize
   the number of hosts on each subnet?

   A. 255.255.255.0

   B. 255.0.0.0

   C. 255.240.0.0

   D. 255.255.240.0

Multiple-Choice Exercise Group

MULTIPLE-CHOICE EXERCISE A

Determining the Address Class

In this exercise, you will determine which class of address is correct for a given IP address and scenario.

1. Write the appropriate address class next to each IP address.

IP Address	Address Class
131.107.2.89	
3.3.57.0	
200.200.5.2	
191.107.2.10	
127.0.0.1	

2. Which address class(es) will allow you to have more than 1000 hosts per network?

3. Which address class(es) will allow only 254 hosts per network?

4. Which address class(es) are not supported by Windows NT?

MULTIPLE-CHOICE EXERCISE B

Identifying Invalid IP Addresses

In this exercise, you will identify which of the following IP addresses cannot be assigned to a host and then explain why an address is invalid.

Review the following IP addresses. Circle the portion of the IP address that would be invalid if it were assigned to a host, and then explain why it's invalid.

A. 131.107.256.80

B. 222.222.255.222

C. 231.200.1.1

D. 126.1.0.0

E. 0.127.4.100

F. 190.7.2.0

G. 127.1.1.1

H. 198.121.254.255

I. 255.255.255.255

MULTIPLE-CHOICE EXERCISE C

Assigning IP Addresses in a Local Area Network (LAN) Environment

In this exercise, you will decide which class of address will support the following IP network, and then you will assign a valid IP address to each type of host to easily distinguish it from other hosts (for example, UNIX, servers, or workstations).

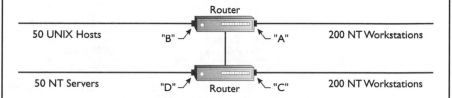

1. Which address classes will support this network?

2. Which of the following network addresses will support this network?

   A. 197.200.3.0

   B. 11.0.0.0

   C. 221.100.2.0

   D. 131.107.0.0

3. Using the network ID that you chose, assign a range of host IDs to each type of host, so that you can easily distinguish the Windows NT Server computers from the Windows NT Workstation computers and from the UNIX workstations.

Type of TCP/IP host	IP address range
Windows NT Server computers	
UNIX workstations	
Windows NT Workstation computers	

Determining the Required Number of IP Addresses

In this exercise, you will decide how many network IDs and host IDs are required to support the network shown below.

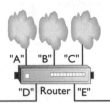

50 NT Servers
200 NT Workstations   "D" | Router | "E"   50 UNIX Hosts

1. How many network IDs does this network environment require?

2. How many host IDs does this network environment require?

3. Which default gateway (router interface) would you assign to the Windows NT Workstation computers?

Defining a Valid Subnet Mask

In this exercise, you're going to define a subnet mask for multiple networks. Keep in mind that not every one requires a subnet mask.

1. Class A network address on a local network

2. Class B network address on a local network with 3800 hosts

3. Class C network address on a local network with 254 hosts

4. Class A address with 14 subnets

5. Class B address with 126 subnets

MULTIPLE-CHOICE EXERCISE E (CONTINUED)

6. Class A network address. Currently, there are 25 subnets that will grow to approximately 55 subnets within the next year. Each subnet will never have more than 40,000 hosts.

7. Using the subnet mask from Step 6, how much growth will this subnet mask provide?

8. Class B network address. Currently, there are 14 subnets that may double in size within the next two years. Each subnet will have fewer than 2000 hosts.

Using the subnet mask from Step 8, how much growth will this subnet mask provide?

Scenario-Based Review

SCENARIO #1 You need to get an IP address assigned so you can broadcast your company on the Internet. Who do you contact?

SCENARIO #2 You need to send a broadcast message on the network informing users that the server is going down. When you send the multicast transmission, which address will IP use to broadcast the message to all users?

SCENARIO #3 The NIC assigns you a Class B address for your company's network. How many octets define the network portion of the address?

SCENARIO #4 The NIC has assigned a Class C address for your new Internet Web server. How many bits can you use for the host address?

SCENARIO #5 You look in your workstation configuration and notice there's an IP address of 127.0.0.1. What does this mean?

SCENARIO #6 You decide you want to subnet your Class B network with an address of 255.240.0.0. When implemented it does not work. Why?

SCENARIO #7 Your boss read in a Microsoft magazine that creating subnets will help her network run more efficiently. She's decided to implement this, and wants you to lead the project. She wants you to outline what the advantages of subnetting the network are so she can justify the project to her superiors in a meeting this afternoon. What will you equip her with? Take a minute to create a list of the benefits of subnetting for her.

SCENARIO #8 You have four offices and 25 nodes at each office. Which subnet mask would you assign to your Class C network address of 201.201.201.0?

SCENARIO #9 You have a Class B network address of 187.32.0.0. Which subnet address would give you at least 200 subnets?

SCENARIO #10 Your network is not assigned an address for the NIC and you do not need to be on the Internet. You create a Class A address of 36.0.0.0 with a subnet mask of 255.255.0.0. How many subnets can you use and how many hosts can be on each subnet?

SCENARIO #11 Your IS manager asks you if there is some kind of computer that will map host names to IP addresses for groups of computers called domains. What do you tell him?

SCENARIO #12 You're called upon to help train a new network help-desk employee who is confused about the Domain Name System. How do you explain it to her?

SCENARIO #13 The CIO of your company is assessing the knowledge level of his network operating system staff. He calls to ask you the difference between NIS and DNS. What do you say?

SCENARIO #14 The host table on your UNIX server needs to be updated. You need to add the recently acquired New York site with an IP address of 132.132.45.98. It also needs an alias of NY. Where is the host table file and in what order would you place the information in the table?

Implementing
IP Routing

ITH TCP/IP BASICS covered and conquered in Chapter 1, our focus is going to both sharpen and shift. Our attention will now be concentrated on Microsoft-specific issues and intricacies. We will begin Chapter 3 with a crisp discussion on IP routing.

Objectives

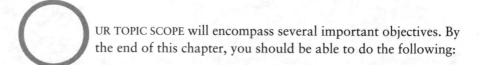

UR TOPIC SCOPE will encompass several important objectives. By the end of this chapter, you should be able to do the following:

- Explain the difference between static and dynamic IP routing.

- Explain the host configuration requirements to communicate with a static or dynamic IP router.

- Configure a computer running Windows NT to function as an IP router.

- Build a static routing table.

- Use the TRACERT utility to isolate route or network link problems.

All readers—even the wizards and gurus in the audience—shouldn't skip class today. Like I said, we're moving into Microsoft Land now, and this chapter is fundamental because it deals with IP routing as spoken in MSNT—an important Microsoft dialect.

What Is IP Routing?

I
P ROUTING IS the process of sending data from a host on one network to a *remote host* on another network through a *router*, or routers. A router is either a specifically assigned computer or a workstation that's been configured to perform routing tasks. In IP terminology, routers are referred to as *gateways*. Gateways are basically TCP/IP hosts that have been rigged with two or more network connection *interfaces*. Outfitted in this manner, they're known as *multihomed hosts,* which we'll discuss more thoroughly later in the chapter.

The path that a router uses to deliver a packet is defined in its *routing table*. A routing table contains the IP addresses of router interfaces that connect to the other networks the router can communicate with. The routing table is consulted for a path to the network that is indicated by the packet's destination address. If a path isn't found, the packet is sent to the router's *default gateway* address— if one is configured. By default, a router can send packets to any network for which it has a configured interface. When one host attempts communication with another host on a different network, IP uses the host's default gateway address to deliver the packet to the corresponding router. When a route is found, the packet is sent to the proper network, then onward to the destination host. If a route is not found, an error message is sent to the source host.

The IP Routing Process

The IP routing process is fairly direct when a datagram's destination is located on a neighboring network. In this kind of situation, a router would follow a simple procedure, as shown in Figure 3.1.

First, when a workstation wants to send a packet to a destination host, in this instance 160.1.0.1 transmitting to 160.2.0.4, host 160.1.0.1 checks the destination IP address. If it determines the address isn't on the local network, it must then be routed. Next, 160.1.0.1 calls on ARP to obtain the hardware address of its default gateway. The IP address of the default gateway is configured in machine 160.1.0.1's internal configuration, but 160.1.0.1 still needs to find the hardware address of the default gateway, and sends out an ARP request to get it. IP then proceeds to address the packet with the newly obtained

FIGURE 3.1

Simple routing

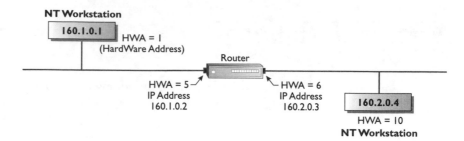

destination hardware address of its default router. The information utilized for addressing the packet includes:

- Source hardware address 1

- Source IP address 160.1.0.1

- Destination hardware address 5

- Destination IP address 160.2.0.4

IP, on the receiving router with the hardware address of 5, establishes that it is not the final, intended recipient by inspecting the packet's destination IP address, which indicates it must be forwarded to network 160.2. Then, IP uses ARP to determine the hardware address for 160.2.0.4. The router then puts the newly identified hardware address into it's ARP cache for easy reference the next time it's called upon to route a packet to that destination.

This accomplished, the router sends the packet out to network 160.2 with a header that includes:

- Source hardware address 5

- Source IP address 160.1.0.1

- Destination hardware address 10

- Destination IP address 160.2.0.4

As the packet travels along network 160.2, it looks for hardware address 10, with the IP address of 160.2.0.4. When an NIC card recognizes its hardware address, it grabs the packet.

It's important to note here that the source IP address is that of the host that created the packet originally, but that the hardware address is now that of the router's connection interface to network 160.1. It's also significant that although both source and destination software IP addresses remain constant, both source and destination hardware addresses necessarily change at each hop the packet makes.

Sounds simple right? Well, it is in a situation like the one we just presented. However, those of you who possess some first-hand experience with this sort of thing may now be finding yourselves just a little distracted with thoughts of a genuinely sarcastic variety. Before turning your nose up and slamming this book shut, let it be known that we too, are fully aware that this isn't a perfect world, and that if things were that straightforward, there wouldn't be a market for books about them! On the other hand, to those readers becoming uncomfortable with the now present implications of potential chaos, we say, relax, make some tea, sit down, and read on.

Start by considering this foul and ugly possibility: What if the destination network is in the dark because it's not directly attached to a router on the delivery path for that nice little datagram? Things come a tumblin' down, that's what! Remember hearing somewhere that there's a reason for everything? Well, we're not sure about that, but the heinous, confusion-producing scenario we just posited is one most excellent reason for the existence of routing tables. With a handy-dandy routing table, the fog clears, clouds part, and destinations sing! Routers, and those dependent on them, again become happy, efficient things. Routing tables are maintained on IP routers. IP consults these to determine where the mystery network is, so that it can send its mystery packet there. Some internetworks are very complex. If this is the case, routing tables should designate all available routes to a destination network, as well as provide an estimate advising the efficiency of each potential route. Routing tables maintain entries of where networks are located, not hosts.

Dynamic vs. Static IP Routing

There are two breeds of routing tables. There are static tables, and there are dynamic tables. Static types are laboriously maintained by a network manager, while the dynamic variety is sustained automatically by a routing protocol. Additionally, static routing tables are the only type supported by the factory-to-you stock version of Windows NT. This is because, at press time, Microsoft version 3.5x doesn't provide support for inter-routing protocols like RIP (RFC 1058) and OSPF (RFC 1131) on Windows NT. Here's a list spotlighting some specific routing table characteristics:

DYNAMIC ROUTING	STATIC ROUTING
Function of inter-routing protocols	Function of IP
Routers share routing information automatically	Routers do not share routing information
Routing tables are built dynamically	Routing tables are built manually
Requires a routing protocol, such as RIP or OSPF	Microsoft supports Multihomed systems as routers
Requires a third-party router	

Dynamic IP Routing

On large internetworks, dynamic routing is typically employed. This is because manually maintaining a static routing table would be overwhelmingly tedious, if not impossible. With dynamic routing, minimal configuration is required by a network administrator. Figure 3.2 shows an example of dynamic routing.

FIGURE 3.2

An example of dynamic routing

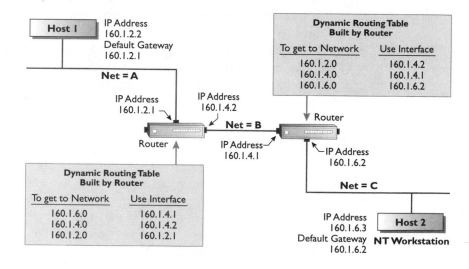

For a host to communicate with other hosts on the internetwork, its default gateway address must be configured to match the IP address of the local router's interface.

In Figure 3.2, Host 1 requires a default gateway address in order to be able to send packets to any network other then Network A. Host 1's default gateway address is configured for the router port attached to Network A. If Host 1 sends a packet that's not destined for the local network, it will be sent to the default gateway address. If no gateway is defined, the packet will be discarded. Host 2 works the same way, however it's default gateway is the router port attached to Network C. When the router receives a packet either from Host 1 or 2, it will observe the destination's IP address and forward it according to the information in its routing table, which is built and maintained through inter-routing protocols.

Dynamic routing is a function of inter-routing, network gossip protocols such as the Routing Information Protocol (RIP) and Open Shortest Path First (OSPF). These routing protocols periodically exchange routes to known networks among dynamic routers. If a given route changes, they automatically update the router's routing table and inform other routers on the internetwork of the change.

Routing Information Protocol (RIP)

RIP is a type of protocol known as a *distance vector routing protocol*. RIP is used to discover the cost of a given route in terms of hops, and store that information in the routing table, which IP uses in selecting the most efficient, low-cost route to a destination. It works by watching for routing table broadcasts by other routers, and updating its own routing table in the event a change occurs. RIP routing tables provide, at a minimum, the following information:

- IP destination address

- A metric (numbered from 1 to 15) indicative of the total cost in hops of a certain route to a destination

- The IP address of the router a datagram would reach next on the path to its destination

- A marker signaling recent changes to a route

- Timers

Some drawbacks to RIP include a problem known as "counting to infinity," as illustrated in Figure 3.3. In certain internetwork configurations, an endless loop between routers can occur if one of the networks becomes unavailable. RIP keeps counting hops each time the broadcast reaches a router in hopes of finding a new route to the formerly available network. To prevent this, a hop-limit count between 1 and 15 is configured to represent infinity, which necessarily imposes size restrictions on networks. RIP can't be utilized on a network with an area consisting of more than 15 hops. In Figure 3.3, Network 6's location was lost between Routers B and D. Router B then looks for a new route to Network 6. Router B already knows that Router C can get to Network 6 with four hops because Router C advertised this information in a broadcast, and all routers save this broadcasted information in their routing tables. Since Router B is looking for a new route to Network 6, Router B references its routing table and finds that Router C can reach Network 6 in four hops. Router B determines it can reach Network 6 in five hops because Router C can make it in four hops. This is because Router B must add an extra hop for itself—four from Router C plus one for Router B. Router B then broadcasts the new route information back out onto the network. Router C receives this information, and enters into its route table that Network 6 is now six hops away—five from Router B, plus one for itself. This process continues until the15 hop limit is reached. At this point, the route to Network 6 is finally dubbed an unreachable destination, and all related route information regarding it is removed from both Router B's and Router C's routing tables.

FIGURE 3.3

"Counting to Infinity"

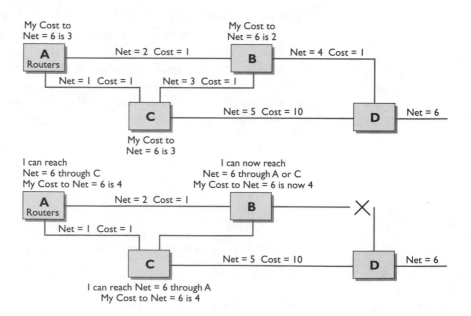

Another problem with large internetworks centers around the fact that RIP routers broadcast routing table advertisements every 30 seconds. On today's gargantuan networks, populated with an abundance of routers, momentous amounts of bandwidth can get gobbled up simply accommodating all the RIP response packet noise.

Open Shortest Path First (OSPF)

Because of these potentially network-hostile characteristics, OSPF is quickly gaining popularity within the Internet community. OSPF is based on *link-state algorithms*, and is therefore known as a *link-state routing protocol*. It's deployed within an *autonomous system*, which is a group of routers that share a certain routing protocol. When that protocol happens to be OSPF, each router retains its own database describing the topology of the autonomous system on which it's located. This kind of system is much more flexible, and has the following advantages as well:

- Network administrators can assign costs to a particular link.

- The total cost for a given path doesn't necessarily have to have a limit.

- Its upper metric limit being 65,535, it has the ability to accommodate vast networks.

- Each node creates a link-state database tree representing the network, and places itself as that tree's root, where it can choose the most direct path to a given destination.

- Related to the above benefit, in the event that more than one route exists of equal cost, OSPF routers can balance the load of network traffic between all available and equally cost-effective routes.

- Link-state routing advertisements are broadcasted much less often—only when a change is detected, thereby reducing network overhead.

- Link-state routing update packets can efficiently carry information for more than one router.

- This type of packet is only sent to *adjacencies,* or neighboring routers selected to swap routing information—a "tell a friend" arrangement that again contributes to network efficiency.

Static IP Routing

Static routing is a function of IP. Static routers require that routing tables are built and updated manually by humans. If a route changes, static routers are secretive and do not share this information to inform each other of the event. They're also very cliquey, and do not exchange routes with dynamic routers.

Windows NT provides the ability to function as an IP router using static routing. NT network administrators must maintain their tables, or acquire a commercial router. A Windows NT-based computer can be configured with multiple network adapters and routes between them. This type of system, which is ideal for small, private internetworks, is referred to as a *multihomed computer*.

Routing tables inventory known networks and the IP addresses used to access them. Windows NT static routing tables are maintained by a route utility, and are comprised of five columns of data, reading left to right. In the list below, the first entry represents the left-most column, the second represents the next one, and so on.

Network Address: A roster of addresses for known networks. Included here is an entry for both the local network (0.0.0.0), and for broadcasts (255.255.255.255).

Netmask: This column lists all subnet masks in use for each network.

Gateway Address: This is a list of the IP addresses employed as the primary datagram receivers for each network.

Interface: Each network card installed in a computer is assigned an interface number.

Metric: This is a list providing an estimate of the number of hops the route would cost. A hop is each pass a datagram makes through a router.

Here are the key things to remember about static routers:

- A static router can only communicate with networks with which it has a configured interface.

- A Windows NT computer can be configured as a multihomed computer.

- A static route can be configured as either a default gateway address or an entry in a routing table.

- A static router, such as a Windows NT multihomed computer, can only communicate with networks to which it has a configured interface. This limits communications to local networks.

Figure 3.4 illustrates static routing.

FIGURE 3.4

Static routers

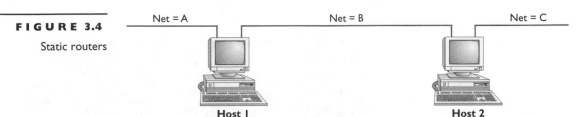

As shown in Figure 3.4, Host 1 has local connections to Networks A and B. This means that hosts on Network A can communicate with hosts on Network B, and vice versa, because Host 1 knows about both networks, and will pass packets destined for either one. Hosts on Network A will not be able to communicate with hosts on Network C.

Host 2 has local connections to Networks B and C and will be able to pass packets destined for either network. However, Network C will not be able to send packets to Network A.

In Exercise 3.1, you'll view a routing table.

After taking all this in, you may have been left with the impression that dynamic routing is the method of choice for everyone's routing needs. While that's certainly true when the network in question is large and complex, providing a multiplicity of paths to destinations and/or growing rapidly, static routing is wonderfully suited for small to moderately sized networks that rarely change. An important consideration is, as is so often the case, cost. All that fabulous intelligence and flexibility, and all those bells and whistles that dynamic routers offer cost a lot—up to around $100k apiece! They're one of the most expensive pieces of equipment one can hook up to a network! Windows NT comes out of the box equipped with static routing built right in—in other words...it's free! It's also free of charge in terms of overhead costs on your network, and it creates the environment for a much closer, more involved relationship between you and your beloved network.

EXERCISE 3.1

Viewing the Routing Table

In this exercise, you'll use the ROUTE utility to view entries in your local routing table.

1. From a command prompt, type **route print** and then press ↵ to view the route table.

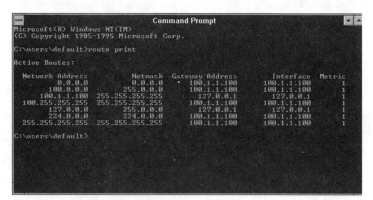

2. Under Gateway Address, what address is listed that is not associated with your local host? This should be your default gateway address—the router interface address atatched to your local network interface.

First Section Summary

THE OPENING OF this lesson presented you with some definitions, beginning with IP routing. IP routing is the process of sending data from a host on one network to a remote host on another network through a router, or routers. In IP terminology, the term gateway essentially means router. A router is either a specifically assigned computer, or a workstation that's been configured to perform routing tasks. When hosts are configured with two or more network connection interfaces, they're known as multihomed hosts.

The path a router uses to deliver a packet is defined in its routing table. You discovered that routing tables contain ledgers with the IP addresses of router interfaces, which connect to the other networks with which a given router can communicate. We then explained the steps a router goes through to deliver a datagram whose destination is located on a neighboring network. Although both source and destination software IP addresses remain constant through this process, both source and destination hardware addresses necessarily change at each hop the packet makes. From here, the discussion led to comparing the differences between static and dynamic routing.

Dynamic routing is usually employed on large internetworks, because the manual maintenance a static routing table requires would be overwhelmingly tedious, if not impossible. Dynamic routing is a function of inter-routing protocols such as Routing Information Protocol (RIP) and Open Shortest Path First (OSPF). RIP is a type of protocol known as a distance vector routing protocol, and is used to discover the cost of a given route in terms of hops, and store that information in the routing table. Some of the drawbacks regarding RIP include a problem known as counting to infinity, where two routers endlessly loopback to each other, attempting to find the proper path to the desination, and the fact that RIP routers broadcast routing table advertisements every 30 seconds, making RIP a potential bandwidth hog.

Using OSPF, a link-state routing protocol, on large, stable internetworks is advantageous because it is deployed on an autonomous system—a group of routers that use and share a chosen routing protocol. Among the benefits of employing OSPF is that each router retains its own database describing the topology of the autonomous system, making it much more flexible.

IP Routing Applied

NOW THAT YOU have a clear picture of exactly what IP routing is, and what it involves, you're ready to learn how it's done. In this section, we'll give you the skinny on configuration and integration issues, and the procedures required for implementation.

Using the Default Gateway Address on a Static Router

Gateways are most often dedicated computers, or routers. The *default gateway* is like a network mediator with connections. It's the node on the local network that knows the network IDs of other networks linked to the greater internetwork. Since it has access to this privileged information, when a given workstation sends out some data that reaches the default gateway, it can forward it along to other gateways as required to reach its proper destination.

One method of configuring a static route without manually adding routes to a routing table is to configure each multihomed computer's default gateway address as the local interface to the other multihomed computer on the common network. It's a type of circular reasoning for computers.

A multihomed computer (a computer with more than one NIC card) can send IP packets to destinations other than those they are locally attached to by setting the internal configuration of the default gateway to the other multihomed computer's network interface. For example, in Figure 3.4, Host 2 would set its default gateway to the network interface on Host 1. Network C would then be able to pass packets to Network A. Host 1 would set its default gateway to the network interface on Host 2, enabling Network A to communicate with Network C.

Whenever Host 1 receives a packet destined for a host on Network C, it'll check its local routing table. If it doesn't find a route to Network C, it forwards the packet to its default gateway, which is a local interface on Host 2. Host 2 will then route the packet to the appropriate interface for delivery on Network C.

Using the default gateway address as a static route only works well with two routers. If more than two are used, you must manually add an entry in the routing table.

Using Additional Default Gateways

Although more than one default gateway can be configured, only the first one will be used for routing purposes. The others will be used only as backup should the primary one become unavailable for some reason. This means you can't use multiple gateways to nab more network bandwidth. However, better fault tolerance is still a definite plus. As I'm sure you are well aware, this backup stuff is by no means unimportant.

Let's say Router A in Figure 3.5 goes on the blink, and is out of commission when the client boots up. The client wants to connect to the server, but the default gateway that the client is defined for is currently unavailable, so it's out of luck. The client has no other default gateway defined, so the client will not be redirected to Router C to connect to the server. However, if the client was to define a second default gateway for Router C, the client would then be directed on towards the server.

FIGURE 3.5

A hypothetical routing dilemma

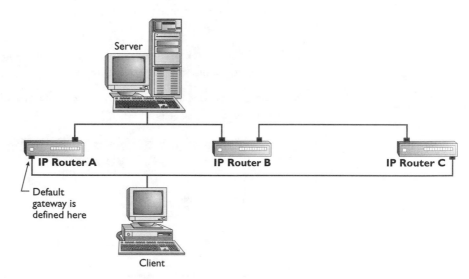

The client is going to have to sit on the other side of the abyss dreaming of multiple default gateways, wishing he or she had a more thorough network administrator who took these kind of precautions. Would that be you? If so, Exercise 3.2 shows you how to create additional default gateways using the Advanced TCP/IP configuration.

Or if you're up for a challenge, Exercise 3.3 shows you how to configure a Windows NT system to use multiple default gateways from the registry.

When one configures one's Windows NT system in this way, retransmission problems at the TCP layer will cause the IP routing software to try the routers listed in the Additional Gateways value. This is again a great backup plan. Why? Well...What if Client and Server were in the middle of an established session, and that troublesome Router A went down again? TCP would send a message to IP to try one of the additional routers in the registry. IP would then try Router C, use a double hop route, and continue exchanging

EXERCISE 3.2

Creating Additional Default Gateways

1. Start the Network utility in the control panel.

2. Select TCP/IP Protocol in the Network Settings dialog box.

3. Choose Configure, which opens the TCP/IP Configuration dialog box.

4. Select the desired adapter to be configured in the Adapter box located in the upper-left corner.

5. In the Default Gateway section of the TCP/IP Configuration dialog box, enter a gateway now, if one doesn't already exist.

6. Select the Advanced button. This allows you to enter advanced configuration for the adapter you've selected.

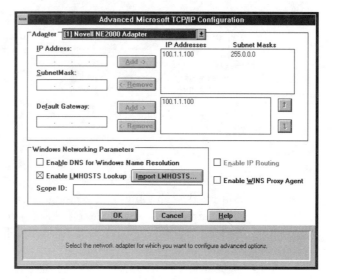

7. Enter the address of the additional default gateway in the Default Gateway address field, and punch the Add button to tack it onto your list.

8. Select OK, then exit the Network utility and restart your computer. The newly added address is now activated.

EXERCISE 3.3

Configuring a Windows NT System to Use Multiple Default Gateways from the Registry

Using the regedit32.exe utility, add a new REG_MULTI_SZ value under the ..\Tcpip\ Parameters key in the registry called Additional Gateways. Provide this value with a list of strings representing your additional default gateways to use in the event the primary default gateway becomes unavailable. You can opt to enter these additions in dotted decimal format (e.g., 160.1.0.1) or as a fully qualified domain name to be resolved by the hosts file or DNS. Be sure to enter your additional gateways in order of preference.

---

data at no cost to the session. When Router A again breathes a breath of life, the inter-routing protocol will force Router C to redirect the session's traffic back through the more optimal, one-hop route provided by the now living Router A.

In order for any host to be able to communicate with other hosts located somewhere out there on the internetwork, its default gateway address positively must be configured to match the IP address of the router's interface on the local segment.

In Exercise 3.4, you will test your default gateway.

EXERCISE 3.4

Testing Communications

Note: This exercise requires access to more than one workstation.

Here, you'll test the configured default gateway address to confirm that internetwork operations are successful.

1. From a command prompt, type **Route Print** to view the route table.

2. Is the default gateway address still listed under Gateway Address?

3. Ping hosts on each network to validate that communications can be established.

Default Routing Table Entries

Windows NT 3.51 and Windows for Workgroups 3.11 routing tables maintain the default entries shown in Table 3.1.

TABLE 3.1

Default routing tables for Windows NT 3.51 and Windows for Workgroups 3.11

ADDRESS EXAMPLES	DESCRIPTION
0.0.0.0	The address used as a default route for any network not specified in the route table
Subnet broadcast 0.0.89.0	The address used for broadcasting on the local subnet
Network broadcast 160.1.0.0	The address used for broadcasting throughout the internetwork
Local loopback 127.0.0.1	The address used for testing IP configurations and connections
Local network 160.1.0.0	The address used to direct packets to hosts on the local network
Local host 160.1.89.56	The address of the local computer; references the local loopback address

Adding Static Entries

The route command is used, as detailed in Table 3.2, to add static entries to a routing table.

TABLE 3.2

Commands Used for Adding Static Entries

TO ADD OR MODIFY A STATIC ROUTE	FUNCTION
route add [*network address*] mask [*gateway address*]	Adds a route
route delete [*network address*] [*gateway address*]	Deletes a route
route change [*network address*] [*gateway address*]	Modifies a route
route print [*network address*] [*gateway address*]	Prints a route
route -s [*gateway address*]	Adds a route to a smart gateway
route -f	Clears all routes

It works like this: To add a static route, enabling communications between a host on network `160.1.89.0` from a host on network `160.1.66.0`, you would run the following command:

```
route add 160.1.24.0 mask 255.255.255.0 160.1.16.1
```

In Exercise 3.5, you will remove your default gateway address, and instead all routing will be done from static routes.

EXERCISE 3.5

Removing the Default Gateway Address

In this procedure, you'll remove the address for the default gateway. This action serves to prevent any sending of packets to the default gateway for routing purposes. Instead, all routing will be achieved from existing route entries.

1. Use the Network application to open the Network Settings dialog box and access the TCP/IP Configuration dialog box.

2. Delete the Default Gateway address.

Close all dialog boxes, and then shut down and restart the computer.

In Exercise 3.6, you'll add a static routing table entry.

EXERCISE 3.6

Adding a Static Routing Table Entry

1. Add a static routing table entry by typing the following command, making sure that it fits on one line:

```
route add 160.1.89.0 mask 255.255.255.0 160.1.89.1
```

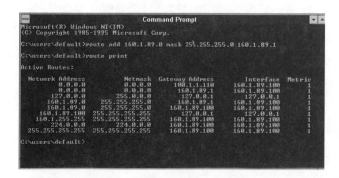

---

2. View the entries in the routing table to verify that the route is listed before you continue.

3. Try to ping the computer (160.1.89.x).

Was the ping successful?

Try to ping a host on another network. Was the ping successful? Why or why not?

Again, it's very important to remember that static routes are not stored in the Registry or in a file. If you restart a multihomed computer, you'll have to rebuild its static routing table.

Using a Static Routing Table

If your internetwork has more than two routers, at least one of which is a static router, you'll need to configure static routing table entries to all known networks on a table at each multihomed computer, as shown in Figure 3.6.

FIGURE 3.6

Proper routing table configuration

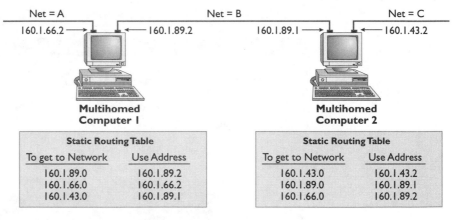

A static routing table for Network C, IP address 160.1.43.0, is created on Multihomed Host 1, directing the router to send the packets to interface 160.1.89.1. This will permit packets to move from Network A to Network C.

Also, a static route is configured on Host 2 to allow Network C to send packets to Network A. This is accomplished by referencing the network address 160.1.66.0, directing the router to send packets on to IP address 160.1.89.2, which can directly deliver packets destined for Network A.

The static routing table is always checked before a packet is routed. If there is no static route to a particular host, the packet is sent to the configured default gateway. For a host to communicate with other hosts on the internetwork, its default gateway address must be configured to match the IP address of the local router's interface.

Integrating Static and Dynamic Routing

As mentioned above, breeds of routers stick to their own and do not speak with those of a different feather. Static routers do not trade routing information with dynamic routers unless they're forced to. As they say, where there's a will, there's a way! To route from a static router through a dynamic router, such as a RIP or OSPF-enabled IP router, one must first add a static route to the routing tables located on both the static and dynamic routers, as shown in Figure 3.7.

- In order to route packets from Network A to the Internet, Host 2 requires that a route be added to its routing table. This addition includes the IP address of the closest interface (in this case, 160.1.66.2) that can access the dedicated IP router to the Internet.

- To route packets from Networks B and C to the Internet, a static entry must be added to Computer B's routing table. This entry includes the IP address of the nearest interface (160.1.89.2) on the dedicated IP router to the Internet.

- To allow computers on the Internet to communicate with hosts on Networks 1 and 2, one must statically configure the dedicated IP router with the IP address of the interface to Host 1. Host 1 then acts as a gateway to other subnets.

It's important to mention here that some implementations of RIP do not propagate static routing tables. Should you find yourself beset with this dilemma, you'd have to statically configure the remote routers in the Internet cloud to achieve your routing goals. Also important to note here is that the exact method for configuring a static route on a RIP router varies with each kind of router. It is therefore very wise to refer to your particular router's vendor documentation for more information.

FIGURE 3.7

Static and dynamic
router integration

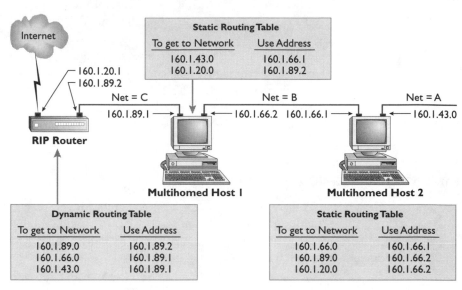

In Exercise 3.7, you will restore your default gateway address.

EXERCISE 3.7

Restoring the Default Gateway Address

In this exercise, you're going to restore the address for the default gateway. This will cause packets to be sent to the default gateway when no route entry is found for the destination network.

1. Use the Network application to open the Network Settings dialog box and access the TCP/IP Configuration dialog box.

2. In the Default Gateway box, type your default gateway address.

3. Close all dialog boxes, and then shut down and restart the computer.

Enabling IP Routing

After each network adapter is configured with a valid IP address and subnet mask, the next step is enabling IP routing for the computer. Assuming that the TCP/IP transport is already installed on your computer, follow the steps in Exercise 3.8 to enable IP routing.

Be aware, this exercise only works if you have more then one NIC card installed in your computer!

EXERCISE 3.8

Enabling IP Routing

1. From the Control Panel, start Network.

2. In the Network Settings dialog box, select TCP/IP Protocol, and then choose Configuration.

3. Then, in the TCP/IP Configuration dialog box, choose Advanced. The Advanced Microsoft TCP/IP Configuration dialog box will now appear.

4. Select the Enable IP Routing check box, and then choose OK. The Enable IP Routing check box is only available on a Windows NT computer that has multiple network cards installed on it.

5. To initialize IP routing, shut down and then restart your computer.

Required here is a note on Registry Entry. It's important to always enable IP routing through the Control Panel Network application rather than through the Registry. Formerly, in Windows NT 3.1, manual editing of the Registry was required.

When the Enable IP Routing check box is selected, the value for the following registry parameter is set to

```
HKEY_LOCAL_MACHINE\System\CurrentControlSet\Services\
    Tcpip\Parameters\IpEnableRouter
```

Implementing a Multihomed Computer

As mentioned, although dynamic routing isn't supported by the Windows NT v3.5x TCP/IP protocol stack, its workstations can be configured as multihomed hosts to support basic, static IP routing through deployment of multiple default gateways. A multihomed workstation is configured with multiple network adapter cards enabling it to route IP datagrams between them. Exercise 3.9 explains how to implement a multihomed computer on a Windows NT computer. Again, two NIC cards are required for this exercise.

EXERCISE 3.9

Implementing a Multihomed Computer

1. Ensure that each adapter card in the multihomed computer is configured with the appropriate driver, valid IP address, and subnet mask.

2. Check that IP Routing is enabled for the computer. (Refer to the last section if you need to.)

3. Configure static routes for all networks to which your multihomed computer has no configured interface already. One must ensure that the new routes are entered into the tables existing on all involved dynamic routers, or sinister things will occur.

Microsoft also supports computers running Windows for Workgroups 3.11 and TCP/IP-32 as a multihomed computer.

The TRACERT Utility

The *TRACERT Utility* is essentially a verification tool. It's used to substantiate the route that's been taken to a destination host. TRACERT is also highly useful in isolating routers and identifying WAN Links that are not functioning and/or are operating too slowly. Here's the relevant command syntax for deploying TRACERT:

    tracert 160.1.89.100

where 160.1.89.100 is the remote computer.

```
                        Command Prompt                       ▼ ▲
C:\users\default>
C:\users\default>tracert 160.1.89.100

Tracing route to TCPIP [160.1.89.100]
over a maximum of 30 hops:

   1    <10 ms    <10 ms    <10 ms  TCPIP [160.1.89.100]

Trace complete.

C:\users\default>_
```

Below is an example of the output that would result from entering the command if the computer was on the network:

```
Tracing route to 160.1.89.100  over 2 hops
1 <10 ms <10 ms <10 ms 160.1.89.2
2 <10 ms <10 ms <10 ms 160.1.89.100
```

TRACERT can aid in determining if a router has failed by the degree of success the command enjoys. For example, if the command is unsuccessful, it is possible to assess router or WAN link problems and identify the point at which routing failed. The response time for the command is returned in the output. The information contained in the output can be readily compared to that recorded for another route to the same destination. This greatly facilitates identifying a slow or ineffective router or WAN link.

For example, the command:

```
tracert 160.1.66.11
```

would display the path taken from the local host to the destination host: 160.1.66.11. The output from the preceding command would confirm that the router address 160.1.66.1 was the route taken from the local host to the destination host. Here's what that output would look like:

```
Tracing route to 160.1.66.11 over a maximum of 30 hops
1 <10 ms <10 ms <10 ms 160.1.66.1
2 <10 ms <10 ms <10 ms 160.1.66.11
```

Second Section Summary

WELL, WE HOPE you've found all of this helpful and enlightening. To make sure none of it got lost in the shuffle, let's take a moment to recap things.

We began this section with a discussion on default gateways. Default gateways are nodes residing on the local network that are aware of other network IDs that are linked into the greater internetwork. Although more than one default gateway can be configured, only the first one will be used for routing purposes. The others will be used only as backup should the primary one become unavailable for some reason, giving your network greater fault tolerance. We also discussed how to create additional default gateways using the Advanced TCP/IP configuration.

Next, we got into the actual building of a static routing table, complete with instruction on adding static entries and default entries. The following commands are important to remember for these procedures:

- Route add

- Route delete

- Route change

- Route print

- Route -s

- Route -f

We then delved into the finer points of integrating static and dynamic routing, noting that in order to route from a static router through a dynamic router, you must first add in a static route to the routing tables located on both types of routers involved.

We then covered how to enable IP routing and how to implement a multihomed computer. We defined multihomed computers as workstations configured with multiple network adapter cards that enable it to route IP datagrams between them. Implementation on a Windows NT 3.5 computer requires that:

- Each adapter card in the multihomed computer is configured with the appropriate driver, valid IP address, and subnet mask.

- IP routing is enabled for the computer.

You finished the section by learning about the highly useful TRACERT utility, finding that TRACERT can be an important diagnostic aid in determining if a router has failed.

Exercise Questions

Multiple-Choice Questions

1. What are the protocols that use dynamic routing?

A. Routing Information Protocol

B. Dynamic Information Protocol

C. Open Shortest Path First

D. Open Safest Path First

2. When configuring multiple default gateways, which is true?

A. Although more than one default gateway can be configured, only the first one will be used for routing purposes. The others will be used only as backup should the primary one become unavailable for some reason.

B. Multiple default gateways cannot be configured with NT.

C. Although more than one default gateway can be configured, only the last one will be used for routing purposes. The others will be used only as backup should the primary one become unavailable for some reason.

D. More then one default gateway can be configured, and NT uses a round-robin approach when choosing the default gateway.

3. What is the TRACERT utility?

   A. The TRACERT utility is essentially a verification tool used to substantiate the route that's been taken to a local host.

   B. The TRACERT utility erases any traces of viruses on Windows NT.

   C. The TRACERT utility works with dynamic routing to help trace the shortest paths.

   D. The TRACERT utility is essentially a verification tool used to substantiate the route that's been taken to a destination host.

4. What is IP routing?

   A. InterProcess Routing is used for delivering e-mail.

   B. IP routing works only on local networks.

   C. IP routing is the process of sending data from a host on one network to a remote host on another network through a router, or routers.

   D. IP routing, a function of the Network Access layer of the DOD reference model, routes packets between hosts.

Scenario-Based Review

SCENARIO #1 Your boss frantically comes up to you and says he put two NIC cards in his NT server, but the workstations on each segment can't see each other. He knows that to route IP packets to other networks, each multihomed computer (static router) must be configured two ways, but he can't remember what they are. What are the two things you need to set on the NT server?

SCENARIO #2 You get a call from a company who thinks they need some routers. They have a small network, and read in a magazine that they should employ static routing. They want to know more about how static routing would meet their networking needs. What do you tell them?

SCENARIO #3 It's your first day on the job at Terrific Technology Teaching Center, and as a co-instructor you are asked to teach on the enabling of IP routers. Take a moment to explain the procedure now.

SCENARIO #4 Later, a student comes up to you confused and asks if she needs to add a routing table to a computer running as a multihomed computer, and connecting two subnet segments. What do you tell her, and why?

SCENARIO #5 You have two NT servers and a router to the Internet. Should you build a static router between the NT servers, or will the dynamic router to the Internet be sufficient?

SCENARIO #6 What information would you put into the static routing table?

IP Address Resolution

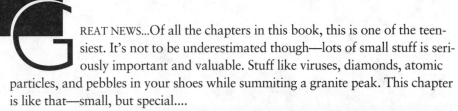

REAT NEWS...Of all the chapters in this book, this is one of the teen-siest. It's not to be underestimated though—lots of small stuff is seri-ously important and valuable. Stuff like viruses, diamonds, atomic particles, and pebbles in your shoes while summiting a granite peak. This chapter is like that—small, but special....

You can't do much before IP address resolution has occurred. It's a primary, fundamental thing. The other types of resolution, host name and NetBIOS, dis-cussed in the next two chapters, can only work for you if the IP address is known first. These operations require the knowledge of IP addresses for the messages they send via TCP/IP to reach their destinations. In short, if commu-nication is to occur, IP addresses must first be resolved. This chapter will focus on how a number assigned to a host system is resolved to find its MAC, or hardware address.

Objectives

FTER YOU'VE MADE short work of this chapter, you should find yourself in possession of sage wisdom about:

- IP address resolution

- How IP address resolution is achieved locally

- How IP address resolution is achieved remotely

- The ins and outs of IP address resolution and ARP caching

- How to deal effectively with some common IP address resolution hang-ups

- The reasons why these hang-ups happened in the first place—and how to prevent them from happening again

IP Address Resolution Defined

THE PROCESS OF resolution involves asking a question and receiving an answer to it. In the case of IP address resolution, the question posed resembles, "Which device is the owner of IP address 192.57.8.8?" The resolution, or answer, to that question would include the MAC address of the NIC (network interface card), as encoded by the manufacturer. In essence, IP address resolution is the linking of an IP, or software, address to a hardware, or MAC, address.

Getting to a specific place first requires knowing where that place is located. Similarly, resolving an IP address is to network managers what locating a certain parcel of land on a planner's grid map is to a city planner or industrial engineer. Suppose your neighbor desired an additional room for their flourishing family, and an expansion was planned. Before the first contractor's hammer fell, a permit for the remodeling would have to be obtained from the city. Those responsible for awarding that permit would then have to "resolve" your neighbor's home address to its physical coordinates—its individual place on their grid. Knowing its "map address," they would then have access to the information they need to proceed with issuing a permit.

The protocol that answers these questions regarding IP address ownership is called ARP. You may recall some discussion about ARP from Chapter 2. In case you don't, ARP stands for "Address Resolution Protocol," and is described thoroughly in RFC 826. ARP is the IP address resolution engine. Regardless of where the ultimate destination is located, ARP always uses a local broadcast to determine where data should be sent. If the destination happens to be on a remote network, the local default gateway's hardware address will be used to hop over to it. Once the mystery address has been resolved, it is recorded in a table called the ARP cache. If additional messages are sent to the same destination, the ARP cache will be checked first so as to prevent unnecessary network traffic generated by a broadcast. This keeps the local network running efficiently as it's examined and logged.

You might also remember our discussion of RARP (Reverse Address Resolution Protocol) in Chapter 2. Like inductive vs. deductive reasoning, it's the inverse operation of ARP—it's used to get an IP address from a Mac Address.

Local Resolution

Each subnet of the network can be thought of as an island that contains a city—say, Maui. So long as you never have to leave that island, you've remained local—or as is the case with computers, on the local network. If you require a service or permit concerning your property on the island, you could contact Maui's local city planning office, and give them your address. They would respond by assigning a permit according to your mapped coordinates. Likewise, whenever a request is made that requires IP address resolution, ARP, IP's city employee, is deployed to the task of confirming your identity and whereabouts.

The process of resolving the IP address of a machine existing on the local network is shown in Figure 4.1, and outlined below. While reading through these steps, notice how ARP works in a way that minimizes network overhead.

FIGURE 4.1

Resolving a local IP address

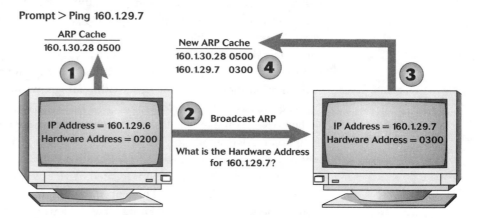

Step One: The destination machine's IP address is checked to see if it's on the local network. If so, the host system will then check its ARP cache for the machine's hardware address.

Step Two: Provided that the ARP address didn't find 0300 in the host system's ARP cache, ARP will attempt to enter it by sending a message requesting the owner of that IP address to send back its hardware address. Because the hardware address is still unknown, the ARP message is sent out as a broadcast that's read by each and every system on the local network. Like a self-addressed envelope that's sent inscribed with all the information necessary to get it back to its sender, both the IP address and the hardware address of the requesting system are included in the broadcast message.

Step Three: The reply message is sent directly to the hardware address of the requesting system. Only the owner of the requested IP address will respond. All other systems will disregard the request.

Step Four: Upon receiving the reply, the requesting machine will append the address into its ARP cache. At this point, communication has been established.

Remote Resolution

When it comes to computer operations, communications are usually much simpler if they involve devices within the local network. These processes can't always be simple though. Complex internetworks with subnets have bridges or routers set up between them that connect them together. These devices are filters that serve to sort data according to its destination—they don't allow all data to cross indiscriminately. To distinguish which data gets to pass through, routers look at the IP address destination located in the packet's header, whereas bridges look at a frame's header for the destination hardware address. Going back to our subnet island of Maui, let's say you find it necessary to contact someone or something that doesn't reside there, but exists on another island—Molokai. Since those who populate Molokai aren't Maui locals, by attempting to make contact with them, you are attempting remote communication. Let's pretend that to reach them, you must cross a draw bridge. Unless you arrive at the draw bridge with a specific, remote Molokai address, the bridge operator will keep the bridge drawn, and you won't be allowed to cross.

Figure 4.2 and the steps immediately following it illustrate the process of resolving the IP address of a machine located on a remote network. These steps are repeated at every router the data encounters en route to its final destination.

Step One: The destination IP address is checked to see if it is on the local network. Once determined otherwise, the system will check its local route table for a path to the remote network. If a path is found, the ARP cache is checked for the hardware address of the default gateway specified in the routing path. Note: In general, the most efficient path to a remote network will be established by a router utilizing OSPF (Open Shortest Path First). This reduces network traffic overhead.

Step Two: When a path is not found, an ARP request is generated to determine the hardware address of the default gateway or router (see Figure 4.2).

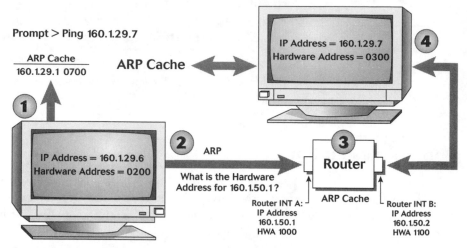

FIGURE 4.2

Resolving a remote
IP address

Since the only thing that is known about the destination is that it is on a remote network, the router will have to be used as the medium to reach the remote destination.

Step Three: The router will reply with its hardware address to the requesting host. The source host will then use ICMP to issue an echo request back to the router, which will then deliver the echo request to the remote network that will eventually reach the destination host. The router will then repeat step one(that is, check if it's local or remote, and then take the correct action. Generally, unless a routing path is found at the server, steps one through three are repeated until the client is on a local network. Note that the router can use either a broadcast or its cache in determining the hardware address of the destination system.

Step Four: The destination machine will also respond to the ARP request with an ICMP echo reply. Since the requesting system is on a remote network, the reply will be sent to the router. As with previous resolutions, if the router (default gateway) is not in the ARP cache, a local IP address resolution scenario will take place to determine the router's address. In turn, the router will then set the route accordingly.

What's more confusing is that there are often multiple bridges to the same location. Finding the shortest path is usually handled by the router, and will remain an issue until the data finds its way to the router directly connected to the destination address's local subnet.

The ARP Cache

The ARP cache is a table used to store both IP addresses and MAC addresses. Each time communication is initiated with another machine, it checks its ARP cache for an entry. If it doesn't find one, an ARP request is broadcasted, the address is resolved, and it is then entered into its ARP cache. The address is now handy, much like an entry in your home address book would be, for the next time communication with that device is necessary. Additionally, the ARP cache maintains the hardware broadcast address (FFFFFFFF) for the local subnet as a permanent entry. Though it doesn't appear when the cache is viewed, this entry allows a host to accept ARP broadcasts.

ARP Entry Lifetimes and the ARP.EXE Utility

Entries in the ARP table include an IP address, a hardware address, and a time stamp. Each entry in the ARP cache is valid for no more than 10 minutes. If an entry isn't used within a ten minute period from its last use, it'll be removed from the cache. With some implementations of TCP/IP, the 10 minute maximum lifetime is automatically extended each time the entry is used. This isn't the case with Windows NT, which simply deletes entries from the cache, starting with the oldest, to make room for new ones as the capacity limits of its ARP table are reached. It will do this to an old entry even if its lifetime hasn't yet expired.

The ARP.EXE utility allows you to view, add, and delete entries in the ARP cache (see Exercise 4.1). Entries are added by typing the command format -s (ip address)(mac address). An example would be arp -s 134.57.8.8 05-20-4a-29-95. These entries are permanently stored in the ARP cache table. Since these entries don't change, they're also referred to as static entries. The only time that these entries will be removed is if the computer is restarted, or if a broadcast is received, indicating that the hardware address has changed. In the latter case, the updated entry becomes dynamic instead of static. Entries can be deleted by typing arp -d 135.57.8.8.

All entries in the ARP cache can be displayed using arp -a or arp -g (-g isn't supported by Windows for Workgroups). These case-sensitive commands can be highly useful when questing for the hardware address of a destination system. For example, if you needed to know the hardware address of a particular workstation, you could use ping to open a communications path to it, and then review the ARP cache to determine the hardware address associated with the pinged IP entry.

The ARP system is kind of like jail. Like all ARP entries—IP addresses having both a hardware address and a time stamp—every jail inmate has a number and exit date. In both cases, depending on the inmate/entry's behavior, the time spent "inside" will vary. Though lifetimes aren't definite for inmates, both ARP entries and inmates have them, along with maximum time periods for their duration. Depending on the jail's capacity, older inmates may be released early, just as old ARP entries are when the ARP cache is full. Occasionally, a judge assigns the death penalty or consecutive lifetime sentences to an individual inmate—like making a manual entry into the ARP table. The only time these special inmates are released is when they're dead (deleted from the ARP cache), a pardon is given, allowing the inmate to begin a new life (restarting the computer), or if the system discovers it has the wrong person (a broadcast notifying ARP of a new, corrected hardware address).

EXERCISE 4.1

Using the ARP.EXE Command to View, Add and Delete Entries in the ARP Cache

To practice viewing the ARP cache:

1. Logon as Administrator.

2. Go to a DOS prompt and type **ARP -a**.

3. Record your results.

To add an entry to the ARP cache:

1. At a DOS prompt, type **ARP -s 160.1.8.18 05-20-4a-29-95**.

2. To view your new entry, type **ARP -a**.

To delete an entry from the ARP cache:

1. At a DOS prompt, type **ARP -d 160.1.8.18**.

2. View your ARP cache to make sure the entry was deleted.

3. Type **ARP -a**.

Common Problems

Many communications problems are in some way related to resolution. The two most common ones are redundant IP addresses and incorrect subnet masks.

A redundant IP address can cause a variety of networking ills. Under Windows NT, it is very obvious indeed when you have duplicate addresses because the host system will simply refuse to initialize TCP/IP. However, not all systems make this problem so deliciously apparent. For example, if a server or gateway were to have their addresses used in more than one place, the wrong system may receive or respond to requests, or even just hang there in suspended animation. Imagine the confusion caused by two people using the same social security number!

The existence of incorrect subnet masks can also make for a gloomy day in Networkland. For example, when a host is attempting to determine if an address is local or remote, it will look to the subnet mask to determine which portions of the address are network-based, and which are node-based. If the system discovers a remote machine on the local network, lots of unnecessary traffic will be created from broadcasts while it attempts to resolve the addresses. Depending on the level at which the broadcast is generated, something called a *broadcast storm* may take place. These are as sinister as they sound—their "storm surges" being capable of destroying network performance by causing systems caught in the deluge to "time-out," and hang there as if frozen.

Summing Things Up

WELL...QUICK AS a desert thundershower, this chapter's over—but hopefully, not before you know it! The IP address resolution process was likened to the human process of asking a question and receiving its answer...the communications equivalent of asking, "What device is the owner of a certain IP address?" and receiving the answer "the MAC address of the NIC card as encoded by the manufacturer." IP address resolution was resolved (pun intended) to be the linking of an IP, or software, address to a hardware, or MAC, address.

You learned, by means of a four step process, how to resolve IP addresses locally. You also noticed how ARP works in a way that minimizes network overhead. Remote resolution, also a four step process, is a bit more complicated because of the involvement of routers, or "bridges."

The ARP cache was then introduced and defined as a table used to store both IP addresses and MAC addresses. It is checked for entries each time communication is initiated with another machine. If no entry is found, an ARP request is broadcasted, and then the address is resolved and entered into the machine's ARP cache for future use. The ARP table includes an IP address, a hardware address, and a time stamp valid for a maximum of 10 minutes. Windows NT doesn't automatically reset an entry's lifetime with each use. Also, as the limits of its ARP table are reached, it selectively deletes entries from the cache, starting with the oldest, to make room for new ones even if the old entry's lifetime hasn't yet expired. We then explored the ARP.EXE utility, the commands associated with it, and its functions. Handy things you can do with ARP.EXE include viewing, adding to, and deleting entries in the ARP cache. The section ended with the discussion of two of the most frequent obstacles to communications, duplicate addresses and incorrect subnet masks, stressing the importance of making sure your addresses are unique, and your subnet masks are valid.

Exercise Questions

Multiple-Choice Questions

1. What is IP address resolution?

   A. Resolving duplicate IP addresses

   B. The successful mapping of an IP address to its hardware address

   C. Resolving invalid subnet masks

   D. Resolving errors when IP tries to resolve an IP address to a hardware address

2. How do you resolve IP addresses locally?

   A. By typing `Resolve IP address ip-address`

   B. By typing `ARP -s ip-address`

   C. With an ARP request and an ARP reply

   D. With a RARP request and a RARP reply

3. How does your computer resolve IP addresses remotely?

   A. It sends an ARP to the destination machine.

   B. It sends a RARP to the destination machine.

   C. It sends a RARP to the default gateway.

   D. It sends an ARP to the default gateway.

4. What is true about the ARP cache?

   A. It's cleared out every time the computer is rebooted.

   B. The ARP cache stores only dynamic IP and hardware addresses.

   C. The ARP cache stores only static IP and hardware addresses.

   D. It's permanent.

5. What's the maximum lifetime of an entry in the ARP cache?

   A. 2 minutes

   B. As specified by the system administrator

   C. 10 minutes

   D. ARP entries are permanent and can only be removed by typing `ARP -d`.

6. Aside from the initial entry into the cache, if the destination system isn't contacted again, how long will the entry remain in the cache?

   A. 10 minutes

   B. 2 minutes

   C. 5 minutes

   D. Until deleted

7. Under Windows NT, if the cache fills up, what happens to old and new entries?

    A. If their lifetime expires, old entries are deleted, and new ones added.

    B. Regardless of whether or not an old entry's lifetime has expired, it is deleted in favor of adding the new one.

    C. Old entries are cached for future use, and new ones added to the ARP table.

Scenario-Based Review

SCENARIO #1 You're a computer science professor at a major university. One of your students wants to know why an IP address needs to be resolved. She asks why it's necessary to know both the software and hardware addresses—why isn't knowing the hardware address enough? Explain.

SCENARIO #2 You're being interviewed for a network specialist position. Your potential employer asks, "In what way could an incorrect subnet mask cause problems? When would these problems occur, and who, if anyone, would notice?" How would you answer?

Host Name Resolution

M OST PEOPLE HAVE more than a little trouble remembering a bunch of 32-bit, binary numbers. The IP address is most commonly represented by four 8-bit numbers instead, but even then, remembering a throng of cryptic number sequences is still, at best, a hassle. TCP/IP allows language-loving humans to use host names for their machines instead. Though TCP/IP hosts do require an IP address to communicate with each other, hosts can be referenced by a handy host name for easy identification by their significant human or humans.

Objectives

S HOULD YOU FIND yourself on the other side of this chapter without total recall regarding this little list, read the chapter again—this time, without *The X-Files* or something else on the tube while "studying" it.

- The definition of host naming

- Host name resolution on both local and remote networks

- Host name resolution and configuration via a DNS

- Host name resolution and configuration via a HOSTS file

- The Microsoft way of achieving host name resolution

- Commonly experienced problems with the above

Host Names Defined

AN OBVIOUSLY CRITICAL first thing to get straight is what, exactly, a host name is. Here it is.... A *host name* is an assigned identifier called an "alias" that's used to designate a specific TCP/IP host in a logical way. This alias can be any string of up to 256 characters of any type. A single host can have many host names which may be the same, or different, from that system's NetBIOS name (we'll discuss this in Chapter 6). The alias allows a given machine to be referenced by name, a function, or anything else that makes the light of recognition burn brightly in the mind of the human who needs to remember which one it is.

Host names are much like NetBIOS names in that their functional uses are the same. For example, a host name such as "Hal" may be resolved to the IP address 160.1.92.26. As we already know, IP addresses can then be resolved to a hardware address, fully identifying the device. This is the same with NetBIOS. Highly noteworthy is the fact that UNIX machines, as well as some others, don't use NetBIOS names. The main difference in referencing the two types of hosts is that with NetBIOS, you must always communicate using the name with Microsoft network commands—not just the IP address. Using TCP/IP utilities to reference a UNIX host will allow you to access the host using the IP address. UNIX has always been TCP/IP-based, and TCP/IP has been specifically tailored to fit the needs of this operating system. However, Microsoft has been backward fitting their operating systems to function with TCP/IP, and with much success. The NetBIOS names used by Microsoft are intended to function under the guidance of different protocols which use a different naming convention, both for user and program-oriented communication.

To a UNIX-based machine, the naming function for both user and program communication may be referenced by anything that is an equivalent to what it's used to seeing. For instance, a UNIX utility like FTP will allow you to contact a host by its host name, domain name, or IP address. To demonstrate this, suppose that you were on the Internet with a UNIX workstation. If you desired to retrieve files from Microsoft's FTP site, you could open FTP.MICROSOFT.COM, or access it by entering its IP address—whichever you prefer.

In the example above, FTP.MICROSOFT.COM is called the FQDN, or Fully Qualified Domain Name. When working with TCP/IP, systems are addressed in a hierarchy that can logically locate a system based on its domain identifier. This system works using host but not NetBIOS names.

The Host Naming Hierarchy

TCP/IP has full support for host naming, which is organized into a hierarchical structure. Each host belongs to a domain, and each domain is classified further into domain types, much like the scientific naming-scheme convention of class, order, phylum, genus, family, and species. `Microsoft.com` is a commercial organization—the "com" standing for "commercial." (See Figure 5.1.)

FIGURE 5.1

Domain name hierarchy

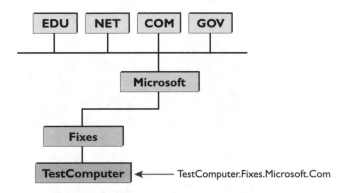

You can tell immediately what type of group you are dealing with by the suffix following the organization name. The following chart lists the various types of organizations suffixed in this manner which you may come across as you explore TCP/IP though the Internet. Some common ones are shown in Figure 5.2.

FIGURE 5.2

Internet top-level domain names

Domain Name	Meaning
COM	**Commercial Organization**
EDU	**Educational Institution**
GOV	**Government Institution**
MIL	**Military Group**
NET	**Major Network Support Center**
ORG	**Organization other than those above**
INT	**International Organization**

Your computer will refer to a DNS server to resolve names listed in the hierarchy. Domain names require a Domain Name Service—a computing service, like UNIX, that requires a *server daemon*, which is a program for UNIX that runs in the background, just like a TSR does for DOS. A Domain Name

Service provides a centralized online database for resolving domain names to their corresponding IP addresses. The base-names like, "Microsoft" in, "Microsoft.com" are registered by the *Stanford Research Institute Network Information Center,* or *SRI International/SRI NIC,* so that they're kept unique on the Internet.

Windows NT 3.5x doesn't provide the server portion of a DNS component. However, Microsoft supports the DNS server daemon for 3.5x through the use of third-party DNS servers.

Resolving Host Names

BEFORE ARP CAN be used to resolve the IP address to a hardware address, a host name must first be resolved to the IP address. The name resolution methods are similar to those used in NetBIOS resolution processes, as you'll see in Chapter 6. Microsoft TCP/IP can use any of six methods to resolve host names. The first three resolution methods—WINS, Local Broadcast, and through the LMHOSTS file—will be discussed in greater detail in the next chapter on NetBIOS. The local host name, and the use of DNS and the HOSTS file are the remaining three. We'll be discussing the last two, the DNS and the HOSTS file methods, as they're applied in the UNIX world. We'll also explore how they translate into the Microsoft environment. The methods that Windows NT can use to resolve a host name are configurable.

Standard Resolution

- **Local host name**   This is the name of the local configured machine as it relates to the destination host. It's typically used for loopback, or recursive connections.

- **HOSTS file**   This is a table stored in a local file and used to resolve host names to IP addresses. It conforms to Berkeley Software Distribution's version 4.3 UNIX's HOSTS file. This file is most commonly used with the TCP/IP utilities FTP, Telnet, ping, etc., to resolve a host's name. It may be used to address a computer by an alias, and in many cases, be placed on multiple computers of varying platforms for host resolution purposes.

- **Domain Name Service (DNS)**   This service is a cornerstone in the UNIX world, and is found on systems running the DNS service daemon. It's commonly employed for the resolution of host name to IP addresses. This file can be thought of as a networked HOSTS file.

Specific Resolution

- **Local broadcast**   An announcement made on a local network requesting the IP address for the system assigned to a specific NetBIOS or host name. It is commonly referred to as a b-node broadcast.

- **Windows Internet Name Service**   This is commonly implemented as a WINS, or Windows Internet Name Server. This type of name resolution service corresponds to RFC 1001/1002, and delivers NetBIOS or host name resolution from a server that's running it.

- **LMHOSTS file**   This is also a table that's stored in a local file and used to resolve NetBIOS or host names to IP addresses on remote networks. It's similar to the HOSTS file discussed in detail next, but offers some functions we'll discuss more in the next chapter on NetBIOS.

Resolution via the HOSTS File

Before getting down to the nitty-gritty on the host name resolution process, it's important to examine in more detail a few particulars regarding the HOSTS file.

The HOSTS File

The HOSTS file is an ordinary text document that can be created or modified using any text editor. It's used by ping and other TCP/IP utilities to resolve a host name to an IP address on both local and remote networks. Each line with a host name or alias can only correspond to one IP address. Because the file is read from top to bottom, duplicate names will be ignored, and commonly used names should be placed nearer the top for speedier access. Older implementations of TCP/IP with Windows NT maintained the case-sensitivity associated with UNIX, but this is no longer the case (pun intended). An entry can be any valid string of up to 256 characters, with comments placed to the right of a pound (#) sign. By default, Microsoft installs a HOSTS file in \systemroot\ SYSTEM32\DRIVERS\ETC, with `127.0.0.1` localhost as a loopback entry.

```
#Sample Host file
#
127.0.0.1    loopback    localhost   #Entries used for loopback diagnostics
#
160.1.27.3   My_Computer             #Entries to describe my System
160.1.4.87   UnixMaster UnixHost     # The Unix system that I talk to

160.1.98.89 Router12                 # My Subnet's Router
```

The HOSTS File Resolution Process

The HOSTS file has long been used for name resolution purposes as implemented with TCP/IP on most UNIX hosts. Since a host can have multiple names, the HOSTS file will commonly contain listings of the local host `127.0.0.1`, as well as other names, called *aliases*, by which the machine may be known when it's referenced by other systems. The HOSTS file will be checked for all host name resolutions, including itself.

Resolution begins when a command is issued requesting resolution. This command can be either machine or user generated. The system will initially check the destination name against is own. If a match is found, it's a done deal—the name's been resolved. However, in some cases, like when the required destination turns out to be on a remote system, or if the request is actually an alias for itself, the system will proceed to check the HOSTS file for a match. If no match is found, and the HOSTS file is the only configured method for resolution, an error will be spawned and sent back. If a match is achieved, the IP address is then used to resolve the destination's IP address to a hardware address with ARP, and the destination host is found. If the destination host is on a remote network, ARP obtains the hardware address of the proper router (default gateway), and the request is then forwarded to the destination host. In Figure 5.3, a user types **Ping Alta** from the host named "Aspen," IP address

160.1.24.3. Aspen first looks into its HOSTS file, and finds an entry for "Alta" of 160.1.29.7. If the name wasn't found in the HOSTS file, an error would be generated reading, no such host. If Aspen has talked with Alta before, the hardware address would be in Aspen's ARP cache. If not, host Aspen would then ARP for the hardware address for the workstation Alta.

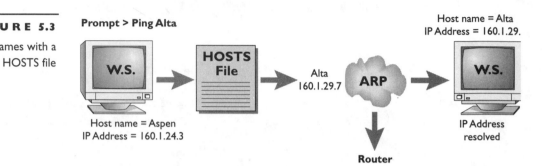

FIGURE 5.3

Resolving names with a HOSTS file

At this point, the process is identical to NetBIOS resolution. We keep comparing the two resolution methods because it's very important for you to understand their similarities and differences. A local machine will resolve to its hardware address, while a remote machine will resolve to the hardware address of the proper default gateway. No local cache is used with host name resolution. You will configure the HOSTS file in Exercise 5.1.

EXERCISE 5.1

Configuring the HOSTS File

1. Open the following file:

    \systemroot\SYSTEM32\DRIVERS\ETC\HOSTS

2. Read the instructions at the beginning of the HOSTS file for adding entries.

3. Go to the end of the file and type in an additional entry.

    example: 160.1.201.22   Unixincharge

4. Save the file as HOSTS.

Resolution via DNS

Although Windows NT doesn't provide a daemon or a server service to behave as a DNS in version 3.51, it does allow itself to act as a client. A DNS can be thought of as a networked version of the HOSTS file. In computing environments such as UNIX, the DNS provides a central reservoir used to resolve fully qualified domain names (FQDNs) to IP addresses.

As shown in Figure 5.4, resolution begins with the issuing of a command requiring resolution. Again, the command can originate from either a machine or a user. In our example, we show a user originated command: `Ping Alta .Fixes.Microsoft.Com`. The DNS receives a request for the IP address of the host system "Alta." If found, the DNS will reply with the matched address. If no match is found, or the DNS server does not respond to requests made at 5, 10, 20, 40, 5, 10, and 20 second intervals progressively, an error will be generated, assuming that DNS is the only configured host name service. If a match is achieved, the IP address is then used to resolve the destination's IP address to a hardware address with ARP. Remember...a local machine—a destination host located on the same subnet as the sending host—will resolve to its hardware address, while a destination for a remote host will resolve to the hardware address of the default gateway.

FIGURE 5.4

Resolution with DNS

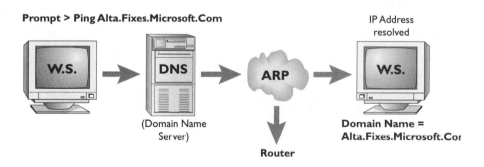

Prompt > Ping Alta.Fixes.Microsoft.Com

IP Address resolved

W.S.

DNS

ARP

W.S.

(Domain Name Server)

Router

Domain Name = Alta.Fixes.Microsoft.Com

A Windows NT machine can be configured to use DNS through the procedure outlined in the following exercise.

EXERCISE 5.2

**Configuring Domain Name Server Support
on a Windows NT Server**

1. From the Main group, open the Control Panel and select Network.

2. In the Installed software section, click on TCP/IP, then select Configure.

3. Select the DNS name button.

4. Type in your system's primary host name (additional ones may be added as aliases in a HOSTS file) in the Host Name box. The default is the name of the Windows NT machine. Assuming you have a domain, enter it, making sure to include its proper extension (i.e., .COM, .EDU, .GOV).

5. Type the DNS server in the DNS search box. The order of priority can be set using the order buttons.

6. Type in the domain suffix that you would like added to your host name. A total of six may be added to search your internetwork. The order of priority can be set using the order buttons.

7. Choose OK.

Additionally, you may set up TCP/IP to use DNS for NetBIOS by clicking on the ENABLE DNS for Windows Networking in the Advanced section of TCP/IP.

The Microsoft Method

Windows NT can be configured to resolve host names using either the HOSTS file or a DNS. If one of them fails, the other is there to provide backup. Microsoft's implementation of TCP/IP under Windows NT supports all forms of resolution mentioned earlier: WINS, b-node broadcasts, and LMHOSTS. In Figure 5.5, we show a system configured to support all forms of name resolution.

Such a system would have the following search order:

Step A: Beginning with a command requiring host name resolution (i. e., Ping, TELNET, FTP, etc.), the local machine's host name will be checked for a match. In the example in Figure 5.5, this would be Ping Alta. If a match is found, no further action is required, and no network traffic is created.

FIGURE 5.5

Microsoft's method of resolving host names

Prompt > Ping Alta

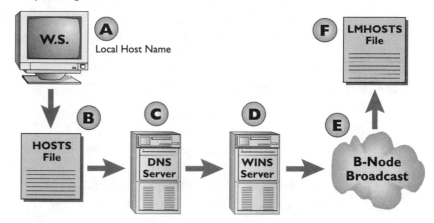

Step B: If the name isn't found, the next step would be to review the HOSTS file on the local machine. Again, if a match is found, no further action is required, and no network traffic is created.

Step C: If the name isn't found, the next strategy will be to attempt resolution though the DNS. If no response is received from the DNS machine, repeat requests will be sent in intervals of 5, 10, 20, 40, 5, 10 and 20 seconds, progressively. If your system is configured for DNS, and the unit is offline or down, all other systems using DNS in some form will experience a considerable slow down—so much so that they may appear to have crashed while attempting to resolve the name.

Step D: If the DNS server was offline, or is unable to resolve the name for some reason, a check is run on the NetBIOS name cache, followed by three attempts to get the WINS server to resolve the name.

Step E: If none of the attempts in Step D successfully resolve the host name, three b-node broadcasts are then sent out.

Step F: If this is also unsuccessful, the final step is to search the LMHOSTS file. This action is very similar to, and corresponds to, the behavior of a Microsoft enhanced b-node system.

If all of these resolution attempts fail, an error will be returned. Since the name can't be resolved, the only remaining way to communicate with the unresolved machine will be to use its specific IP address.

The action path of host name resolution closely resembles that of NetBIOS name resolution. The key difference between them is that NetBIOS name resolution methods generate less network traffic, whereas host names are resolved by standard UNIX methods.

Some Common Problems

There are several problems associated with host name resolution. Commonly, `ping` is used to verify entries. This works extremely well unless a different client has the IP address, resulting in the dismal fact that you are actually checking the wrong machine. There is a great degree of similarity between the following list of headaches plaguing host name resolution, and those experienced with NetBIOS name resolution.

HOSTS / DNS Does Not Contain a Name

Like the search for Atlantis, you just can't find something if it isn't there. If the name doesn't exist, the system can't find it. Quite often, companies will implement DNS as a solution. It's important to remember that if your system is configured for the wrong DNS server, you won't be successful in resolving the filename, and therefore will also fail to resolve the host name to an address. This same predicament occurs when backup copies of the HOSTS file are created, but the wrong one is modified.

HOSTS Contains a Misspelled Entry

People who tell you not to let little things bug you have never spent the night in the same room with a thirsty mosquito. Little things are capable of great destruction, and host name resolution can fail because of something as simple as a spelling error in a command or an entry in the HOSTS file. Be sure to back up the HOSTS file before making changes. HOSTS files can become large, containing a multitude of entries—a very daunting, confusing thing to encounter late at night when it's easy to make mistakes like typing in the wrong IP addresses or host names. These entries just won't work if the host names are spelled incorrectly.

HOSTS Entry Has the Wrong IP Address

Most often, it's not that the IP address is wrong in the HOSTS file or DNS, so much as the host's IP address has changed. If this is the case, then you are trying to reach a host at an IP address that either no longer exists, or has been reassigned elsewhere. When you come across this problem, be sure to verify that you really do have the right IP address. Commonly, in our busy world, when systems are moved and IP addresses are changed, small things like the HOSTS file are overlooked. Sure, the DNS was changed and a memo was sent to management, but if the numbers don't match, your memo was a lie. If you change a machine's IP address, pay close attention to these numbers—sometimes the only way to know for sure is to check the host itself. This applies to a wrong IP address attached to a DNS server.

HOSTS File or DNS Contains Repeat NetBIOS Name Entries

Once the host name has been found with an IP address, there is no further need to search any further. The systems involved consider the name to be resolved. Unfortunately, if the IP address recorded in the file is an old one, and the correct entry located below it contains the right one, the proper system will never be reached. Make sure you have only one up-to-date entry for each host name entered in the file.

Summing Things Up

A HOST NAME IS defined as an assigned identifier, called an *alias*, that is used to designate a specific TCP/IP host in a logical way. This alias can be any string of up to 256 characters of any type. It allows a given machine to be referenced by a name, function, etc., that's more easily recalled by the user than an abstract number.

TCP/IP host naming is organized into a hierarchical structure. Each host belongs to a domain, and each domain is classified further into domain types. For example, `Microsoft.com` is a commercial organization—the "com" stands for "commercial."

Microsoft TCP/IP can use any of six configurable methods to resolve host names, some used for standard resolution, and others for specific resolution. Standard resolution is accomplished through:

■ Local host name

■ HOSTS file

■ Domain Name Service (DNS)

Specific resolution is achieved through:

■ Local broadcasts

■ Windows Internet Name Service (WINS)

■ LMHOSTS file

We explored host name resolution in action, pausing to examine the HOSTS file itself in greater detail. The HOSTS file is an ordinary text document that can be created or modified using any text editor, and also by Ping and other TCP/IP utilities used to resolve host names to IP addresses on both local and remote networks. Older implementations of TCP/IP with Windows NT maintained the case-sensitivity associated with UNIX, but this is no longer the case. An entry can be any valid string of up to 256 characters, with comments placed to the right of a pound (#) sign.

We then discussed resolution through DNS. Although Windows NT doesn't provide a daemon or a server service to behave as a DNS in version 3.5*x*, it does allow itself to act as a client.

The action path of host name resolution closely resembles that of NetBIOS name resolution. The key difference between them is that NetBIOS name resolution methods generate less network traffic, whereas host names are resolved by standard UNIX methods.

We closed the chapter with news on some of the problems commonly encountered with host name resolution:

1. The HOSTS file / DNS does not contain a name. If the name doesn't exist, the system can't find it.

2. The HOSTS file contains a misspelled entry.

3. The HOSTS entry has the wrong IP address.

4. The HOSTS file or DNS contains repeat NetBIOS name entries.

Exercise Questions

Multiple-Choice Questions

1. What is a domain name?

   A. The Microsoft implementation of a NetBIOS name server

   B. A text file in the same format as the 4.3 BSD UNIX file

   C. A hierarchical name that is implemented using a Domain Name Server (DNS)

   D. A flat name that is implemented using a Domain Name Server (DNS)

2. What is Host name resolution?

   A. A b-node broadcast on the local network for the IP address of the destination NetBIOS name

   B. The process of mapping a host name to an IP address

   C. A hierarchical name that is implemented using a Domain Name Server (DNS)

   D. A local text file that maps IP addresses to the NetBIOS computer names

3. What is true of a host name? Choose all the correct answers.

   A. The NAMEHOST utility will display the host name assigned to your system.

   B. It is an alias assigned to a computer by an administrator to identify a TCP/IP host.

   C. A host name never corresponds to an IP address that is stored in a HOSTS file or in a database on a DNS or WINS server.

   D. Host names are not used in Windows NT commands.

   E. A host name cannot be used in place of an IP address when using Ping or other TCP/IP utilities.

4. Which are common problems associated with host name resolution?

   A. Multiple entries for the same host on different lines

   B. Host name is misspelled

   C. Case-sensitivity

   D. IP address is invalid

Scenario-Based Review

SCENARIO #1 You have enabled all Windows NT name resolving techniques: WINS, b-node broadcast, and LMHOSTS, in addition to the HOSTS file and DNS. But none of these methods resolves a host name. What is the only way to communicate with this host?

SCENARIO #2 When resolving names with a HOSTS file, the local names are being resolved while none of the remote host names are being resolved. What would stop the remote host names from being resolved?

SCENARIO #3 When resolving names with a HOSTS file, you notice that a host name is being resolved incorrectly. When checking the HOSTS file, you don't see a problem, as the name is spelled correctly and the IP address is correct. What else could be wrong?

SCENARIO #4 Your company needs to resolve names on the Internet for it's customers trying to look up information on the state of the company. What service will you use to resolve names?

NetBIOS
Name
Resolution

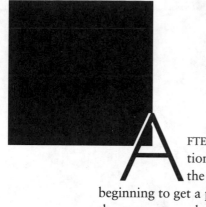

AFTER CHAPTER 4's initiation into the realm of address resolution, followed by Chapter 5's introduction into exploration of the next layer—host name-to-IP addressing—you're probably beginning to get a pretty clear picture of how naming and the resolution of those names works. This chapter will delve deeper into this theme, offering you another view of resolution as achieved through NetBIOS.

Objectives

BY THE TIME you're finished reading this chapter, the items listed below should be as easy to recall as your best friend's phone number. You should have a working knowledge of:

- NetBIOS naming

- The various NetBIOS over TCP/IP node types

- NetBIOS name resolution via broadcasts

- NetBIOS name resolution via LMHOSTS

- NetBIOS name resolution via NetBIOS Name Server

- NetBIOS name resolution configuration on both local or networked LMHOSTS files

- Common problems concerning NetBIOS names, and their likely causes

NetBIOS Naming

WHEN PEOPLE REFER to the place where the U.S. President lives in everyday conversation, most would simply say "the White House" rather than refer to his actual address of 1600 Pennsylvania Avenue. Furthermore, it would indeed be a rare bird who would reference the White House by noting its lot number as defined in a city planning grid for Washington, DC.

It's the same with computer programs, especially those that human beings interact with. That's because for us, it's just easier to recall and keep track of a name, as opposed to an impersonal and nondescript number. This given, a logical name is referred to as a *NetBIOS name*. A NetBIOS name may be up to 15 characters in length, with an additional 16th character which internally represents the service or application that was utilized to enter the name.

When communicating with each other, systems such as Windows NT, Windows for Workgroups, LAN Manager, and LAN Manager for UNIX use NetBIOS names rather than IP addresses. NetBIOS names are generally registered when a service or application requiring use of NetBIOS is started up. A good example is Windows NT, in which the NetBIOS name is registered during the initialization phase of the server or workstation that's running it.

NetBIOS naming is widely employed in Microsoft's suite of operating systems. In Windows NT, the NetBIOS name can be viewed by typing nbtstat -n or by clicking the Network icon in Control Panel. It can also be accessed in the registry under

```
\CurrentControlSet\Control\ComputerName
```

Another common use for NetBIOS names in Windows NT is in command line entries which enable connections through File Manager by using the *UNC* (Universal Naming Convention) with the NET command. This naming scheme serves to make connectivity management more simple and efficient. Let's say you wanted to see exactly which shared directories were available on a certain NetBIOS computer named "Bill." On a Windows NT computer, you'd begin by entering the command prompt NET VIEW \\BILL. If all goes well, from there you'd see that there's also a shared directory appropriately named Share. To connect to this directory, you would type NET USE Z: \\BILL \Share. You'd then find yourself privy to all directories located therein.

The Name Resolution Process

BEFORE ARP (Address Resolution Protocol) can be used to resolve an IP address to a hardware address, a NetBIOS name must first be resolved to that IP address. Again, looking to the White House analogy, suppose you'd like to send a letter to the U.S. President. In order to make it possible for your note to reach him, you'd need to resolve the name "White House" to its actual, physical location of 1600 Pennsylvania Ave., Washington, DC, plus the zip code. To find the proper address information, you could look in a telephone book, ask a buddy, or call a government office. NetBIOS names are resolved much the same way, and just as in the above scenario, there are several ways to accomplish that goal. These possible resolution avenues can be sorted into two categories: *standard resolution* and *specific resolution*. Under Windows NT, all methods by which resolution may be achieved are configurable.

Standard NetBIOS Resolution

Standard NetBIOS Name Resolution, which is the process of mapping a NetBIOS name to an IP address, is done dynamically by Windows NT. Standard resolution comes in three forms:

Local Broadcast A request sent out on a local network announcing a specific device's NetBIOS name with the goal of discovering its IP address. Commonly referred to as a b-node broadcast.

NetBIOS Name Cache A listing comprised of both locally resolved names and names, other than local ones, that have been recently resolved.

NBNS, or NetBIOS Name Server Commonly implemented as a *WINS (Windows Internet Name Service)*, this type of name resolution conforms to RFC 1001/1002, performing NetBIOS naming resolution from a server that's running it.

Specific NetBIOS Resolution

Alternately, specific resolution is a manual process. It is the Microsoft-specific NetBIOS Name Resolution method of building a set of tables, and referring to them for resolution. As with standard resolution, specific resolution also comes in three different varieties:

LMHOSTS file A table stored in a local file used in resolving NetBIOS names to IP addresses on remote networks. Though similar to the HOSTS file listed below, it offers further functionality that will be explained more thoroughly later in the chapter.

HOSTS file Remember our discussion in Chapter 2 about the table stored in a local file used to resolve host names to IP addresses? A fact we didn't mention there is that this file conforms to BSD UNIX Version 4.3's HOSTS file. Because of its versatility—it's at home on many a different platform—this is the file most commonly used with the TCP/IP utilities FTP, Telnet, and Ping for host name resolution. It may additionally be used to address a computer by an alias.

Domain Name Service (DNS) Here's another one we discussed earlier. It's also common in the UNIX world, and used for resolving a host name to an IP address. This file can be functionally thought of as a networked HOSTS file.

NetBIOS over TCP/IP Node Types

As is certainly apparent by now, there exist different modes and means by which NetBIOS names can be resolved. Just as in other forms of problem resolution, the process chosen implies, and sometimes determines, the tools that must be used. For example, when faced with a numbingly boring T.V. show, we may: A) turn off the tube, or B) fall asleep. If we opt for choice A, we'll either employ hands, fingers, and a remote control; or legs and feet or a wheelchair, etc., to personally deactivate it. Option B would require mentally tuning it out and closing our eyes. Similarly, the modes by which a client resolves a host address are also different and named accordingly. Collectively, there are five modes for resolving names, of which four are defined by RFC 1001/1002, and one by LMHOSTS as specified by Microsoft. They are as follows:

- B-node (broadcast)

- P-node, or peer-to-peer

- M-node (mixed)

- H-node (hybrid)

- Microsoft enhanced b-node

B-Node (Broadcast)

Operating in this mode resolves and registers names via the broadcast of UDP datagrams. On small networks, this works well. However, as the networking environment grows, UDP data broadcasting both increases traffic and falls short of achieving its goal when routing is introduced. Typically, routers won't pass broadcasts, creating the undesirable consequence of only local systems receiving messages. One way around this is to configure the router to pass b-node broadcasts. Unfortunately, the vast amount of traffic generated by doing so quickly defeats the whole purpose of having a functional network in the first place, and is therefore not recommended.

P-Node, or Peer-to-Peer

This method of operation provides an effective and efficient means for resolving names directly from a NetBIOS Name Server (NBNS) such as WINS—with only one major draw back: The WINS IP address must be specified at each client, leading to major issues if the IP address is ever changed or the server goes offline. Microsoft does provide for a secondary server, but this causes a performance reduction while waiting for the primary server to time-out. Also, since broadcasts aren't used, local communication isn't possible in the event a WINS server is unavailable as specified in the TCP/IP configuration at each host.

M-Node (Mixed)

NetBIOS over TCP/IP Name Resolution *M-mode* (*Mixed*) is a composite mode wherein a client behaves as both a b-node and a p-node system. In the event the system is unable to find the IP address of a given destination machine via the broadcast mode, it'll switch to using the NBNS p-mode method to directly resolve the name.

H-Node (Hybrid)

NetBIOS over TCP/IP Name Resolution *H-node (Hybrid)* is a combination of b-node and p-node. Here, we see the inverse operation of the m-node mode, and by default, an h-node functions as a p-node. Employing h-node, a system will first query the NBNS, only sending a broadcast as a secondary name-resolution strategy.

Microsoft Enhanced B-Node

When Microsoft TCP/IP is initialized, it will load the #PRE portion of the LMHOSTS static map file into the address cache. During operation, a Microsoft enhanced b-node system first attempts to resolve names by checking the address cache before a broadcast is sent out. The system will only issue a broadcast if the name isn't found in the cache. If these efforts are unsuccessful, the system will examine the LMHOSTS file directly to achieve resolution as a last resort.

NetBIOS Name Registration, Detection, and Discharge

We have the option to have our names listed in the telephone book, to look to see if we're listed in it, and if desired, to remove our names from it. NetBIOS naming is similar in this respect. All modes of NetBIOS over TCP/IP use a form of registration and duplicate detection, and all discharge obsolete or otherwise unwanted names. Operations such as these are commonly resolved through broadcasts, or by contacting a NetBIOS name service. There are three ways NetBIOS names are registered, released, and discovered as part of the NetBIOS Name Resolution process. They are as follows:

Name registration   As a NetBIOS over TCP/IP host starts up, it registers its name through a NetBIOS name registration request. If the designated name is found to be a duplicate, the host, or NetBIOS Name Server to which the client is registering, will counter with a negative name registration response. An initialization error will result.

Name detection   When communicating between NetBIOS hosts, a name query request is issued for resolution. Depending on how the request was issued, either the host that possesses that name or the NetBIOS Name Server will reply with a positive name query response.

Name discharge   At the conclusion of a NetBIOS over TCP/IP host-assisted session, the NetBIOS name that the system has used is discharged. This prevents the system from issuing negative name registration responses resulting from duplicates when later attempts are made to register that same name by a different system. This catharsis takes place when the unit is either taken offline or workstation service ends.

B-Node: Resolving NetBIOS Names Locally

The steps listed below are crucial in understanding NetBIOS Name Resolution, and why it functions the way it does. A solid grasp of how NetBIOS names are resolved when the destination host is on the local network will equip you with much more than answers to basic questions—it provides a foundation for understanding later topics that evolve from it. The process for achieving the resolution of NetBIOS names on the local network is shown in Figure 6.1 and described below:

FIGURE 6.1

A local NetBIOS name is resolved to an IP address using a b-node broadcast

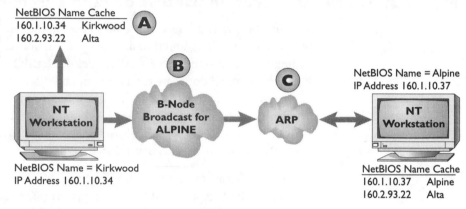

DOS Prompt > NET USE K: \\Alpine\public

Step A: Systems operating in b-node mode initiate a command with a NetBIOS requirement like NET USE K: \\Alpine\public (see Figure 6.1). To prevent costly name-resolution transactions, the system will first check the local address cache. If the name is found there, adding traffic to the network and thereby reducing its speed and efficiency can be successfully avoided. If no match is found, the system moves on to Step B.

Step B: At this stage, name query broadcasts are sent out on the local network carrying the request for the destination's NetBIOS name.

Step C: The broadcast is received by all systems on the local network. They will all begin to check to see if their name matches the one broadcasted. If the owner is found, that device will prepare a name query response. This response is sent out as soon as ARP resolves the hardware address of the system that initiated the name query. As the requesting system receives the positive response, a NetBIOS connection is established.

Recall that, typically, routers won't pass broadcasts, resulting in only the local systems getting the message. Broadcasts that are passed increase network traffic, thereby decreasing performance. Because of this, even though many routers can support broadcasts, the function is usually disabled.

Enhanced B-Node: Resolving Remote NetBIOS Names

When a host resides on a remote system, a local broadcast will still be issued in an attempt to resolve the name. If the broadcast is passed by the router, the request will be answered and processed in the same manner as a local b-node resolution request. If this effort fails, the LMHOSTS file is examined in a further attempt to locate the specific address (see Figure 6.2).

FIGURE 6.2

Resolving remote NetBIOS names (enhanced n-node)

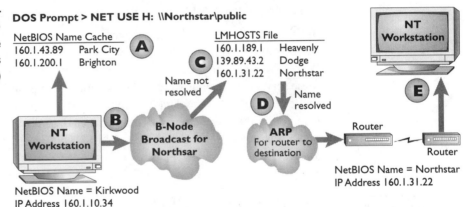

Step A: Systems operating in enhanced b-node mode initiate a command with a NetBIOS requirement—again, as an example: NET USE H: \\ NorthStar\public (see Figure 6.2). As in regular b-node mode, the system checks the local address cache, looks no further if found, and moves on to the next step if this endeavor is unsuccessful.

Step B: Again, as in non-enhanced b-node mode, at this stage, the system broadcasts a name query request on the local network looking for \\NorthStar. Assuming the destination system resides on another network, and the mediating router won't pass b-node broadcasts, the resolution request will again fail, requiring things to proceed to Step C.

Step C: Here, the LMHOSTS file is searched, and the corresponding entry is found. NorthStar, IP address `160.1.31.22`. The address is resolved.

Step D: Once the IP address is revealed to the requesting remote system, the local routing table is consulted for the most efficient path to it. If one isn't found, an ARP request is made to obtain the hardware address of the default gateway. Whenever a remote address is identified, it will be sent to the gateway for delivery. Because the gateway is used frequently, its hardware address is usually acquired from the local cache. Alternately, if it's not present in the cache, it can be located via broadcast.

Step E: A response is sent out as soon as ARP resolves the hardware address of the router. When the response is received by the requesting system, a NetBIOS connection is established.

Resolving NetBIOS Names with a NetBIOS Name Server

In this section, we'll look at how name resolution works when using a NetBIOS Name Server (NBNS). A common implementation of an NBNS is a WINS (Windows Internet Name Service) server. An NBNS is highly flexible, so these servers enjoy wide usage. They'll function in p-node, m-node, and h-node modes of NetBIOS over TCP/IP. Another reason for their popularity is that using an NBNS extends better performance than does traditional broadcast resolution. Figure 6.3 illustrates how NetBIOS names are resolved to an IP address using a NetBIOS Name Server.

FIGURE 6.3

Resolving names with a NetBIOS Name Server

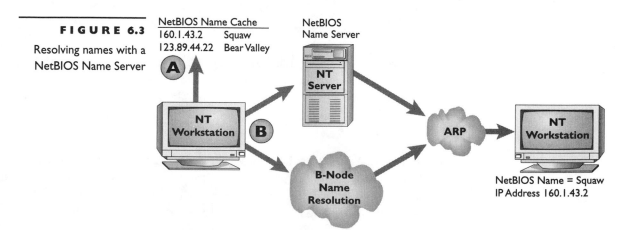

As in prior examples, the process of resolving a NetBIOS name begins with entering a command that triggers the initiation of it (e.g., NET USE, NET VIEW, etc.). It also parallels previous methods in the following ways:

Step A: NET USE L: \\SquawValley\public. The system will explore the local address cache to try to resolve the name.

- If found, resolution is achieved, and the ARP process will commence for the additional resolution of the hardware address.

- The object of things functioning thus is to avoid creating any additional traffic on the network.

- In this mode of operation, no matter what's done, the local cache will always be checked before any further resolution efforts are begun.

Step B: Depending on the mode by which TCP/IP is configured, the step that comes next varies. Following is a list organizing these special circumstances for you.

P-Node (Peer to Peer)   After Step A collectively fails to resolve the name, a request is sent directly to the NetBIOS Name Server. If found, the identified name is returned in a response to the requesting system.

M-Node (Mixed)   If Step A fails to resolve the name, the steps outlined for b-node broadcasts are followed. If this strategy also misfires, the host will then attempt to resolve the NetBIOS name as if it were configured as a p-node.

H-Node (Hybrid)   Again, as with M-Node, should Step A attempts prove unsuccessful, the steps detailed earlier in the section for p-nodes are then followed. If these also flop, the host will then attempt to resolve the NetBIOS name as if it were a b-node—by using a broadcast.

Step C: As soon as the host name is resolved, as in steps A or B, ARP is used to determine the hardware address.

First Section Summary

N THE FIRST section of this chapter, you learned that NetBIOS naming is widely employed in Microsoft's suite of operating systems because for us, it's easier to recall a name as opposed to an abstract number. You also learned that this given, a logical name is referred to as a NetBIOS name, which may be up to 15 characters in length, with an additional 16th character to represent the service or application used to enter it. Before ARP can be used to resolve an IP address to a hardware address, a NetBIOS name must be resolved to that IP address first. You found that, under Windows NT, all methods by which resolution may be achieved are configurable.

Two possible avenues to achieving resolution were then explored, beginning with a look at three types of standard resolution:

Local Broadcast   A request sent out on a local network, commonly referred to as a b-node broadcast

NetBIOS Name Cache   A listing of locally, as well as recently, resolved names

NBNS, or NetBIOS, Name Server   A type of name resolution that conforms to RFC 1001/1002

We then moved on to describe specific resolution—a manual process that is also the Microsoft-specific NetBIOS Name Resolution method, involving building a set of tables and then referring to them for resolution. You learned that specific resolution also comes in three flavors:

LMHOSTS file   A table stored in a local file used in resolving NetBIOS names to IP addresses on remote networks

HOSTS file   A versatile file that conforms to BSD UNIX Version 4.3's HOSTS file

Domain Name Service   Also common in the UNIX world—can be functionally thought of as a networked HOSTS file

The section then progressed into a discussion on node types, wherein you discovered there to be five modes for resolving names—four defined by RFC 1001/1002; one by LMHOST, as specified by Microsoft:

B-node (broadcast)   Resolves and registers names via the broadcast of UDP datagrams

P-node, or peer-to-peer   Resolves names directly from a NetBIOS Name Server (NBNS), such as WINS

M-node (mixed)   A composite mode wherein a client behaves as both a b-node and a p-node system

H-node (hybrid)   The inverse operation of m-node mode

Microsoft enhanced b-node   First attempts to resolve names by checking the address cache before sending out a broadcast

From there, discussion moved to investigate three ways NetBIOS names are registered, released, and discovered as part of the NetBIOS Name Resolution process. They were:

Name registration   Occurs as a NetBIOS over TCP/IP host starts up and registers its name through a NetBIOS name-registration request.

Name detection   Occurs during communication between NetBIOS hosts; a name query request is issued for resolution.

Name discharge   Occurs at the conclusion of a NetBIOS over TCP/IP host session. At this time, the NetBIOS name that the system has used is discharged, preventing the system from issuing negative name registration responses as a result of the existence of duplicates when later attempts are made to register the same name by a different system.

You were then introduced to step-by-step procedures which outlined and guided you through the various processes for NetBIOS Name Resolution both on the local network, employing b-node, and on remote networks, using enhanced b-node. You finished the section with a discussion on how name resolution is accomplished when employing a NetBIOS Name Server.

NetBIOS Name Resolution in Action

M ICROSOFT'S IMPLEMENTATION OF TCP/IP under Windows NT supports all forms of resolution mentioned earlier. If your system has been configured in this fashion, you will find that Microsoft has designated that name searches follow the sequence shown in Figure 6.4, and outlined below.

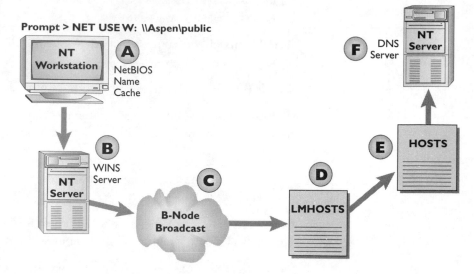

FIGURE 6.4

The Microsoft method of resolving NetBIOS names

Step A: The process begins by entering a command initiating NetBIOS Name Resolution, such as NET USE W: \\Aspen\public (see Figure 6.4). At this point, the local address cache will be checked for the destination host.

Step B: Assuming the name wasn't found, the next step is to contact the WINS server following the process outlined under p-node in this chapter.

Step C: If the WINS server was unable to locate the name, or if it did, and identified it as unavailable, Microsoft's TCP/IP would then issue a b-node type broadcast.

Step D: If the broadcast fails to hit paydirt, the next step is to search the LMHOSTS file. The action taken corresponds to that of a Microsoft enhanced b-node system.

Step E: At this point, the HOSTS file, which resides on the local hard drive, will be examined.

Step F: The last gasp efforts that will be made are done though DNS. If the DNS machine is ignoring you and not responding, a repeat request will be sent to it at intervals of 5, 10, 20, 40, 5, 10, and 20 seconds. If your system's configured for DNS, and the unit has crashed or is offline, all systems on the network that are using DNS in some form or another will experience a considerable operational slow down. The delay can be so pronounced that systems can appear to have crashed while resolving the name. This sinister effect is most commonly seen with Windows for Workgroups, and isn't nearly as nasty with Windows NT. NT's process managing is much more efficient.

If all attempts at resolution fall short of the target, an error message will be sent in reply. However, it should be pointed out here that Microsoft's implementation provision for name resolution is not only tenacious, it's efficient. Its system's sequence of resolution strategies prioritize in such a way that it first chooses the quickest method, requiring the minimum cost in network overhead. Also important to note is that once resolution is achieved, no further steps are taken—it does not simply complete a predetermined process, it monitors that process, only doing that which is required to accomplish success, and no more.

Local NetBIOS Resolution via LMHOSTS

LMHOSTS is a static table that's stored in a local file used to resolve NetBIOS names to IP addresses on remote networks. Just like any other table, LMHOSTS has a specific format, and supports special functions based on the commands entered therein. Functionally, LMHOSTS offers the following:

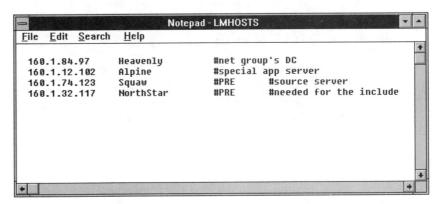

- Name resolution, when called upon

- A single entry for names-to-IP addresses. All other following entries will be ignored if the same NetBIOS name is used in combination with a different IP address.

To avoid constant reboots for changes in the LMHOSTS file, entries can be manually loaded by typing `nbtstat -R`. *Note that the* `-R` *is case-sensitive.*

- You can load the IP addresses of frequently accessed host machines into memory by using the #PRE remark after the entry. This is a handy little feature for reducing network traffic, since it warrants that no broadcasts need to be made to access the host. The information intended for the lines with the #PRE remark is loaded when NetBIOS over TCP/IP is initialized.

- The LMHOSTS file can support domain validation, account synchronization, and browsing by adding #DOM to an entry line.

All statements in Microsoft TCP/IP32 that begin with a # sign are treated as comments.

- Supports old LMHOSTS files originating from older implementations of Microsoft TCP/IP, such as LAN Manager.

- On Windows NT systems, LMHOSTS is maintained in \windir\SYSTEM32\ DRIVERS\ETC, where windir is the directory where Windows NT has been installed. The default directory is WINNT35. If it is installed from an upgrade, it will be in the previous versions of the Windows directory.

Networked NetBIOS Resolution via LMHOSTS File

As mentioned earlier, Microsoft has created enhanced flexibility with their implementation of TCP/IP. Conforming to this standard is the expanded functionality of LMHOSTS. Microsoft has added features to LMHOSTS, like the unprecedented ability to use it within a networked, or centralized, configuration. This not only makes the file readily accessible, and easily amended and expanded, but facilitates and simplifies the entire TCP/IP management process.

A networked LMHOSTS file can be added to a local LMHOSTS file by adding #INCLUDE to the beginning of the line that precedes the file you desire to add.

The following graphic demonstrates how to use a networked LMHOSTS file.

Windows NT 3.51 automatically examines the LMHOSTS file prior to users logging on. Because the NetBIOS Helper service starts at boot-up, when it doesn't yet have a username to retrieve the LMHOSTS file from a remote system, a null username is substituted. Unlike Windows NT 3.1, Version 3.51 must be specifically configured to support null usernames.

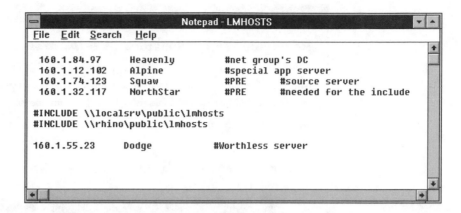

```
─                          Notepad - LMHOSTS                        ▼ ▲
File  Edit  Search  Help
                                                                       ↑
  160.1.84.97      Heavenly         #net group's DC
  160.1.12.102     Alpine           #special app server
  160.1.74.123     Squaw            #PRE      #source server
  160.1.32.117     NorthStar        #PRE      #needed for the include

#INCLUDE \\localsrv\public\lmhosts
#INCLUDE \\rhino\public\lmhosts

  160.1.55.23      Dodge            #Worthless server



                                                                       ↓
◄ ▒                                                                 ► ▒
```

Shared LMHOSTS files should be accessible by all users. To make a share accessible by a null user, use REGEDT32 to modify:

\HKEY_LOCAL_MACHINE\SYSTEM\CurrentControlSet\Services\
LanmanServer\Parameters\NullSessionShares

On a new line in NullSessionShares, type the name of the share for which you want NULL session support, such as Public. This complete, you can now activate it by either rebooting, or stopping and then starting, the server service.

This process sounds rather long, however in practice, these steps go by rather quickly.

An alternative to modifying the registry is to manually run the NBTSTAT -R command to include the remote LMHOSTS files. Depending on your requirements, you could place this command in a batch file such as a LOGIN script, if used, or place an icon in the startup group to automate a manual process. If you opt for the latter, keep in mind that the startup group is kept on a per user basis, and is not a COMMON group. You will therefore have to add the icon for each user that works on that particular machine. This can get more than a tad tedious if that group of users numbers many! Consequently, the best approach is to either modify the Registry, or place the file in a Login Script. Here's your chance to get your hands dirty and experience for yourself the stuff of NetBIOS name resolution. In Exercises 6.1 and 6.2, you'll practice configuring LMHOSTS, as well as gain some insight into the workings of both local and remote name resolution.

EXERCISE 6.1

Resolving NetBIOS Names to IP Addresses

In the next two exercises, you will configure the LMHOSTS file to resolve NetBIOS names to IP addresses. You will see what happens when you attempt to resolve a remote NetBIOS computer name using just a local broadcast.

You will need two computers for both exercises 6.1 and 6.2, an NT Server, and an NT Workstation.

1. From the File Manager, choose Connect Network Drive.

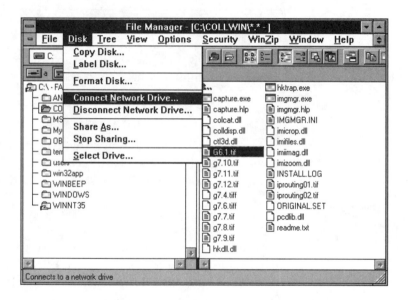

2. The Connect Network Drive dialog box appears.

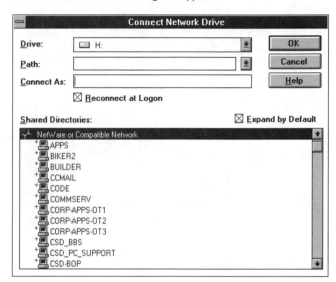

3. In the box, type **\\remote workstation name** and then choose OK. You should receive an error message stating that the name cannot be found.

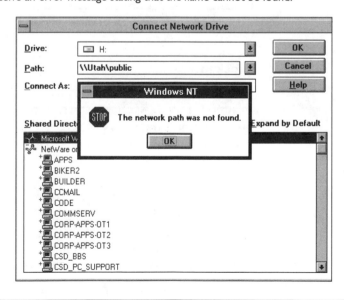

EXERCISE 6.2

Configuring LMHOSTS for Remote Computer Names

Here you will see what happens when you attempt to resolve a remote NetBIOS computer name with a properly configured LMHOSTS file.

1. Open the file \systemroot\SYSTEM32\DRIVERS\ETC\LMHOSTS.SAM.

2. Read the instructions at the beginning of the LMHOSTS file for adding entries.

3. Go to the end of the file and add the following entry:

   160.1.x.x *computer_name* (where *computer_name* is the name of the second computer)

4. Save the file.

5. From File manager, choose Connect Network Drive. The Connect Network Drive appears.

6. Type **computer_name** (the name of the second computer).

Success is indicated by a list of shared resources, or an empty list. If you receive an error message, compare the command syntax to the spelling of the LMHOSTS file entry.

Block Inclusion

The LMHOSTS file has one final feature that we haven't yet discussed—block inclusion. This is a special, last resort, reconnaissance-type feature that enables you to spy into another system's LMHOSTS file and look up unresolved names. The only time block inclusion is used is after all other LMHOSTS search path possibilities have been exhausted. If the system is unable to find the name you desire resolved in the local cache, and additionally fails through use of any #PRE tags and preexisting file entries to the block inclusion, only then should you use block inclusion.

A block inclusion is designated by placing #BEGIN_ALTERNATE and #END_ALTERNATE at the beginning and end of the block, respectively. During a search, the first system listed in the inclusion block is checked for a match to a requested name. Whether that name is successfully resolved or not, no additional systems will be searched in the block unless that first system is unreachable, and perhaps offline. Only then would the next entry in the inclusion block be read. Lines that are typically found in the block inclusion are usually started with #include, which designates a remote system. When deciding whether or not to search LMHOSTS files recorded in a block inclusion, keep in mind that this feature exists more for purposes of fault tolerance than it does for facilitating group searches. Doing multiple recursive searches may progressively lead to longer and longer resolution times as your list grows.

Speaking of performance, when initially designing the LMHOSTS file, it's very important to keep in mind that the names of the most commonly used systems should be placed at the top of the file, and all #PRE entries at the bottom. Since the LMHOSTS file is read top to bottom, doing this will help you to find your more commonly accessed machines more quickly. The #PRE entries can be ignored after TCP/IP initializes.

The following graphic is an example of an LMHOSTS file with block inclusion:

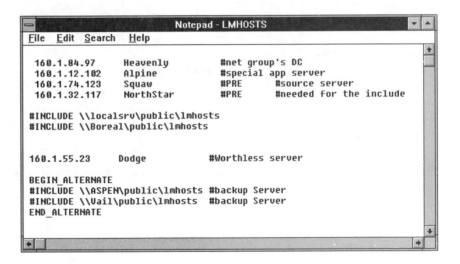

```
                         Notepad - LMHOSTS
 File   Edit   Search   Help

    160.1.84.97      Heavenly        #net group's DC
    160.1.12.102     Alpine          #special app server
    160.1.74.123     Squaw           #PRE     #source server
    160.1.32.117     NorthStar       #PRE     #needed for the include

 #INCLUDE \\localsrv\public\lmhosts
 #INCLUDE \\Boreal\public\lmhosts


    160.1.55.23      Dodge           #Worthless server

 BEGIN_ALTERNATE
 #INCLUDE \\ASPEN\public\lmhosts #backup Server
 #INCLUDE \\Vail\public\lmhosts  #backup Server
 END_ALTERNATE
```

NetBIOS Name Resolution Headaches

Just as it is with so many things (too many?) in this ol' world, you have to follow certain guidelines in order for things to operate smoothly. For example, if, like so many people, you fail to change your car's oil every 3500 miles, you spend far too much time with your mechanic, and bring about premature death to your car. It's much the same with the LMHOSTS file, as it is with TCP/IP in general. Not understanding or following guidelines and proper procedure, and failing to maintain things well causes problems. Here are a few common ones:

Case Study #1: A Horse With No Name—When NetBIOS Names Cannot Be Resolved

We know you'll be absolutely stunned to hear that when a NetBIOS name can't be resolved, it's usually because a user has forgotten that a specific entry is required for each device that needs to be resolved by the system that's been asked to resolve it. For instance, a company that uses both a WINS server and an LMHOSTS file may find that they can only access some of their computers when their WINS server is taken offline. Why? Because the WINS server was nicely up-to-date, but the LMHOSTS file wasn't.

THE MORAL OF THE STORY Ignore it, and it will go away... Maintain it, and it's here to stay.

Case Study #2: Spell Check

...Or the case of mistaken identity. It's amazing how many times people will add a host name containing a one, and replace it with a lower case L, or the roman numeral one (I). The way a NetBIOS name is spelled in the system is exactly the way it must be entered when trying to resolve it.

THE MORAL OF THE STORY Don't get creative with host names—keep 'em the same.

Case Study #3: Return to Sender—No Longer at This Address

Usually it's not that the IP address is entered incorrectly in the LMHOSTS file, but that the host's IP address has changed. If it has, then you are trying to reach a host at an IP address that either no longer exists, or has now been reassigned. It's important to be sure—verify that you really do have the right

IP address. During a big undertaking, such as the movement of an entire network system, or when IP addresses on hosts are changed, small things like LMHOSTS files are commonly overlooked. Sure, the DNS was changed, memos were e-mailed to management, etc., but even the most efficient folks can make mistakes. Pay close attention to the numbers—sometimes the only way to know is to check the host itself.

THE MORAL OF THE STORY Make your list, and check it twice.

Case Study #4: Sorry—I Thought You Were Someone Else

As we've pounded into you, once the name has been found, accompanied by its corresponding IP address, there's no need to search any further. Resolution has been achieved. Unfortunately, if the name listed in the file is associated with the wrong, or more commonly, obsolete IP address, the correct entry below it will never be reached. Just as you're sometimes judged by the company you keep, so are computers!

THE MORAL OF THE STORY Don't procrastinate—stay up to date. Make sure that you have only one, *current* entry, for each NetBIOS name.

Words to the Wise

Debugging problems in TCP/IP is easy if you have a clear understanding of each part's function. While each element and its role is pretty straightforward stuff, trying to put it all together to grasp the Big Picture can be difficult and confusing. Small, simple details can grow to become really big problems if overlooked, or are otherwise hidden from you. For instance, if a certain host was moved, and another device was put in its place using the same IP address, when pinging diagnostically, you'd get the impression that the server was up and running. However, what's really happening is that the address no longer represents the server you think it does—you're not talking to the server, you're talking to some mysterious other machine! All in all, understanding how all the pieces of the TCP/IP puzzle fit together, paying attention to details, and considering an action's consequences will make you better able to both prevent problems before they occur, and equip you with solutions to solve them when they do.

Second Section Summary

THE SECOND SECTION of this chapter began with introducing NetBIOS in action—giving you a picture of how NetBIOS works, and what it is exactly, that it does. Microsoft's implementation provision for name resolution is not only tenacious, it's efficient. Its system's sequence of resolution strategies prioritizes in such a way that it chooses the quickest method first, requiring the minimum cost in network overhead. Also, it's intelligent—it doesn't simply complete some possibly unnecessary, predetermined process unless success requires it to.

Next, you looked into NetBIOS resolution via LMHOSTS—a static table that's stored in a local file used to resolve NetBIOS names to IP addresses. You found that LMHOSTS is used for name resolution on both local and remote networks. You also discovered that Microsoft has added snazzy new features to LMHOSTS, like the unprecedented ability to fool around with it within a networked, or centralized configuration. The file can be amended and expanded with the greatest of ease, soundly simplifying the entire TCP/IP management process. We then showed you in a couple of exercises how to resolve NetBIOS names to IP addresses and configure LMHOSTS for remote computer names.

We wrapped up the section on the LMHOSTS file with a discussion on block inclusion—a last resort, reconnaissance-type innovation that enables you to spy into another system's LMHOSTS file and look up unresolved names. The only time block inclusion is used is after all other LMHOSTS search path possibilities have been exhausted.

Bringing Chapter 6 to a close, we presented four case studies delimiting disaster avoidance in the NetBIOS world. In addition to these scenarios, we included a paragraph of worldly advice that encouraged you to pay close attention to details—or else—and to carefully consider an action's ramifications before hopping ahead with it.

In general, this chapter's goal was to provide a more comprehensive grasp of how perfectly meaningful names can be translated into obscure and meaningless—to humans, that is—numbers and addresses. To make sure you understand, we suggest working through the questions that follow.

Exercise Questions

Multiple-Choice Questions

1. What is NetBIOS naming?

   A. A b-node broadcast on a local network

   B. A local text file used for addressing

   C. Computer names used to communicate with other hosts

   D. Entries in the LMHOSTS file

2. Which of the following are NetBIOS over TCP/IP node types?

   A. NBNS

   B. P-node

   C. L-node

   D. M-node

3. What is NetBIOS name resolution?

   A. The local cache containing locally registered computer names

   B. A server configured with the DNS daemon

   C. The process of successfully mapping a computer's NetBIOS name to an IP address

   D. A broadcast used for registration and resolution

4. What is NetBIOS Name Resolution via the LMHOST method?

   A. A local text file in the same format as the 4.3BSD UNIX/etc/hosts file

   B. A static file used to resolve NetBIOS names to IP addresses

   C. Stored in the registry, and used in Windows NT commands

   D. A computer name assigned during Windows NT installation

Scenario-Based Review

SCENARIO #1 You're trying to connect to an NT server with the NET USE\\server_name command. That works OK, but when you try NET USE\\IP_address, it gets a bad command or filename. You checked the IP address, and it's correct. What could the problem be?

SCENARIO #2 You get calls from users complaining that NetBIOS names are not being resolved all the time. "It's flaky," as one user puts it. You open the LMHOSTS file and find some errors: a misspelled name, some old IP addresses, and a couple of misplaced comments. What effect can these erroneous entries have on the LMHOSTS file?

SCENARIO #3 While cleaning out the LMHOSTS file, you find entries that start with #PRE. Where should you locate the LMHOSTS entries with the #PRE identifier? Why?

SCENARIO #4 You have been promoted to network manager. Your first job is to make sure you are using all of the company's bandwidth properly. Which node modes should you use? Which mode will be the most efficient for your network?

SCENARIO #5 Someone in your office deleted the # signs in the LMHOSTS file because they thought they were comments. After you replaced the # signs, and the phones stopped ringing (two hours later!), this staff member wanted to know what the # identifiers that are used in the LMHOSTS file are used for. What do you tell them?

DHCP : Dynamic Host Configuration Protocol

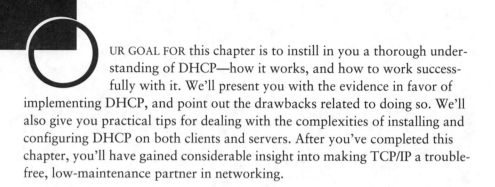

UR GOAL FOR this chapter is to instill in you a thorough understanding of DHCP—how it works, and how to work successfully with it. We'll present you with the evidence in favor of implementing DHCP, and point out the drawbacks related to doing so. We'll also give you practical tips for dealing with the complexities of installing and configuring DHCP on both clients and servers. After you've completed this chapter, you'll have gained considerable insight into making TCP/IP a trouble-free, low-maintenance partner in networking.

Objectives

PON COMPLETION OF this section, you should have the following items indelibly written into your memory:

- The definition of DHCP

- How to install DHCP

- DHCP in action

- DHCP requests and leasing

- How DHCP is configured for multiple subnets

- DHCP clients

- DHCP and the IPCONFIG utility

- DHCP database backup and recovery issues

- The DHCP database JETPACK compression utility

DHCP Defined

DHCP'S PURPOSE IS to centrally control IP-related information and eliminate the need to manually keep track of where individual IP addresses are allocated. Choosing whether or not to use DHCP is like choosing whether or not to use a database. For example, imagine that you're the local telephone company busily assigning telephone numbers to your customers. Suppose that for some strange reason, you choose to keep track of your assignments on paper—without the aid of a computer. As customers come and go, voids develop in your list where numbers that have been assigned, and then dropped, are no longer anywhere to be found. Still others begin to be assigned duplicate numbers—further confusing matters. Clearly, storing your customer information in a central database would prevent this chaos, automatically enabling you to keep abreast of all these changes. DHCP can also help in a situation where a network is running out of IP addresses. For example, if an administrator assigns static IP addresses for network hosts on a class C network, that leaves the administrator only 254 addresses to assign hosts—even less if the administrator subnets. If the amount of hosts number near 300, the administrator can use DHCP to assign hosts and lease IP addresses for a short period of time. This is a terrific, serviceable benefit of DHCP—the ability to actually have fewer IP addresses than hosts.

This only works on a network whose hosts can function well when using IP addresses periodically.

DHCP has a history. Originally, it was called BootP protocol and was designed to provide IP addresses to diskless workstations. Today, DHCP is built onto the BootP protocol (RFC 951) in an effort to simplify and centralize IP addressing. DHCP is formalized and defined by RFCs 1533,1534, 1541, and 1542.

When TCP/IP starts up on a DHCP-enabled host, a special message is sent out requesting an IP address and a subnet mask from a DHCP server. The contacted server checks its internal database, then replies with a message offer comprised of the information the client requested. DHCP can also respond with a default gateway address, DNS address(es), or a NetBIOS Name Server, such as WINS. When the client accepts the IP offer, it is then extended to the client for a specified period of time, called a lease. If the DHCP server is out of IP addresses, no IP addressing information can be offered to the clients, causing TCP/IP initialization to fail.

The lease procedure can be likened to that of leasing a car. After negotiating acceptable terms with an automobile dealer, a lease is secured, permitting you use of a certain car for a specific period of time. If the car dealership doesn't have the terms or vehicle you want, you don't drive off the lot with one.

DHCP—the Good, the Bad, and the Ugly

If we were to pause here and ask you whether or not you should opt to utilize DHCP, based upon the telephone company example given earlier, you might think it's a no-brainer, and answer with a resounding "Yes!" Recall, though, that we mentioned there were some drawbacks to doing so. If so, you're probably getting pretty curious about what exactly those drawbacks might be. To help you understand these, as well as why you would choose to use DHCP, here's a list of both the pros and cons associated with using DHCP.

To Use or Not to Use DHCP?

THE GOOD

- No additional services are required by the computer to assign numbers.

- No additional computer is needed when assigning addresses.

- It's inexpensive!

- IP configuration information is entered electronically by another system, eliminating the human-error factor. No more typing in the wrong address, subnet mask, gateway, DNS addresses, and NetBIOS Name Server addresses—Yippee!

- Configuration problems are minimized, clearing up a labyrinth of possible situations that lead to big messes and obscure, hard-to-find problems.

- IP becomes a "plug and play operation." We, the members of the world-wide Now Society, collectively concur that getting things up and running sooner is certainly better. Most often, when running DHCP, new or moved systems can instantly be plugged into a network segment with no additional configuration requirements—no strings attached!

THE BAD

- Users with a new machine may randomly select an IP address to gain immediate access to the network. Later, that number may be assigned to a different user and show up as a duplicate. This will not be fun for the network's caretaker to find.

- Because input for the IP address, subnet mask, gateway, DNS addresses, and NetBIOS Name Server address is done by a human on a PC, it can easily be entered incorrectly. There are quite a number of required entries allowing little or no margin for error. As if that weren't bad enough, these erroneous numbers appear to work initially, schmoozing you in for the kill with friendly, false effectiveness. Later, you may find that you have someone else's IP address, are incapable of resolving NetBIOS names, or find yourself marooned—unable to get to another subnet.

- Having all one's eggs in one basket. Exclusive reliance on the DHCP server during the TCP/IP initialization phase could potentially result in an initialization failure if that server is down, or otherwise unavailable.

- Certain applications of TCP/IP, like logging in to a remote network through a firewall, require the use of a specific IP address. DHCP allows for exclusions and holes that prevent certain IP address ranges from being used. If your needed address happens to be found in a specified exclusive range, you're beef.

THE UGLY

- There's an extensive amount of incredibly tedious work involved in maintaining an accurate roster of both used and free IP addresses. To those detail-oriented individuals in the audience whose greatest joy is to stay up all night keeping records, this may not sound too appalling—until you find out that once the information goes into error, it's almost impossible to fix it. What does this vile fact translate to in reality? Well, it means that you may find yourself forever in the dark regarding the status of a given computer. Whether it's on, off, or other, will be an eternal mystery to you. It could, therefore, easily cause you not to register a certain IP address (the mystery node's). After all, how could you register something you didn't know existed? Of course, it could also simply be that the wrong one was entered in the first place, but knowing this still wouldn't help you. Your only option at this point would be to go host-to-host, one at a time, checking IP addresses.

FINAL ANALYSIS All things considered, that which is gained when using DHCP does outweigh that which is lost. However, it should be noted that it's ultimately up to you—the network professional—whether or not DHCP is the best choice for your particular networking environment. Generally, unless your network is very tiny, or is running applications that are incompatible with DHCP (e.g. routers that can't handle the BootP/DHCP protocol), you should opt to utilize this feature.

Further Considerations about Implementing DHCP

As stated, DHCP's purpose is to make IP address management a breeze. However, as we just established, it's not for everyone, or every situation. Here are a few more points to ponder before you dive right into implementing DHCP:

- What kind of IP information will the DHCP server deliver? Is it possible to deliver IP addresses for all the different scenarios that are required?

- Are all machines on the network, regardless of operating system or function, going to utilize DHCP? If, for applicational purposes, some will not, are you well aware of the static addresses for each of those devices?

- Will the DHCP server support subnets other then its own? If so, it will obviously operate via a router. Does that router support the BootP protocol? If not, it won't pass BootP broadcasts, and a DHCP server will have to be placed on every segment.

- Regarding the dual, pivotal issues of performance and reliability... How many DHCP servers would your network require? DHCP servers are selfish, secretive, and possessive devices that do not share their information with other machines.

If you find that yours is a situation that will require multiple DHCP servers, consider the following as an implementation forethought: For reasons of performance and fault tolerance, every DHCP server should have 75% of the available IP addresses on it own subnet, and 25% of those from a remote subnet. This arrangement is highly beneficial, and provides for a backup in the event that any one DHCP server becomes unavailable.

DHCP in Action

DHCP IS A simple process by which a host system obtains an IP address. This address is a necessary prerequisite to performing any communications with the rest of the network, and depends on the number of NIC's *(network interface cards),* that are configured with the TCP/IP and DHCP protocol. The number of NIC cards necessarily equals the number of instances that the DHCP process runs, and additionally determines the number of IP addresses received. Each card has its own IP address. In order for DHCP to operate on remote networks, the router must support the forwarding of DHCP broadcasts (RFC 1542). To fully understand the operation of DHCP, it's necessary to assess the steps by which it operates. These steps can be organized into four operational stages as follows:

Stage One: IP Lease Request

This is the first step for a system seeking to acquire an IP address under DHCP. It's triggered whenever TCP/IP, configured with DHCP, is started for the first time. It also occurs when a specific IP address is requested but unavailable, or an IP address was used and then released. Since the requesting client isn't aware of its own IP address, or that belonging to the DHCP server, it will use 0.0.0.0 and 255.255.255.255, respectively. This is known as a DHCP discover message. The broadcast is created in a scaled down TCP/IP with UDP ports 67 (BootP client), and ports 68 (BootP server). This message contains the hardware address and NetBIOS name for the client system to be used in the next phase of sending a lease offer. If no DHCP server responds to the initial broadcast, the request is repeated three more times at 9, 13, and 16-second intervals, plus a random event occurring in the period between 0 and 1000 milliseconds. If still no response is received, a broadcast message will be made every five minutes until it is finally answered. If no DHCP server ever becomes available, no TCP/IP communications will be possible.

Stage Two: IP Lease Offer

The second phase of DHCP involves the actual information given by all DHCP servers that have valid addressing information to offer. Their offers consist of an IP address, subnet mask, lease period (in hours), and the IP address of the proposing DHCP server. These offers are sent to the requesting client's hardware address. The pending IP address offer is reserved temporarily to prevent it from being taken simultaneously by another machine, creating horrid address-clone duplicates and interminable chaos. Since multiple DHCP servers can be configured, it also adds a degree of fault tolerance, should one of the DHCP servers go down.

Stage Three: IP Lease Selection

During this phase, the client machine will select the first IP addressing offer it receives. Clients reply by broadcasting an acceptance message, requesting to lease IP information. Just as in Stage One, this message will be broadcast as a DHCP request, but this time, it'll additionally include the IP address of the DHCP server whose offer was accepted. All other DHCP servers will then revoke their offers.

Stage Four: IP Lease Acknowledgment

The accepted DHCP server proceeds to assign an IP address to the client, then sends an acknowledgment message, called a *DHCPACK*, back to the client. Occasionally, a negative acknowledgment, called a *DHCPNACK,* is returned. This type of message is most often generated if the client is attempting to lease its old IP address which has since been reassigned elsewhere. Negative acceptance messages can also mean that the requesting client has an inaccurate IP address, resulting from physically changing locations to an alternate subnet.

After this final phase has been successfully completed, the client machine integrates the new IP information. It endows it with a fully functional TCP/IP configuration, usable with all utilities, as if the newly acquired information had been in its possession prior to using DHCP. In Windows for Workgroups, DHCP information is stored in an encrypted format inside the Windows directory, in a file called *DHCP.BIN*. In Windows NT, this DHCP information can be found in:

HKEY_LOCAL_MACHINE\SYSTEM\CurrentControlSet\Services\
adapter\Parameters\Tcpip

The different steps undergone in this process of sending and receiving offers are not just formalities. They're quite necessary. Following them ensures that only one offer is accepted—preventing duplicate addressing pandemonium, as well as producing a good measure of fault tolerance. Additionally, if every machine that sent out an offer immediately assigned it to a requesting workstation, there would soon be no numbers left to assign. Furthermore, if the acceptance response to these offers was controlled by the client instead of the server, there would be a much greater risk of creating duplicate IP addresses. The server could misinterpret a slow response from the engaged client, caused by the network, and propose the offer information to another client. Two or more clients would then be receiving the same offer from the same server simultaneously—Networkland bigamy, resulting in Networkland polygamy, causing ultimate chaos for Networkland officers (you)! With these logistical conditions in mind, it's clear that DHCP's an honorable pragmatist, and it's above outlined method of operation is indeed sensible, and functionally sound.

DHCP Lease Renewal

Recalling the fact that with DHCP, IP addresses are leased for a period of time—not indefinitely—would necessarily bring up questions about what happens when the lease ends, or needs to be renewed. Regardless of the length of time an IP address is leased, the leasing client will send a *DHCPREQUEST* to the DHCP server when its lease period has elapsed by 50%. If the DHCP server is available, and there are no reasons for rejecting the request, a DHCP acknowledge message is sent to the client, updating the configuration and resetting the lease time. If the server is unavailable, the client will receive an "eviction" notice stating that they had not been renewed. In this event, that client would still have a remaining 50% lease time, and would be allowed full usage privileges for its duration. The rejected client would react by sending out an additional lease renewal attempt when 87.5% of its lease time had elapsed. Any available DHCP server could respond to this DHCPREQUEST message with a DHCPACK, and renew the lease. However, if the client received a DHCPNACK (negative) message, it would have to stop using the IP address immediately, and start the leasing process over, from the beginning.

When a client initializes TCP/IP, it will always attempt to renew its old address. Just like any other renewal, if the client has time left on the lease, it will continue to use the lease until its end. If, by that time, the client is unable to get a new lease, all TCP/IP functions will cease until a new, valid address can be obtained.

DHCP Lease Release

Yes, it's true...All good things must come to an end. Such is the case with leases. Since they specify a certain period of time, it's obvious that at some point, the lease will end. Although they can be renewed repeatedly, it's important to keep in mind the fact that the lease process is an "at will" process. This means that if the client elects to cancel the lease by using the IPCONFIG/ RELEASE utility, which is discussed later in this chapter, or is unable to contact the DHCP server before the lease elapses, the lease is automatically released. This is an important function that's useful for reclaiming extinct IP addresses formerly used by systems that have moved or switched to a non-DHCP address. An additional condition would occur when the IP address you're trying to snatch is reserved for a different system. In this case, you would find yourself unable to renew the lease, and eventually lose it as time expires.

Note that DHCP leases are not automatically released at system shutdown. A system that has lost it lease will attempt to re-lease the same address that it had previously used.

Making DHCP Function

Now that you have an idea of what DHCP is, and what it can and can't do for you, the next step is to understand what's required to implement it and make it work. First, you need to make sure you have the right stuff on hand. There are three components essential for successful implementation:

A server. Under Windows NT, a DHCP server can be any Windows NT server, provided that it's running TCP/IP, and is not itself a DHCP client. The server must have the DHCP server service up and running with a designated scope or range of available IP addresses to assign.

A client machine. The client can be practically any machine, including a Windows NT server, as long as it's not running the DHCP Server Service.

Compatible running mates include Windows NT Workstation 3.5*x*, Windows 95, Windows for Workgroups 3.11 with TCP/IP-32, and LAN Manager 2.2c (not the OS/2 version). Another potential candidate is Microsoft Network Client 3.0 for DOS, complete with a Real Mode TCP/IP driver.

A router. If the DHCP server will function for multiple subnets, the router must support forwarding BootP broadcasts (RFC1542).

These requirements met, you can now move on to installing and configuring a DHCP server.

DHCP Server Installation and Configuration

Relax! As you will soon see, installing a DHCP server is much easier than you'd think—so don't be intimidated. Begin with any Windows NT server. After booting up and logging onto your server, proceed with the steps in Exercise 7.1.

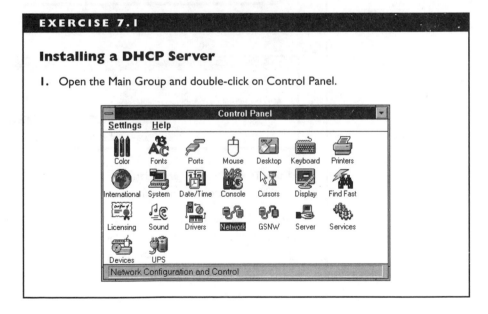

EXERCISE 7.1

Installing a DHCP Server

1. Open the Main Group and double-click on Control Panel.

EXERCISE 7.1 (CONTINUED FROM PREVIOUS PAGE)

2. Double-click on Network. The Network Settings dialog box appears.

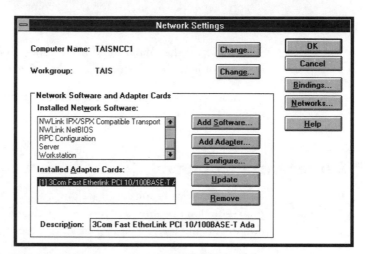

3. Click on Add Software. The Add Network Software dialog box appears.

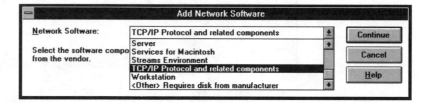

4. Select TCP/IP Protocol and related components from the list. The Windows NT TCP/IP Installation Options dialog box appears.

5. Select DHCP Server Service from the list of options, and click on Continue. Whatever you do, do not select Enable Automatic DHCP Configuration! The DHCP server must be manually configured.

Windows NT TCP/IP Installation Options

Components: | File Sizes:

TCP/IP Internetworking — 0KB

☐ Connectivity Utilities — 0KB

☐ SNMP Service — 123KB

☐ TCP/IP Network Printing Support — 57KB

☐ FTP Server Service — 131KB

☐ Simple TCP/IP Services — 20KB

☒ DHCP Server Service — 345KB

☐ WINS Server Service — 499KB

Space Required: 345KB
Space Available: 222,864KB

☐ Enable Automatic DHCP Configuration

The DHCP Server service provides automatic configuration and addressing for Windows TCP/IP computers on your internetwork. Choose this option to make this computer a DHCP server.

[Continue] [Cancel] [Help]

6. In the Windows NT Setup dialog box, type in the source path for the Windows NT installation disk(s).

Windows NT Setup

Please enter the full path of the Windows NT distribution files. If you want to install files from the original Setup floppy disks, type a drive path (such as A:\i386) and Setup will prompt you for the correct disk. Then choose Continue.

E:\i386\

[Continue] [Cancel]

7. Exit the Network Control Panel, and select Restart the system.

At this point DHCP is installed, but must still be configured before it's actually operational. To accomplish this, begin by logging back into the server, and starting the DHCP manager program. You can also configure the DHCP server from a command line by using the manager that's distributed with the Windows NT Resource Kit. Most of the operational configuration is accomplished by performing these four activities:

- Defining the address scope

- Specifying a client exclude list

- Enabling the client

- Setting up the backup strategy

In the following sections, we'll cover these configuration steps, beginning with instruction on how to define an address scope.

Defining the DHCP Scope

At a minimum, at least one scope must be defined per DHCP server, but you can assign multiple scopes. Since DHCP servers operate independently of each other and don't share information, it's very important to be sure that the IP addresses listed in that scope are unique. It's that sinister Networkland Law of Duplicates again! If two DHCP servers have a scope comprised of the same IP addresses, duplicates will be dispersed over your network, causing the grisly crash of one or both of the hapless clients that possess the same address. In Exercise 7.2, you will define the scope of a DHCP server.

EXERCISE 7.2

Defining the Address Scope of a DHCP Server

1. Double-click on the Network Administration group icon.

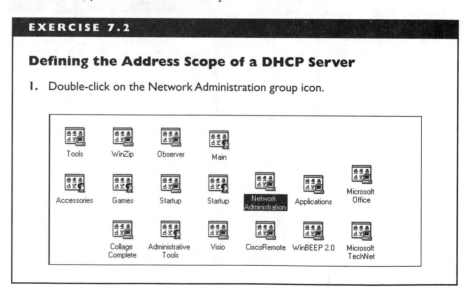

EXERCISE 7.2 (CONTINUED FROM PREVIOUS PAGE)

2. In the Network Admistration (Common) dialog box, double-click on the DHCP Manager program.

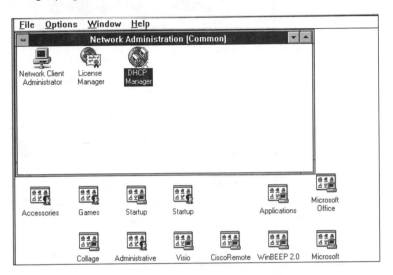

3. In the DHCP Manager - (Local) dialog box, select Scope ➢ Create.

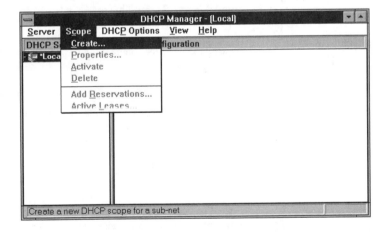

4. Then define the following options in the Create Scope - (Local) dialog box:

```
┌─                        Create Scope - (Local)                        ─┐
┌─IP Address Pool──────────────────────────────────────────────────────
  Start Address: │160 .1    .200 .1  │      Excluded Addresses:
                                              ┌──────────────────────┐
  End Address:   │160 .1    .200 .25 │        │                      │
                                              │                      │
  Subnet Mask:   │255 .255 .255 .0   │        │                      │
  Exclusion Range:                            │                      │
  Start Address: │  .   .   .    │  [ Add -> ]│                      │
                                              │                      │
  End Address:   │  .   .   .    │  [<- Remove]└──────────────────────┘
─────────────────────────────────────────────────────────────────────
┌─Lease Duration──────────────────────────────────────────────────────
  ○ Unlimited
  ● Limited To: [3 ▲▼] Day(s) [00▲▼] Hour(s) [00▲▼] Minutes
─────────────────────────────────────────────────────────────────────
Name:    │                                                   │
Comment: │                                                   │
```

Start Address: This will become the first IP address in the range available to be assigned to a DHCP client.

End Address: This will become the last IP address in the range available for assignment to a DHCP client.

Subnet Mask: This will become the subnet mask assigned to all DHCP clients of this server.

Exclusion Range Start Address: This will designate the first IP address in a special, exclusive range unavailable for assignment to DHCP clients. These addresses are generally reserved for hosts which must maintain a static IP address for extended periods (e.g., the IP address for the DHCP or WINS server). If these addresses aren't corralled away from the normal available range, operation of both the client with the static address and the DHCP client may fail.

Exclusion Range End Start Address: This will designate the last IP address in the above mentioned reserved range, unavailable for assignment to a DHCP client.

Lease Duration: This will designate the amount of time a client system can lease an IP address. This option can be set to a specific number of days, hours, and minutes, or even an unlimited span.

EXERCISE 7.2 (CONTINUED FROM PREVIOUS PAGE)

Name: To ease management, it's advised to assign a name to the scope you're defining.

Comment: This optional field is for identification purposes, and is used to describe your scope.

Once you've filled out the above information in the Create Scope dialog box, click on OK. You'll then be asked to activate the scope. If you're ready to implement the scope at this time, select Yes.

If you are just now preparing a DHCP server and are not yet ready to start this scope, select No. You can start the scope at a later time by selecting Scope ➢ Active in the DHCP Manager program.

DHCP Scope Options

For each scope member, options can be configured for the scope to provide additional configuration information to the scope members. The scope options contain an array of parameters that the DHCP administrator may configure. After the DHCP scope has been defined, there are three levels of scope options that become available for configuration.

GLOBAL OPTIONS These exist at the default selection level. They provide the ability to deliver common information to all DHCP clients located on all subnets that access that particular DHCP server. An example of a global option is all the network's clients using the same WINS or DNS server.

SCOPE OPTIONS These secondary level options are used to define information specific for a particular scope of IP addresses. A good example is appointing a specific gateway for each subnet to use. Scope options are always given priority over global options.

CLIENT OPTIONS Client options are specific to a certain IP address. For example, a client using a reserved IP address may have a specific configuration requirement. This option is given the highest priority—over both scope and global options.

Both global and scope options can be delineated from the DHCP Manager window by selecting from the Options pull-down menu. The options are listed as either active or unused. To control your selection, click on the desired option, and then select Add or Remove. When options are highlighted, values may be assigned by clicking on the Value button.

Because Microsoft clients only support a limited number of the DHCP functions, only those relative to Microsoft's TCP/IP implementations will be discussed. All other DHCP functions, such as Time Offset, Time Server, Name Servers, Log Servers, Cookie Servers, LPR Servers, Impress Servers, etc, will only function on other operating systems, such as UNIX.

The Microsoft-compatible DHCP functions are discussed below:

003 Router   assigns a default gateway to the client. This function is only enabled when the default gateway hasn't already been manually defined on that client.

006 DNS Servers   indicates the IP address(es) of DNS servers to the client

046 WINS/NBT Node Type   designates NetBIOS name resolution configuration

- Broadcast/B-node

- Point to Point/P-node

- Mixed/M-node

- Hybrid/H-node

044 WINS/NBNS Servers   designates the IP address(es) of WINS servers to the client. This option is only used if the client hasn't already been manually configured for a WINS server.

047 NetBIOS Scope ID   verifies the local NetBIOS scope ID in a way that a NetBIOS over TCP/IP host will only communicate with other identically configured NetBIOS hosts.

After selecting from the various options listed above, one must appoint an appropriate value for your selection. These value types are similar to those found in common computer programming, as well as in the Windows NT registry. There are a total of six value types available to choose from. The data types can be thought of in the same context as setting up a database field type. For example, where you'd use a date field to express time, you'd instead use an IP address to designate a system's logical location. We've listed the data types for you below:

IP Address   specifies the IP address of an object, such as a server or router that is added to the options list. Typically, options with server or router in the name tend to use this value.

Long   specifies a 32-bit numeric value commonly used as a value for the designation of timings such as an *ARP Cache Time-out*.

String   defines a collection of *characters*, normally used as a value type for object names (e.g., a domain name).

WorD   sets a 16-bit number value of a designated block size. "Max DG Reassembly Size" is an example of an option that uses this value type.

BytE   establishes a numeric value designated by a single byte. Typically used in situations where a single character (a character is one byte long) represents an option such as *WINS/NBT node* type. In this case, the value will be equal to 1, 2, 4, or 8.

Binary   This value, set to on or off, designates that a value is binary. It's commonly used when the need arises to enable or disable a specific set of functions or options. An example of a circumstance requiring this kind of action is when one is dealing with vendor-specific information.

DHCP Client Reservation

Often in many networks, there are certain change-resistant machines such as servers that must always use the same IP address. To fulfill this need, and shelter these sensitive devices, a special arrangement called a client reservation must be made with the DHCP server. Typically, client reservations are made so that machines that access other networks through a *firewall*, a device that secures a network by allowing only authorized systems to access the network, can function.

Another example of the need to reserve a particular IP address concerns systems that utilize DHCP, but not any additional services, such as WINS.

A system such as this must have a manual entry in the WINS server so that other systems can be aware of its existence. Secondly, these nonWINS type clients must use some method of resolution, like a WINS proxy agent, so that they can communicate with other machines. Since DHCP is dynamic in nature, and the LMHOSTS file is static, they're incompatible—they won't communicate without help. Simply placing address entries in LMHOSTS on a system using DHCP without WINS, etc., would result in their incorrect resolution—perhaps (perish the thought), to an extinct IP address...Ouch! To make a client reservation, follow the steps in Exercise 7.3.

EXERCISE 7.3

How to Make a Client Reservation

1. Run the DHCP Management program.

2. Select Scope ➢ Add Reservations. The Add Reserved Clients dialog box will appear.

Add Reserved Clients
IP Address: `160.1 .200.`
Unique Identifier:
Client Name:
Client Comment:
[Add] [Close] [Help] [Options...]

You will then be prompted for the following information:

IP Address   This is the IP address that you wish to reserve for a client.

Unique Identifier   This is the hardware address of the client's network interface card. This is the most important entry in the reservation since it will contain the address that the DHCP server responds to. A mistake in this entry will cause the server to assume that the client is not the machine in the reservation, and assign it another IP address. Trust us. You don't want to go there! There's more than one way to determine the NIC card's hardware address, but all three ways listed below are begun from the command line.

First way: From the command line, type **IPCONFIG /ALL**.

Second way: Again from the command line, type **NET CONFIG RDR**.

Another way: Use a utility provided by the card's manufacturer. This information is not hard to find, but the number you'll unearth may be hard to under-stand. You may also notice this number making a cameo in utilities such as Microsoft Diagnostics and Microsoft's WINDIAG program.

Client Name   This entry is an identification tool for reservations, and is used to increase their manageability. It's much easier to identify a machine by name than by an abstract number. Imagine yourself sitting there trying to figure out which hardware address goes to which machine. (Warning!...If you think that's a cool way to spend an evening, you might be a nerd.)

Client Comments   One may feel so moved as to make a statement about the entry. These should be short, but they don't need to be sweet.

All DHCP servers should be set with the same reservation information.

DHCP Client Configuration

There are many different kinds of clients that support DHCP. Typically, installation procedures are similar from type to type. For brevity, we'll outline the specifics for installation as they apply to Windows NT and Windows For Work-groups. With respect to both of these operating systems, and regardless of what's in place prior to enabling DHCP, the subnet mask and IP address must be replaced when DHCP is enabled. All other options, such as DNS server, WINS server, Default Gateway, etc., will be used over DHCP's specifications. In Exercise 7.4, you will install a DHCP client under Windows NT.

EXERCISE 7.4

Installing a DHCP Client Under Windows NT

1. Select Main ➤ Control Panel ➤ Network.

If TCP/IP was not installed, select Add from the list, and then choose TCP/IP and related components. The Windows NT TCP/IP Installation Options dialog box will appear.

2. Check the Enable Automatic DHCP Configuration box.

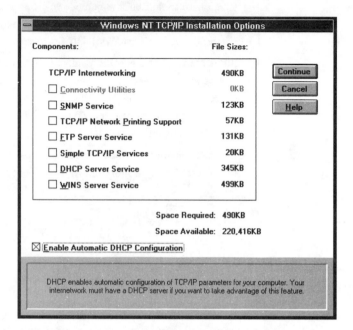

3. If needed, provide a path in the Options program for a source file.

4. Select OK from the Network Configuration program, and restart as a DHCP client.

If you already have TCP/IP (in Windows NT), the configuration procedure is similar to that for a new installation:

1. Select Main ➤ Control Panel ➤ Network.

2. Select TCP/IP Protocol from the list of installed components, and then choose Configure.

3. In the options box located near the top of the screen, select Enable Automatic DHCP Configuration and then choose Continue.

4. Exit the Network Configuration Program, and restart as a DHCP client.

In Exercise 7.5, you will install DHCP with Windows for Workgroups.

EXERCISE 7.5

Installing DHCP with Windows for Workgroups

The procedure to configure a client for DHCP is slightly different than that for Windows NT.

1. If TCP/IP has not been installed, run the Network Setup program (Winsetup /Z) in the Network group.

2. Select Add Protocol from the network subdialog box.

3. In the Microsoft TCP/IP Configuration dialog box, select Enable Automatic DHCP Configuration, and then choose Continue.

4. When finished, you will be prompted to restart Windows. After doing so, your machine will restart as a DHCP client.

If you already had TCP/IP (in Windows for Workgroups), the procedure is similar to that for a new installation:

1. Run the Network Setup program (Winsetup /Z) in the Network group.

2. Select Microsoft TCP/IP 3.11 from the list of installed protocols in the network subdialog box.

3. Click on Enable Automatic DHCP Configuration, then select Continue.

4. When finished, you will be prompted to restart Windows. Your machine will restart as a DHCP client.

DHCP and the IPCONFIG Utility

TCP/IP is very adaptable, presenting its users with many opportunities for customization. It's fully routable, and supports multiple internal functions. Unlike *NetBEUI,* which is nonroutable, and virtually nonconfigurable, traditional TCP/IP has not been *plug and play*. Plug and play means that when a software or hardware item is installed, it configures itself. You've plugged it in (installed it) and you're now free as a bird to work with it without further ado. For TCP/IP, DHCP has changed all this. TCP/IP now realizes unprecedented ease in implementation. Unfortunately, as invention and progress often serve to create efficiency and simplify things, they also tend to author whole new sets of problems. Suppose that for whatever reason, you need to find out about the IP address, subnet mask, and default gateway that your system has been assigned. To answer this dilemma, Microsoft uses a command line utility called IPCONFIG. When IPCONFIG is executed, it displays all the basic, can't live without it, IP information you most often need:

- IP address

- Subnet mask

- Default gateway

If only things were always that simple! Nope—sad, but true, knowing this basic stuff may fail to do the trick when it comes to situations like the blood pressure-increasing inability to resolve a NetBIOS name. The good news is that Microsoft thought of that one. Should this unfortunate, yet commonplace event happen to you, type **IPCONFIG /ALL**. This will access the advanced listing information you may find highly useful in curing what ails your network. This beneficial information includes:

- Your system's host name

- NetBIOS node type (b-node, p-node, m-node, h-node)

- The assigned NetBIOS scope ID

- The IP address(es) of designated DNS servers

- NetBIOS resolution via DNS Enabled Status

- The IP address(es) of designated WINS servers

- IP Routing's Enabled Status

- WIN Proxy's Enabled Status

- DHCP's Enabled Status

- The Network Adapters Description

- The Hardware address of the Network Adapter

Renewing a Lease Through IPCONFIG

As discussed earlier in this chapter, a DHCP lease is automatically renewed when 50% of the lease time gets used up. In the same vein—adhering to the same availability proviso—one can also renew a DHCP client's IP address lease manually via the IPCONFIG utility by executing IPCONFIG/RENEW. This function can be especially critical when a DHCP server goes down and you wish to maintain a new lease once the server is brought back up. This happens more often than one might think. For example, suppose you were upgrading the server and intended to have it down more than half of your client's lease period. Here's when IPCONFIG/RENEW hits a homer. With this cool little command, you can schedule a time for the server to be up, making it possible for all your users to renew their leases.

Releasing a Lease Through IPCONFIG

In addition to renewing leases, you may need to cancel them. For example, if you want to move a system from one subnet to another, that system's IP address, subnet mask, and default gateway will probably all need to be changed. As a result, the machine's old information becomes obsolete, requiring lease cancellation. Typing IPCONFIG/RELEASE from the command line will generate a DHCPRELEASE message, and immediately cause all TCP/IP functioning on that client to cease.

Also noteworthy is the fact that the DHCPRELEASE message isn't automatically generated when you shutdown a DHCP client. So, if one of your users is going to the Bahamas, resulting in their system's extended dormancy, IPCONFIG/RELEASE again comes in handy. Releasing their lease gives the server an opportunity to assign the lucky sap's IP address to some less fortunate being's computer.

Maintaining the DHCP Database

There are three basic functions involved in maintaining the DHCP database—backup, restore, and compact. In most cases, you'll only be performing backups occasionally, and compacting the database on a weekly basis, or less. Only volatile, problematic, or extremely complicated network environments will require more vigilance on your part. To a degree, some functions described in this section are automatic. For example, if the system detects a corrupted database, it will automatically revert to its backup. Should this occur in a neglected network where no backup exists—it's curtains...you're in trouble! The following procedures are essential for ensuring your network's health, and optimizing its performance. Understanding this section will help you prevent problems and preserve your sanity, as well as that of those who depend on you.

Backup

You can keep a backup copy of all information that is entered when configuring the server. This information includes scopes, client reservations, options, etc. The DHCP database will be backed up automatically every hour to the *\systemroot*SYSTEM32\DHCP\BACKUP\JET directory. Even so, savvy, jaded network types make their own—just in case. Exercise 7.6 shows you how:

EXERCISE 7.6

Backing Up the DHCP Database

You can change the backup interval by modifying the registry entry key located in: HKEY_LOCAL_MACHINE\SYSTEM\CurrentControlSet\Services\DHCPServer\ Parameters\BackupInterval

Note that a duplicate of the registry key for DHCP is stored in \systemroot\system32\ DHCP\Backup, in a file called DHCPCFG.

Restore

This function of DHCP ensures that reliable data is served. If, for example, the DHCP server determines when initializing that its data is corrupt, it will automatically revert to the backup. You can force the DHCP server to manually restore the database in two ways, as shown in Exercises 7.7 and 7.8.

EXERCISE 7.7

Restoring the DHCP Database—First Way

1. Set the Restore Flag Option to 1. This option is stored in: HKEY_LOCAL_MACHINE \ CurrentControlSet\ Services\DHCPServer\Parameters

2. Restart the computer. Once the system has rebooted, it will change the flag back to a 0.

Restoring the DHCP Database—Second Way

Copy the contents of the backup directory, *systemroot*\SYSTEM32\DHCP\BACKUP\
JET, to the DHCP directory, *systemroot*\SYSTEM32\DHCP.

Compact

The ubiquitous Computerdom issue of More Space Needed is what this handy function addresses. One executes it by running the JETPACK.EXE utility. This economical tool should be run periodically to keep your database a compact and efficient thing. There's no set period for how often you should run this utility. It depends on how compulsive you are. Things that indicate it's a good time to run the compactor are more users and/or workstations moving onto your network (your company is growing and hiring), or less users (layoffs, and reorganization). Large, volatile networks may need to be compacted once a week, whereas smaller ones changing rarely may only need to be compacted every couple of months. Generally, the rate of change is a good barometer of when to run JETPACK.EXE. To compact your database, follow the steps in Exercise 7.9.

Compacting the Database

1. Stop the DHCP server through the Service Manager in the Control Panel, or type **net stop dhcpserver** at a command prompt.

2. Change to the DHCP directory *systemroot*\SYSTEM32 \DHCP, and run JET-PACK DHCP.MDB temp_file.MDB.

Note that the temp filename is not important. Once JETPACK has completed compacting the database, the temp_file (regardless of name), will have its contents copied back to the DHCP.MDB file, and will then be deleted.

3. Finally, restart the DHCP server either by rebooting, or by selecting Control Panel ➢ Service Manager, or by typing **net start dhcpserver** at a command prompt.

Knowledge of which files you're working with, and how they perform with a DHCP server, can be useful, so we've included this little resource of DHCP files. It's provided for your information only—not as an exercise.

This alphabetical listing includes the filenames with a brief description of them, and should help you get a clear picture of the DHCP database.

DHCP.MDB This is the main DHCP database file. It's arguably the most important file in the DHCP directory that you'll work with.

DHCP.TMP This file is used internally by the DHCP server for temporary storage while running.

JET.LOG/JET*.LOG These are transaction log files which can be used in a jam by DHCP to recover data.

SYSTEM.MDB A storage file used by the DHCP server to track the structure of the database.

Summing Things Up

THE PURPOSE OF DHCP is to centrally control IP-related information and eliminate the need to manually keep track of where individual IP addresses are allocated. Unless your network is very tiny, or is running applications that are incompatible with DHCP (e.g., routers that can't handle the BootP/DHCP protocol), using DHCP is generally a good idea.

There are four stages to the DHCP lease process: The lease request, lease offer, lease selection, and finally, its acknowledgment. In order to make DHCP function, you need to have some spare equipment on hand—a server, a machine to act as your client, and a router. When it comes to defining the DHCP scope, at least one of these must be delimited per server since DHCP servers operate independently of each other, and don't share information. There are three different kinds of scope options: global, scope, and client. The global variety exists at the default selection level, and provides the ability to deliver common information to all DHCP clients located on all subnets which access a particular DHCP server. Scope options are given priority over the global kind, and are, as their name suggests, used to define information specific for a particular scope of IP addresses. Client options are the most individualized and privileged of all.

Certain machines common to most networks must always use the same IP address. To fulfill this need, and shelter these sensitive devices, this special client reservation arrangement must be made with the DHCP server. Typically, client reservations are made so that machines that access other networks through a firewall can function. (Recall that a firewall is a device that secures a network by allowing only authorized systems to access the network.) You learned how to install and configure DHCP through a host (pun intended) of exercises outlining the specifics for installation as they apply to Windows NT and Windows For Workgroups.

IPCONFIG is a cool utility that can be very useful in resolving a mysterious NetBIOS name. Typing IPCONFIG /ALL. IPCONFIG /RENEW can be especially useful at critical times such as when a DHCP server goes down and you wish to maintain leases once the server is brought back up.

We closed the chapter with a discussion on maintaining the DHCP database. The functions involved in doing so are backup, restore, and compact. The very cool and economical JETPACK.EXE utility should be run periodically to keep your database working for you as the compact and efficient thing it should be.

Now is a good time to pause, look over the list below, and find out what you've learned. You should be able to discuss:

- The definition of DHCP

- How it's installed

- DHCP functions

- DHCP requests and leasing

- What steps are involved in the lease process, as well as each step's corresponding message(s)

- How DHCP is configured for multiple subnets

- DHCP clients

- How the IPCONFIG utility relates to DHCP

- DHCP database backup and recovery

- The JETPACK compression utility

Exercise Questions

Multiple-Choice Questions

1. What are the four steps in the DHCP lease process?

    A. Contact, Offer, Selection, Acknowledgment

    B. Request, Offer, Election, Acceptance

    C. Request, Offer, Selection, Acceptance

    D. Petition, Offer, Election, Acknowledgment

    E. Request, Offer, Selection, Acknowledgment

2. Why are initial broadcasts used, and what uses them?

    A. Routers use them to update the routing tables of all DHCP servers on the network.

    B. Client machines use them to secure leases and notify all DHCP servers that they now have one, so the servers won't send out more DHCPACK's and thus create duplicate addresses.

    C. DHCP servers use them to secure client leases, and release them if they're not renewed when 50% of the lease has expired.

    D. Client machines use them to locate a DHCP server in order to acquire an IP address for a specific period of time.

3. What is the default period of time a DHCP lease is extended to a client?

    A. 24 hours

    B. 48 hours

    C. 72 hours

    D. 3¼ days

    E. Unlimited

4. How often should the JETPACK utility be used?

   A. An administrator should use it when the leases of the client machines on the network have expired.

   B. Depending on the size of the network, and how many changes typically occur on it, the requirement varies from every few days to every couple of months.

   C. As often as possible. Changes that aren't recorded and updated can go into error, causing chaos on the network.

   D. Because space in the DHCP.MDB file is valuable and fills up fast, the JETPACK utility should be run every 72 hours to remove obsolete IP address entries.

5. How many DHCP servers are required for a network that possesses three subnets, each with DHCP clients on it, and whose routers are supportive of the BootP protocol?

   A. One DHCP server is all that's required.

   B. Since there are three subnets on the network, three DHCP servers would be required in order to ensure fault tolerance.

   C. Two servers are required in order to ensure the network's fault tolerance.

6. Does Microsoft support DHCP server options that Microsoft clients will not support? Explain.

   A. Yes. The additional DHCP server options are there for other IP-based platforms, such as UNIX, which necessarily utilize different information.

   B. Yes. Additional server options exist in order to enable communication on the Internet.

   C. No. DHCP servers are for DHCP clients only. Machines operating under different platforms, like UNIX, utilize servers that correspond to theirs—never DHCP servers.

   D. Yes, but only if Power PCs, which support all types of software platforms, exist as client machines on that network.

7. Once configured, what are the administrative functions performed on a DHCP server?

A. Backup, renew, release

B. Backup, restore, delete

C. Backup, restore, compact

D. Backup, renew, compact

Scenario-Based Review

SCENARIO #1 It's late—almost time to go home. You've only got one more DHCP client to get a lease for, and that's almost done. Just as you kick back and throw your tired dogs up onto the desk, DHCPNACK appears on your screen. What does this mean, and what are the possible reasons for it appearing on your screen?

SCENARIO #2 As Network Manager, you find yourself needing to bring down one of your DHCP servers—the one that just happens to serve the CEO's client machine. You've checked, and sure enough, that client's lease will most certainly expire, causing all the Big Cheese's TCP/IP functions to come to a grinding halt before you could possibly complete your work on the troubled server. To complicate things, if you don't bring down and repair that server, all the clients using it—including the CEO—will be in big trouble. Are you about to become unemployed, or are there solutions to this dilemma? Explain.

WINS: Windows Internet Name Service

I N A TCP/IP-BASED environment, resolving names using a network service is most often achieved with DNS. Windows NT 3.5*x* doesn't support DNS; instead, it utilizes a more efficient and powerful service—WINS (Windows Internet Name Service). In its 3.5*x* versions, the WINS has more than one advantage over DNS. Most importantly, WINS servers are dynamic; they're able to automatically add and change entries as needed.

Objectives

B Y THE TIME you've made it to the other side of this chapter, you'll be armed with all you need to know regarding:

- WINS functions

- How WINS handles the resolution of NetBIOS names

- Installing and configuring WINS

- WINS client setup

- WINS replication

- How to maintain a WINS database

WINS Defined

NETBIOS B-NODE BROADCASTS create lots of traffic on networks. This being a less than desirable thing, Microsoft counter-created something called an *NBNS (NetBIOS Name Server)* as a solution, dubbing it *WINS (Windows Internet Name Service)*—and it works! A WINS server acts as network support by intercepting the legions of name-query broadcasts and processing them internally. This prevents inundating the network and consuming precious bandwidth. As a result, the network is relieved of stress—freed to function efficiently, unencumbered by its broadcast-related burdens. There's a whole bunch of interesting documentation about WINS in RFC 1001 and RFC 1002 that you can browse through sometime if you're interested. Figure 8.1 details a WINS function.

FIGURE 8.1

The functions of WINS

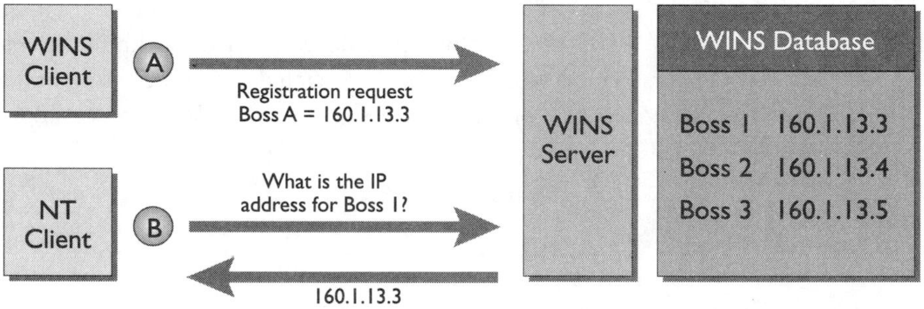

Before two NetBIOS-based hosts can communicate, the destination Net-BIOS name must be resolved to an IP address. This is necessary because TCP/IP requires an IP address in order to establish communications. It can't achieve them through using a NetBIOS computer name. The procedure is as follows:

Step A: In a WINS environment, each time a WINS client starts up, it registers its NetBIOS name and IP address with the WINS server.

Step B: When a WINS client initiates a command to communicate with another host, the resulting name query request is sent directly to the WINS server instead of being broadcast all over the local network.

Step C: If the WINS server finds the destination host's NetBIOS name and concurrent IP address mapping in its database, it returns this information to the WINS client. Because the WINS database obtains name/IP address mappings dynamically, its database entries are always current.

Why Use WINS?

Ahhh...Why do we love WINS? Let us count the ways! Yes, indeed. There's an abundance of benefits gained through employing a WINS server. The stand-out is its exceptional ability to substantially reduce traffic and effectively promote overall resolution speed. Since network broadcasts are sent directly to the WINS server, there is no need for congestion-producing b-node broadcasts. These broadcasts only darken the network doorstep if the server is unavailable or unable to resolve the needed address. Since WINS servers are the first contact, and are, in most cases, ready, willing, and able to satisfy name queries, the time spent resolving a NetBIOS name is markedly reduced. Additionally, Microsoft clients using WINS automatically register with the WINS server upon start-up, ensuring totally pristine, right off the vine freshness of the contents of its database—more so than any other resolution service! Finally, because it's dynamic in nature, employing a WINS server fully eliminates a lot of the agonizingly boring work normally associated with database maintenance. As an extra bonus, you can even assign a second WINS server to a client for purposes of fault tolerance.

WINS in Action

WHEN A WINS client starts, messages will be sent between the WINS client and the WINS server in order to register each of the WINS client's names. Like DHCP, WINS messages occur in four modes: name registration, name renewal, name release, and name query/name resolution, as illustrated in Figure 8.2.

Name Registration

In the WINS environment, each client registers its name and corresponding IP address with its designated WINS server when it starts up. When a NetBIOS-based application or service is started, the client's NetBIOS name is also included

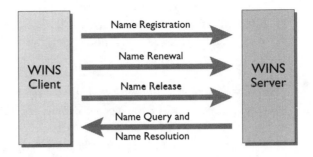

FIGURE 8.2

WINS works in
four modes

in that package of information (See Figure 8.3). One type of service that is NetBIOS-dependent is the Messenger service used for the delivery of print notices, system events, and the like.

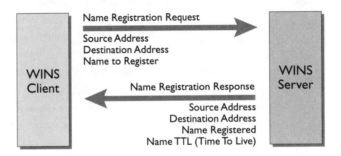

FIGURE 8.3

Name registration

When a unique and valid name is received by the WINS server, it returns a message confirming registration, plus a specified *Time To Live (TTL) period* designating the duration of time that name can be used. With WINS, as with everything else in Computerdom, the existence of duplicate names is an offensive, frowned upon thing. If one of these dirty buggers is discovered during the WINS registration process, a WINS server will send out a challenge to its database's registered owner of the name in the form of a name query request. The challenge message is repeated three times, at 500 millisecond intervals—less if the server receives a reply. When the client happens to be a multihomed system, the above process is repeated for each IP address until the server either receives a reply or tries each address three times. If the current owner of the name responds, the WINS server will reject the request by sending a negative name request back to the machine attempting to claim the already in-use NetBIOS name. If the current registered owner doesn't reply, then the name is deleted from the database, and a positive acknowledgment is sent to the requesting machine. If the primary WINS server doesn't respond after three tries, an attempt will then be made to contact a secondary server. If this effort is also frustrated, and no available server is found, the client will send out a b-node broadcast to validate its name and achieve registration among its peers.

Note: The phrase "Time To Live" (TTL) is a common one in TCP/IP. Most often, it refers to notices sent out delimiting a period of time, or specifying the number of hops a message may go through before it's discarded. Obviously highly useful, it serves to phase out obsolete messages, and also prevents them from looping endlessly in circles among two or more routers. (Recall the "Counting to Infinity" scenario we presented earlier!)

Renewing Names

Similar to lease renewal, the process of renewing a name begins when a WINS client notifies the WINS server that it desires to continue its use of that name, and so, its current Time To Live period now needs to be reset. Registered names associated with the WINS client are always done so on a temporary basis. This prevents confusion or worse if the name's current owner moves, receives a new IP address, or otherwise discontinues use of its name. Temporary registration permits the server to reassign the name elsewhere should any of these events occur. It's sort of an environmentally-friendly, Networkland recycling program that's so popular, traffic gets really heavy en route to the recycling center. The name renewal process is shown in Figure 8.4.

FIGURE 8.4

The name renewal process

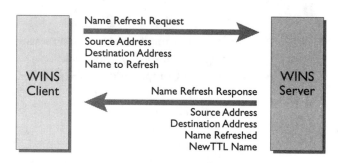

When the TTL period lapses to 50 percent of its original lease time, the WINS client sends a name renewal message to the primary WINS server. This message contains the client's name and both the source and destination IP address. If there's no response, the message will be resent once more at one eighth of the TTL. If there's still no response from the primary server, the client will then attempt renewal through the secondary WINS server, if one's configured. If the effort is successful, the WINS client will attempt to register with the secondary server as though it were the first attempt. If, after four attempts, the WINS client fails to contact the secondary WINS server, it'll switch back to the primary one. Once successful contact is made, either the primary or secondary WINS server will respond by sending the client a new TTL period. This process will continue as long as the client computer is powered-on, and as long as it remains a WINS client.

Releasing Names

WINS clients can also relinquish ownership of its name. It can accomplish this by sending a name-release message, containing its IP address and name, during a proper shutdown. This will cause the entry to be removed from the WINS server's database. The WINS client will wait for confirmation in the form of a positive release message, comprised of the released name and a new TTL of zero, from the WINS server. At this point, it'll stop responding to its former NetBIOS name. If the IP address and name sent by the client don't match, the WINS server will return a negative release message. If no confirmation is received from the WINS server, the WINS client will then send up to three b-node broadcasts notifying all other systems, including nonWINS clients, to remove the now invalid name from their NetBIOS name caches. This process is illustrated in Figure 8.5.

FIGURE 8.5

The name
release process

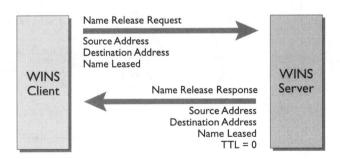

Name Query and Response

The WINS process is central to communication. Through it, names are resolved to IP addresses, which clearly identifies the devices involved, and forms the basis for them to communicate. To get a picture of this process, think of making a phone call, and what you need to know to make it. First, you need the right number for the person you're trying to contact. For the call to be successful, you need an acknowledgment from the other end that you have, in fact, reached them. Think about phoning up someone who isn't home and doesn't have an answering machine. Because you didn't receive an acknowledgment from them, or their machine, you're left wondering if you actually reached them or not. Without the right access coordinates, plus a response from whomever or whatever's been contacted, communication just doesn't happen. This process describes name query and response, and the reason it's set up the way it is. Ideally, when a network is populated solely with WINS clients, the need for congestion-producing b-node broadcasts all but vanishes. Equipped with a fully functioning WINS server, most resolution traffic should be h-node over UDP port 137- NetBIOS Name Service. In Figure 8.6, we've detailed an expansion of how WINS, a NetBIOS Name Server, processes a request, or query. Try to make mental notes of how similar this process is to the one outlined for NetBIOS name servers covered in Chapter 6.

FIGURE 8.6

Name query and
name resolution

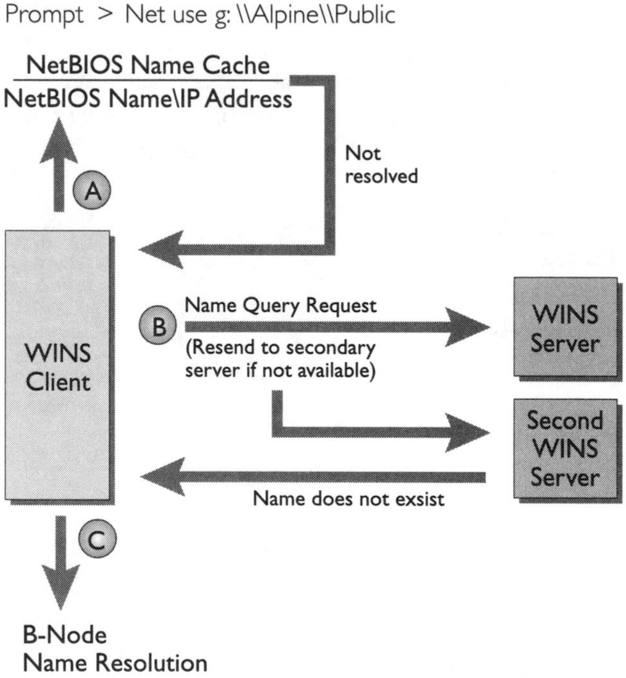

Prompt > Net use g: \\Alpine\\Public

NetBIOS Name Cache
NetBIOS Name\IP Address

Not resolved

(A)

WINS
Client

Name Query Request
(Resend to secondary
server if not available)

(B)

WINS
Server

Second
WINS
Server

Name does not exsist

(C)

B-Node
Name Resolution

By default, WINS uses the h-node implementation of NetBIOS over TCP/IP. The NetBIOS Name Server is always checked for a NetBIOS name/IP address mapping before initiating a b-node broadcast. The process is as follows:

Step A: Again, as with NetBIOS name resolution, begin with a command like NET USE or NET VIEW. We'll use net use g: \\Alpine\public. Initially, the system will always check the local address cache to try to resolve the name. If it's found there, ARP will then proceed to resolve the hardware address. This deftly avoids adding unnecessary traffic on the network.

Step B: If the process in Step A fails to resolve the name, a request is sent directly to the WINS server. If the primary server is up, and the name is found in its database, the information is returned to the requesting system. If the server fails to respond, the request is repeated twice before the client then switches to the secondary WINS server.

Step C: If both the primary and secondary WINS servers fail to resolve the name, the client will revert to using a broadcast. If this is also unsuccessful, the system will then try checking the LMHOSTS file, HOSTS file, and finally, DNS.

As soon as the host name is resolved as in steps A or B, ARP kicks in to ferret out the hardware address.

WINS Implementation

BEFORE DECIDING WHETHER or not to switch to or install WINS, it's wise to first assess your needs and be sure you understand the requirements necessary to implement it.

Prior Considerations

While it may be true that WINS servers are usually a helpful asset, they're not for every network. An example would be a small NetBIOS network existing within a larger, primarily UNIX-based internetwork. That network would likely be best off just using the DNS server and avoiding the cost of implementing a couple of WINS servers. Most often, if the decision is made to adopt

WINS, two or more WINS servers need to be configured. This is because even though only one is actually required, the network will enjoy the advantages of fault tolerance in the event one of the servers goes down. The performance of each WINS server will vary according to that particular machine's hardware. For instance, the average high-end Pentium 166 MHz can process about 1500 name registrations and 750 name queries per minute. You can enhance the performance of each WINS server by an estimated 25% by adding an auxiliary CPU. This is because each additional CPU adds a new, separate WINS process thread. It's also important to remember that your NIC card and disk drives can be the cause of bottlenecks. Performance for name registration can also be augmented by disabling logging though the WINS manager. However, this is generally a bad idea, because if the system crashes, you could lose your recent updates.

With the recommended two-server minimum execution of WINS, it's reasonable to expect to service up to roughly 10,000 clients. A good tactic to optimize performance is to set half the clients to one WINS server as their primary contact, and the other half to the other WINS server as their primary. For their secondary server, each client group would be configured with the opposite group's primary server.

Server Requirements

By now you've decided to answer the pressing information processing question: "To WINS, or not to WINS?" If you've decided in favor of implementing WINS, you now need to know just what it'll take to do so.

For optimum performance, WINS servers should be Cray super-crunchers. (We warned you—we told you this would be expensive!) Just kidding. There really aren't a lot of requirements placed on a WINS server, therefore, it can and should be added to any Windows NT 3.5x server that is running TCP/IP with a static, nonDHCP assigned IP address. If you elect to use DCHP, it changes things, but we'll tell you more about that a little later. For now, suffice it to say, if you're running DHCP, the WINS server will only function with a reserved address—using the same subnet mask and default gateway each time. The problem with using DHCP is each client absolutely must know the WINS server's IP address. This can become a problem if its address should change.

There's no requirement for a WINS server to become a domain controller of any type.

Server Installation

The WINS service comes ready with Windows NT and will integrate seamlessly into the existing operating system as we shall soon see. It's a beautiful thing!

EXERCISE 8.1

Installing a WINS Server

In this exercise, you'll be installing a WINS server for the automatic resolution of Net-BIOS names to IP addresses for WINS clients.

1. Load the LMHOSTS file entries into the NetBIOS Name Cache, then type **nbstat -R** and press ↵.

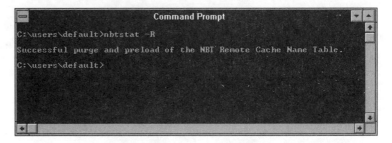

2. Select Control Panel ➤ Network Settings, and then click on Add Software.

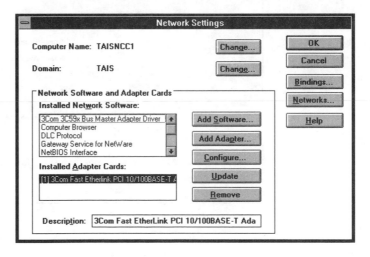

EXERCISE 8.1 (CONTINUED FROM PREVIOUS PAGE)

3. In the Network Software box, select TCP/IP Protocol and related components, then choose Continue.

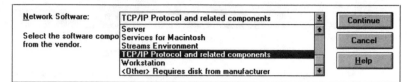

The Windows NT TCP/IP Installation Options dialog box appears, displaying all available component choices.

4. Select WINS Server Service, then choose Continue.

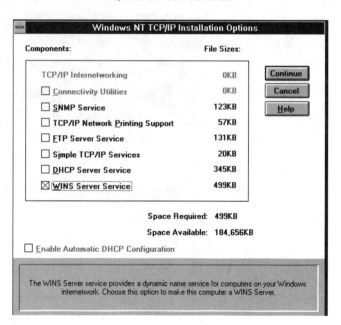

The Windows NT Setup box appears, asking for the full path of the Windows NT distribution files.

5. Type **winntroot** and then choose Continue.

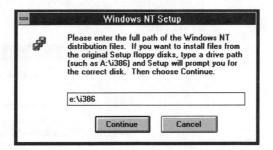

The appropriate files will now be copied to your workstation, and the Network Settings dialog box will appear.

6. Under Installed Network Software, select TCP/IP Protocol, then choose Configure. The TCP/IP Configuration dialog box appears.

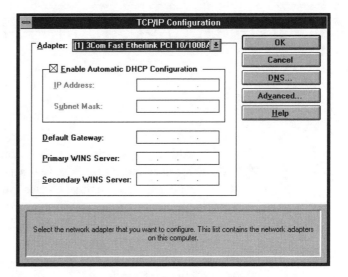

7. In the Primary WINS Server box, type your IP address, then choose OK. The Network Settings dialog box will appear.

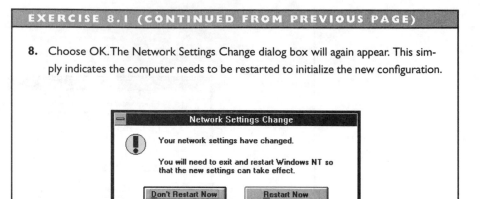

8. Choose OK. The Network Settings Change dialog box will again appear. This simply indicates the computer needs to be restarted to initialize the new configuration.

9. Choose Restart Now.

WINS Server Configuration—Static Mapping for Clients

MOST CONFIGURATION FOR the WINS Server Service settings are automatic. Normally, few changes need to be made. However, things get a little more complicated when systems configured as WINS clients need to talk to those that aren't. For communication to happen in a mixed environment, manual entries must be made to the WINS server. This is due to the fact that nonWINS clients don't automatically register their names and so won't be recognized, making resolution for them impossible. The only alternative to manually adding entries to the WINS server is to add them to the workstation's LMHOSTS file. To add a static mapping for any type of client, see Exercise 8.2.

EXERCISE 8.2

Configuring Static Entries for NonWINS Clients

1. From Network Administration (Common), start WINS Manager.

2. From WINS Manager - (Local), select Mappings ➤ Static Mappings.

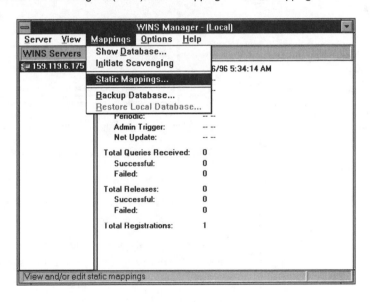

3. Choose Add Mappings from the Static Mappings - (Local) screen.

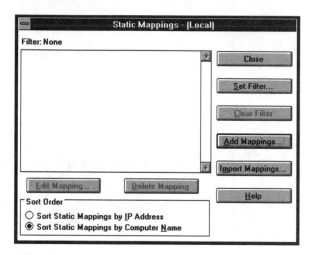

The Add static Mappings dialog box will then appear.

4. In the Name box, type the computer name of the nonWINS client.

5. In the IP address box, type the IP address of the nonWINS client.

6. Under Type, select an option indicating whether this entry is a unique name or a type of specially named group described in the following list:

- **Unique**   will make an entry into the WINS database allowing for only one address for the given name. This is the most common choice for specifying non-WINS clients.

- **Multihomed**   This is an extension of the unique name option that defines a name by referencing a system. However, since a multihomed system can have multiple addresses (up to 25), it can be included with a given name. This type of computer is connected to more than one physical data link. The data links may or may not be attached to the same network.

- **Group**   This is the same as a normal group, where the IP addresses of individual clients are not stored. A normal group is the name to which broadcasts are sent, and is the domain name used for browsing purposes. It's where domains and workgroups can be specified. This option is useful for functions involving broadcasts, and required lists, as in domain browsing. This function provides the means to define the group name for a group of WINS clients to be able to talk to a non-WINS domain.

EXERCISE 8.2 (CONTINUED FROM PREVIOUS PAGE)

■ **Internet Group** This is an extension of the normal group option and is used to gather up to 25 domain controllers, enabling them to communicate with each other. Like the group function above, a domain name is registered so it can be recognized as a single unit for purposes of creating cohesion among domain servers.

7. After verifying the information you've entered, select Add. If you select Add, then realize you've made a mistake—you've got to close the current box and delete the entry from the static entry dialog.

The entry is now in the database. The template will clear, allowing you to make additional entries.

Note that this procedure is not valid for systems that use DHCP if their IP addresses are not reserved. For example, if a nonWINS DHCP client were to change its IP address, the static name mapping would not be valid.

Short Cut: Suppose you've got this hideously long list of static mappings to add to your system. Employing the above procedure, you'll be ordering pizza for weeks, and your dog will forget who you are, and go into attack mode upon your arrival back home. A quick alternative to plinking each one in is to use the WINS Manager's import function. It'll work with any text file that's in the same format as an LMHOSTS file. All keywords with the exception of #DOM will be ignored. Those that are specified with the #DOM will be marked as an Internet group whose IP addresses will be added to a little group for that specified domain. With this short cut, you can create unique group and Internet group settings.

Client Requirements

To implement WINS, the client machine requires configuration. A WINS client needs a computer running any of the following supported operating systems:

■ Windows NT Server 3.5*x*

■ Windows NT Workstation 3.5*x*

■ Windows 95

■ Windows for Workgroups with TCP/IP-32

- Microsoft Network Client 3.0 for MS-DOS (with TCP/IP)

- LAN Manager 2.2c for MS-DOS

Sorry—LAN Manager 2.2c for OS/2 isn't supported. Essentially, the only requirements for WINS clients are: They must be able to run a supported operating system/IP stack, and be configured with the IP address of both the primary and secondary (if there is one) WINS servers.

TCP/IP drivers are available on the distribution CD for Windows NT Server 3.5x.

WINS Client Configuration

AFTER THE WINS server setup is complete, WINS clients can begin accessing it. In order for a client machine to be able to do this, it must first become a WINS client, configured with TCP/IP, with WINS enabled. This is accomplished by entering the IP address(es) for the WINS system(s) the client will be accessing. Exercise 8.3 illustrates the installation of WINS on NT clients and Windows for Workgroups.

For those clients who are also DHCP clients: When values (addresses) are entered into the WINS address slots, they will be given priority, automatically overriding any DHCP values.

Client Installation

Configuring a computer to be a WINS client requires that you add the IP address of the primary WINS server, and optionally, the IP address of a secondary WINS server. This can be done manually or automatically using DHCP. Exercises 8.3 and 8.4 assume that the TCP/IP transport is already loaded.

EXERCISE 8.3

Installing WINS Clients

1. From the Main group, open the Control Panel, and select Network.

2. Locate TCP/IP Protocol from the list of installed software, then select Configure.

3. Under TCP/IP configuration, type in the addresses of both the primary and secondary WINS servers (if one exists), then select OK.

4. Exit all applications—Control panel, etc.—then shutdown and restart your computer.

Windows for Workgroups Clients

EXERCISE 8.4

Installing Windows for Workgroups As a Client

From the Network group, open Network Setup.

1. Locate TCP/IP-32 3.11, then select setup.

2. Inside TCP/IP configuration, enter the addresses for both the primary and secondary WINS server (if one exists), then select OK.

3. Exit all applications, then shutdown and restart your computer.

The DHCP Client

Clients can be configured for WINS even if they're also DHCP clients. DHCP uses two information fields to define WINS support. The first field is defined by the addresses of the primary and secondary WINS servers in the 044 WINS/NBNS Servers blank. The second source is clarified by the type of node they've been configured to behave as. A WINS/DHCP client must be configured to act as a hybrid node, specifying it thus: 046 WINS/NBT Node to 0x8 (h-node).

0x8 is the NetBIOS specification to define an h-node system. If you don't recall this, or need to review the various node types, refer back to Chapter 6.

Configuration for the NonWINS Client

If you have computers on your internetwork that are not supported as WINS clients, they can resolve NetBIOS names on a WINS server using a WINS proxy agent (see Figure 8.7). NonWINS clients can be configured to use WINS in an indirect manner. This process doesn't require changing anything on the non-WINS client itself. Instead, a WINS client that's located on the same network or subnet is used to act as a relay between the nonWINS machine and the WINS server. The machine acting as the relay is known as a WINS proxy agent. Using a WINS proxy agent to extend name resolution capabilities of a WINS server requires one proxy agent on each subnet that has nonWINS clients. This is not required if the network's routers are configured to forward b-node broadcasts (UDP 137 and 138), but is recommended to reduce broadcast traffic. You should have no more than two proxy agents per subnet, and the proxy agent must be a Windows-based WINS client—it cannot be a WINS server.

FIGURE 8.7

Using a WINS proxy agent

Non WINS Client → WINS Proxy Agent → WINS Server

A WINS proxy agent performs the two focal tasks of NetBIOS Name Registration and NetBIOS Name Resolution. The part these machines play in name registration is limited—they don't achieve actual, complete name registration of the nonWINS client. The proxy agent serves only to verify that no other machine is currently registered with the name being requested. It then proceeds to forward the query on to the WINS server for true registration. This method is more thorough and fault tolerant because two machines, both the proxy agent and the WINS server, check up on the proposed name. The Proxy agent detects the resolution request, checks its own name cache for it, and sends the request on to the WINS server if the name isn't already in use.

The WINS server then sends the actual resolution response back to the proxy agent, which then forwards it onward and back to the nonWINS client completing the process.

Exercise 8.5 shows you how to add the WINS proxy function.

EXERCISE 8.5

Configuring a WINS Proxy Agent

1. From the Main group, start Control Panel, and select Network.

2. Locate TCP/IP Protocol from the list of installed software, then select configure.

3. Examine the WINS IP address boxes. The primary WINS server must be defined for the proxy agent to have a WINS server to work with.

4. Click on the Advanced button. Select Enable Proxy Agent, then click OK.

5. Exit all applications, then shutdown and restart your computer.

Database Replication

UNLIKE DHCP SERVERS that don't communicate with each other, WINS servers can be configured to replicate their database entries, sharing them with each other so that all servers across the network have synchronous name information. This also facilitates communication between WINS clients that've registered with different WINS servers. As an example, suppose your system has registered with the WINS server "Alpine" (see Figure 8.8), and your buddy's system registers with the WINS server "Aspen." Not only will these systems enjoy full communication, they'll be able to resolve the names directly for each other because the WINS database is replicated between servers. This feature is not automatic, and requires configuration to become operative. When it has been, replication is automatically triggered any time the database changes (e.g., when names are registered and/or released). To configure a WINS server to function in this manner, it must be ordained as either a push or pull partner.

Push or Pull Partners

Push partners are WINS servers that function by sending update notices to pull partners whenever changes are made. Pull partners—also WINS servers—function by sending out requests to push partners, asking them for entries more recent than their current listings when they want to update their database contents. WINS servers can be defined as both push and pull, ensuring the most up to date information is registered. Only new listings added since the last time an update occurred will be replicated—not the entire database. To get a picture of this, take a peek at Figure 8.8.

Determining If a Server Is a Push or Pull Partner

WINS database replication types can be determined by how a WINS server is used and the architecture of the network. If your network spans multiple sites across slow links, you'll want your servers to pull each other for updates. This is because pull requests can be predetermined to occur at specific times, like during lunch or evening, when the network's traffic is likely to be light. Alternately, if the links are fast, your concerns would have less to do with traffic, and your servers should be ordained as push partners. If you choose to set the server as a push, it's often a good idea to go ahead and configure it as both push and pull. By doing so, you'll be ensuring yourself that you're in possession of the most up-to-date WINS entries available.

FIGURE 8.8

Determining whether a
WINS server is a push
or pull partner

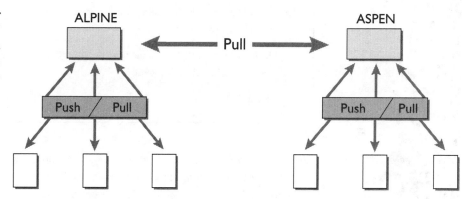

In all, there are four ways in which replication takes place:

- Once configured as a replication partner, each server will automatically pull updates during initialization at startup.

- As a pull partner, the machine will query other WINS servers for updates at a chosen and specified time.

- As a push partner, the machine will advertise its updates when it reaches its threshold for number of changes. Both the threshold and the update interval are user definable.

- Finally, WINS databases may be manually replicated through the WINS Manager.

Exercise 8.6 should help clarify things....

EXERCISE 8.6

Viewing the NetBIOS Name/IP Address Mappings That Have Been Registered in the WINS Database

1. Under Network Administration, double-click on WINS Manager.

2. Select Mappings ➤ Show Database.

The Show Database dialog box will now appear, displaying all NetBIOS names that have been registered in WINS.

3. Notice which NetBIOS names have been registered at the WINS server by the client and when they will expire.

4. Choose Close.

The WINS Manager interface utility can be a little confusing the first time you work with it. It's helpful to understand that you have the ability to list, configure, and trigger replication partners from the Replications Partner dialog box.

Configuring Replication

To add a replication partner for a WINS server, try Exercise 8.7:

EXERCISE 8.7

Adding a Replication Partner for a WINS Server

1. Start WINS Manager, then select Replication Partners from the server menu.

2. Choose Add, then enter the name or IP address of the new WINS server Partner.

3. Select OK to continue. Once the current WINS server communicates with the new partner, they'll appear in the address listing.

At this point, you can either add additional servers by repeating the steps above, or set the partner type by selecting a WINS server from the list.

To set the partner type...

4. Elect either one or both of the Push/Pull Partner boxes from servers to list at the bottom of the dialog box, then select the related configure button.

Push partners are configured by setting the number of changes before the server sends out change notices. The number of requests a server receives should be used to determine the number of changes entered before the change notices are sent. The minimum setting is five changes. For a server that receives hundreds of registrations to be required to have every five changes notified across the network would be very wasteful and highly unnecessary. Although there are no wrong answers to what number of changes should occur before notices are sent, there are some that are more efficient and wiser than others. The same old network-oriented common sense applies here: Only send stuff out across the network as needed, avoiding unnecessary traffic. Always consider speed and efficiency—the things of performance. Don't create a setting that will require so many update notices—the replication process will be slowed to the point of decreased functionality.

As for pull partners...Here, your concerns are similar—defining a start time and an interval for replication. The determining factors for pull partner should be how much bandwidth you have at your disposal, and your transfer time. Again, there aren't any wrong settings for replication, but plan your update schedule for when the network is less busy.

5. When complete, select OK to continue.

6. From the Send Replication Now box, choose either push or pull to replicate your selected partners. You can also select Replicate Now to configure all systems at once. If you select Push with Propagation, those systems that receive updates will automatically share them with all their pull partners. If the partner finds no new entries, the Propagation command will be ignored.

7. Select OK to enter your changes.

Automated Cleanup

I'S PROBABLY BECOMING pretty apparent by now that most of the data managed by WINS machines is maintained automatically, with the option for the network administrator to intervene at certain times. Often, it's best to leave the majority of management functions to the internal system control of the WINS server, unaided by us humans. Controlling a WINS server pretty much comes down to setting things up, adding names, and removing them when necessary. There are some exceptions though. The related duties of database backup, restoration, and compression are definitely going to suffer without good 'ol fashioned human support. Understanding that the name registration process is automatically handled by each WINS client may lead you to wonder about its opposite function—that of removing obsolete or incorrect names from the database.

Most of the database cleanup is accomplished automatically by controls set though the Configuration menu in the WINS Manager program. Once in, you'll be presented with a configuration screen listing four different timers:

Renewal Interval This delimits the intervals at which a WINS client is cued to renew its name with the WINS server. It's similar to the DHCP lease period discussed in Chapter 5. The default setting for this value is four days, or 96 hours.

Extinction Interval This sets the period of time between an entry being marked to be released and its subsequent extinction. Names are marked "release" when a WINS client terminates its session, changes its name, etc. At this point, the entry is considered deleted, but it's not automatically removed from the database. The default setting for this value is also four days, or 96 hours.

Extinction Time-out This option describes the time elapsed between an entry being marked as extinct, and when that entry is removed, or "zapped." This setting is the Lysol of database cleanup. The default setting for this value is again four days, or 96 hours, but it can also have a minimal value set for one day.

Verify Interval This sets the frequency at which a WINS server verifies the entries it doesn't own are still active (i.e., those depicting shared information from other servers). Both the default and minimal settings for this value equal 24 days, or 576 hours.

That's not all folks—there are two more options involved in the whole push or pull configuration fest. Let's say you want your server to pull other WINS servers for any new database entries, or other replication related stuff upon initialization. To do this, select the initial replication box located under Push Parameters, inside of which you'll find the spiffy option to set a retry count. This is like a replication insurance policy that ensures important changes are made even if your server is extremely busy, or temporarily unreachable. However, it's generally effective to simply push changes upon initialization, notifying other available WINS servers of changes when your server starts up. Since, in most cases, the servers that are up have more current information than those that are down, you may want to consider using both these methods. One final thing on push parameters—you can also set updates to automatically occur upon any IP address change. This is a highly mutable area, since when an entry is changed, it's often because DHCP has assigned a new address to it, or because the device has been moved to a different subnet.

If you're professionally managing this server, you should also select the Advanced button from the WINS Manager configuration panel to display additional options. This will reveal additional control opportunities described in the list below.

Logging Enabled   turns on WINS server database event logging. As the name suggests, whenever changes are made to the database, they're recorded in the log.

Log Detailed Events   specifies whether log entries are to be short and sweet or long-winded. It's used to add potentially telling details in the log, which can become quite handy when troubleshooting. Be warned, however... Nothing worthwhile in life is free! There's an abundance of overhead associated with this function that can turn your Porsche of a network into a Volvo. Steer clear of this one if speed and performance tuning are your goals.

Replicate Only with Partners   determines whether your WINS server will communicate with other servers with which it's not already configured to push or pull entries. This is a really cool feature if you're running separate networks that shouldn't be communicating with each other. This function is enabled by default.

Backup On Termination   automatically backs up the database when WINS Manager is closed.

Migrate On/Off replaces static information with the dynamic variety in the event of a conflict. For example, if you've made static entries, and the information you entered eventually changes, the WINS server will cause the database entries to "migrate" from static (S) to active/dynamic (A). A better name could be "evolve." If you're upgrading systems to Windows NT, use this option.

Starting Version Count (hex) Specifies the highest version ID number for the Database. Usually, you will not need to change this value unless the database becomes corrupted and needs to start fresh.

Database Backup Path defines a local, nonnetwork directory to which the WINS database will be backed up. This variable will be used along with automatic restore if the database is ever corrupted.

Maintaining the WINS Database

NOW THAT YOU know the ins and outs on configuring replication partners, we'll give you the skinny on database control. The WINS Manager provides you with the tools you need to list, filter, and control name mappings. You'll learn to use them, as well as gain insight into what's involved in these processes, in Exercise 8.8.

EXERCISE 8.8

To Open and View the Contents of the WINS Database

1. **Startup** Open the WINS Manager, and select Show Database from the Mappings Menu. Call mappings on the currently selected WINS server will then be displayed.

2. **Filter** To streamline and arrange the scope of displayed mappings, select Show Only Mapping from Selected Owner from the display options box. Then select an owner from the owners list, and choose a sort order. The options for determining the sort order can be established by IP Address, Computer Name, Expiration date, Version ID, or Type. This function can be used independently of whether a filter is applied or not. You can also customize the filter by using the Set Filter button. This will specify a limited range of mappings for names and IP addresses.

3. **Information**   This allows you to examine the information you've entered. Notice each line entry is designated by a little computer icon indicating a unique name, or by a computer with an echo trail denoting a group, Internet group, or multihomed computer. You'll notice the registered NetBIOS name, located to the right of the symbol and followed by the IP address, plus a check mark under A for active/dynamic, or S for static mapping. If you see an ominous little cross (like one on a tombstone) appear in the A column, it means the entry is doomed on death row, and will soon be deleted. The cross icon never appears for static entries because they're immortal and permanent. The remaining information consists of the Expiration Date equaling the current WINS server time, plus the TTL and the version ID—a unique hexadecimal number used to determine how fresh an entry is when communicating with other WINS servers.

4. **Removal**   If you're seeking to delete a certain WINS server, plus all related database entries owned by it, choose it from the select owner list, and click on delete owners list.

5. **Exit**   Click the Close button to exit back to the WINS Manager Main menu.

As you now know, a NetBIOS name is 15 characters long, and up to 16 characters in total length. When reviewing the information list generated while showing the database mappings, you can determine what the 16th character is by examining the value in block brackets, located next to the NetBIOS name. Listed below are the five different types of entries possible for a registered name:

\\Computer-Name[00h]   The registered name on the WINS client of the Workstation Service

\\Computer-Name[03h]   The registered name on the WINS client of the Messenger Service

\\Computer-Name[20h]   The registered name on the WINS client of the Server Service

\\User-Name[03h]   The name of the user currently logged on to the computer, this name is used along with the messenger service for activities and communications like print notifications, net send, system events, etc. If a duplicate name is discovered because a user is logged on to more than one machine, only the first name will be registered.

\\Domain-Name[1Bh]   This is the domain name as registered by the *Primary Domain Controller,* or *(PDC),* that's acting as the domain Master browser. It's useful for remote domain browsing. When prompted, a WINS server will produce the IP address of the system that registered the name.

Backing Up

Be a good scout—be prepared—back your stuff up! Doing so is the hallmark of the seasoned, "been there—done that," commemorative hat-wearing network professional. It is an aspect of the WINS database not to be ignored. Always keep a backup copy of all information entered when configuring the server. This backup becomes automatic after a 24 hour period lapses, and after a backup directory has been specified. To specify your backup directory, follow the steps in Exercise 8.9.

EXERCISE 8.9

Backing Up the WINS Database

1. From the WINS Manager Mapping menu, select Backup Database.

The Select Backup Directory dialog box appears.

2. Under Directories, select *\systemroot*\SYSTEM32\WINS.

3. Cancel Perform Incremental Backup and choose OK.

The WINS Manager window appears, followed by a message box indicating the backup was completed successfully.

4. Choose OK.

5. Switch to File Manager, then select \systemroot\SYSTEM32\WINS.

6. View the contents of the WINS_BAK directory, then exit File Manager.

In addition to backing up the database, you should also backup all the registry entries (see Exercise 8.10).

EXERCISE 8.10

Backing Up the Registry Entries

1. Run the Registry Program REGEDT32.

2. Open HKEY_LOCAL_MACHINE\SYSTEM\CurrentControlSet\Services\WINS.

3. Choose Registry ➢ Save Key.

4. Type in the path to where the WINS files are backed up.

Restoration

Restoration ensures that reliable data is served. If the WINS server determines upon initialization that its data is corrupt, it will automatically revert to the backup. You can also manually force the WINS server to restore the database in two ways. The first way is by selecting Restore Database from the WINS manager mapping menu, and specifying the path where the backup directory is located. The second way is begun by deleting JET*.LOG, WINSTMP.MDB, and SYSTEM.MDB from the \systemroot\SYSTEM32\WINS directory. That done, proceed to copy SYSTEM.MDB from the Windows NT server distribution CD-ROM to the \systemroot\SYSTEM32\WINS directory. Finally, copy WINS.MDB from the backup directory to \systemroot\SYSTEM32\WINS. (See Exercise 8.11.)

EXERCISE 8.11

Restoring the WINS Database

1. Go to WINS Manager.

2. From the Mappings menu, choose Restore Local Database.

The Select Directory to Restore dialog box will appear.

3. Under Directories, select \systemroot\SYSTEM32\WINS, then choose OK. The WINS Manager window then appears, followed by a message box indicating the restore was completed successfully.

4. Choose OK.

5. Use Control Panel Services, Server Manager, or a command prompt to start the Windows Internet Name Service.

Compacting

This management function is executed by running the JETPACK.EXE utility. This program should be run periodically when the database grows over 30MB in size to keep the database efficient. The size of the database depends on both the number and the type of entries in it. A unique or group entry uses only 50 to 70 bytes to record it, but an Internet group or multihomed entry will use a whopping 50 to 300 bytes depending on the number of IP addresses associated with it. On top of that, there are about 50 to 100 bytes of overhead needed to track time stamps and the other information that supports each entry. To compact a database, follow the steps in Exercise 8.12.

EXERCISE 8.12

Compacting the Database

1. Stop the WINS Server through the Control Panel or Server Manager, or by typing **net stop WINS**.

2. Change to the WINS directory, \systemroot\SYSTEM32\WINS, and run JETPACK WINS.MDB temp_file.MDB instead. Once JETPACK has completed compacting the database, the temp_file (regardless of name) will have its contents copied back to the WINS.MDB file, and will then be deleted.

3. Finally, restart the WINS server either by rebooting from Control Panel or Server Manager, or typing **net start WINS**.

Below is a list of some of the files you'll be working with along with some information on how they perform in relation to the WINS server.

JET.LOG/JET*.LOG   This file contains transaction log files which may be used by WINS to recover data if necessary.

SYSTEM.MDB   This is a storage file that is used by the WINS server to track the structure of the database.

WINS.MDB   This is the main WINS database file. It's the most important file you'll work with in the WINS directory. You'll most likely find yourself performing all maintenance operations with this file.

WINSTMP.MDB   This temporary file is used and created internally by the WINS server. In the event of a crash, this file does not have to be removed.

Summing Things Up

THE WINDOWS INTERNET Name Service has an important advantage over DNS because WINS servers are dynamic; they're able to automatically add and change entries as needed. A WINS server acts as network support by intercepting the legions of name-query broadcasts and processing them internally, preventing these broadcasts from inundating the network and consuming precious bandwidth.

Key benefits to implementing WINS include:

- WINS servers are the first contact for name queries, and are most often able to satisfy them, so the time spent resolving a NetBIOS name is markedly reduced.

- Microsoft clients using WINS automatically register with the WINS server upon start-up, ensuring a current database better than any other resolution service.

- Because WINS is dynamic in nature, using a WINS server eliminates much of the tedious work normally associated with database maintenance.

- You can assign a second WINS server to a client for purposes of fault tolerance.

Some important facts about the name registration process:

- When a unique and valid name is received by the WINS server, it returns a message confirming registration, plus a specified Time To Live period (TTL) designating the duration of time that name can be used.

- If a duplicate name is discovered during the WINS registration process, WINS servers send out a challenge in the form of a name query request.

- The challenge message is repeated three times, at 500 millisecond intervals—less if the server receives a reply.

- For multihomed systems, the above process is repeated for each IP address until the server either receives a reply or tries each address three times.

- If the current owner of the name responds, the request will be rejected by sending a negative name request back to the requesting machine.

- If the current registered owner doesn't reply, then the name is deleted from the database, and a positive acknowledgment is sent to the requesting machine.

- If the primary WINS server doesn't respond after three tries, an attempt will then be made to contact a secondary server.

- If no available server is found, the client will send out a b-node broadcast to validate its name and achieve registration among its peers.

- Registered names associated with the WINS client are always done so on a temporary basis, preventing confusion or worse if the name's current owner moves, receives a new IP address, or otherwise discontinues use of its name.

When the TTL period lapses to 50 percent of its original lease time, a WINS client that desires to continue use of its name needs its current Time To Live period reset. The client sends a name renewal message to the primary WINS server containing the client's name, and both the source and destination IP address. Once successful contact is made, either the primary or secondary WINS server will respond by sending the client a new TTL period. This process will continue as long as the client computer is powered-on, and remains a WINS client. WINS clients can also relinquish ownership of its name by sending a name-release message, containing its IP address and name, during a proper shutdown.

Some important things to consider before and during the implementation of WINS include:

- The size of your network. A small NetBIOS network existing within a larger, primarily UNIX-based internetwork would likely be better off just using the DNS server to avoid the cost of implementing WINS servers.

- For reasons of fault tolerance, at least two WINS servers need to be configured.

- The performance of each WINS server will vary according to that particular machine's hardware.

- You can enhance the performance of each WINS server by an estimated 25% by adding an auxiliary CPU because each additional CPU adds a new, separate WINS process thread.

- Your NIC card and disk drives can be the cause of bottlenecks.

- A two-server minimum execution of WINS can service up to roughly 10,000 clients.

- To optimize performance, set half the clients to one WINS server as their primary contact, and the other half to the other WINS server.

There aren't a lot of requirements placed on a WINS server, therefore, it can and should be added to any Windows NT 3.5x server that is running TCP/IP with a static, nonDHCP-assigned IP address. If you're also running DHCP, the WINS server will only function with a reserved address—using the same subnet mask and default gateway each time. The problem with using DHCP is that each client must know the WINS server's IP address, which can become problematic if its address should change. There's no requirement for a WINS server to become a domain controller of any type.

Most configuration for the WINS server service settings are automatic. Communications become more complicated when systems configured as WINS clients need to talk to those that aren't. To ensure communication in a mixed environment, manual entries must be made to the WINS server. The only alternative to manually adding entries to the WINS server is to add them to the workstation's LMHOSTS file.

A WINS client requires configuration and needs a computer running any of the following supported operating systems:

- Windows NT Server 3.5x

- Windows NT Workstation 3.5x

- Windows 95

- Windows for Workgroups with TCP/IP-32

- Microsoft Network Client 3.0 for MS-DOS (with TCP/IP)

- LAN Manager 2.2c for MS-DOS

To become a WINS client, the machine must be prepped by being configured with TCP/IP, with WINS enabled. This is accomplished by entering the IP address(es) for the WINS system(s) the client will be accessing.

For clients that are also DHCP clients, addresses are entered into the WINS address slots, where they will be given priority, and automatically override any DHCP values. DHCP uses two information fields to define WINS support: One, defined by the addresses of the primary and secondary WINS servers in the 044 WINS/NBNS Servers blank, and the other, clarified by the type of node they've been configured to behave as. A WINS/DHCP client must be configured to act as a hybrid node, specifying: 046 WINS/NBT Node to 0x8 (H-node).

NonWINS clients can resolve NetBIOS names on a WINS server using a WINS proxy agent. These alien clients can be configured to use WINS in an indirect manner, by using a WINS client that's located on the same network or subnet to act as a relay between the nonWINS machine, and the WINS server. This machine acting as the relay is known as a WINS proxy agent. Using a WINS proxy agent to extend name resolution capabilities of a WINS server requires one proxy agent on each subnet that has nonWINS clients, but is not required if the network's routers are configured to forward b-node broadcasts (UDP 137 and 138). However, it's recommended to reduce broadcast traffic. You should have no more that two proxy agents per subnet, and the proxy agent must be a Windows-based WINS client—it cannot be a WINS server. A WINS proxy agent performs the two focal tasks of NetBIOS name registration and NetBIOS name resolution in a limited manner—they don't achieve actual, complete name registration of the nonWINS client. The proxy agent serves only to verify that no other machine is currently registered with the name being requested, and then forwards the query on to the WINS server for true registration. This method is more thorough and fault tolerant because two machines, both the proxy agent and the WINS server, check up on the proposed name.

Unlike DHCP servers that don't communicate with each other, WINS servers can be configured to replicate their database entries, sharing them with each other so that all servers across the network have synchronous name information. When this feature has been configured, replication is automatically triggered any time the database changes. To function in this manner, the WINS server must be designated as either a push or pull partner. Push partners function by sending update notices to pull partners whenever changes are made, and pull partners function by sending out requests to push partners, asking them for entries more recent than their current listings when they want to update their database contents. You can set up the server as both push and pull to ensure possession of the most up-to-date WINS entries available.

The duties of database backup, restoration, and compression require human support. Most of the database cleanup is accomplished automatically by controls set though the Configuration menu in the WINS Manager program where there's a listing of four different timers:

- Renewal Interval
- Extinction Interval

- Extinction Time-out

- Verify Interval

There are two more options involved in push or pull configuration. To cause a server to pull other WINS servers for any new database entries upon initialization, select the initial replication box located under Push Parameters. If you're professionally managing this server, select the Advanced button from the WINS Manager configuration panel to display additional control customization options:

- Logging Enabled

- Log Detailed Events

- Replicate Only with Partners

- Backup On Termination

- Migrate On/Off

- Starting Version Count (hex)

- Database Backup Path

The WINS Manager provides you with the tools you need to maintain the WINS database:

- List name mappings

- Filter name mappings

- Control name mappings

It's very important to keep a backup copy of all information entered when configuring the server. This backup becomes automatic after a 24-hour period lapses, and after a backup directory has been specified.

Restoration ensures that reliable data is served. If the WINS server determines upon initialization that its data is corrupt, it will automatically revert to the backup. To manually force the WINS server to restore the database, select Restore Database from the WINS Manager mapping menu, and specify the path where the backup directory is located.

The compacting function is executed by running the JETPACK.EXE utility. This program should be run periodically when the database grows over 30MB in size to keep the database efficient.

Exercise Questions

Multiple-Choice Questions

1. How many WINS servers are recommended for a network of 10,000 clients?

   A. 1000

   B. 50

   C. 1

   D. 2

   E. 10

2. What are two benefits to a WINS server?

   A. IP addressing to multiple clients

   B. Reduces traffic

   C. Can only be updated statically, so it's very secure

   D. Internetwork and Inter-domain browsing capabilities without configuring and maintaining an LMHOSTS file at each computer

3. How can WINS support a nonWINS client?

   A. Using DHCP

   B. Using a proxy agent

   C. Using an LMHOSTS file

   D. Using a push partner

   E. Using a pull partner

4. How must WINS be configured to support an environment of multiple nonWINS clients spread across a wide area network at two different sites?

A. One WINS server should be configured for both locations.

B. Two WINS servers should be configured, one per location. The WINS servers should be set as pull partners with static entries for the nonWINS clients. A proxy agent should also be configured on each subnet that has nonWINS clients.

C. Three WINS servers should be configured: two servers in one location, and one server in another, running as pull partners with static entries for the nonWINS clients. A proxy agent should also be configured on each subnet that has nonWINS clients.

D. Two WINS servers should be configured, one per location. The WINS servers should be set as push partners with static entries for the nonWINS clients. A proxy agent should also be configured on each subnet that has nonWINS clients.

Scenario-Based Review

SCENARIO #1 You work at a large retail computer shop. A customer asks if a 386DX-25MHZ system with 12MB of memory would be enough to run the WINS service process. Is it? What should you ask of your customer before answering his question (besides his credit card number)? What suggestions should you make?

SCENARIO #2 You are a network administrator for a computer manufacturer. They have a large network and need to install WINS on it to help keep traffic down. They have a few O/S2 and UNIX computers, and need to register them in the WINS database. How do you do this?

SCENARIO #3 You are installing two NT computers at your home office. After installing an NT server running DHCP and WINS, you want to backup the WINS database. What are the steps to do this?

Internetwork
Browsing

THIS CHAPTER'S ALMOST as teensy as the one on IP address resolution. We thought you might appreciate a little breather after WINS, but again, don't underestimate its importance. Size isn't everything! Chapter 9's focus is on how to successfully browse for network resources across routers. It'll also examine some important issues centered around supporting this activity. We'll give you the skinny on configuring the LMHOSTS file to make browsing possible across domains for nonWINS clients, and how to prime LMHOSTS for use in logon validation and password changes in a domain. By the end of this chapter, Microsoft's Computer Browser service, and several other different types of browsers, should be as familiar as old friends.

Objectives

WHEN CRUISING THROUGH this chapter, you should aim to become a wiz regarding the following:

- The Microsoft Windows NT Computer Browser service, and how it works

- How the different types of browsers—master, preferred master, and backup—function

- How to configure LMHOSTS so nonWINS clients can browse across domains

- Configuring LMHOSTS for logon validation and password changes in a domain

A Browsing Brief

BEFORE YOU CAN share something, you must first be aware of it, know how to find it, and know how to obtain it. Browsing plays an important role in both finding and sharing currently available network resources. By providing a list of these resources, the Computer Browser service works to free most of the network's computer population from the burden of individually maintaining their own. This saves time and memory because this resource list is only distributed to a few specially designated machines that exist to support the network by performing browsing for it, along with other services. It's highly efficient. Through using the Windows NT Computer Browsing service, the network operating system can swiftly locate active resources—connecting to them seamlessly.

Let's say you want to print something. Before you can, you need to locate a printer on your network to connect to. Without the help of a browser, your system would be reduced to a door-to-door solicitor, petitioning each system along the network corridor about what resources it has available until finally finding what it needs. It would then be required to record and maintain that information for future use. All of this would take up lots of CPU time, while reducing available memory on your workstation. NT's Browsing service also reduces costs and adds efficiency in terms of network overhead. To find a particular resource, your workstation can simply contact the network's designated browser instead of generating a whole bunch of network traffic to find the treasure you're after.

How They Work

Here's a step-by-step outline of basic Browser service behavior and operation:

Step 1: After startup, every machine running a Browser service checks in with the Master browser of their domain or workgroup. They're required to do so even if they don't have any shared resources to offer their group. Sometimes, under Windows NT, a system will possess hidden, administrative shares, like c$.

Step 2: Like any introduction, the client's first time contacting the Master browser is special. The first time the client tries to locate its available network resources, it asks the Master browser for a list of Backup browsers.

Step 3: The client then asks for a list of network resources from one of the Backup browsers.

Step 4: The Backup browser then provides the client with a list of domains and workgroups, plus a list of local servers appointed for the client's particular workgroup or domain.

Step 5: The client's user then picks a local server, domain, or workgroup in order to view another list of available servers.

Step 6: Lastly, the client's user chooses a server to look for the right machine with which to establish a session for using their desired resource. The user then contacts that server.

Browser Forms and Functions

Browser services have a hierarchy to them. The task of providing a list of network resources to clients is broken down into various roles, which are carried out by the corresponding computer. Systems running Windows NT Workstation or NT Server can perform any of the following roles:

Master browser   This is the machine that builds, maintains, and distributes the *browse list*—the master list of all available network resources.

Preferred Master browser   This is a system specially cast and designated to play the role of Master browser by a network administrator. At startup, this system arrogantly proclaims itself to be the network's Master browser. If it finds another machine trying to horn in on its rightful network position in its absence, the preferred Master browser will force an election between itself and the upstart. Networks not being democracies, these elections most often result in the preferred Master browser reclaiming its throne. The only exception to this being if that "little upstart" machine also happens to be a *primary domain controller (PDC)*. PDCs always function as the Master browser of the domain—their reign is not to be challenged.

Backup browser   These systems act as relay stations. They receive copies of the browse list from the Master browser, and upon request, distribute them to clients.

Potential browser   This is a system that has the capacity for becoming a browser, but isn't one, and won't become one unless specifically commanded to do so by the Master browser.

Non-browser   This computer is configured so that it won't maintain a browser list. These are most often client systems.

Browser Criteria

Browser criteria serve as a means of determining the hierarchical order of the different types of computer systems in the workgroup or domain. Each browser computer has certain criteria, depending on the type of system it is. These criteria include:

- The operating system

- The operating system version

- Its current role in the browsing environment

The following is a hypothetical list of computers in a domain. They're presented in the order in which they would win an election, and organized into three criteria categories.

Criteria category #1: Operating system

- Windows NT Server

- Windows NT Workstation

- Windows for Workgroups

Criteria category #2: Operating System Version

- 4.0/3.51

- 3.5

- 3.1

Criteria category #3: Current Browser Role

- Preferred Master browser

- Master browser

- Backup browser

- Potential browser

This criteria ranking is observed and referred to during an election. These elections are held to determine which computer should be the Master browser in the event the current Master browser becomes unavailable.

The Browser Election

As its title would suggest, the Master browser oversees the entire browsing environment. There is only one Master browser for each domain or workgroup. In a domain that spans subnets, there is a Domain Master browser. If the computer that's designated as the Master browser shuts down for any reason, another computer needs to be selected to be the Master browser. This is done through a browser election, which ensures that only one Master browser exists per workgroup or domain. An election is instituted when any of the following events occur:

- A client computer can't locate a Master browser

- A Backup browser attempts to update its network resource list, and can't locate the Master browser

- A computer that's been designated as a Preferred Master browser comes on line

Configuring Browsers

To determine whether a Windows NT computer will become a browser, the Browser Service looks in the registry when the computer initializes for the following parameter:

\HKEY_LOCAL_MACHINE\SYSTEM\CurrentControlSet\Services\ Browser\Parameters\MaintainServerList

For performance tuning and optimization purposes, it's possible to both configure and prevent a computer from becoming a browser.

The MaintainServerList parameter can contain the following values:

PARAMETER	VALUE
No	This computer never participates as a Browser server.
Yes	This computer becomes a Browser server. At startup, it attempts to contact the Master browser to get a current browse list. If the Master browser cannot be found, the computer forces one to be elected. This computer either is elected as the Master browser or becomes a Backup browser. Yes is the default value for Windows NT Server domain controller computers.
Auto	Depending on the number of currently active browsers, this computer may or may not become a Browser server. It's referred to as a Potential browser. This computer is notified by the Master browser as to whether it should become a Backup browser. Auto is the default value for Windows NT Workstation and Windows NT Server—nondomain controller computers.

Browser Announcements

Master browsers and Backup browsers each have their own roles to play in the operation of the browsing environment. Browsers need to communicate with each other and must provide service to client computers. When a computer that's running the Server Service comes online, it must inform the Master browser that it's available. It does this by announcing itself on the network.

Servers

Each computer periodically announces itself to the Master browser by broadcasting on the network. Initially each computer announces itself once per minute. As the computer stays running, the announcement time is extended to once every 12 minutes. If the Master browser hasn't heard from a computer after three announcement periods elapse, it'll remove the computer that hasn't kept in touch from the browse list.

Important! This means that there could be a 36-minute delay between the time a server goes down and the time that server is removed from the browser list. Computers appearing in the list could possibly be unavailable.

Backup Browsers

In addition to announcing themselves, Backup browsers contact the Master browser every 15 minutes to obtain an updated network resource (browse list), and a list of workgroups and domains. The Backup browser caches these lists, and forwards them to any clients that send out a browse request. If the Backup browser can't find the Master browser, it forces an election.

Master Browsers

Master browsers also announce themselves to Backup browsers with a broadcast periodically. When Backup browsers receive this announcement, they refresh their Master browser name with any new information.

Master browsers receive announcements from the following systems:

- Windows NT 4.0/3.51 Workstation

- Windows NT 4.0/3.51 Server

- Windows NT 3.1 Workstation

- Windows NT 3.1 Advanced Server

- Windows for Workgroups

- Lan Manager systems

Master browsers will return lists of backup browsers to these systems for their local subnet:

- Windows NT 4.0/3.51 Workstation

- Windows NT 4.0/3.51 Server

- Windows NT 3.1 Workstation

- Windows NT 3.1 Advanced Server

- Windows for Workgroup clients

When a system starts and its Maintain Server List parameter is set to Auto, the Master browser is responsible for telling the system whether to become a Backup browser or not.

The list of resources that the Master browser maintains and returns to the Backup browsers is limited in size to 64K of data. This limits the number of computers that can be in a single workgroup's or domain's browse list to 2000-3000 computers.

Cruising an Internetwork

MANY A PROBLEM can arise when trying to browse around networks that require a hop or two across routers to reach. You see, Master browsers receive notices via b-node broadcasts, and as you've learned, routers, by default, won't let those pass through to different subnets. Also, domains that span routers are very prevalent in TCP/IP internetworks. On Microsoft networks, the Browser Service relies heavily on NetBIOS name broadcasts for getting information from connecting systems. Microsoft has come up with two great solutions for machines with that ol' Travelin' Jones—one dependant on WINS, and the other on the LMHOSTS file.

On the Wing with WINS

Again...it's WINS to the rescue! And again it does so ever so elegantly, without gumming up the network with all those broadcasts! If you didn't fall asleep during the last chapter and call it "read" anyway, you'll recall that WINS solves the whole NetBIOS broadcast jam by dynamically registering names. Machines running WINS maintain and store all that name-related stuff, like addresses, etc., in their databases, where the information is readily available to the remote TCP/IP hosts requiring it when contacted to establish communications. WINS clients, configured to operate compatibly with a WINS Server, automatically register their names with them upon startup. This makes clean, broadcast-less identity referencing routinely available to all—except, of course, nonWINS clients, which we'll be discussing next. For a visual reference to what we've been talking about, see Figure 9.1 below.

FIGURE 9.1

Browsing with WINS

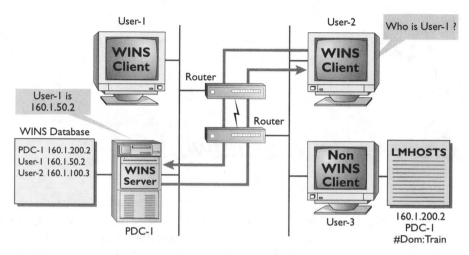

If you happen to be running the client component Windows for Workgroups with TCP/IP-32, you'll have to replace the VREDIR.386 file with the one supplied on the Windows NT Server 3.5x distribution CD.

The LMHOSTS File and Domain Functions

NonWINS clients can be Internetwork browsing's problem children. But look on the bright side...Knowing how to work with them effectively could prove useful in leveraging that raise you've been after—so don't fall asleep just yet! The fact that nonWINS clients register using b-node broadcasts presents a major problem if the system designated as the domain's Master browser is somewhere over the rainbow on a different subnet. Its registration broadcast won't be forwarded. On the client end of things, receiving messages that the Browser Service isn't available or viewing empty resource lists are also potential pitfalls.

To address these dilemmas, Microsoft added a pair of tags to the LMHOSTS file: #PRE and #DOM. These tags enable the nonWINS client to communicate with a domain controller to do three very important things:

- Register with it

- Verify a user account

- Change passwords

Because user validation is required to operate login scripts and user profiles, and because broadcasts are used for replication of the domain database, special care should be used when configuring domain controllers when there isn't a WINS Server around. To ensure your nonWINS clients will function well, be sure an entry is added for each domain controller present in the domain. Domain controllers that are also nonWINS machines should have a listing of all other domain controllers in their databases. This will prove very handy if one of the servers is ever promoted to primary domain controller at any point in the future.

LMHOSTS file entries on each subnet's Master browser must first list the IP address, followed by the domain browser's NetBIOS name. Then come the tags, #PRE and #DOM, followed by the domain name. They should look something like this:

```
137.37.9.9   master-browser_name #PRE #DOM: domain-name
137.37.9.10  domain-controller_name #PRE #DOM: domain-name
```

Domain Functions

The #PRE tag tells TCP/IP to preload the resolution information into memory, while the #DOM tag alerts the client machine that it has reached a domain controller. #DOM is significant for the directing of data during broadcasts. These addresses indicate to the router to forward broadcasts to certain addresses. All this means that you're essentially making a broadcast and then directing it to a special place, so the #PRE tag must always precede the #DOM tag. Check out Figure 9.2 for a visual illustration of LMHOSTS in action.

Certain tasks executed by Windows NT network services will cause broadcasts to be sent out to all computers located within a Microsoft domain. For instance, when logging into a domain or changing a password, a broadcast will be transmitted to the domain to find a domain controller able to authenticate the logon request, and/or change the user's password. Another situation that

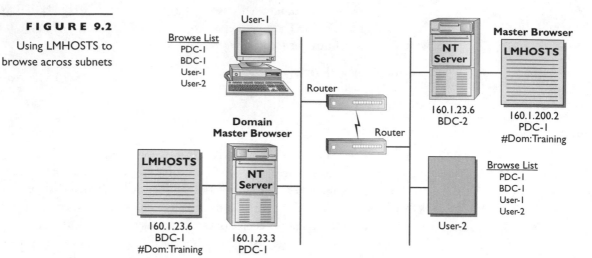

FIGURE 9.2

Using LMHOSTS to browse across subnets

will induce broadcasts is when a domain controller replicates the domain user account database. To do this, the primary domain controller sends a broadcast out to all backup domain controllers that populate the domain, directing them to request a replication of updated changes made in the domain accounts database (see Figure 9.3).

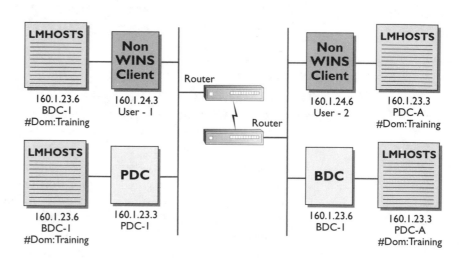

FIGURE 9.3

NonWINS clients domain functioning in an internetwork

Remember that for Windows for Workgroups, the presence of a Windows NT server Domain is required for WAN browsing, since Workgroups do not define a domain controller. For a Windows for Workgroups client to be capable of WAN browsing, it must first log onto a domain.

Exercise 9.1 will help you try your hand at configuring the LMHOSTS file for browsing.

EXERCISE 9.1

Configuring the LMHOSTS File

This exercise requires more then one computer. Prepare your LMHOSTS file with the appropriate entry to logon to another computer on your domain.

1. Stop the WINS Server Service. From the command prompt, type **net stop wins**.

2. From the command prompt, verify that you have no existing connections to your other computer. Type **net use \\othercomputername\ipc$ /d.**

3. Purge the NetBIOS name cache. Type **nbstat -R** and then press Enter (the "R" must be in upper case).

4. Try to browse **Net View \\othercomputername**.

5. Notice the error that occurs when a remote host does not exist in the LMHOSTS file or when the entry is invalid.

6. Use Notepad to create a file in the \winroot directory named LMHOSTS.

7. Add the following entry to the file:

   IP_Address othercomputername #PRE #DOM:DOMAIN

8. Save the file, and then exit Notepad.

Now, you're going to add the LMHOSTS file mapping for the other computer's domain controller to the NetBIOS name cache for browsing and logon validation.

1. Clear the NetBIOS name cache and load #PRE entries. Type **nbstat -R** and then press Enter.

2. View the NetBIOS name cache. Type **nbstat -c** and then press Enter.

3. Notice the entry that appears. Hopefully, it's your other computer!

Summing Things Up

MICROSOFT'S COMPUTER BROWSING service works to free most of the network's computer population from the burden of individually maintaining their own network resource database lists. This saves time and memory because this resource list is only distributed to a few specially designated machines. Windows NT Computer Browsing service is a highly efficient way of swiftly locating active network resources.

Systems running Windows NT Workstation or NT Server can perform any of the following roles:

- Master browser
- Preferred master browser
- Backup browser
- Potential browser
- Nonbrowser

Browsers use various criteria to determine the hierarchical order of the different types of computer systems existing in a workgroup or domain. Each kind of computer has certain criteria, including its operating system and version, and its present role in the browsing environment.

A browser election is instituted when any of the following events occur:

- A client computer can't locate a Master browser
- A Backup browser attempts to update its network resource list, and can't locate the Master browser
- A computer that's been designated as a Preferred Master browser comes online

The following are the types of announcements the different browsers make:

Servers   When a computer that's running the Server service comes online, it must announce itself over the network. Initially, it announces itself to the Master browser once per minute. As it stays running, the announcement time is extended to once every 12 minutes. If the Master browser hasn't heard from a computer after three announcement periods elapse, that computer will be removed from the browse list.

Backup browsers   These contact the Master browser every 15 minutes to obtain an updated network resource (browse list), and a list of workgroups and domains. The Backup browser caches these lists, and forwards them to any clients that send out a browse request. If the Backup browser can't find the Master browser, it forces an election.

Master browsers   These computers announce themselves to Backup browsers with a broadcast periodically. When Backup browsers receive this announcement, they refresh their Master browser name with any new information.

Many problems can arise when trying to browse around internetworks. Master browsers receive notices via b-node broadcasts, which can pass through routers to different subnets without help from you. Microsoft's solutions to browsing dilemmas are found in WINS, and through configuring the LMHOSTS file.

The WINS solution method is a piece of cake—machines running WINS maintain and store everything necessary in their databases, where it's readily available to the remote TCP/IP hosts that require the information upon contact. WINS clients automatically register their names with the servers upon startup. WINS makes clean, efficient, broadcast-less registration and easy browsing available to all systems running it.

The LMHOSTS strategy is a different story. Being that a nonWINS client's registration broadcasts aren't forwarded, ensuring smooth browsing with one requires a little finesse. So, Microsoft has added a pair of tags to the LMHOSTS file: #PRE and #DOM. These tags enable the nonWINS client to communicate with a domain controller to accomplish three very important things:

- Registration

- Verification of a user account

- Changing of passwords

It's important to note that LMHOSTS file entries on each subnet's Master browser must first list the IP address, followed by the domain browser's Net-BIOS name, and then the tags #PRE and #DOM, followed by the domain name. They should look like this:

```
137.37.9.9    master-browser_name #PRE #DOM: domain-name
137.37.9.10   domain-controller_name #PRE #DOM: domain-name
```

The #PRE tag tells TCP/IP to preload the resolution information into memory, while the #DOM tag alerts the client machine that it has reached a domain controller. #DOM is significant for the directing of data during broadcasts, and can be thought of in the same context as *helper addresses* found in routers.

Certain tasks executed by Windows NT network services will cause broadcasts to be sent out to all computers located within a Microsoft domain. This happens when logging into a domain or changing a password, or when a domain controller replicates the domain user account database.

Exercise Questions

Multiple-Choice Questions

1. Which Windows NT service provides browsing capabilities requiring no extra configuration?

A. The Windows 95 Computer Browser service

B. The Windows NT Computer Browser service

C. The Windows NT Computer LMHOSTS service

D. The Windows NT Computer WINS service

2. What's the function of the Master browser?

   A. The Master browser collects information and puts it in the LMHOSTS file.

   B. The Master browser collects and maintains the LMHOSTS list of available network resources. It also distributes this list to Backup browsers.

   C. The Master browser collects and maintains the master list of available network resources. It also distributes this list to Backup browsers.

   D. The Master browser collects and maintains the backup list of available network resources. It also distributes this list to Master browsers.

3. What's required in the LMHOSTS file for a nonWINS client to browse resources on another subnet, and to ensure interdomain activity?

   A. The following entry for each domain controller located on a different subnet:

   ```
   master_browser ip_address #PRE #DOM:domain_name
   ```

   B. The following entry for each domain controller located on a different subnet:

   ```
   ip_address master_browser #DOM:domain_name #PRE
   ```

   C. The following entry for each domain controller located on the same subnet:

   ```
   ip_address master_browser #PRE #DOM:domain_name
   ```

   D. The following entry for each domain controller located on a different subnet:

   ```
   ip_address master_browser #PRE #DOM:domain_name
   ```

4. What's required on domain controllers to ensure account synchronization can be accomplished in an internetwork?

   A. Each domain controller requires an LMHOSTS file with the following entry:

   ```
   ip_address master_browser #PRE #DOM:domain_name
   ```

   B. Each domain controller requires a HOSTS file with the following entry:

   ```
   ip_address master_browser #PRE #DOM:domain_name
   ```

   C. Each domain controller requires an LMHOSTS file with the following entry:

   ```
   master_browser ip_address #PRE #DOM:domain_name
   ```

   D. Each domain controller requires a HOSTS file with the following entry:

   ```
   ip_address master_browser #DOM:domain_name #PRE
   ```

5. A user calls you and says she can see that the server she wants to connect to is listed, but she is unable to connect to it. How could a server appear in the browse list but not be available?

   A. She can connect. It's user error.

   B. The server could be down. It is possible that the server has shut down but has not yet been removed from the list.

   C. The administrator has not yet purged the browser list.

   D. The user needs to reboot her workstation.

Scenario-Based Review

SCENARIO #1 You have three networks tied together with a router. The router has a capacity for NetBIOS name broadcasts. For optimum performance, should you use the LMHOSTS file and WINS, or simply let the router pass NetBIOS name broadcasts?

SCENARIO #2 Unclear on the issue of browsers, Management invites you into a meeting to shed some light on the matter. They want to know what types of browsers systems that are running Windows NT Workstation or NT Server become. What do you tell them?

SCENARIO #3 A student of yours knows that Microsoft has added a pair of tags to the LMHOSTS file: #PRE and #DOM, and remembers that these tags enable the nonWINS client to communicate with a domain controller to accomplish three very important things. However, this student is unable to recall exactly which three things, and asks you. What would your explanation be?

Connectivity in Heterogenous Environments

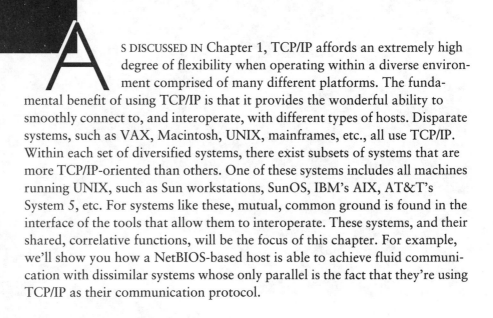

A<small>S DISCUSSED IN</small> Chapter 1, TCP/IP affords an extremely high degree of flexibility when operating within a diverse environment comprised of many different platforms. The fundamental benefit of using TCP/IP is that it provides the wonderful ability to smoothly connect to, and interoperate, with different types of hosts. Disparate systems, such as VAX, Macintosh, UNIX, mainframes, etc., all use TCP/IP. Within each set of diversified systems, there exist subsets of systems that are more TCP/IP-oriented than others. One of these systems includes all machines running UNIX, such as Sun workstations, SunOS, IBM's AIX, AT&T's System 5, etc. For systems like these, mutual, common ground is found in the interface of the tools that allow them to interoperate. These systems, and their shared, correlative functions, will be the focus of this chapter. For example, we'll show you how a NetBIOS-based host is able to achieve fluid communication with dissimilar systems whose only parallel is the fact that they're using TCP/IP as their communication protocol.

Objectives

B<small>ELOW ARE SOME</small> things to focus on while working through this section. Make sure you're comfortable with each of them upon completion of this chapter.

- Dissimilar communication environments

- Communication between NetBIOS and foreign host systems

- Software requirements for achieving communication with Microsoft operating systems

- Usage of TCP/IP utilities as provided by Microsoft

- The Windows NT FTP server
- TCP/IP printing issues

Connectivity in Dissimilar Environments

TCP/IP PROVIDES A flexible means by which dissimilar computing environments may effectively communicate with each other. Without thinking in terms of a network, think of two systems communicating through asynchronous modems. Regardless of what operating systems these two systems may be running, they can "talk" provided they do so using the same parameters and protocols for communication. TCP/IP serves as an organizational model by establishing a set mode of communication despite the operating system in use. The following is a sample list of some common operating systems that can use Microsoft TCP/IP to interoperate for file and print services.

- Apple Macintosh
- DEC VAX systems
- DOS systems with TCP/IP
- IBM mainframes (among others)
- Internet objects
- LAN Manager
- NFS HOSTS
- OS/2 Systems with TCP/IP
- TCP/IP-based printers
- Windows 95
- Windows NT
- Windows for Workgroups
- UNIX-based systems

The only requirements for connecting between these disparate operating systems are that they're running TCP/IP as their communication protocol, and that they're using their respective utilities and services in some specific ways that will be described later in the chapter.

A Microsoft client such as Windows NT, Windows 95, or Windows For Workgroups can interoperate with an *RFC-compliant,* NetBIOS-based *SMB (Server Message Block)* server using the *Windows Redirector.* It accomplishes interoperation through use of standard windows commands over a common set of communication protocols like TCP/IP or NetBEUI. Two examples of machines that can operate in this manner are a UNIX host that's running LAN Manager for UNIX, and a DEC VAX, running Pathworks. Both LAN Manager for UNIX and DEC's VAX system running Pathworks operate similarly to Windows NT when it's running on platforms other than Intel.

TCP/IP Utilities and the WINDOWS NT Command

Many of the TCP/IP-based networking features are built directly into Windows NT. The type of network function you're attempting to perform will also determine whether you'll be using a Windows NT internal function or a TCP/IP utility. The chosen function will further define the requirements for carrying it out. Here are a few network truisms to keep in mind while working with Windows NT and TCP/IP commands:

- The same protocol must be used on both systems attempting communication with each other for connectivity and communication to result.

- Network connections from a command line are achieved through the NET USE command.

- Applications on other systems are accessed though Windows NT's native environment, and are processed at the client (distributed) rather than processed by the server host (centralized).

- Windows NT must use NetBIOS names (not IP address names) to communicate via the NET USE and NET View line commands. This is done for reasons of maintaining compatibility with other protocols, like with NetBEUI, which doesn't use IP addresses, and doesn't accommodate the overhead of additional program processing well.

- The NetBIOS scope parameter must match all other host's scope parameters. This allows NetBIOS networks to be divided and organized. Systems set for one scope don't communicate with those set for another scope. Therefore, two systems can have the same NetBIOS name as long as they're using different scopes.

- Remote hosts—those located on other subnets—must be resolved by a supported method such as WINS, LMHOSTS, etc.

How to Interoperate with an RFC-Compliant NetBIOS Host

When Windows NT isn't attempting to communicate with an RFC-compliant NetBIOS-based host (Windows for Workgroups, Windows 95, Windows NT, LAN Manger, LAN Manager for UNIX, etc.), but is trying to talk to a foreign TCP/IP system, different rules apply. While it's true that a number of common functions work great within a common realm, they're not understood and shared among foreign hosts that use tools uniquely and specifically defined for their way of communicating. Here are some ins and outs to know when communicating with foreign TCP/IP hosts.

- You must use TCP/IP—NetBEUI won't talk to TCP/IP, and nor will IPX or any other non-IP protocol.

- Only commands supported by the specific TCP/IP utility, such as FTP, TELNET, etc., may be used to communicate with the foreign system.

- Applications that are accessed on the foreign system are run centrally at the foreign system—not at your local system. This is because different systems use different compilers, CPU commands, and memory instructions which generally are not platform-independent.

- TCP/IP utilities can use either the host name or the IP address.

- Both local and remote host names that are used in TCP/IP utilities must be resolved in the HOSTS file, DNS, WINS, b-node broadcast, or LMHOSTS file.

There's a distinct difference in how TCP/IP communication is established between similar and foreign hosts While these differences may seem trivial, they're important to understand. Grasping these similarities and differences will greatly assist you later in debugging and configuring large TCP/IP environments.

TCP/IP Utilities the Microsoft Way

TCP/IP UTILITIES FOLLOW their own specific set of rules. This conformity provides for standardization and ease of use when moving from one machine to the next through various operating systems. Microsoft provides FTP, LPQ, LPR, REXEC, RSH, RCP, Telnet, and TFTP TCP/IP utilities. The majority of the commands presented here are similar in implementation to their UNIX-based counterparts. And yes, just like UNIX, they're usually case-sensitive. These utilities can be divided into three categories:

- Command utilities: REXEC, RSH, and Telnet

- Transfer utilities: RCP, FTP, and TFTP

- Printer utilities: LPR and LPQ

Command Utilities

REXEC (Remote Execution)

The Remote Execute connectivity command will run a process on a remote system equipped with the REXEC server service. The REXEC service is password protected. Only upon receiving a valid password will this function proceed. The command format is as follows:

```
REXEC host {-l username} {-n} command
```

This command line is broken down as follows:

host   specifies the host name or IP address of the system that is not the default.

-l username   specifies a valid user on the remote system when this is not the default.

-n   redirects the input for REXEC to NULL, if you don't want input.

command   specifies the execution line you wish to run on the host.

RSH (Remote Shell)

The Remote Shell utility allows a user to issue a command to a remote host without logging into it. Password protection is not provided, however the designated username must exist in the *.rhosts file* on the UNIX server that's running the RSH daemon. This command is commonly used with UNIX systems for executing program compilers. The command format is as follows:

```
RSH host {-l username} command
```

host specifies the host name or IP address of the system where the remote commands are run.

-l username designates a valid user on the remote system when this is not the default. (It must be in a .rhosts file located in the user's home directory.)

command is the UNIX command to be run on the remote host.

Telnet

The Telnet connectivity command initiates terminal emulation with a remote system running a Telnet service. Telnet provides DEC VT 100, DEC VT 52, or TTY emulation through the connection-based services of TCP. This program provides a way for users to execute any command as if sitting right there in front of the host it's to be performed on. Telnet has similarities to Novell's Rconsole utility, but can also be thought of as a text-based network version of Symantec's PC Anywhere remote control utility in that it's limited to those machines (a workstation or server) running a Telnet server program. The Telnet program requires TCP/IP on both the client and server, and requires an account set up on the server being contacted. Microsoft Windows NT doesn't provide the server process, however, it does provide a client interface. Security is furnished by the requirement of a username and password identical to those used when logging into the system directly. Telnet sometimes serves up a full graphical display beyond text. If this occurs, it's usually a form of X Windows.

If you have installed TCP/IP and connection utilities from Windows NT, you have access to the Telnet program. To establish a connection, simply type **Telnet** plus the destination name or IP address. If no destination is specified, the Telnet terminal screen will be displayed. At this point, choose Remote System from the Connect menu. The Connect dialog box will appear. Then, in the Host Name box, type the host name or IP address of the Telnet server, and choose OK. Selecting Connect ≻ Remote System would then prompt you for the connection destination. Again, either an IP address or host name can be used. When logging onto the Telnet server, enter your user account and the corresponding password. You will then be able to talk to the remote host as though you were sitting there in front of it.

By default, Telnet uses port 23. Depending on the service, SMTP, FTP, Telnet, Time, Login, Whois, BootP etc., can be redirected by a command line, through which you can use a different port. (A port specifies the remote port you want to connect to, providing compatibility with applications.) This is very handy for talking to other services—for example, direct communication to an SMTP mail port 25. You would type TELNET host 25 to connect SMTP with an Internet mail server.

RCP (Remote Copy)

RCP is used to copy files between local and remote UNIX hosts, or between two remote hosts. The Remote Copy tool is used in a similar manner as FTP for copying files, except it doesn't require user validation. Like RSH, the designated username must exist in the .rhosts file located on the UNIX server that's running the RCP daemon. It's also commonly used with UNIX systems. The command format is as follows:

```
RCP {-abhr}{host1.}{user1:}source {host2.}{user2:}path/
    destination
```

Host1/host2 is the name, or IP address, of the destination or source system. If the host .user: portion is omitted, the host is assumed to be the local computer.

User1/User2 specifies valid users that exist on the destination and source systems (usernames must be in .rhosts file), and source/destination is the full path designating where files are copied.

The switch options are as follows:

-a Set by default, this option sets transfers to ASCII, and specifies for translation UNIX/DOS text formatting for cr-lf (carriage return/linefeed, DOS hex 0d 0a), and lf (linefeed, UNIX hex 0a).

-b Sets transfers to binary with no translation.

-h Sets the transfer of hidden files.

-r recursively copies the contents of all subdirectories of the source to the destination. Both the source and destination must be directories. It's equal to the DOS' /S command with XCOPY.

FTP

Discussed in Chapter 2, The File Transfer Protocol is used to copy files to and from a system running an FTP server over TCP, and is therefore quite obviously connection-oriented. The host may be UNIX, VAX, Windows NT, or any other system running an FTP server process. Although this utility uses both user and password protection, it can be configured to allow anonymous usage. Unlike Telnet, Microsoft does provide a daemon or server service for FTP to run. In most Internet applications, when using FTP with "anonymous" as a user ID, an e-mail account is used as the password, as it can be logged to show an audit trail.

If you've installed TCP/IP and connection utilities with Windows NT, you already have the FTP program. Since no icon is created from a command prompt, type **ftp**, and the destination name or IP address.

The Command line with options is:

```
ftp {options} host command
```

If no destination host is specified, the FTP terminal screen will appear. When it does, type **open** to establish your connection. As with Telnet, you'll then be prompted for a login name and password. Once connected, you have a variety of options available to you. You can view these options by typing, **help** or **?**. Doing so will yield the following information:

! DOS shell to command prompt. Type Exit to return.

? Command listing or ? Command displays the command description. It works the same as help.

append Allows you to add to a file.

ASCII Sets the transfer mode type to ASCII. Used for text files.

bell Inserts a little beep when the command is completed.

Bye Closes an FTP session and exits the FTP program.

Binary Sets the transfer mode type to binary. Used for files other than text.

cd   Change directory on FTP server (must include a space following cd; also uses .. (double dots) for going back a directory, and / for specifying root).

close   Closes an FTP session.

debug   Toggles the debug mode.

delete   Removes a remote file.

dir   Lists a directory of files—similar to ls -l in UNIX.

disconnect   Closes an FTP session.

get   Retrieves a file.

Glob   Toggles meta-character expansion of local filenames.

hash   Toggles printing. '#'(hash signs) for each data block transferred.

help   Command listing or help Command displays the command description. Same as ?.

literal   Send arguments, verbatim, to the remote FTP server. A single FTP reply code is expected in return.

lcd   Changes directory locally.

ls   Lists a directory of files. (Use ls -l for all information.)

mdelete   Removes multiple remote files.

mdir   Provides a directory of multiple remote directories.

mget   Downloads multiple files from remote system.

mkdir   Makes a directory on the remote system.

mls   Provides a directory of multiple remote directories.

mput   Uploads multiple files to remote system.

open   Begins an FTP session.

prompt   Forces interactive prompting on multiple commands.

put   Uploads a file.

pwd   Prints a working directory (like CD in DOS).

quit Exits the FTP session.

Quote Sends arguments, verbatim, to the remote FTP server. A single FTP reply code is expected in return. Quote is identical to Literal.

recv Downloads a file.

rename Renames a file.

rmdir Removes a directory.

remotehelp Gets a help listing from the FTP server.

send Uploads a file.

status Shows the current status of FTP connections.

trace Toggles packet tracing.

type Sets the transfer type.

user Sends new user information.

verbose Toggles the verbose mode.

As you can see, there are a ton of commands. While it is not important to memorize them, you should be aware of their existence and how to find them. Many new GUI FTP programs have been created by third parties in an effort to simplify the FTP process. However, most FTP systems use the same commands in a manner that complies to the standard. Exercise 10.1 will help you practice installing and configuring the Windows NT FTP server service onto your computer.

TFTP

The Trivial File Transfer Protocol, also discussed in detail in Chapter 2, is equal to FTP without security. Using UDP to communicate in place of TCP, this program will communicate with a host running the TFTP server software. As with Telnet, Microsoft only provides the client portion of TFTP. The server part must come from a third party source, or be used from another operating system such a UNIX server. The command format is as follows:

```
TFTP [-i] host [GET | PUT] source [destination]
```

-i specifies binary image transfer mode, also called octet. If -i is omitted, the file is transferred in ASCII mode.

source/destination is the full path designating where files are copied to and from.

GET transfers destination (specifies where to transfer) on the remote computer to source (specifies what file to transfer) on the local computer.

PUT transfers source (specifies what file to transfer) on the remote computer to destination (specifies where to transfer) on the local computer.

Printer Utilities

LPQ

Line Printer Queue allows a user to view the print queue on an LPD (Line Printer Daemon) server. It displays the state of a remote LPD queue. The command format is as follows:

```
lpq  -Sserver -Pprinter [-1]
```

-S*server* is the name, or IP address, of the host providing the LPD service.

-P*printer* is the name of the print queue.

-l specifies that a detailed status should be given.

LPR

The Line Printer utility allows jobs to be sent to a printer that is serviced by a host running an LPD server. The command format is as follows:

```
lpr -Sserver -PPrinter [-CClass] [-JJobname] [-oOption]
    [-x] [-d] filename
```

-S*Server* is the name, or IP address, of the host providing the LPD service.

-P*Printer* is the name of the print queue.

-C*Class*   is the job classification for use on the banner page.

-J*Job*   is the job name to be printed on the banner page.

-o*Option*   indicates the type of file (the default is text file; use -ol for binary files such as postscript, etc.).

-x   is for compatibility with SunOS 4.1.*x* or a prior version.

-d   is for sending a data file first.

The FTP Server—Installation and Configuration

TP GIVES USERS the ability to send and receive files. This action is often compared to uploading and downloading files from a *BBS,* or Bulletin Board System, via modem. BBS and FTP sites differ in a couple of ways. First, the FTP site is usually connected via network line rather than voice-graded phone cable. Second, FTP is a specific service for file transfer communications, whereas a BBS can use a number of various transfer protocols, provided the client supports them.

For example, to download a file with a BBS, you dial it up and get your listing of files. You then select a file for downloading, and the protocol to use, for example, Z-Modem. Alternatively, FTP can be used between two computers on the same network just by specifying the name or IP address. It can also be used to gain access to systems on a different network, such as Microsoft's FTP site, FTP.MICROSOFT.COM. Because FTP is a service, it is platform-independent. Even though Microsoft's is run on Windows NT, while many others are run on UNIX, you won't find any major differences in them from the client viewpoint. On a network that's directly connected to the Internet, you can retrieve a file from a remote FTP site simply by typing **start ftp**, opening the site by name, or IP address, listing the file, and then using the `get` command. Exercise 10.1 will help you practice these things.

EXERCISE 10.1

Installing, Configuring, and Testing the FTP Server Service

1. From the Control Panel, start Network.

2. Choose Add Software.

3. In the Network Software box, select TCP/IP Protocol and related components.

4. Choose Continue.

5. Select FTP Server Service, then choose Continue.

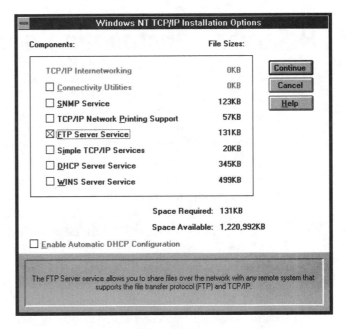

The Windows NT Setup dialog box prompts you for the location of the distribution files.

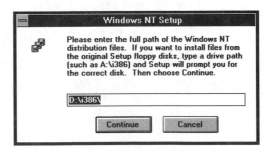

6. Type in the path.

The Windows NT message box appears to inform you that FTP does not encrypt passwords, and asks if you want to continue installing the software.

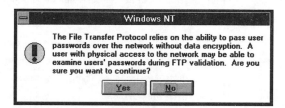

7. Choose Yes.

Files are copied to your computer, and the FTP Service dialog box appears with the following options:

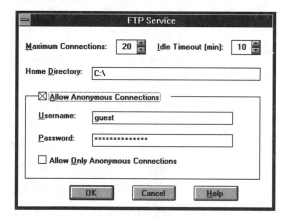

- **Maximum Connections**: This equals the maximum number of synchronous connections to the FTP server, and must be within the range of 1 to 50.

- **Idle Timeout (min)**: This delimits the period of time in which no activity occurs until a session is closed by the system. This must be within the range of 1 to 60.

- **Home Directory**: This is the standard default directory for a connection. If an anonymous or other directory isn't found with the connecting users, the default is C:\USERS\DEFAULT. Otherwise, users will be changed to their named directory automatically.

EXERCISE 10.1 (CONTINUED FROM PREVIOUS PAGE)

- **Allow Anonymous Connections**: This option allows users to connect to the system with the username "anonymous." This function does not block valid usernames and passwords from being used. It should be done by also selecting Allow Only Anonymous Connections. This function is great for allowing anyone access to a server. It's the type of connection most Internet FTP sites, such as FTP.MICROSOFT.COM, use.

- **Username**: By default, this is the equivalent to the guest account. It may, however, be changed to represent any user so that FTP access will provide an appropriate level of security for a particular user. This is the account the anonymous user will portray.

- **Password**: This is the password for the anonymous user. When an FTP session is opened, the system will use this password to connect the user to the operating system as if they were the user listed above in Username. If the user account password is changed, it must be changed here as well.

- **Allow Only Anonymous Connections**: Limits FTP log in connections to the username "anonymous." Valid user accounts will be rejected. This is implemented mainly due to the fact that passwords are too easily stolen, since they're not encrypted.

8. In the Home directory box, type **C:\Users\Default**.

9. Select Allow Anonymous Connections (make sure you don't select Allow Only Anonymous Connections), then choose OK.

The Network Settings dialog box appears.

10. To save the configuration, choose OK.

A Network Settings Change dialog box appears, indicating the computer needs to be restarted.

11. Choose Restart Now.

Configuring the FTP Server Service

1. From the Control Panel, start FTP Server.

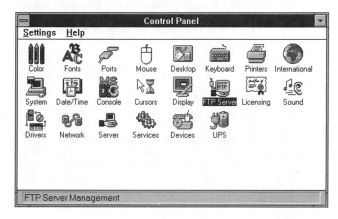

The FTP User Sessions window appears.

2. Choose security.

The FTP Server Security dialog box appears.

3. In the Partition box under Security Access, select C:.

4. Select the Allow Write check box.

5. Verify that Allow Read is still selected, then choose OK.

The FTP User Session window appears. Leave the FTP User Sessions window open while you continue with the exercise.

EXERCISE 10.1 (CONTINUED FROM PREVIOUS PAGE)

Testing the FTP Server

1. From the command prompt, verify that the FTP server was installed correctly using the FTP command and the loopback address. Type **ftp 127.0.0.1**.

If it is installed correctly, you will see the following prompt: **User (127.0.0.1:(none)):**.

2. At the prompt, type the username **administrator** and then press Enter.

A prompt appears for the administrator password.

3. At the password prompt, press Enter.

The message confirms that the administrator is logged in, and the ftp> prompt appears. This confirms that the Windows NT FTP server was installed correctly.

FTP Management

There are three basic functions to Windows NT FTP Management—Session, Security, and Logging.

User Sessions

Sessions management is performed by first selecting the FTP Server icon in the Control Panel. Upon opening the subprogram, you'll be presented with a list of users that are connected to your server, including their IP address and the length of time they've been connected. From this screen, you can disconnect all users listed, or target individually selected sessions. Because this screen doesn't update automatically, it's important to click on the refresh button to get the most current information.

Security

Although FTP has username and password security (unless configured for Anonymous), there still remains a large security concern—passwords aren't encrypted. This means that anyone with network access, and in possession of some type of packet analyzer, such as Lanalyser for Windows (Microsoft's Network Analyzer to be shipped with NT Server 4.0) or a Network General Sniffer, etc. can view your password when you log into an FTP server. If you're using a nonanonymous Windows NT implementation with FTP, you'll have blabbed your network name and your password, since they're one and the same. If security is a major concern, limit FTP access to a single account, and design your *Internet firewall* to block foreign, non-registered IP addresses.

A firewall is a protection filter put in place to keep unauthorized users from hacking into a company's system from the outside.

The Session Manager

This is the program that's used to configure security. Recall that the FTP Session Manager is accessed though the Control Panel by selecting the FTP server icon. Security is the process by which you can restrict an FTP user of any type, either valid or anonymous, to certain limited accessibility. All drives will be displayed in the partition box of the FTP Server Security dialog box. Select Allow Read to let users see file listings, and/or Allow Write to let users upload and delete files and directories. Since each FTP session is logged in as a user (the default is guest), access will be limited accordingly to the security specified in the dialog box.

For best results, you should use FTP on NTFS volumes, since security is more manageable with them. Note that either Allow Read or Allow Write must be selected in order for access to be granted to the volume, regardless of who the user is.

In Exercise 10.2, you get to practice restricting user access to drive C by removing "write" access and configuring the FTP server security. You'll also practice testing it afterward.

EXERCISE 10.2

Restricting User Access

To configure the FTP server service, take the following steps:

1. From the FTP User Sessions window, choose Security.

The FTP Server Security dialog box appears.

2. In the Partition box, select C: from the list.

3. Clear Allow Write, then choose OK.

The FTP User Sessions dialog box appears.

To test the FTP security from an FTP client, do the following:

1. To see what happens when you don't have the proper access, try to transfer a file to the FTP server. Type **put filename.txt myfile.txt**.

Notice the error message received. This is because you don't have "Write" access.

2. Type **quit**, then choose Close to exit the FTP User Sessions window.

Logging

The last FTP management issue we'll discuss is logging—a more manual process to implement since it must be done though the Registry Editor (regedt32). There are two types of logging—user and file access. Depending on your requirements, you can apply user access to find out who's accessing your servers and file access to determine which files are used the most, or both. You may opt to use no logging if you don't especially care who accesses your server. There are three possible registry value entries that may be used with logging:

LogAnonymous   This command logs FTP sessions with the anonymous user.

LogNonAnonymous   This one logs FTP sessions with users that are using their Windows NT accounts.

LogFileAccess   This one logs the files accessed by FTP clients.

Again, using the Windows NT Registry Editor (regedt32), these entries should be added to:

```
HKEY_LOCAL_MACHINE\SYSTEM\CurrentControlSet\Services\
    FTPSVC\Parmeters.
```

If the value listed above does not appear in the Registry, simply add the entry, and send the value to 1. The value type is REG_DWORD.

The FTP log files detailing user access can be examined though the Event Viewer in the Administrative Tools group. Each connection will appear as a line item in the Event Viewer. Depending on the information you're looking for, you might find using filter events from the View pull-down menu helpful. They'll allow you to view only the data relevant to your purposes, instead of reading through all that's recorded.

You'll find file access recorded in FTPSVC.LOG, which is stored in \systemroot\SYSTEM32. The report will begin with a heading describing the FTP server service start time and date, followed by individual lines stating the client's IP address and name. The file also includes information on which file was accessed, and the date and time it was opened. In Exercise 10.3, you'll enable logging, and then proceed to view the logs.

EXERCISE 10.3

Configuring FTP Logging

1. Open regedt32 and maximize HKEY_LOCAL_MACHINE.

2. Select SYSTEM\CurrentControlServices\FTPSVC\Parameters.

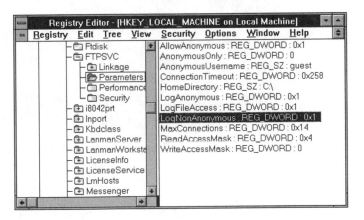

3. Add the following parameters to enable logging:

Value Name	Value type	Value
LogFileAccess	REG_WORD	I
LogAnonymous	REG_DWORD	I
LogNonAnonymous	REG_DWORD	I

4. Exit the Registry Editor, and then restart the computer.

Viewing FTP Logs

1. From the Administrator tools group, start Event Viewer.

The Event Viewer window appears.

2. Verify that the System Log is displayed. If not, choose Log ➤ System.

3. Next select View ➤ Filter Events.

The filter dialog box appears.

4. In the source box, choose FTPSVC, and then choose OK.

The Event Viewer window appears, displaying only events generated by the FTP Server service (FTPSVC).

5. Display the details of the events listed. Notice that the administrator has logged on.

Internetwork Printing

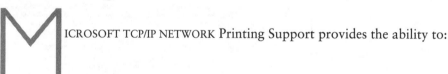

ICROSOFT TCP/IP NETWORK Printing Support provides the ability to:

- Print to a printer attached to a Windows NT 3.5 print server from a UNIX host (LPDSVC service).

- Print to printers attached to UNIX hosts from any computer that can connect to a Windows NT computer. The Windows NT computer communicates with the UNIX printer using the LPR and LPQ utilities.

- Print to printers that use a network interface with TCP/IP (see Figure 10.1).

Implementation

Implementing printing support for TCP/IP is a three-step process. First, you add network printing support to a computer that will both print to a printer connected to a UNIX host and control a TCP/IP-based printer. The next step is

FIGURE 10.1

Internetwork Printing

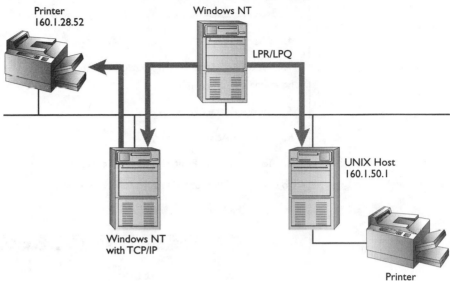

to use Print Manager to create a printer using the LPR (Liner Printer) port print monitor. Lastly, you start the TCP/IP Print Server service (LPDSVC service).

Exercise 10.4 is designed to help you to practice these steps. Take a moment to work through it now.

EXERCISE 10.4

Printing to a TCP/IP-Based Printer

To install the TCP/IP-based printer, do the following:

1. Access the Windows NT TCP/IP Installation Options dialog box.

The Windows NT TCP/IP Installation Option dialog box appears, displaying the TCP/IP components available to be installed.

2. Select TCP/IP Network Printing Support, then choose Continue.

The Windows NT Setup box appears, prompting you for the full path of the Windows NT distribution files.

3. Type in the path, and then choose Continue.

The appropriate files will be copied to your workstation. The Network settings dialog box appears.

4. Choose OK.

The Network Settings Change dialog box appears, indicating the computer needs to be restarted.

5. Choose Restart Now.

6. Logon as Administrator.

7. To start TCP/IP Print Server, use Control Panel Services or Server Manager.

To create a TCP/IP-based printer, follow these steps:

1. From the Main group, start Print Manager.

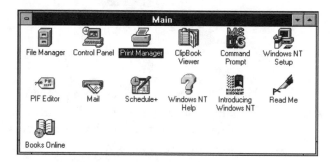

2. Choose Printer ➤ Create Printer.

The Create Printer dialog box appears.

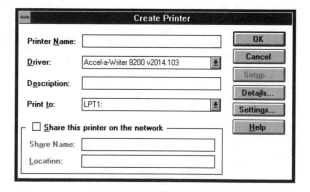

EXERCISE 10.4 (CONTINUED FROM PREVIOUS PAGE)

3. Complete the Create Printer dialog box by typing in the following information:

- Printer Name: **TCPPRT**
- Printer Driver: **printer_driver**

The Print Destination dialog box appears.

4. Select LPR Port, and then choose OK.

The Add LPR Compatible Printer dialog box appears.

5. In the Name or Address of Host Providing LPD box, type your own IP address.

6. In the Name of Printer on that Machine box, type **tcpprt,** and then choose OK.

The Create Printer dialog box appears.

7. Select Share This Printer on the Network, and then choose OK.

A Windows NT Setup dialog box appears, prompting you for the location of the Windows NT Server distribution files.

8. Type in the path of the distribution files.

9. To complete the setup of the printer, choose OK.

Print Manager appears with the TCP/IP Printer created.

Printing to a TCP/IP-Based Printer

Once you have installed and configured TCP/IP printer support, you will connect to the printer using Print Manager or the LPR command, depending on whether the printer is attached to a Windows NT computer or a UNIX host. In Exercise 10.5, you'll learn how to use Print Manager to connect to a TCP/IP-based printer.

EXERCISE 10.5

Printing to a TCP/IP-Based Printer

1. Select Printer ➤ Connect Printer.

The Connect to Printer dialog box appears.

EXERCISE 10.5 (CONTINUED FROM PREVIOUS PAGE)

2. In the Shared Printers list, select \\servername\TCPPRT, and then choose OK.

The Print Manager window appears with the connected printer displayed.

3. Start Notepad and create and print a short document on \\servername\TCPPRT.

4. Switch back to Print Manager.

Notice your document in the queue.

5. Exit Print Manager.

Using LPR and LPQ to Access a TCP/IP-Based Printer

1. From the command prompt, view the remote print queue, and then type **lpq -Sip_address -Ptcpprt -l**.

Note that the -S and -P switches must be in uppercase.

The Windows NT 3.51 LPD Server print queue status appears.

2. To send a new job to the print queue, type **lpr -Sip_address -Ptcpprt c:\config.sys**.

The job will be sent to the print queue.

3. View the remote print queue to check that the new job has been spooled.

Notice the new job lists the LPR client documents as the Jobname.

4. Exit the command prompt.

Summing Things Up

THE FIRST CONCEPT we focused on in this chapter was how communication occurs within a diversified communication environment. TCP/IP provides a flexible means by which dissimilar computing environments may effectively communicate with each other. It serves as an organizational model by establishing a set mode of communication despite the operating system in use. Different systems, such as NetBIOS-based hosts and Sun workstations are able to achieve fluid communication in spite of their differences because of the fact that they're using TCP/IP as their communication protocol. Microsoft clients such as Windows NT, Windows 95, or Windows For Workgroups can interoperate with an RFC-compliant, NetBIOS-based SMB server using the Windows Redirector. This is achieved through the use of standard windows commands like NET USE and NET VIEW over a common set of communication protocols like TCP/IP or NetBEUI. Some important things to remember when communicating to foreign TCP/IP hosts are:

- You must use TCP/IP. NetBEUI won't talk to TCP/IP, and nor will IPX.

- Only commands supported by the specific TCP/IP utility, such as FTP, TELNET etc., may be used to communicate with the foreign system.

- Applications that are accessed on the foreign system are run centrally at the foreign system—not at your local system.

- TCP/IP utilities can use either the host name or the IP address.

- Both local and remote host names that are used in TCP/IP utilities must be resolved in the HOSTS file, DNS, WINS, b-node broadcast, or LMHOSTS file.

Microsoft provides FTP, LPQ, LPR, REXEC, RSH, RCP, Telnet, and TFTP TCP/IP utilities, which can be organized into three divisions as follows:

- Command utilities: REXEC, RSH, and Telnet

- Transfer utilities: RCP, FTP, and TFTP

- Printer utilities: LPR and LPQ

The majority of the commands presented in the chapter for these utilities are similar in implementation to their UNIX-based counterparts, and like UNIX, they're usually case-sensitive.

In the next section, we discussed installing and configuring an FTP server, beginning with an introduction on the platform-independent FTP service. Even though Microsoft's is run on Windows NT, and others are run on UNIX, there aren't any major differences between them from the client viewpoint. On a network that's directly connected to the Internet, you can retrieve a file from a remote FTP site simply by typing start ftp, opening the site by name or IP address, listing the file, and using the get command.

There are three basic functions to Windows NT FTP Management: Session, Security, and Logging.

Sessions management is performed though the Control Panel by selecting the FTP Server icon. Upon opening the subprogram, you'll be presented with a list of users that are connected to your server, including their IP address, and the length of time they've been connected. This is the program that's used to configure security, which is a definite concern because although FTP has username and password security (unless configured for Anonymous), passwords aren't encrypted. Anyone with network access, and in possession of some type of packet analyzer, such as Lanalyser for Windows (Microsoft's Network Analyzer to be shipped with NT server 4.0), or a Network General Sniffer, etc., can view your password when you log into an FTP server. Security is accomplished by restricting user access and mobility.

There are two types of logging—user and file access. Depending on your requirements, you can apply user access to find out who's accessing your servers, and file access to determine which files are used the most, or both. There are three possible registry value entries that may be used with logging:

- LogAnonymous

- LogNonAnonymous

- LogFileAccess

The FTP log files detailing user access can be examined though the Event Viewer in the Administrative Tools group. Each connection will appear as a line item in the Event Viewer.

The last issue we covered was internetwork printing. Microsoft TCP/IP Network Printing Support provides the ability to:

- Print to a printer attached to a Windows NT 3.5 print server from a UNIX host (LPDSVC service).

- Print to printers attached to UNIX hosts from any computer that can connect to a Windows NT computer. The Windows NT computer communicates with the UNIX printer using the LPR and LPQ utilities.

- Print to printers that use a network interface with TCP/IP.

Exercise Questions

Multiple-Choice Questions

1. What are some common machines that use TCP/IP to interoperate for file and print services?

   A. Apple Macintosh

   B. DEC VAX systems

   C. DOS systems with TCP/IP

   D. TCP/IP-based printers

   E. Windows 95

2. What does the RCP command do?

   A. Request for Copy (a client requesting a file)

   B. Remote Compression

   C. Remote Copy (similar to FTP, except doesn't require a user validation)

   D. Request for Copy Protocol (a file transfer protocol)

3. What are the three basic functions to Windows NT FTP Management?

   A. Session

   B. Security

   C. Logging

   D. Fragmentation

Scenario-Based Review

SCENARIO #1 Your company has just purchased a communications server which has been installed with an IP address of 160.1.8.8. Although the communications unit has NASI (a network specification for a networked pool of modems) support, you do not have any NT-based software to support this function. All that you really want to do is just get to any dumb terminal that can dial a BBS so you can get the latest instructions on how to install a software package that was shipped without an addendum. You call the software company and ask them to fax it to you, but the tech tells you they only have it on their BBS. You then decide to call the communication server manufacture to find out if it can be accessed by anything else aside from the NASI compliant software. They tell you that you can Telnet to the communications server's IP address on ports 232 to 248 (16 ports), and access it as a dumb terminal using "AT" modem commands. Using Microsoft's Telnet program, how do you Telnet to that server on port 232?

SCENARIO #2 Suppose that you have full Internet access and wish to get some compressed executable files from Microsoft's FTP site, which is running on Windows NT. Given proper access, would you be able to retrieve the files, and if so, how?

SCENARIO #3 Suppose that you have full Internet access, and wish to get some compressed text files from Novell's FTP site, which is running on a UNIX-based system. Given proper access, would you be able to retrieve the files, and if so, how?

SCENARIO #4 A Windows FTP server is configured so that only an anonymous user (defined as Administrator instead of Guest) can access the server. The default access has been cleared from the home directory partition, and no other access has been assigned. What can the user see as an anonymous administrator?

Microsoft SNMP
Services

THIS CHAPTER PROVIDES an overview of the Simple Network Management Protocol (SNMP), including the functions performed by an SNMP management station, and the Microsoft SNMP service (SNMP agent). Detailed information is provided on installing and configuring the Microsoft SNMP service as a tool for monitoring network performance and activity.

Objectives

KEEP THESE IMPORTANT points in mind while you're working through this chapter. They're basics, as well as being major elements of focus for the exam. After working through this section, you should be able to:

- Explain the purpose of SNMP

- Describe the different operations performed by an SNMP agent and an SNMP management system

- Define the Management Information Base (MIB)

- Install and configure the Microsoft SNMP service

Presenting SNMP

SNMP (SIMPLE NETWORK MANAGEMENT PROTOCOL) is a very important protocol in the TCP/IP suite. It allows you to monitor and manage a network from a single workstation or workstations called SNMP managers.

SNMP is actually a family of specifications that provide a means for collecting network management data from the devices residing in a network. It also avails a method for those devices to report any problems they're experiencing to the management station. From an SNMP manager, you can query the network's devices regarding the nature of their functions. Examples of machines you'd want to keep an eye on include:

- Computers running Windows NT

- Lan Manager servers

- Routers and gateways

- Minicomputers or mainframe computers

- Terminal servers

- Wiring hubs

Figure 11.1 shows the network administrator at an SNMP management station making queries to various devices on the internetwork. A router can be queried for the contents of its routing table, or for statistics relating to the amount of traffic it's forwarding. A mainframe computer can be surveyed to determine which ports are listening for requests, or for what connections have been established with clients. A Windows NT computer can also be monitored, and can alert the manager of pertinent events, like when a particular host is running out of hard disk space. Regardless of the type of device that is queried, the SNMP agent on the device is able to return meaningful, highly useful information to the manager.

FIGURE 11.1

SNMP managers
and SNMP agents

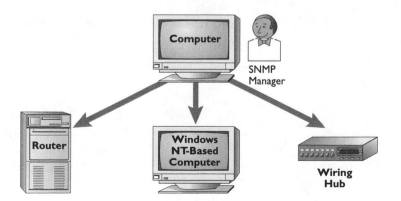

There are two documents you can read for a complete description of SNMP:
1. RFC 1098: The Simple Network Management Protocol
2. RFC 1213: Management Information Base for network management of TCP/IP-based internets: MIB-II

Management Systems and Agents

SNMP uses a distributed architecture consisting of management systems and agents that works like this: The manager first submits a request to the agent. This request is either to obtain, or to set the value of, a networking variable within the agent's *Management Information Base (MIB)*. The agent satisfies the request according to the community name accompanying the request. A community name can be compared to a password, and will be discussed more thoroughly later in the chapter.

The SNMP protocol is simple in that only five types of commands are defined within it. They are:

GetRequest   The command used by the manager to request information from an agent.

GetNextRequest   Also employed by the manager, this command is used if the information desired is contained within a table or array. The manager can use this command repeatedly until the complete contents of the array have been acquired.

GetResponse   The queried agent uses this command to satisfy a request made by the manager.

SetRequest   The manager uses this command to change the value of a parameter within the agent's MIB.

Trap   A special command the agent uses to inform the manager of a certain event.

Figure 11.2 outlines the primary function of the management system—requesting information from an agent. A management system is any computer that's running the SNMP management software. This system can initiate the `GetRequest`, `GetNextRequest`, and the `SetRequest` operations.

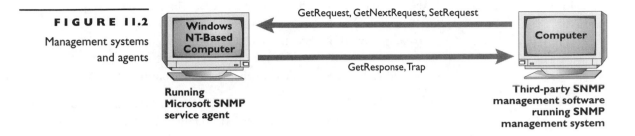

FIGURE 11.2

Management systems
and agents

An SNMP agent is any computer that's running SNMP agent software—
most often, a server or router. The chief obligation of an SNMP agent is
to perform the tasks initiated by the `GetRequest`, `GetNextRequest`, and
`SetRequest` commands, as required by a management system. The Microsoft
SNMP service is the SNMP agent software. The only operation initiated by an
agent is the `trap` command, which alerts management systems of an extraordinary event, like a password violation.

MIB: The Management Information Base

A MIB describes the objects, or entries, that are to be included in the SNMP
agent database. For this reason, SNMP agents are sometimes referred to as
MIBs. Objects in a MIB must be defined so that developers of the management
station software will know which objects are available, the object names, and
their related values. This information is included in a MIB specification.

A MIB records and stores information about the host it is running on. An
SNMP manager can request and collect information from an agent's MIB, as
well as inspect or alter the objects it contains. For example, from the SNMP
manager, you can find out the number of sessions that have taken place on a
certain remote host. The Microsoft SNMP service supports Internet MIB II,
Lan Manager MIB II, DHCP MIB, and WINS MIB. Below is a description of
each of these tools:

Internet MIB II   is a superset of the previous standard, Internet MIB I.
It defines 171 objects essential for either fault or configuration analysis.
Internet MIB II is defined in RFC 1213.

LAN Manager MIB II for Windows NT   contains a set of objects specifically designed to support computers running Windows NT. It defines approximately 90 objects that include items such as statistical, share, session, user, and logon information. Most LAN Manager MIB II objects have read-only access because of the nonsecure nature of SNMP.

DHCP MIB   Windows NT includes a DHCP MIB that defines objects to monitor DHCP server activity. This MIB (DHCPMIB.DLL) is automatically installed when the DHCP server service is installed. It contains approximately 14 objects for monitoring DHCP, including the number of DHCP discover requests received, the number of declines, and the number of addresses leased out to clients.

WINS MIB   Windows NT includes a WINS MIB that defines objects to monitor WINS server activity. This MIB (WINSMIB.DLL) is automatically installed when the WINS server service is installed. It contains approximately 70 objects for monitoring WINS, such as the number of resolution requests successfully processed, the number of resolution requests that failed, and the date and time of the last database replication.

Microsoft's SNMP Service

I N ORDER TO take advantage of Microsoft's NT SNMP services, you must have an SNMP manager that can monitor and display SNMP alerts. The Microsoft SNMP service provides SNMP agent services to any TCP/IP host that's running the SNMP management software. Microsoft SNMP service can run on Windows NT, as long as it's also running TCP/IP.

There are two methods that the Microsoft SNMP service management software can employ to collect information about devices. One way is to have devices send alerts to an SNMP manager, or to any other manager within the community. Another method is to have the SNMP manager poll devices every few seconds, minutes, or hours.

By adding the public community to the alert list, any management station within the community will receive alerts, and be able to make changes to the configuration.

Microsoft's SNMP service can use a HOSTS file, DNS, WINS, or the LMHOSTS file to perform host name to IP address translation, and to identify which hosts it will report information to, and receive requests from. It also enables *counters* for monitoring TCP/IP performance with *Performance Monitor*.

Planning and Preparing for Implementation

F YOU PLAN on using the SNMP service with a third-party manager, you'll need to:

- Record the IP addresses and host names of participating hosts.

- Add host name/IP address mappings to the appropriate name resolution resource.

- Identify the third-party management systems and Microsoft SNMP agents.

HOST NAMES AND IP ADDRESSES When installing the SNMP service on an agent, make sure you have the host names, or IP addresses of the hosts to which your system will send SNMP traps, as well as those to which your system will respond regarding SNMP requests.

HOST NAME RESOLUTION The SNMP service uses normal Windows NT host name resolution methods to resolve host names to IP addresses. If you use host names, be sure to add all host name/IP address mappings of the participating computers to the appropriate resolution sources (such as the HOSTS file, DNS, WINS, or the LMHOSTS file).

MANAGEMENT SYSTEMS AND AGENTS A management system is any computer running the TCP/IP transport and third-party SNMP manager software. The management system requests information from an agent. To use the Microsoft SNMP service, you need at least one management system.

An SNMP agent is a Windows NT-based computer running the Microsoft SNMP service. The agent provides the management system with requested status information and reports any extraordinary events.

Defining SNMP Communities

Before you install SNMP, you will need to define an SNMP community. A community is a group to which hosts running the SNMP service belong. A community parameter is simply the name of that group. SNMP communities are identified by their community parameter. The use of a community name provides some security and context for agents receiving requests and initiating traps. It does the same for management systems and their tasks. An agent will not respond to a request from a management system outside its configured community, but it can be a member of multiple communities at the same time, allowing for communications with SNMP managers from various communities. Figure 11.3 illustrates how a community name is used.

FIGURE 11.3

How an SNMP community is used to group hosts

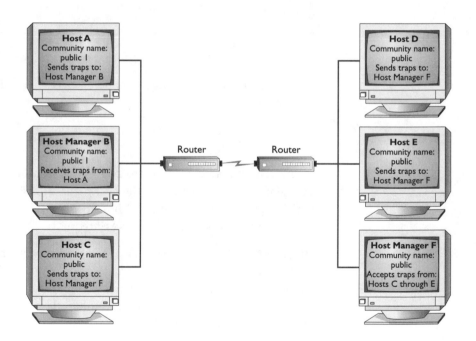

In Figure 11.3, Host A can receive and send messages to Host Manager B because they are both members of the public1 community. Host C through Host E can receive and send messages to Manager F because all these machines are members of the default public community.

SNMP Installation and Configuration

NEXT, WE'LL TALK about installing and configuring the SNMP service on a Windows NT computer. Before installing SNMP, make sure the TCP/IP protocol suite is installed. This will also enable you to monitor TCP/IP with the Performance Monitor.

SNMP Service Security

There is minimal-level security available with SNMP, inherent in the processes of management and agent systems when initiating and receiving requests and traps. However, don't allow yourself to be lulled into a false sense of security! If your SNMP-managed network is connected to the Internet, or any public internetwork, a firewall should be in place to prevent intrusion from outside SNMP management consoles. When installing SNMP, keep the following security configuration options in mind:

Send Authentication Trap   This is used if you want the computer to send a trap for a failed authentication. When the SNMP service receives a management request that does not contain or match the community name, the SNMP service can send a trap to the trap destination.

Accepted Community Names   This specifies community names from which the computer will accept requests. A host must belong to a community that appears in this list for the SNMP service to accept requests from that host. Typically, all hosts belong to the community named public.

Accept SNMP Packets from Any Host   By default, this option is checked. It accepts packets from everybody.

Only Accept SNMP Packets from These Hosts   If checked, the computer should only accept packets from hosts that have specific IP or IPX addresses, plus the host name that's in the associated box.

To install SNMP and specify security options, see Exercise 11.1.

Installing and Configuring the SNMP Service

1. Select Control Panel ➤ Network.

2. Choose Add Software in the Network Settings dialog box.

3. Select TCP/IP protocol and related components in the Network Settings box, then choose Continue.

4. Check SNMP Service in the Windows NT TCP/IP Installation Options dialog box, then choose Continue.

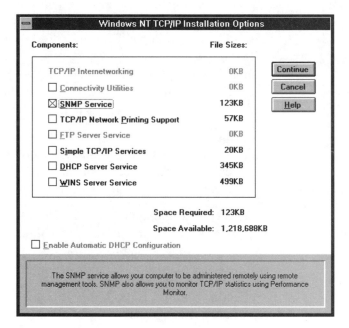

5. Type in the path of the distribution files.

6. Choose OK to close the Network Settings dialog box.

7. The SNMP Service Configuration dialog box screen appears:

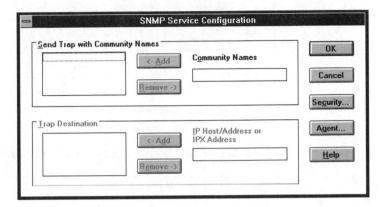

8. First specify the SNMP community to which this computer will belong. The default community is public. Enter SNMP community names in the Community name box and choose ADD to move them to the Send Traps with Community Names box.

9. Second, specify the trap destinations for the computer. To do this, enter the desired IP addresses in the IP Host/Addresses or IPX Addresses box, and choose Add to move them to the Trap Destination box.

10. To specify security settings, choose the Security button to open the SNMP Security Configuration dialog box:

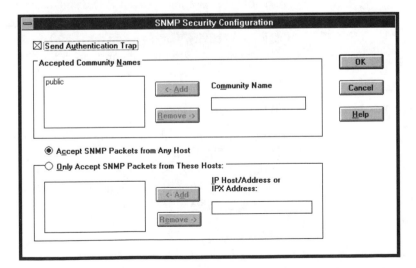

11. Check the Send Authentication Trap box if you want the computer to send a trap for a failed authentication.

12. In the Accepted Community Names box, specify community names from which this computer will accept requests. Typically, all hosts belong to public.

13. By default, the Accept SNMP Packets from Any Host option is checked. If this computer should only accept packets from hosts that have specific IP or IPX addresses, check Only Accept SNMP Packets from These Hosts, then add the chosen hosts in the associated box.

14. Choose OK after entering the security information.

SNMP Agent Services

A Simple Network Management Protocol agent is a database of information about a device and/or its environment which is installed on the device designated for management or monitoring. Data contained in the agent database depends on the specific function of the devices that are to be monitored. The agent in the managed device doesn't volunteer information because doing so would take away from its primary function. The only exception to this rule is that an agent will send an alarm to the management station if a critical threshold is crossed. Microsoft SNMP agent services give a Windows NT-based computer the ability to provide an SNMP management system with the information on activity that occurs at different layers of the Internet Protocol suite.

In Exercise 11.2, you will configure SNMP agent services.

How to Spot SNMP Service Errors

After SNMP is installed, you can then view SNMP errors from the Event Viewer system log. The Event Viewer will record all events occurring with the system components of SNMP—even failure of the SNMP service to start. The Event Viewer is the first place you should look to identify any possible problems related to the SNMP service.

EXERCISE 11.2

Configuring SNMP Agent Services

1. In the SNMP Service Configuration dialog box, choose the Agent button to open the SNMP Agent dialog box.

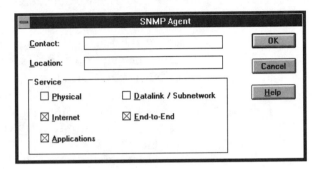

2. In the Contact and Location boxes, enter the name of the computer user and the computer location, as well as any other identification information.

3. If additional TCP/IP services have been installed on the computer, check an SNMP service option in the Service box. Each service provides information on activity at the different layers. The default services are Application, End-to-End, and Internet. The options are as follows:

- **Physical** This computer manages a physical layer TCP/IP device such as a repeater.

- **Datalink\Subnetwork** This computer manages a datalink layer such as a bridge or a subnetwork.

- **Internet** This computer manages an Internet layer device, that is, it functions as an IP gateway (router).

- **End-to-End** This computer acts as an IP host. This option should be selected for all Windows NT computers.

- **Applications** This computer supports applications that use TCP/IP. This option should be selected for all Windows NT computers.

4. Choose OK, then exit the SNMP Service Configuration dialog box and the Network Settings dialog box.

How SNMP Works

THE FOLLOWING STEPS outline how SNMP works and responds to a third-party management system request (see Figure 11.4):

Step 1: A third-party SNMP management system running on Host 1 requests the number of active sessions from a Microsoft SNMP agent. The SNMP management system uses the host name to send the request. The request is passed by the application to socket (UDP port) 161. The host name is then resolved by using the HOSTS file, DNS, WINS, b-node broadcast, or LMHOSTS.

Step 2: An SNMP message that contains the `GetRequest` command is formed to discover the number of active sessions with the community name public.

Step 3: The Host 2 Microsoft SNMP agent receives the message, and verifies the community name, as well as whether the message has been corrupted in any way. If the community name is incorrect, or the message has been corrupted somewhere along the way, it's discarded. If the message is valid, and the community name is correct, then the host verifies the IP address to make sure the address is authorized to accept massages from the management station.

Step 4: An SNMP message stating that eight sessions are active is then sent back to the SNMP manager.

FIGURE 11.4

How SNMP works

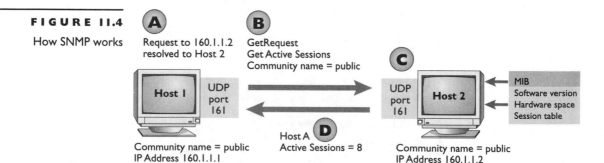

Summing Things Up

S NMP PERMITS THE monitoring and managing of a network from a single workstation or workstations called SNMP managers. It's a family of specifications that provide a means for collecting network management data from the devices residing in a network. With an SNMP manager, you can query the network's devices regarding the nature of their functions.

SNMP uses a distributed architecture consisting of management systems and agents. A management system is any computer running the SNMP management software. Its primary function is requesting and gathering information from an agent. This system can initiate the `GetRequest`, `GetNextRequest`, and `SetRequest` operations.

An SNMP agent is any computer running SNMP agent software—most often, a server or router. The chief obligation of an SNMP agent is to fulfill the requests and tasks required of a management system. The only operation initiated by an agent is to collect data centering on an extraordinary event, such as a password violation, through the `trap` command. Only five types of commands are defined within SNMP:

- `GetRequest`

- `GetNextRequest`

- `GetResponse`

- `SetRequest`

- `Trap`

A MIB describes the objects, or entries, that are to be included in the SNMP agent database. SNMP agents are sometimes referred to as MIBs. An SNMP manager can request and collect information from an agents MIB. It can also inspect or alter the objects contained in it. The Microsoft SNMP service supports Internet MIB II, Lan Manager MIB II, DHCP MIB, and WINS MIB.

The two methods that Microsoft SNMP service management software can employ to collect information about devices are:

- To have devices send alerts to an SNMP manager, or to any other manger within the community

- To have the SNMP manager poll devices every few seconds, minutes, or hours

To use the SNMP service with a third-party manager, you must:

- Record the IP addresses and host names of participating hosts

- Add host name/IP address mappings to the appropriate name resolution resource

- Identify third-party management systems and Microsoft SNMP agents

An SNMP community is a group to which hosts running the SNMP service belong. A community parameter is simply the name of that group. An SNMP agent will not respond to a request from a management system outside its configured community, but it can be a member of multiple communities simultaneously.

The security available with SNMP is minimal. If your SNMP-managed network is connected to the Internet, or any public internetwork, a firewall should be in place to prevent intrusion from outside SNMP management consoles. When installing SNMP, keep the following security configuration options in mind:

- Send Authentication Trap

- Accepted Community Names

- Accept SNMP Packets from Any Host

- Only Accept SNMP Packets from These Hosts

Now that you've worked through this section, take a moment to review the following items:

- Explain the purpose of SNMP.

- Describe the different operations performed by an SNMP agent and an SNMP management system.

- Define the Management Information Base (MIB).

- Review the process for installing and configuring the Microsoft SNMP service.

Exercise Questions

Multiple-Choice Questions

1. Which MIBs are supported by Microsoft Windows NT?

A. Internet MIB II

B. Lan Manager MIB II

C. Microsoft WINS MIB

D. Microsoft LMHOSTS MIB

E. Microsoft DHCP MIB

2. What does the Microsoft SNMP service use to resolve a host name to an IP address?

A. LMHOSTS

B. HOST

C. DNS

D. p-node broadcast

E. b-node broadcast

F. WINS

3. What is the default community name?

A. public1

B. public

C. community

D. send agent

E. GetRequest

4. What is a MIB?

   A. An information base of errors

   B. An information base of packets sent to the default gateway

   C. A set of manageable objects representing device data

   D. A set of manageable objects representing network data

Scenario-Based Review

SCENARIO #1 You want to add SNMP to your NT workstation, but you don't want just anybody getting in and changing your MIBs. What security option should you put in place to stop SNMP packets from being tweaked by unwanted visitors?

SCENARIO #2 You've decided to install TCP/IP on your NT server. You also want to add SNMP for monitoring purposes. How do you do this?

SCENARIO #3 Your company's network manager has set up your NT workstation to respond to SNMP requests coming from an SNMP management system. While doing so, she told you all about the sort of stuff the management system will be requesting. What are the operations she told you will be requested by the SNMP management system?

Fine Tuning and Optimization

CHAPTER

12

THIS CHAPTER PROVIDES detailed information on Microsoft TCP/IP parameters that affect performance and optimization in an internetwork. Emphasis is placed on TCP sliding windows, how they work, and how the size of the sliding window can have the greatest impact on performance. Exercises peppered throughout will give you an opportunity to use Performance Monitor to oversee performance using various sliding window sizes, and to configure a NetBIOS scope ID to isolate NetBIOS traffic in an internetwork.

Objectives

ON THE OTHER side of this chapter, you should feel comfortable with the following items, and be able to perform the functions related to them.

- Identify the factors in a network environment that have the greatest effect on performance.

- Identify the goals in tuning TCP/IP for performance.

- Explain the effects a TCP window that is too small may have on performance.

- Explain the effects a TCP window that is too large may have on performance.

- Identify the TCP/IP parameters that affect performance and describe when and how to change them.

- Configure a scope ID to isolate NetBIOS traffic.

Factors That Affect Performance

I N MOST NETWORKING environments, Microsoft TCP/IP can dynamically tune and optimize itself. Tuning Microsoft TCP/IP parameters basically comes down to choosing the best values for a particular network's needs. Different factors need to be taken into consideration to enhance the performance of the individual network on which you are working. The key to making the proper choices in fine tuning a Microsoft TCP/IP network is a solid understanding of the different parameters, and the ramifications of utilizing them.

Here are some factors that can affect performance. All of these can be improved by adjusting certain Microsoft parameters:

FACTORS	EFFECT
Physical Topology	*Token ring* uses 4202 byte frames on a token-passing network. *Ethernet* uses 1514 byte frames on a contention-based topology. Because of this, more data can be transmitted with Token ring.
LAN/WAN	Data typically can run at around 10MB on a LAN (soon to be around 100), and usually only up to 1.544MB on a WAN.
Slow-link or *fast-link*	WAN data links average from 56kbs to 1.544kbs for a T1. WANs in the future will be over 2GB on Sonet.
Router throughput	Routers like Cisco's IGS or AGS have a small amount of Random-access memory (RAM) and slower CPUs. Routers need to look at the packets received to determine the destination network. If there isn't enough random-access memory on board, the router can delay sending out the packet to its final destination and the packet could *time-out*. Newer routers like Cisco's 4000 and 7000 series have more on-board random-access memory and faster processors and can therefore analyze and send out packets faster to the final destination.

FACTORS	EFFECT
Asynchronous	Terminal Emulation, like that seen with the Telnet program, makes a PC into a *dumb workstation* running *asynchronous data transmission* one character at a time.
Synchronous	Synchronous applications like FTP can typically transfer large chunks of synchronous data at one time. Frequent and large file transfers could require a large amount of buffers to receive the data.

Performance Tuning Goals

When working on a Microsoft NT TCP/IP environment, it's important to keep in mind that performance can be improved by eliminating delays, allowing data to be continuously transferred. For example, TCP requires an acknowledgment for the data it transmits, and must wait for it before transferring more data. If the sender has to wait for an acknowledgment after sending each segment of data, throughput will be low. Because time is available after the sender finishes transmitting the data segment, and before the sender finishes processing any received acknowledgment, the interval can be used for transmitting more. The number of data segments the sender is allowed to have outstanding without receiving an acknowledgment is known as the *window,* or *sliding windows*. The size of TCP sliding windows can have the greatest effect on this performance, but only when configured properly. Sliding windows will be discussed thoroughly in the next section.

Performance can also be improved on a TCP/IP host by keeping data from being retransmitted. Positive acknowledgment with retransmission is one technique that guarantees reliable delivery of data from one host to another. Positive acknowledgment requires the receiver to communicate with the source, sending back an acknowledgment message when it receives data. The sender keeps a record of each packet it sends and waits for an acknowledgment before sending the next packet. In addition, the sender also starts a timer when it sends a packet, and retransmits a packet if the timer expires before an acknowledgment for it arrives. If the router at which the packet is received is overworked, the packet could time-out and be retransmitted. Retransmissions can create a lot of traffic, taking up bandwidth and causing performance problems on the network.

Sliding Windows and How They Work

In a reliable, connection-oriented data transfer, the sequence of data segments must be delivered to the receiver in the same sequence that they were transmitted. TCP uses sliding windows to buffer data for transmission between two hosts. Each TCP/IP host maintains two sliding windows: one for receiving data, and the other for sending data. The size of the window indicates the amount of data that can be buffered on a computer. In Figure 12.1, sliding windows are used with a window size of one.

FIGURE 12.1

Sliding windows with a window size of one

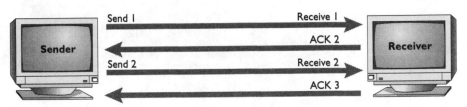

With a window size of one, the sender waits for an acknowledgment for every data segment that is transmitted. Notice that when the receiver receives Packet 1, the receiver acknowledges Packet 2. This lets the sending station know what the receiver is expecting next. When the receiver receives Packet 2, the host acknowledges Packet 3, and so on, until the transfer is complete.

In Figure 12.2, the window size is set for three.

FIGURE 12.2

Sliding windows with a window size of three

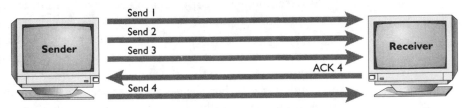

Notice that with a window size of three packets, the sender can transmit three data segments before expecting an acknowledgment. Also notice that after three packets, the host responds with an acknowledgment of four. During the TCP initial 3-way handshake, the size of the send window on each host is set to the size of the other host's receive window, unless the local send window is smaller than the destination receive window.

Figures 12.3 and 12.4 illustrate how sliding windows work on the sending and receiving hosts.

FIGURE 12.3

How sliding windows work on the transmitting host

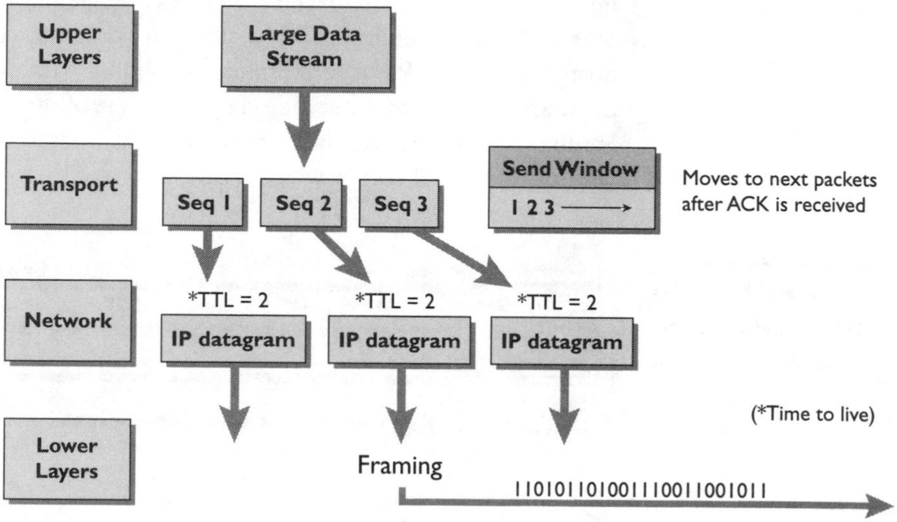

| Upper Layers | | Large Data Stream | | | | |

Send Window

Moves to next packets after ACK is received

1 2 3 ⟶

Transport

| Seq 1 | Seq 2 | Seq 3 |

*TTL = 2   *TTL = 2   *TTL = 2

Network

| IP datagram | IP datagram | IP datagram |

(*Time to live)

Lower Layers

Framing

11010110100111001100101I

TCP accepts a data stream from the upper layers, breaks large streams of data into smaller messages, sequences each message, and places this stream in a send window. TCP adds this information in the Transport layer's header, and then hands it down to IP to be formed into datagrams.

When TCP transmits each packet to IP, the TCP protocol sets a timer, specifying how long it'll wait for an acknowledgment (an ACK) before the packet is retransmitted. A copy of each packet remains inside the send window until an acknowledgment is received.

The sequence numbers that TCP adds to each message are used to put the message back together at the receiving end. An acknowledgment for each message is sent back to the transmitting host along with the status of the current window size. When the acknowledgment is returned and received by the transmitting host, the window slides (hence the name sliding windows) pass the acknowledged data to the remaining data stream waiting to be sent. If the transmitting host does not receive an acknowledgment within the time originally set, the packets will be resent. Retransmitting packets takes up precious bandwidth on the network.

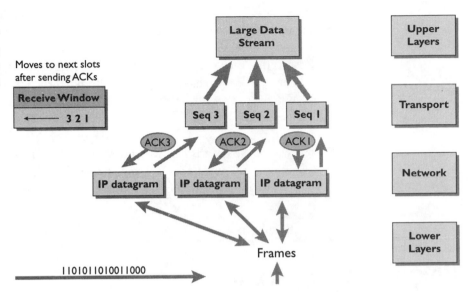

FIGURE 12.4

How sliding windows work on the receiving host

If by chance a packet does not reach the other side, as in Figure 12.5 (where packet 5 does not arrive at the destination), the receiving host acknowledges with a request to resend the missed packet. The transmitter must resend packet 5 and receive an acknowledgment before transmitting number 7.

FIGURE 12.5

Retransmitting

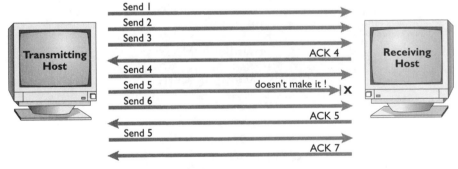

Some Specifics For Windows NT and Sliding Windows

Windows NT implements TCP sliding windows with a default window size of 8760, and with an acknowledgment of every two segments received. The delayed ACK timer is hard-coded for one-fifth of a second (200 milliseconds).

Windows NT 3.5 implements the *Van Jacobson Slow Start algorithm* to determine the initial retransmit timer value. When a host transmits a packet to a receiving host, the time it takes for the packet to get from the transmitting host to the receiving host, then back to the transmitting host with an acknowledgment, is known as the *Smoothed Round Trip Time (SRTT)*.

When a packet is transmitted from a host, an SRTT value is added to the segment. If an ACK is not received within the SRTT, the packet is retransmitted and the timer is set to two times the original SRTT. If an ACK is still not received, the packet is resent again, with the SRTT being set to four times the original. If still no ACK is received, it resends the packet. Resending the packet will be attempted a total of five times, taking approximately 16 seconds.

Performance Tuning

A S YOU ALREADY know, Microsoft TCP/IP dynamically tunes itself. So in most cases, changing parameters isn't necessary. However, in some networks, the following Registry parameters can be changed to affect the performance of your Microsoft host.

These parameters are:

- TcpWindowSize

- ForwardBufferMemory

- NumForwardPackets

- DefaultTTL

TcpWindowSize

The size of the sliding window that TCP uses to buffer data is determined by the TcpWindowSize parameter. On WANs with high bandwidth and low-delay links, large windows often lead to better performance. Since small windows can only be capable of buffering fewer than two segments, both the network and the computer can become bogged down, resulting in a higher frequency of ACKs being sent. On LANs, the window size doesn't affect performance much. The default window size is 8760 REG_DWORD for Ethernet. This parameter can be found in the \Tcpip\Parameters subkey.

ForwardBufferMemory

The amount of memory allocated for an IP router to store packets in the router queue is determined by the ForwardBufferMemory parameter. If a multihomed computer has a buffer that's too small, it can drop packets. The default value of 74,240 can accommodate storing 50 packets of 1,480 bytes each. If you require continuous transfers of large files, increasing this value could be necessary. If IPEnableRouter isn't implemented, this parameter will be ignored. It's found in the \Tcpip\Parameters (REG_DWORD) subkey.

NumForwardPackets

This parameter defines how many IP packet headers can be stored in an IP router packet queue. If packets are being dropped because an excessive amount of packets is overloading the router queue, the value of NumForwardPackets should be expanded. Slow links, and/or congestion at the router, is a common cause of this type of event. The default value is 50 packets (REG_DWORD). This parameter is in the \Tcpip\Parameters subkey, and is ignored if IPEnable-Router is not enabled.

DefaultTTL

This parameter determines how long a packet is allowed to live on the network before it's discarded. The packet's TTL (time to live) correspondingly decreases by the number of seconds the packet resides on each router, with a minimum of one second for each router that processes the packet. Increasing, the DefaultTTL on a network with many slow links can help to enable communications between the hosts they separate. The default value is 32 seconds (REG_DWORD). This parameter is also found in the \Tcpip\Parameters subkey.

The Registry parameters for TCP/IP are added in:

HKEY_LOCAL_MACHINE\SYSTEM\CurrentControlSet\Services

Once this type of parameter is added to the registry, it's easy to change its value. In Exercises 12.1 and 12.2, you'll learn how to add TCP/IP registry parameters and then change their values.

EXERCISE 12.1

Adding TCP/IP Parameters to the Registry

1. Start the Registry Editor.

2. Maximize the HKEY_LOCAL_MACHINE.

3. From this window, select \SYSTEM\CurrentControlSet\Tcpip\Parameters.

4. Select Edit ➤ Add Value.

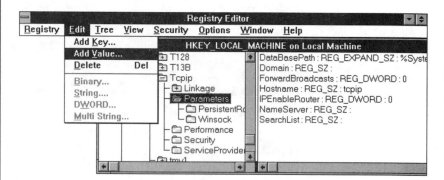

5. In the Add Value box, type **TcpWindowSize**.

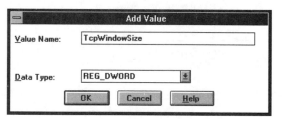

6. In the Data Type box, select REG_DWORD, and then choose OK. The DWORD Editor box will appear.

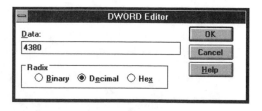

---

7. In the Radix box, choose Decimal.

8. In the Data box, type **4380** (the default is 8k). Click OK.

TcpWindowSize:REG_DWORD: 0x111c appears in the window.

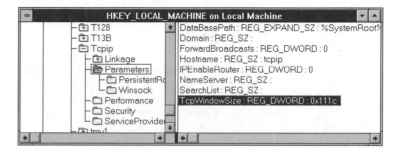

If you select the value before the Radix, the value will default to hexadecimal and then convert incorrectly.

9. Shut down and restart your computer.

EXERCISE 12.2

Changing an Existing TCP/IP Value in the Registry

1. Go to the Registry Editor and from the HKEY_LOCAL_MACHINE\System\ CurrentControlSet\Services\Tcpip\Parameters, find the value TcpWindowSize in the right pane.

2. Double-click on the parameter.

3. In the Data type Editor dialog box, type **2920** and then choose OK.

This will set the window size to 2920 bytes.

4. Shut down and restart your computer.

Some Guidelines for Optimizing Performance

THERE AREN'T ANY concrete, set rules for properly tuning parameters in a Microsoft NT TCP/IP network. These parameters will necessarily vary according to the needs of each individual network. Nevertheless, there are some important points to keep in mind that will help you optimize your TCP/IP network.

- Your goal should be to improve performance whenever possible, the exception being if you need to reduce memory usage.

- Use Performance Monitor to baseline your network. Find out what the normal manner of operation is for your network by running it at different times of the day, and keeping records. Look for patterns—find out where bottlenecks are, or where a potential bottleneck might occur, by using SNMP to gather statistics.

- Make only one change at a time to your parameters, noting the results. Monitor the network closely to discover how your changes are affecting its overall performance, while considering future needs and growth.

- Lastly, test, test, then test some more. Double check to make sure the change you made actually took affect, and if it made any difference. If your change didn't solve a certain problem or improve performance, try another parameter.

In Exercise 12.3, you'll practice doing some performance testing on your NT host. You'll learn how to use Performance Monitor to create a log, generate network traffic, then view the log file in chart form to determine a baseline for network traffic. The parameters for the default window size are assumed to be 2920, as set from the last exercise.

EXERCISE 12.3

Testing Performance Tuning on TCP/IP

1. First start Performance Monitor.

2. Select View ➤ Log.

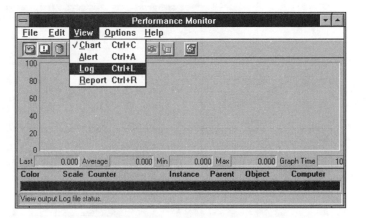

3. Next select Options ➤ Log. The Log Options box appears.

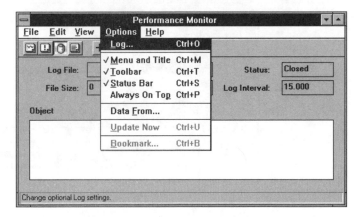

4. In the File Name box, type **TEST2.LOG** (2 for 2k byte window size).

5. In the Update Time box, change the Periodic Update to 2 seconds, and then choose OK.

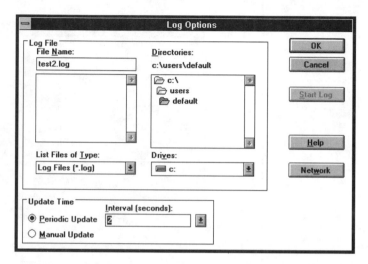

The Performance Monitor window appears with C:\USERS\DEFAULT\TEST2.LOG in the Log File box.

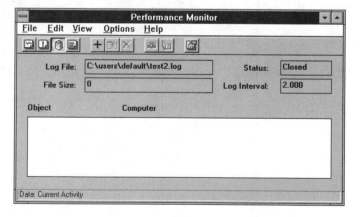

6. Choose Edit ➢ Add To Log. The Add to Log box appears.

7. Select Redirector in the Objects box, then choose Add.

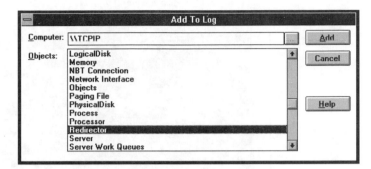

8. Choose Done.

9. Select Performance Monitor Option ≻ Log.

10. In the Log Options box, choose Start Log.

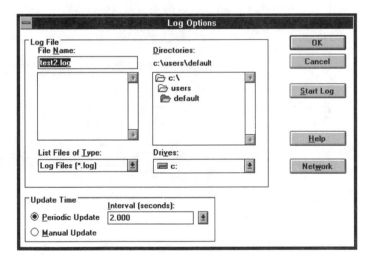

11. From the command prompt, create and run a batch file that will copy files from one directory to another. For example, type **Edit batch.bat**.

12. Next type **copy c:\users\default *.* c:\test** (this assumes you have some files in the default directory, and you have a c:\test directory).

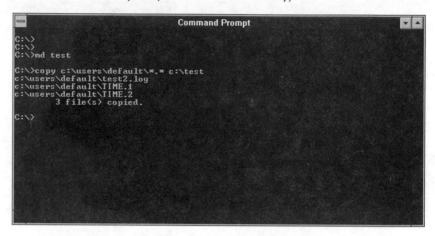

13. When the files have been copied, select Options ➣ Stop Log.

14. Next select Options ➣ Data From.

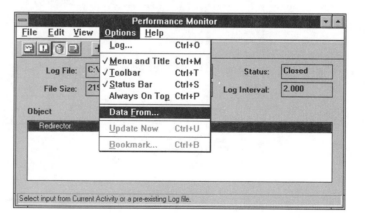

15. In the Data From box, select Log File, then choose the ellipsis button next to perfmon.log.

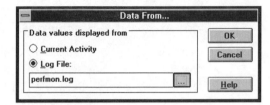

16. Select TEST2.LOG under File Name, then OK twice.

17. Choose View ➤ Chart.

18. Then select Edit Add To Chart. The Add to Chart box appears.

19. In the counter box, choose Bytes Received/sec, then Add.

20. Choose Done.

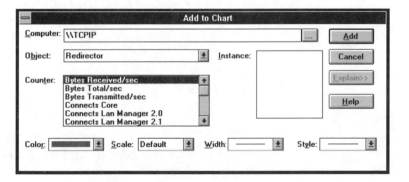

21. Document the average and maximum bytes per second that were transferred.

22. Change your TcpipWindowSize back to 4380, and then run through this exercise again, this time changing the name to TEST4.LOG.

23. Document the average and maximum bytes per second that was transferred.

24. Change your TcpipWindowSize to 8760 (the default) and then run through this exercise again, this time changing the name to TEST8.LOG.

25. Document the average and maximum bytes per second that was transferred.

As illustrated in the last exercise, Performance Monitor can be a very useful tool in troubleshooting TCP/IP problems on your network. Performance Monitor can also be used for monitoring many different settings in the TCP/IP suite if the SNMP services are installed on the computer. Some of the other settings that can be monitored are:

COUNTER TYPE	DESCRIPTION
Network Interface	The Network Interface counters describe the rates at which bytes and packets are sent and received over a network TCP/IP connection. They also describe various error counts for the same connection.
ICMP and IP	The ICMP and IP counters describe the rates at which ICMP messages and IP datagrams are sent and received on a host. They also describe various error counts for the ICMP protocol.
TCP and UDP	The TCP and UDP counters describe the rates at which TCP segments and UDP datagrams are sent and received on a host. The TCP counters also describe the number of TCP connections that are in each of the possible TCP connection states. The UDP counters also describe the various error counts for the UDP protocol.
NBT connection	This counter describes all NetBIOS over TCP/IP sessions, and the bytes sent and received over these connections.
DHCP, WINS, and FTP servers	These counters describe the rate of requests for services provided by the DHCP server service, WINS Server service, and Server service.

SNMP

As you recall from Chapter 11, if you're implementing SNMP as an internetwork management tool, the Microsoft SNMP service will automatically provide information on Internet MIB II, LAN Manager MIB II, WINS MIB, and DHCP MIB. This information can be useful in determining whether a host is active or inactive, how many connections there are, and how many NetBIOS name resolution requests have been successfully resolved.

NetBIOS Traffic Control

The way to stop NetBIOS traffic from being seen by everyone that has a browsing service is to create scope IDs. The NetBIOS scope ID is simply a group of characters that are added on to your NetBIOS name. The primary purpose of a NetBIOS scope ID is to isolate NetBIOS traffic on a single network. Using a NetBIOS scope will not decrease traffic on the network, but it will decrease packets that are accepted by a particular host. The NetBIOS scope ID on two hosts must match, or they won't be able to communicate with each other using NetBIOS over TCP/IP. Adding scope IDs to hosts allows you to use the same NetBIOS name on two hosts. Because the scope ID becomes part of the NetBIOS name, it makes the name unique.

Since adding a scope ID does not cut down on NetBIOS traffic, and you don't really want to have two hosts with the same NetBIOS name, why create scope IDs in the first place? The answer—security! It's not a miracle cure, or a perfect product, but it can prevent two computers sitting right next to each other from seeing each other on the network.

In Figure 12.6, two NetBIOS scopes are used to cut down on NetBIOS traffic. The two scopes named MNGR and ENGR can communicate with hosts in their scope, but not computers in the other scope. Notice that HOSTA.MNGR and HOSTA.ENGR are named the same, but with different scope IDs.

FIGURE 12.6

Isolating NetBIOS traffic

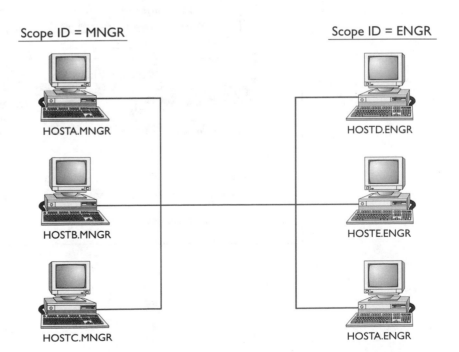

Scope ID = MNGR

Scope ID = ENGR

HOSTA.MNGR   HOSTD.ENGR

HOSTB.MNGR   HOSTE.ENGR

HOSTC.MNGR   HOSTA.ENGR

In Exercise 12.4, you'll learn how to create and activate a scope ID on an NT host.

EXERCISE 12.4

Configuring a NetBIOS Scope ID

1. Select Control Panel ➤ Network.

2. Choose TCP/IP from the Installed Network Software box, then choose Configure.

3. Choose Advanced in the TCP/IP Configuration box. The Advanced Microsoft TCP/IP Configuration box appears.

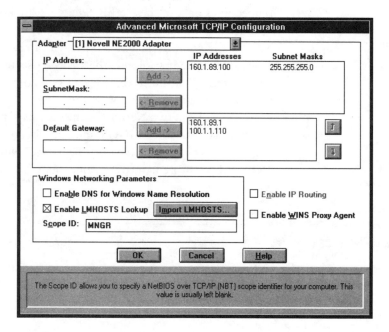

4. In the Scope ID box, type a character string that will append your NetBIOS name. Remember the scope ID must match with the other hosts you want to communicate with or they will not be able to see each other on the network.

5. Choose OK, and then Restart Now.

Summing Things Up

HOPEFULLY, YOU'VE LEARNED a thing or two about how to turn that Ol' Gray Mare of a network into a prize-winning thoroughbred—without the weak ankles! As the gates swung open, you found that tuning Microsoft TCP/IP parameters is about choosing the best values for an individual network's needs. There are several factors that need to be taken into consideration, all of which can be improved by adjusting certain Microsoft parameters. Factors that can affect performance are:

- Physical topology

- LAN/WAN

- Slow-link or fast-links

- Router throughput

- Asynchronous data transmission

- Synchronous data transmission

Performance can be improved on a TCP/IP host by keeping data from being retransmitted. Though it guarantees reliable delivery of data from one host to another, positive acknowledgment with retransmission can create a lot of traffic, taking up bandwidth and causing performance problems on the network. Performance can also often be improved by eliminating delays, allowing data to be continuously transferred. The interval between the transmission of a packet and processing the acknowledgment for receiving it can be used for transmitting more data. The number of data segments the sender is allowed to have outstanding without receiving an acknowledgment is known as the window, or sliding window. The size of TCP sliding windows varies. Each TCP/IP host maintains two sliding windows—one for receiving data and one for sending data. The size of the window indicates the amount of data that can be buffered on a computer. TCP accepts a data stream from the upper layers, breaks large streams of data into smaller messages, sequences each message, and places this stream in a send window. TCP then adds this information to the transport layers header, and then hands it down to IP to be formed into datagrams. For NT, the default window size is 8760, with an acknowledgment of every two segments received. The delayed-ACK timer is hard-coded for one-fifth of a second (200 milliseconds).

We also discussed the performance tuning Registry parameters that can be changed to positively affect the functioning of your Microsoft host.

TcpWindowSize   The size of the sliding window that TCP uses to buffer data

ForwardBufferMemory   The amount of memory IP allocates for an IP router to store packets in the router queue

NumForwardPackets   Defines how many IP packet headers can be stored in an IP router packet queue

DefaultTTL   Determines how long a packet is allowed to live on the network before it's discarded

You were then advised of some tips for optimizing a network's functioning:

- Improve performance whenever possible, barring the need to reduce memory usage.

- Use Performance Monitor to baseline your network.

- Find out what the normal manner of operation is for your network by running it at different times of the day, and keeping records.

- Look for patterns—find out where bottlenecks are, or where a potential bottleneck might occur by using SNMP to gather statistics.

- Make only one change at a time to your parameters, noting the results.

- Consider future networking needs and growth.

- Test, test, then test some more. Double-check to make sure the change you made actually took affect, and if it made any difference.

- If your change didn't solve a certain problem or improve performance, try another parameter.

Performance Monitor can be a very useful tool in troubleshooting TCP/IP problems on your network. Some of the other settings that can be monitored are:

- Network Interface

- ICMP and IP

- TCP and UDP

- NBT connection

- DHCP, WINS, and FTP servers

Approaching the home stretch, we discussed creating scope IDs to control NetBIOS traffic and keep it from being sent all over the network and seen by everyone that has a browsing service on. The NetBIOS scope ID is a group of characters that are added to a NetBIOS name. The NetBIOS scope ID on two hosts must match, or they won't be able to communicate with each other using NetBIOS over TCP/IP. Adding a scope ID affords the benefits of security by preventing two computers sitting right next to each other from being able to see each other on the network.

Exercise Questions

Multiple-Choice Questions

1. What TCP parameter do you set to control the size of the sliding window?

   A. DefaultTTL

   B. ForwardBufferMemory

   C. NumForwardPackets

   D. TcpWindowSize

   E. SizeWindowTcp

2. What happens to your host if you set the window too small?

   A. It can cause delays in transmission and create a higher number of ACKs.

   B. It will cause improvement in transmission rates.

   C. It will cause a smaller number of ACKs.

   D. It can cause improvement in transmission and create a smaller number of ACKs.

3. What happens to your host if you set the window too large?

    A. It can find packets that are lost.

    B. It can lose packets if routers become congested from too much data being transmitted.

    C. Your workstation will work faster from more data being received.

    D. Your workstation will work more slowly from more data being received.

4. In what hive do you set the TcpWindowSize?

    A. HKEY_LOCAL_MACHINE\SYSTEM\CurrentControlSet\Tcpip\Services\Parameters

    B. HKEY_LOCAL_MACHINE\SYSTEM\SetControlCurrent\Services\Tcpip\Parameters

    C. HKEY_LOCAL_MACHINE\SYSTEM\CurrentControlSet\Services\Tcpip\Parameters

    D. HKEY_LOCAL_MACHINE\SYSTEM\CurrentControlSet\Parameters\Services\Tcpip

Scenario-Based Review

SENARIO #1 Your workstation on the Microsoft TCP network seems to be working more slowly than when you first added TCP/IP onto it. After putting a network probe on the network, you see alot of ACKs coming from your workstation. What could the problem be, and how can you fix it?

SENARIO #2 Your Microsoft NT workstation with TCP/IP has been running fine for the last couple of weeks. However, this morning you notice sluggish response time from the server, and people around you are complaining. When looking at the router you notice the utilization is over 80 percent of average. What could the problem be, and how can you fix it?

Shooting Trouble

13

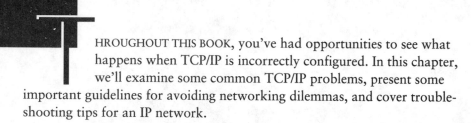

T HROUGHOUT THIS BOOK, you've had opportunities to see what happens when TCP/IP is incorrectly configured. In this chapter, we'll examine some common TCP/IP problems, present some important guidelines for avoiding networking dilemmas, and cover trouble-shooting tips for an IP network.

Objectives

B Y THE TIME you've reached the end of this chapter, you should be able to:

- Accurately identify common TCP/IP related problems.

- Use Microsoft Windows NT utilities to successfully diagnose TCP/IP related problems.

Getting to the Source

A LTHOUGH IT MAY certainly seem during a major network outage that you've found and are experiencing an entirely new, never before encountered network problem, 99% of the computer puzzles you'll experience on the job won't be new ones at all. Rest assured. It's highly likely your hand up isn't unique, but rather common—with a proven, successful method to lead you happily toward its solution. In the networking industry, contacts are your best friends, so the old adage of never burning your bridges at work strongly applies. The network world is a small world after all, and you just never know when you might need the insights of a former colleague!

When an outage occurs on a network large or small, time-honored problem solving strategies like staying calm, thinking logically, and the good ol' process of elimination also apply. Lots of network problems can be grouped into categories. It's important to understand these different categories, and then work deductively through them until the culprit's exposed. Many Microsoft TCP/IP-related problems can be grouped into the following categories:

SOURCE CATEGORY	TYPICAL ASSOCIATED PROBLEMS
Configuration	If your network configuration is incorrect, it can result in one or more services not starting when you bring up your NT workstation or server.
IP addressing	The host can hang when trying to communicate with other hosts. This could be caused by the existence of an improper subnet address or duplicate IP address. Windows NT will give you a pop-up message if there are duplicate IP addresses on your network.
Subnet addressing	Related to the above, if your host has an improper subnet address assigned to it, it may not be able to talk to other local or remote hosts.
Resolution	You can ping a host with an IP address, or connect to a network drive using a host's IP address, but you cannot establish a connection using only its host name.

The source of the problem implicates the problem itself. Identifying the source narrows down the field of possible causes, and expedites finding a solution. For example, if you ping to "Host Bob," and receive an error stating host unknown, you can then ping Host Bob from the host's IP address: 160.1.56.89. If the ping is successful, a resolution problem is the culprit, and you can begin troubleshooting the resolution methods used on your network. If the ping was unsuccessful, you can start troubleshooting Host Bob for connectivity issues.

Tools for Diagnosis

TCP/IP'S BEEN AROUND for quite a while, so there's a whole bunch of tools around to help you in troubleshooting problems related to it. Some of these tools can be used to locate the source, while others can be employed to track errors. Microsoft Windows NT includes plenty of utilities that can prove very helpful when attacking a TCP/IP network related problem.

The following TCP/IP tools are included with Microsoft NT:

TOOL	PURPOSE
PING	Ping is used to verify connections between hosts by sending ICMP echo packets to the specified IP address.
ARP	Used to gather hardware addresses of local hosts and your default gateway. You can view the ARP cache and check for invalid or duplicate entries.
NETSTAT	You can check your current connections and protocol-related statistics of your TCP/IP host.
NBTSTAT	Reports statistics and connections for NetBIOS over TCP/IP
IPCONFIG	The Ipconfig command displays TCP/IP configuration settings for a host. This utility is particularly useful when the host obtains address information dynamically from DHCP, or a host name from WINS.
TRACERT	TRACERT is a route-reporting utility that sends ICMP echo requests to an IP address, and reports ICMP errors that are returned. TRACERT produces a report that lists all of the routers crossed in the process.
ROUTE	Used to view or modify the local routing table
SNMP	Simple Network Management Protocol is used to remotely manage network devices by collecting, analyzing, and reporting data about the performance of network components.

TOOL	PURPOSE
EVENT LOG	You can use the Event log to track errors and certain noteworthy events.
PERFORMANCE	Performance Monitor is a versatile tool that can be used to analyze MONITOR performance and detect bottlenecks. Remember, Microsoft SNMP must be enabled on a host in order to monitor TCP/IP counters.
REGISTRY EDITOR	The Registry is the fault-tolerant database in which configuration data is stored for Windows NT. REGEDIT32 is the editor that allows you to browse and edit the configuration of the host.

General Guidelines to Follow

WHEN FACED WITH a troubleshooting dilemma, it's a good idea to keep some simple guidelines in mind to help you stay focused. In a difficult, high pressure situation, they can prevent you from duplicating your efforts. Often, in a "network down" predicament, people panic and just start recklessly resetting routers, rebooting servers, and so on. After these attempts, when the network still doesn't function, they call on someone else, who then enters the situation and begins resetting routers and rebooting servers—taking up critical time with redundant approaches, and getting everyone nowhere fast! It's so important to approach these often complicated quandaries in a sensible, logical manner—with a plan, so if you do get stumped, you can turn the problem over to someone and equip them with organized knowledge of exactly what you've already done. Also important is to document the error and solution path for other colleagues who may come across that very problem again later. Figure 13.1 shows the different layers of the DOD reference model and the different protocols related to each layer. A firm understanding of the different layers and the protocols that are specified at each layer will help you intelligently troubleshoot network problems—and make you sound smart in meetings too!

FIGURE 13.1

Protocols at each
layer of the Internet
Protocol suite

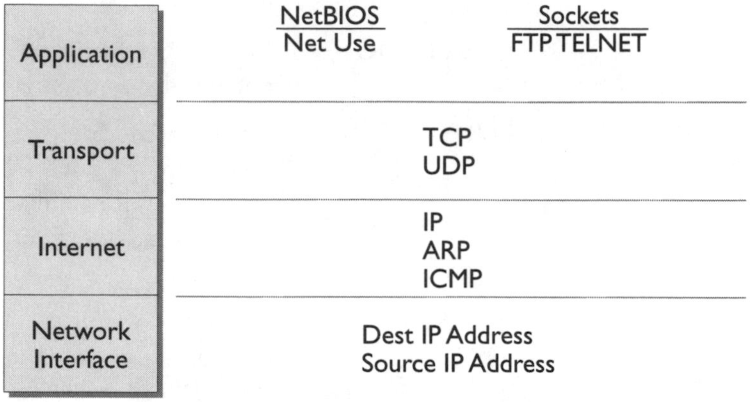

| Application | NetBIOS / Net Use | Sockets / FTP TELNET |

```
              ┌──────────────┐   NetBIOS        Sockets
              │ Application  │   Net Use        FTP TELNET
              ├──────────────┤
              │              │        TCP
              │  Transport   │        UDP
              ├──────────────┤
              │              │        IP
              │   Internet   │        ARP
              │              │        ICMP
              ├──────────────┤
              │   Network    │   Dest IP Address
              │  Interface   │   Source IP Address
              └──────────────┘
```

Using Figure 13.1 as a troubleshooting guide, let's say that a user calls complaining that they can't log on to the NT domain. Begin by analyzing the bottom layer of the DOD model, working up through the model to the Application layer until a likely problem source is established. You must determine that the protocols at each layer of the TCP/IP suite can communicate with those operating at the layers above and below.

- First, try to ping the device in question. If you can ping the host, then you have verified IP communication between the Network Interface layer and the Internet layer. Why? Because Ping uses ARP (Address Resolution Protocol) to resolve the IP address to a hardware address. If pinging worked, then the resolution was successful, meaning the culprit isn't in the lower layers.

- Next, try to either Telnet or Net Use to the host. If you can establish a session, you have successfully verified TCP/IP communication from the Network Interface layer through the Application layer. At this point you will have to go to the host in question to find out what the user is typing in. The problem can sometimes be something as simple as a domain name being spelled incorrectly.

- If you are unable to resolve the problem, try using a network analyzer like Network General's Sniffer, or Microsoft Network Monitor to help you discover the problem.

Verifying IP Communications

Pinging a host is a very popular way of troubleshooting problems. It can be a great place to start—sometimes leading you straight to the problem. If you can ping a host on a remote network, you have verified connectivity through routers, gateways, bridges, and possibly other network devices. That's a pretty good test. Your first weapon when trouble strikes is to try to ping the host. If pinging the host by its host name doesn't work, then try pinging with the host's IP address. If pinging is successful when using just the IP address, then you have a resolution problem.

Here are some general guidelines to keep in mind when pinging a host:

- First, ping the local host address of 127.0.0.1. This will tell you if the host can see itself on the network, and whether TCP/IP is loaded correctly.

- Next, ping your IP address to check the correct configuration. If this doesn't work, select Control Panel ➢ Network, and check for IP address, subnet, and default gateway entry errors.

- If you're successful pinging your own IP address, ping the default gateway next. If this doesn't work, check your configuration again, and then check to make sure the router is up and working.

- Next, ping the IP address of a remote host located on the other side of the router to verify that the router and WAN is working correctly. If this doesn't work, make sure that IP routing is enabled on all router interfaces. (Typically this is on by default, but someone could have accidentally disabled it.) Also, make sure the remote host is up and functioning.

If all is successful and all problems seem to be fixed, throw caution to the wind and try pinging the host by its host name. If things still aren't working, it's time to troubleshoot your resolution methods, like the HOSTS file, WINS, LMHOSTS and DNS. Refer to previous chapters if you get stuck.

Verifying TCP/IP Session Communications

After you ping your network to death and fix the problem, or find that all is well, the next step is to establish a session with the remote host. You can use a few different methods to verify communication between the Network Interface layer and the Application layer.

- To connect to a host using it's NetBIOS name, make a connection using the NET USE or NET VIEW command. An example would be NET USE G: \\Alpine\share. If this isn't successful, make sure you're using the correct NetBIOS name, or that the host even has a NetBIOS name. Also, make sure the destination host is in your LMHOSTS file (entered correctly) if the destination host is located on a remote network.

- If you're still having problems connecting with the NetBIOS name, it's time to check Scope IDs. Each host can be given an extension on their NetBIOS name to keep hosts from seeing each other on the network. Check to make sure that the Scope ID is the same as yours.

- To connect to a host that is not NetBIOS-based, use the Telnet or FTP utility to make a connection. If by chance this was unsuccessful, make sure the remote host has TCP/IP running, and that it also has a Telnet or FTP daemon running. Additionally, make sure you have the correct permission on the remote host to enable you to perform Telnet or FTP. If you're still unsuccessful, check your HOSTS file to make sure the entry for the remote host is correct.

Summing Things Up

NETWORK PROBLEMS CAN be grouped into categories. Solid problem solving skills begin with an understanding of the different categories, and how to work deductively through them until the culprit's exposed. Microsoft TCP/IP-related problem categories are:

- Configuration

- IP addressing

- Subnet addressing

- Resolution

Remember—the source of the problem implicates the problem itself. Therefore, identifying the source narrows down the field of possible causes and expedites finding a solution.

Microsoft Windows NT includes plenty of utilities that can prove very helpful when attacking a TCP/IP network-related problem. Some of these tools can be used to locate the source, while others can be employed to track errors. They are:

- PING

- ARP

- NETSTAT

- NBTSTAT

- IPCONFIG

- TRACERT

- ROUTE

- SNMP

- EVENT LOG

- PERFORMANCE

- MONITOR

- REGISTRY EDITOR

Next, we explored some general guidelines to keep in mind when going after nasty network gremlins. The basic key to success is to approach networking puzzles in a logical manner—with a plan, so if you get stumped, you can turn the problem over to someone who knows what you've already done. It's important to document the problem and the solution path for other colleagues who may come across it later. Your order of defense is as follows:

- First, try to ping the device in question. If you can ping the host, then you have verified IP communication between the Network Interface layer and the Internet layer.

- Next, try to either Telnet or Net Use to the host. If you can establish a session, you have successfully verified TCP/IP communication from the Network Interface layer through the Application layer.

- If you are unable to resolve the problem, try using a network analyzer like Network General's Sniffer, or Microsoft Network Monitor to help you discover the problem.

General guidelines to keep in mind when pinging a host:

- First, ping the localhost address of 127.0.0.1. This will tell you if the host can see itself on the network, and whether TCP/IP is loaded correctly.

- Next, ping your IP address to check the correct configuration. If this doesn't work, select Control Panel ➤ Network, and check for IP address, subnet, and default gateway entry errors.

- If you're successful pinging your own IP address, ping the default gateway next. If this doesn't work, check your configuration again, and then check to make sure the router is up and working.

- Next, ping the IP address of a remote host located on the other side of the router to verify that the router and WAN are working correctly.

The next step is to establish a session with the remote host. You can use the following methods to verify communication between the Network Interface layer and the Application layer:

- To connect to a host using its NetBIOS name, make a connection using the NET USE or NET VIEW command. An example would be NET USE G: \\Alpine\share.

- If this isn't successful, make sure you're using the correct NetBIOS name, and that the host has a NetBIOS name.

- Also, make sure the destination host is in your LMHOSTS file, and entered correctly if the destination host is located on a remote network.

- If you're still having problems connecting with the NetBIOS name, check scope IDs.

- To connect to a host that is not NetBIOS-based, use the Telnet or FTP utility to make a connection.

- If unsuccessful, make sure the remote host has TCP/IP and a Telnet or FTP daemon running.

- Make sure you have the correct permission on the remote host to enable you to perform Telnet or FTP.

- Check your HOSTS file to make sure the entry for the remote host is correct.

Exercise Questions

Multiple-Choice Questions

1. Which utility in TCP/IP communications is used to check connectivity between the Network Interface layer and the Internet layer?

   A. ARP

   B. NETSTAT

   C. PING

   D. NBTSTAT

2. What are two popular ways to troubleshoot a TCP/IP host problem?

   A. PING

   B. NETSTAT /a

   C. Establish a session

   D. NBSTAT /r

3. What does NBTSTAT do?

   A. Verify that TCP/IP is configured correctly and that another host is available.

   B. Check the state of current NetBIOS over TCP/IP connections.

   C. Browse and edit the parameter configurations.

   D. View the ARP cache to detect invalid entries.

Scenario-Based Review

SCENARIO #1 Your Windows NT workstation cannot talk to a host in another building, but it works locally. Your co-workers' workstations are working fine. What is the troubleshooting step you should take?

SCENARIO #2 Your Windows NT workstation cannot talk on the network either locally or remotely. What are the troubleshooting steps you should take?

SCENARIO #3 You have just installed TCP/IP and cannot ping hosts by their NetBIOS name on your network. Your IP address, subnet mask, and default gateway are correct. What is the problem?

SCENARIO #4 When pinging any host on your network, you get a `request timed out` message. You check your configuration in the local host and your IP address is `201.89.57.37`. Your subnet mask is `255.255.0.0`, and your default gateway is `201.89.57.1`. What is the problem?

SCENARIO #5 When starting your Windows NT hosts, the following message appears:

```
At least one service or driver failed during system
startup. Use Event Viewer to examine the event log for
details.
```

What could the problem be?

SCENARIO #6 When attempting to connect to a server by it's host name, you get the following message:

```
network path was not found
```

What could the problem be?

SCENARIO #7 When trying to connect to a host on another network, you receive the following error message:

```
The network path was not found.
```

You can connect to all hosts on your local network. What is the problem?

SCENARIO #8 You are copying large files from a server to your workstation and it is extremely slow. All other hosts are fine. What is the problem?

Microsoft NT 4.0

NTRODUCING...MICROSOFT NT Version 4.0! This snappy upgrade has made a good thing even better, and this chapter will not only provide a complete overview of 4.0, it'll give you the skinny on what the important changes are. As you've probably noticed, regardless of which Windows operating platform you use, the configuration is very similar. There are two types of Windows interfaces available: The Windows NT 3.5x interface that you've been studying so far in this book, and the Windows 95-style interface which you will soon be reading about. In terms of changes to existing utilities, differences between Windows NT 3.5x and Windows NT 4.0 are very minor. The greatest changes are found in the arena of new tools like 4.0's DNS or Web server enhancements. When reading this section, keep in mind that TCP/IP is a collection of protocols that must meet standard requirements in order to communicate with other hosts. Therefore, most of what you'll be presented with that contrasts the 3.5x implementation of TCP/IP can be met through third-party software suppliers. To avoid confusion about the two interfaces, we've created a separate section exclusively for Windows NT 4.0 which follows the same context order as the 3.5x portion of the book.

Objectives

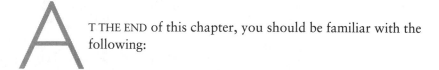

T THE END of this chapter, you should be familiar with the following:

- TCP/IP with Windows NT 4.0
- IP Routing

- IP Filtering
- Name Resolution
  - NetBIOS
  - WINS
  - DNS
- DNS Server
- DHCP Relay
- SNMP
- Microsoft Internet Information Server
- Internet Server Manager
  - FTP
  - Gopher
  - WWW
  - Key Manager

TCP/IP with Windows NT 4.0

THE CREATION OF the popular Windows 95 interface began a new era in software development. Windows NT 4.0, with its Windows 95-like interface, is much easier to use than Windows NT 3.5x. If you're at all accustomed to the Windows 95 interface, navigating and customizing NT will be a snap! The reason for creating the new user interface was to provide some organization to make it easier for people to multitask on the job. While the internal programs have undergone a facelift, they're still essentially the same interface. Considering the differences between Windows 3.1x and Windows 95, it may come as a surprise that Windows NT 3.5*x* is already a 32-bit operating system. The transition between the two interfaces is therefore mostly cosmetic, with the exception of 4.0's additional utilities. To ease administrative burdens, a Network Monitor for analyzing and capturing network traffic is now included, along with an enhanced Task Manager that provides memory and processor utilization at a glance. The existing Diagnostics tool has been improved, and now displays information about device drivers, network usage, and system resources in a more straightforward manner. Administrative wizards automate the most common management tasks, such as adding user accounts. There are also wizards for adding or removing programs, modems, and printers.

The above graphic illustrates one of the differences between the NT 3.5*x* and 4.0 interfaces: The START button shows up in Windows NT 4.0 in the side bar.

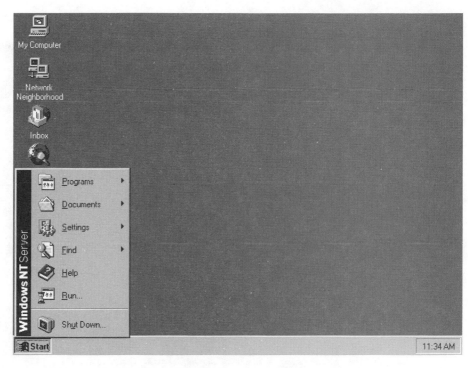

To configure TCP/IP addresses under Windows NT 4.0, select Start ➤ Settings ➤ Control Panel ➤ Network.

Once selected, a menu will appear with tabs at the top of the screen.

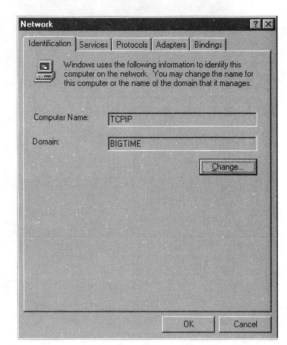

Note that the configuration buttons that were previously on the configuration screen are now tabs located along the top of the screen.

When you begin managing Windows NT, your first question may be, "Where have all the 3.5x TCP/IP add-ons gone?" Table 14.1 shows where TCP/IP is configured in NT 4.0.

TABLE 14.1 Windows NT 3.5x and 4.0 TCP/IP Configuration	**WINDOWS NT 3.5X**	**WINDOWS NT 4.0**
	Connectivity utilities	Automatic with TCP/IP installation
	SNMP Service	Services tab
	TCP/IP Network Printing Support	Services tab - Microsoft TCP/IP Printing
	FTP Server Services	Services tab - Microsoft Peer Web Services
	Simple TCP/IP Services	Services tab
	DHCP Server Services	Services tab
	WINS Server Services	Services tab

Let's take a look at the tab screens under the Network icon.

The Identification tab appears whenever you double-click on the Network icon in Control Panel. Windows uses the information in the Identification tab screen to identify a particular computer on the network. You can change the name for the computer, or the name of the domain it logs into or manages. The Services tab lists the network services installed on your computer. Clicking on a service allows you to view or change its properties, or to remove or update it. Just click the appropriate button for the function you wish to view or change. Network services supports the network operations performed by Windows NT. One type of service enables you to share your files and printers with other people on the network. Examples of other services are automatic system backup, remote registry, and network monitor support.

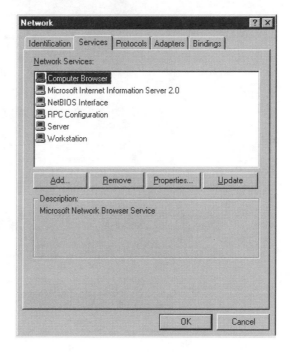

The Protocols tab lists the protocols that are installed on your computer. Clicking on one of them allows you to view or change its properties, or to remove or update it. Again, just click the appropriate button for the protocol you wish to modify. Remember—protocols designate the language a computer uses to communicate over a network. Computers must speak the same language—they must use the same protocol to be able to communicate with each other.

In the Protocols tab, TCP/IP can be installed, if it isn't already, by clicking on the Add button and then selecting TCP/IP Protocol from the list of protocols.

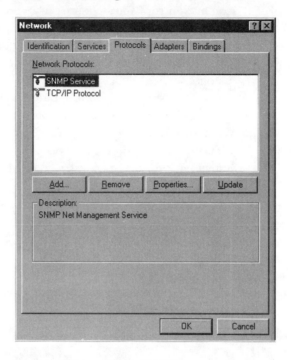

In Exercise 14.1, you'll install the TCP/IP protocol.

EXERCISE 14.1

Installing TCP/IP on Windows NT 4.0

1. Double-click on the Network icon, and choose the Protocol tab.

2. Click on Add…, then choose TCP/IP Protocol from the list of protocols.

EXERCISE 14.1 (CONTINUED FROM PREVIOUS PAGE)

3. Click on Properties.

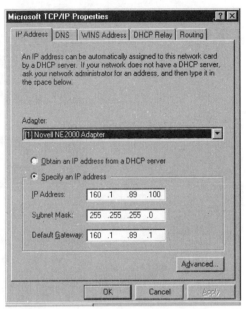

You'll promptly be notified that TCP/IP can be dynamically configured if a DHCP server is available on your network.

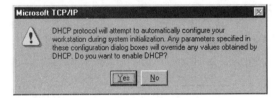

4. Choose No.

5. Type in your IP address, subnet mask, and default gateway.

6. Click on OK.

From this point, you'll proceed just as if you were under Windows NT 3.5*x*, except that additional options can be opened up by selecting the Advanced button, which is located on the IP Address tab page.

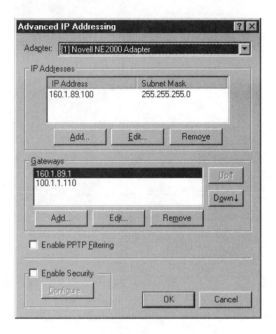

Clicking on the Advanced button will open a dialog box where you're allowed to assign additional IP addresses and gateways; enable a special type of filtering called PPTP, which we'll discuss later; and configure security options. You control the address entries by clicking on the Add, Edit, and Remove buttons. Each additional IP address will require a subnet mask companion. Additional IP addresses can only be added if DHCP is *not* enabled on your client, otherwise, a message will appear in the IP box stating that DHCP is enabled. Depending on the order in which you access your various networks, you'll want to use the Move buttons to place each Gateway address according to the most used at the highest location. When you work with these addresses, click on the IP address itself to select it for editing or removal. Clicking on the line, a blank space, or a subnet mask won't work.

The Adapters tab lists the adapters installed on your computer. Click an adapter to view or change its properties or remove or update the card, then click the appropriate button. An adapter is the hardware device that physically connects your computer to the network.

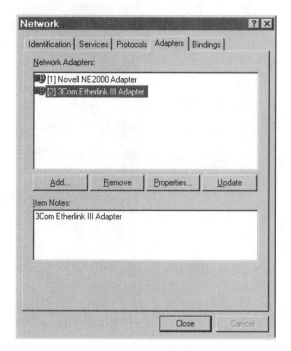

Network bindings are connections between network cards, protocols, and the services that are installed on your computer. You can use the Bindings tab to disable network bindings or to arrange the order in which the computer finds information on the network. Click a binding path in the list, then click the appropriate button to enable or disable the binding, or to move up or move down the binding. A red symbol at the left of a binding indicates that all connections for that binding are disabled.

IP Routing with Windows NT 4.0

ROWING RIGHT ALONG with the rapidly expanding Internet, intra-nets and distributed client/server computing is the order for inex-pensive, easily operated routing support across both LANs and WANs. The word routing makes most folks think of special hardware-based, costly devices. Though hardware-based routers are indispensable for many, as a company grows its routing needs often change. This can sometimes mean replacing its present router, and trading it in for a more powerful model—an expensive undertaking at best! Many times, other important considerations come into play as well. This brings up another great feature of Windows NT—its routing capability. Just adding the appropriate LAN/WAN card or cards to a Windows NT Server allows you to configure it as a router! The Windows NT

Multi-Protocol Routing service provides flexible and economical routing solutions that answer the call for costly, dedicated routers. RIP for TCP/IP, RIP for Internetwork Packet Exchange (IPX), and the BootP relay agent for DHCP combine to make up *MPR (Multi-Protocol Router)* in Windows NT. A Windows NT router employs the BootP relay agent for the task of forwarding DHCP requests along to DHCP servers located on other subnets. Because of this, one DHCP server can service many IP subnets, making MPR a terrific, cost-effective solution for evolving organizations in need of high performance routing support. Because Windows NT machines normally don't behave as routers, MPR must be installed after TCP/IP onto your 3.5*x* or 4.0 computer.

MPR is part of the Windows NT Server and Windows NT Workstation Version 4.0 package. You can get your hands on MPR for Windows NT Version 3.51 from ftp.microsoft .com. It's included in Service Pack 3 and later under the MPR directory. When used for routing, Windows NT Version 3.5 or earlier doesn't provide support for RIP.

In Exercise 14.2, you'll practice enabling RIP routing.

EXERCISE 14.2

Enabling RIP Routing

1. Double-click on the Network icon, and choose the Services tab.

2. Choose Add, and then RIP for Internet Protocol.

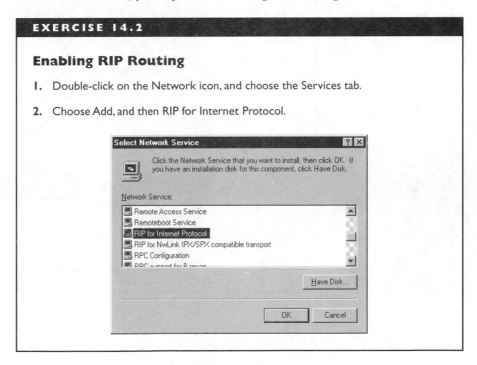

EXERCISE 14.2 (CONTINUED FROM PREVIOUS PAGE)

3. Insert the path to the distribution files and then choose Continue.

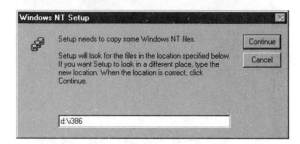

4. Go to the Protocol tab, and choose Properties on TCP/IP.

5. Choose the Routing tab, and click Enable IP Forwarding.

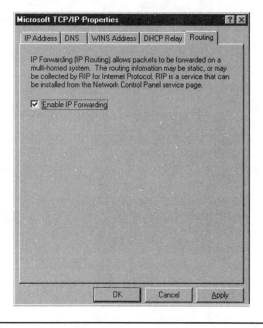

Selecting this option should only be done if you have two or more network cards, and your network uses dynamic RIP routing. This is a big change from the way NT 3.5*x* handled the task of routing IP packets by default. Because an NT multihomed host is able to exchange information with RIP routers, the multihomed host can be aware of remote networks. It's thereby equipped to deliver packets destined for remote hosts without the tedious task of adding static routes—definitely cause for celebration!

IP Filtering in Windows NT 4.0

THE ADVANCED SECTION under TCP/IP Protocol Configuration in the Network Control panel also has the ability to perform some of the security tasks typically handled at a firewall, or router. The first security measure we'll explore involves the Point-to-Point Tunneling Protocol (PPTP). Point-to-Point Tunneling Protocol (PPTP) is a recently developed tool that supports multiprotocol Virtual Private Networks (VPN). It works by enabling users to both remotely and securely access corporate networks via the Internet. Virtual Private Networks is a new feature to Windows NT that's installed as a service. Using PPTP, remote users are able to use Microsoft Windows 95 and Windows NT Workstation systems, dial into a local Internet service provider, and achieve a secure connection into their corporate network.

This feature is obviously quite handy for those who telecommute. Folks who travel a lot or work from home and require access to their corporation's networks can use PPTP to remotely check their e-mail and perform other important job-related tasks. Instead of dialing long distance for remote access into the company network, they can simply dial a local number using PSTN, ISDN, or X.25 to obtain an Internet service provider *point of presence*. Their PPTP session provides a secure connection via the Internet back to the corporate network. For example, take Renee, a user working in Paris, France who needs to work with a database on an NT 4.0 Server in Los Angeles, California. To achieve her goal, she would simply need to make a local call in Paris to access the Internet and then be connected to the corporate server in Los Angeles. Easy!

PPTP is also economical to implement. Doing so doesn't require any changes to the network addressing that's already in place. This is accomplished by Virtual WAN support, using PPTP over IP backbones. PPTP is also quite flexible because it supports multiple protocols like IP, IPX, and NetBEUI. So being, it can be used to access a whole salad of various LAN infrastructures. Though Microsoft intends to provide PPTP support for Windows 95, it's included free of charge in Windows NT Server 4.0 and Windows NT Workstation 4.0—such a deal!

Exercise 14.3 will help you install the PPTP driver onto your host.

EXERCISE 14.3

Installing the Microsoft PPTP Driver

1. Go to the Control Panel and double-click on the Network icon.

2. Next click on the Protocols tab.

3. Choose Microsoft PPTP Driver, and then click Add.

4. Choose OK.

5. Type the path to the distribution files and then choose OK.

6. Enter the number of connections (VPN's) you want available to PPTP.

This is a very cool technology you can use to create a multiprotocol, Virtual Private Network which allows secure access to your network from the Internet. With it, you can enable filtering on PPTP, allowing you to limit network access simply by clicking on Enable PPTP Filtering. Doing so disables communications for the network adapter with all other protocols except PPTP.

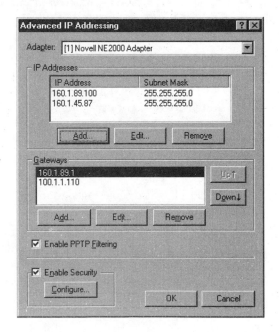

If you select Enable Security and then choose the Configure button, you'll have access to the Advanced Security Configuration button. You'll then be presented with a set of three lists—TCP Ports, UDP Ports, and IP Protocols. Each of these lists have the options available to Permit All or Permit Only, allowing you to specify the TCP, UDP, and IP protocol entries to be passed. These numbers can be found in the services and protocol files located in winroot\system32\drivers\etc\protocol files. Both the UDP and TCP entries use the services file; the IP entries use the protocol file. The only awkward thing about the configuration of this security section is that all blocks are inclusive only. This means you can include all entries that use a specified port, but you can't single out a particular entry and exclude it. You're stuck with including all of them. Use the Add and Remove buttons to control the lists. Exercise 14.4 will demonstrate how to install PPTP filtering.

EXERCISE 14.4

Installing PPTP Filtering

1. Double-click on the Network icon in the Control Panel.

2. Chose the Protocols tab.

3. Choose TCP/IP Protocol.

4. Click on Properties.

5. If using more then one IP address, make sure to click on the correct IP address, and then choose Advanced.

6. In the adapter box, choose the adapter for which you want to provide PPTP filtering.

7. Click on Enable PPTP Filtering.

8. Restart the computer.

Name Resolution

OU WILL READ about two Windows NT Server services that can manage all name resolution issues. You will also read about two types of names, NetBIOS and DNS. Windows NT network applications use a naming convention known as NetBIOS. In general, NetBIOS computer names consist of a single part. TCP/IP protocols rely on the DNS naming convention. DNS computer names consist of two parts: A computer name and a domain name, which combine to make the Fully Qualified Domain Name (FQDN).

NetBIOS names can be made compatible with DNS computer names, making interoperation possible between the two. Windows NT combines the NetBIOS computer name with the DNS domain name to form the FQDN.

DNSNetBIOS

Network Basic Input\Output System (NetBIOS) defines a software interface and a naming convention—not a protocol. The NetBIOS namespace is flat, meaning that all names within a network must be unique. Resources are identified by NetBIOS names that are registered dynamically when computers start, services start, or users log on. A NetBIOS Name Query is used to locate a resource by resolving the name to an IP address. They're 15 characters long—16 if you include the type—and both Windows NT 3.5x and 4.0 machines use the same methods for NetBIOS name resolution. Again, if this or other NetBIOS-related issues are cloudy in your mind, refer to Chapter 6 to clear things up.

WINS

Windows Internet Name Service (WINS) is a NetBIOS name service. When a Windows NT computer is configured as h-node (the default for WINS clients), it attempts to use a WINS Server for name registration and resolution first. If that fails, it resorts to subnet broadcasts, the HOSTS file, LMHOSTS, etc.

Using WINS for name services dramatically reduces the number of IP broadcasts used by Microsoft network clients. WINS is especially helpful on DHCP-enabled networks. One of the DHCP-provided parameters can be the address of a WINS Server. When this is so, as soon as the client is configured by DHCP, it registers its name and address with the WINS Server, making it easy to locate by the other computers on the network. This combination of DHCP and WINS is ideal for dynamic situations.

Both Windows NT 3.5*x* and 4.0 use the same system for WINS resolution. If there are still questions floating around in your mind regarding WINS resolution, thumb back to Chapter 8 for a second dose.

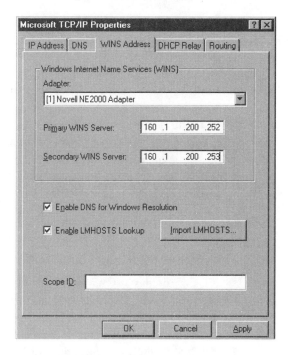

The graphic above shows the WINS Address tab. Following is an explanation of the selections you can make.

- The WINS Address tab allows you to pick a primary WINS Server and a secondary WINS Server. This permits you to use WINS protocol in combination with name query broadcasts to resolve computer names to IP addresses.

- If you want to use Domain Name System (DNS) for NetBIOS name resolution on Windows networks, simply select Enable DNS for Windows Resolution. This option uses the IP address specified in the TCP/IP Connectivity Configuration dialog box to identify the DNS Server.

- Select Enable LMHOSTS Lookup to use the LMHOSTS file for name resolution. Click Import LMHOSTS to specify the location of the LMHOSTS file to import.

- Type in the computer's scope identifiers, if for some god-knows-what reason you are using scope IDs. To be able to communicate, all computers on a TCP/IP internetwork must have the same scope ID. Usually this value is left blank. The network's administrator should provide the correct value for this parameter.

DNS

The Windows NT-based DNS server provides connectivity between WINS and DNS. In addition to providing an RFC-compliant DNS service, the Windows NT-based DNS server can pass through an unresolved DNS name query to a WINS Server for final name resolution. This occurs transparently—the client doesn't need to be aware of whether a DNS or a WINS Server processed the name query. In a Windows NT-based network that's running both DNS and WINS Servers, you can perform something called *forward look-up* (IP address resolution using a friendly NetBIOS or DNS name), and *reverse look-up* (NetBIOS or DNS name resolution using an IP address).

Dynamic WINS and Static DNS

WINS provides a dynamic, distributed database for registering and querying dynamic NetBIOS name-to-IP address computer mappings. DNS provides a static, distributed database for registering and querying static, FQDN name-to-IP address mappings.

DNS depends on static files for name resolution, and doesn't yet support dynamic name and IP address mapping updates. In other words, DNS requires the static configuration of IP addresses to perform name-to-IP-address mapping. WINS supports DHCP's dynamic allocation of IP addresses, and can resolve a NetBIOS computer name to a dynamic IP address mapping.

DNS Server

D NS IS THE traditional and widely-used name resolution service for the Internet and other TCP/IP networks. Windows NT Server Version 4.0 has expanded support for DNS by implementing a DNS Server. DNS and NetBIOS names are similar in that they're user-friendly names for computers and other network devices. However, as discussed earlier, the DNS name is based on a hierarchical naming structure that's more flexible than the flat structure of NetBIOS names. DNS computer names consist of two parts—a host name and a domain name—which when combined, form the fully qualified domain name, or *FQDN*. A DNS name can be as long as 255 characters, while the NetBIOS name is limited to 15 user-definable characters. Under Windows NT, the DNS host name defaults to the NetBIOS computer name. Windows NT combines the NetBIOS computer name with the DNS domain name to form an FQDN by removing the 16th character in the Net-BIOS name, and adding a dot followed by the DNS domain name. It's easy to change the default host name from the NetBIOS computer name. To do this, reconfigure TCP/IP by selecting the DNS page in the Microsoft TCP/IP Properties dialog box, and change the host name displayed on the DNS page. With Windows NT 4.0, it's now possible to connect to a NetBIOS over TCP/IP (*NetBT) resource* by using an IP address, FQDN, or NetBIOS computer name. For example, if you're using the Event Viewer, you will be prompted to select computer, at which point you will have the option to enter an FQDN, IP address, or NetBIOS name. This also means you can use an IP address with any Net command like Net Use 160.1.23.56, instead of Net Use Aspen.

DNS is one of the Windows NT Server services. You will install the DNS server service in Exercise 14.5.

EXERCISE 14.5

Installing a DNS Server on an NT 4.0 Server

1. Click Start, point to Settings, then click Control Panel.

2. Double-click the Network icon.

3. Click the Services tab.

4. Click Server, and then click Add.

5. Choose OK.

6. Type the path to the Windows NT 4.0 Server DNS files, and then choose OK.

7. Restart the computer.

Managing DNS Servers

A key feature of the DNS service in Windows NT Server 4.0 is a snazzy graphical interface from which the database files can be managed. Use of this graphical tool should help eliminate some of the errors associated with making changes directly to a zone database file using a file editor. Dynamic name resolution will only work on networks with at least one computer running Windows NT Server that have DNS and WINS enabled on them. Once a Windows NT DNS Server is installed, the DNS Manager is added to the Administrative menu. Using DNS Manager, you can add servers that are running the Windows NT Server 4.0 DNS service to the server list. Once added, you can view and change the parameters of any of the Windows NT Server 4.0 DNS servers included in the list. Exercise 14.6 will teach you to manage DNS Server with DNS Manager.

EXERCISE 14.6

Managing Windows NT 4.0 DNS Servers

To open the DNS Manager:

1. Click START.

2. Go to Program ➢ Administrative Tools, and click on DNS Manager.

3. To add a DNS server, click Server List in Domain Name Server. In Domain Name Service Manager, click Server List.

4. On the DNS menu, click New Server. The Add DNS Server dialog box appears.

5. In DNS server, type the IP address of the DNS server to be added to the server list, then click OK.

DHCP Relay

DHCP RELAY IS an exceptional, money-saving feature for networks peppered with older routers that don't support this function. When a dynamic client computer that's located on the same subnet as a BootP relay agent requests an IP address, its request is forwarded right to the subnet's BootP relay agent. This agent is configured to forward the request directly to the correct computer—as long as it's running the Windows NT Server DHCP service. That computer then returns an IP address directly to the requesting client.

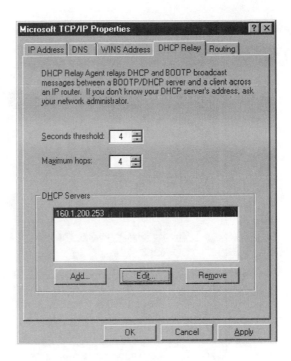

Configuration of the DHCP BootP relay agent is a two-step process. The first step is to install the DHCP Relay Agent Service onto the computer chosen to work as a BootP relay agent. Using the Microsoft TCP/IP Protocol Properties dialog box, the BootP agent can then be configured with the IP address of the computer that's running the Windows NT Server DHCP service. When that's done, the agent will know where to forward client requests for available IP addresses.

The DHCP Relay Agent Service is a Windows NT Server service.

The relay function is built into the Protocol module of TCP/IP, and has two configuration options. The first is Seconds threshold, a time to live option restricting the time span a request must be answered within. The second is Maximum hops, which specifies the maximum distance—in terms of routers—that a request can be forwarded. To configure this option, first select a seconds threshold (the default is 4) and then specify a maximum number of hops (the default is also 4). Next, select the Add button, specifying the IP address of the DCHP server that will answer client requests. You will install the DHCP Relay Agent Service in Exercise 14.7.

Regarding BootP Relay... This is the software service component that enables a Windows NT server to forward BootP broadcasts. Unlike the DHCP Relay Agent Service, it's not configurable. It's essentially an intermediate step towards contacting a DHCP Server.

EXERCISE 14.7

Installing the DHCP Relay Agent Service

1. Select Control Panel ➤ Network.

2. Choose the Services tab.

3. Choose Add.

4. Choose DHCP Relay Agent, then choose Have Disk, if you're loading from CD-ROM.

5. Choose OK, if you're downloading from the network.

6. Type the path to the distribution files.

7. Choose Close.

8. Shut down and restart your computer.

You will add an IP address to the BootP relay agent in Exercise 14.8.

EXERCISE 14.8

Adding an IP Address to the BootP Relay Agent

1. Select Control Panel ➤ Network, then choose the Protocols tab.

2. Choose TCP/IP Protocol, and then click Properties.

3. Choose the DHCP Relay tab.

4. Notice that the Seconds threshold and Maximum hops settings are set at 4.

5. Under DHCP Servers, type the IP address of the server that will provide the IP address to the subnet's requesting clients.

6. Choose Add, then OK.

SNMP and Windows NT 4.0

S IMPLE NETWORK MANAGEMENT Protocol (SNMP) is a network management standard widely used in TCP/IP networks, and more recently, with the Internet Packet Exchange (IPX) networks. Both Windows NT Server and Windows NT Workstation 4.0 include an SNMP service that allows windows NT-based computers to be managed using SNMP network management programs. Again, if SNMP stuff is foggy to you, refer back to Chapter 11 for full details.

Assuming that TCP/IP has already been installed, SNMP may be added as a service by selecting Control Panel Services Configuration ➤ Add. From the resulting list, select SNMP, and continue. You will be presented with a menu that is broken down into three parts: Agent, Traps, and Security. The SNMP configuration that you'd enter is the same information that you would under Windows NT 3.5*x*.

Under Windows NT 3.5x, SNMP is added by selecting Add Software and TCP/IP and related components rather than by adding it under Services.

Before installing the SNMP service, an administrator must identify the following information:

- The contact person and location for the administrator of the local computer

- Community names that can be shared by hosts on the network

- IP address, IPX address, or the network computer name of the SNMP management console that will be the destination for trap messages generated by computers within a specific community

To configure the SNMP Agent, select the Agent tab on the Microsoft SNMP Properties page. Under Service, select the type of service to report. Select all boxes that indicate network capabilities provided by your NT computer. SNMP must have this information to manage the enabled services. Notice that Applications, Internet, and End-to-End are default services.

The SNMP agent generates trap messages, which are then sent to an SNMP management console—the trap destination. Trap destinations are identified by a computer name, IP address, or IPX address of the "host of hosts" on the network to which you want the trap messages sent. The trap destination must be a host that is running an SNMP manager program. To configure the trap destination on a Windows NT 4.0-based computer, use the Traps tab in the Microsoft SNMP Properties page to enter the host name, IP address, or the IPX address of the computer(s) running an SNMP manager program.

Community names provide a rudimentary security scheme for the SNMP service. You can add and delete community names by using the Security tab on the Microsoft SNMP Properties page. You can also filter the type of packets that the computer will accept. You must configure the SNMP service with at least one community name. The default name is Public.

In Exercise 14.9, you'll install the SNMP agent onto your NT 4.0 computer.

EXERCISE 14.9

Configuring the SNMP Agent

1. Go to Control Panel ➢ Network.

2. Choose Services, then Add.

3. Under Select Network Service, choose SNMP Service.

4. Type in the path to the distribution files.

5. The Microsoft SNMP Properties page appears.

6. Type in the Contact and Location Information on the Agent page.

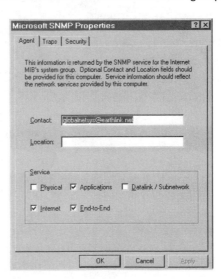

7. Choose the Service types, or accept the defaults.

---

8. Choose the Traps tab.

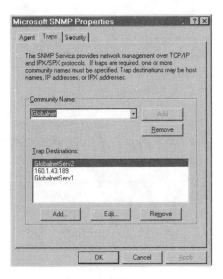

9. In the Traps tab, add a new Community name if needed. Public is the default.

10. Add the Trap destination Host or Hosts.

11. Choose the Security tab.

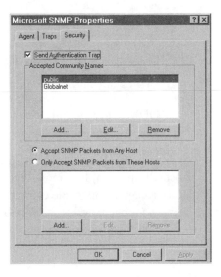

EXERCISE 14.9 (CONTINUED FROM PREVIOUS PAGE)

12. In the Security tab, add any new Community names, then choose Add.

13. Choose OK.

14. Restart the computer

Microsoft Internet Information Server

WINDOWS NT 4.0 introduces the Microsoft Internet Information Server. It's both a network file and an application server. This next section explains the design principles and architecture behind the Internet Information Server, which supports three protocols: HTTP, FTP, and Gopher. We've included some exercises to give you experience installing the Internet Information Server and configuring the protocols. To install the following items, select Control Panel ➤ Network ➤ Services tab.

- Internet Service Manager: Installs the administration program for managing services

- World Wide Web Service: Creates a WWW publishing server

- Gopher Service: Creates a gopher publishing server

- FTP Service: Creates a File Transfer Protocol (FTP) publishing server

- ODBC Drivers and Administration: Installs Open Database Connectivity (ODBC) drivers

Before installing the Microsoft Internet Information Server, you need to close all open applications—even the Control Panel window—or you're likely to get an open file error message. Also, if you're intending on installing the Gopher service, it's a good idea to declare an Internet domain name in the TCP/IP configuration (under the DNS tab). If you don't define an

Internet domain name, you'll be notified to set one during the installation to ensure that Gopher operates properly.

Exercise 14.10 will help you install Microsoft's Internet Information Server.

EXERCISE 14.10

Installing Microsoft's Internet Information Server

1. Select Control Panel ➢ Network ➢ Services tab, click your right mouse button on Network Neighborhood, and then choose Properties. Select Add. You will be presented with a list of services.

2. Select Internet Information Server v2.0.

NOTE: When installing Microsoft NT Version 4.0 Server, the Install Internet Information Server icon appears by default on the desktop. Double-click the icon.

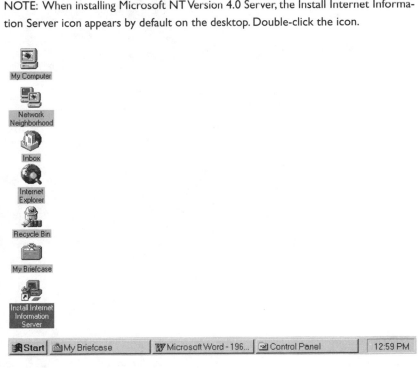

3. Type in the path to the Distribution files.

EXERCISE 14.10 (CONTINUED FROM PREVIOUS PAGE)

A Welcome screen will appear, notifying you to close all background applications. Close all other programs and then click OK.

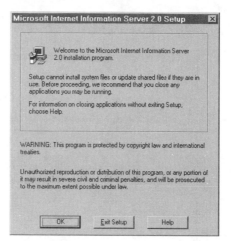

4. You'll be given a menu listing all the service components (as listed above). Click on the adjacent box to select each desired component. Note that there's one extra item—Help and Sample Files. Select this option if you want to install online Help and sample HyperText Markup Language (HTML) files. Then click OK to continue.

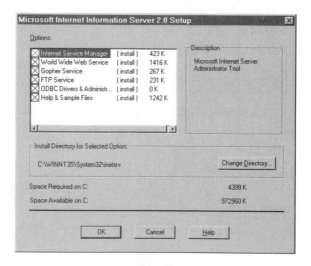

A list of directories is presented for the locations of World Wide Web, FTP, and Gopher Publishing.

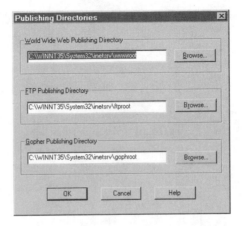

This is the path of the home (root) directory for each service you're installing. It's your option to accept the default directory, and place all files to be published in that directory. By default, and unless configured otherwise, the files in that directory, plus all subdirectories, will be available to clients. If you have existing files to be published, as in HTML files, type the fully qualified path to them or relocate the files to the new home directory, making adjustments where necessary in the documents to reflect the directory change. Of note—the Setup program doesn't allow network shares to be specified as root publishing directories. If your files are stored on a network share, you'll need to use Internet Service Manager to configure your publishing directories after setup's completed.

5. Click OK to continue.

6. You'll then be asked to if it's OK to create directories. Choose Yes.

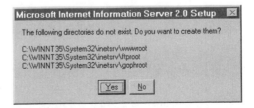

If you're installing the Gopher service and haven't declared an Internet Domain Name, you will receive a warning at this point. Click OK.

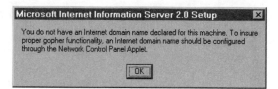

Also, if you're configuring your system with FTP, you may receive the following warning regarding the anonymous user account: Your computer's guest account is enabled for network access. This means that any user can access the FTP service, regardless of whether they've been granted access to do so. Do you want to disable the guest access to the FTP service on this computer? This question is an individual judgment call. Do you want anonymous access? This is your decision.

The final phase in configuring the Installation involves the *ODBC (Open Database Connectivity)* drivers.

ODBC allows the Internet utilities to interface with a database—usually via *SQL Server*. In the Install Drivers dialog box, you'll be prompted to select SQL Server. Then select OK to complete the installation.

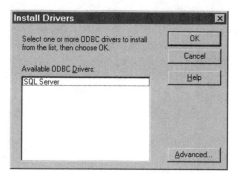

You'll need to provide access to set up the ODBC drivers and data sources by using the ODBC *applet* icon in the Windows NT Control Panel. If you have an application running that uses ODBC, you may see an error message telling you that one or more components are in use. If so, close all applications and services—in this case the ones that use ODBC. You have the option of entering the Advanced section of the SQL dialog box to gain access to how the selected drivers are installed, managed, and translated.

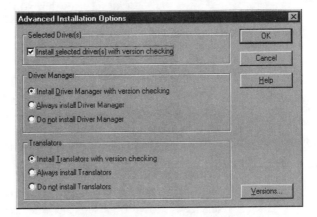

In the Advanced Installation Options dialog box, you'll choose whether you want to perform a version check, install the driver manager, or look manually at each module's version by clicking on the Versions button. This will reveal the currently installed version of the MS Code Page Translator, the ODBC Driver Manager, and SQL Server. Click OK to complete the installation.

If after installation is complete, you decide to remove a Microsoft Internet Information Server component, you'll need to use the procedure in Exercise 14.11:

Removing the Microsoft Information Server

1. Choose Start ➤ Programs, then choose Microsoft Internet Server (Common).

2. Run the Internet Information Server Setup.

3. A Welcome screen will appear, notifying you to close all background applications. Close all other programs and then click on OK.

4. A menu will appear, asking you if you would like to Add/Remove Components, Repeat last install, or Remove All. If you add components, the instructions are the same as in the last exercise. If you select to remove all components or repeat the last installation, you will be prompted for confirmation before continuing.

Internet Service Manager

ALL OF THE services that you've installed for the Microsoft Internet Information Server can be managed by the Internet Services Manager, located in the Microsoft Internet Server (Common). This program is designed to assist you in the configuration and enhancement of your internetwork services. By using a single program to manage Internet services, you're able to manage all Internet services running on any Windows NT system in your network in a streamlined manner. Depending on the number of systems running internetwork services, you can choose from three control view formats, found in Microsoft Internet Service Manager's View menu.

Report view   This selection provides an alphabetical listing of all selected computers. A host's name may appear more than once since each installed service is shown on a separate line. While in the Report view, you may sort by any column simply by clicking on the header. This view tends to be most useful when you're managing one or two systems running Internet Server. This is the default view.

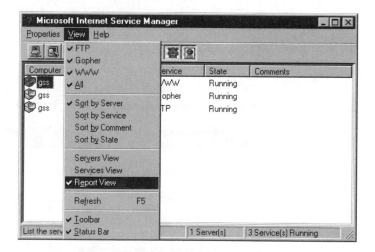

Servers view   This view is ideal for larger installations of Internet Information Server. It's the computer name of all systems running any of the Peer Web services. Click the plus symbol next to a server name to display which services that server is running. You can also double click on the server name. Double-click a service name to see its property sheets. This display is an easy to view tree which displays the services as traffic lights—Red (stopped), Yellow (paused), and Green (running).

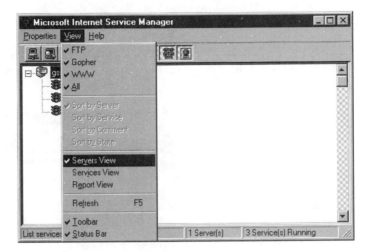

Services view   This is the most efficient way to determine where a particular service is running. All systems running a service such as FTP will be listed under that grouping. Click the plus symbol next to a service name to see which servers are running that service, or double-click on the service. Double-click the computer name under a service to see the property sheets for the service running on that computer.

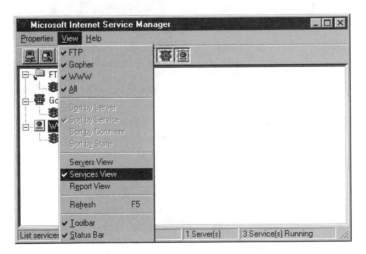

No matter which view you choose, you'll be able to perform similar functions. The main reason behind changing views is to refine and assist the management process. You'll notice that the all functions are included in the button bar, and that they're identical to those in the pull-down menus. The three functions performed in the manager are Connecting to a Server, Services Control, and Service Configuration.

Connect to Server can be selected through either the connect button, or the pull-down menu under Properties. This function is used to enable you to attach to the server you wish to manage. Use the Find All Servers button, or pull-down menu to locate systems dynamically.

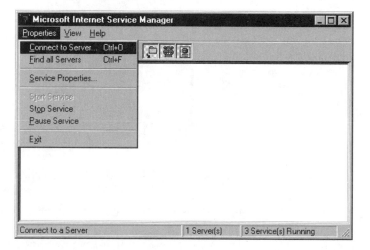

Services Control provides the ability to stop, start, or pause a service. Ordinarily, this type of function is done though the Server Manger or Control Panel. However for many users, this activity is difficult and cumbersome. Because of this, improvements were in order, and you can now simply use either the button bar or the pull-down menus.

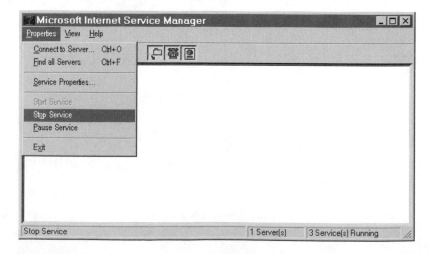

Service Configuration is only accessible by double-clicking on the leaf item in the displayed tree—there is no button bar or pull-down menu for this one. When you double-click the desired item, you'll access a setup page. The page is very similar to other service pages. They only vary slightly from service to service.

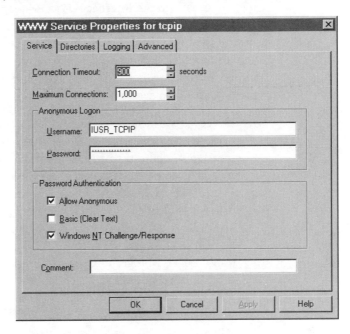

The configuration for each service is discussed in the following sections.

Unlike Windows NT 3.5x, the services are configured with a new anonymous account created by setup, rather than defaulting to the guest account. The new account name is called IUSR_computername. It uses a randomly generated password and privilege to log on locally. When Peer web services are installed on domain controllers, this account is added to the domain database automatically. After setup has completed installation, you can change the username and password for the account from the Service Property sheet inside the Internet Service Manager. The new username and password must match the same username and password in the Windows NT User Manager. The WWW, FTP, and gopher services use the IUSR_computername user account by default when anonymous access is allowed (not Guest). Rights for this account can be configured like all others through User Manager. File permissions can be set on NTFS drives for IUSR_ computername, with Windows NT Explorer.

FTP

U NDER MICROSOFT WINDOWS NT 4.0, FTP management is performed though the Internet Service Manager. As With Windows NT 3.5*x*, you can use any FTP client, including most Web browsers, to connect to the FTP server. To see the configuration of a host system with the FTP service, double-click on the server from the Services View. You'll then be presented with the property sheets, including Service, Messaging, Logging, Directories, and Advanced.

Service   This sheet is the same as the configuration screen in Windows NT 3.5*x*. However, there are a few minor differences. First, maximum connections defaults to 1,000 rather than 20. Also, the connection timeout has increased from 10 minutes (3.5*x*) to 15, which is now measured in seconds (900 by default). Additionally, anonymous username, as discussed earlier, has been changed to IUSR_computername. Two new features to this screen are the addition of a comment field to describe the purpose of the FTP service, and the Current Sessions manager—previously managed from the FTP Manger in Control Panel under Windows NT 3.5*x*. No additions or changes have been made to the Current Sessions Manger.

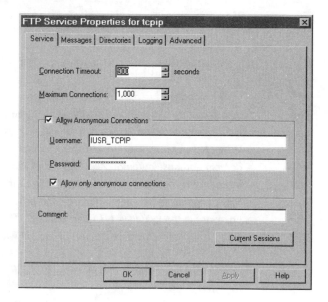

Messages isn't a truly new feature to the FTP service, since previously you could make these entries though the Registry editor under 3.5*x*. However, what's new about this sheet is that it now provides a Welcome message (logging on), an Exit message (logging off), and a Maximum connections message (limit of users logged on).

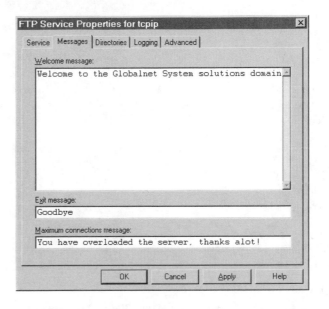

Directories this sheet offers the configuration of directories—a feature not fully offered by Windows 3.5*x*. By default, all files and subdirectories will be available, if placed in the home directory. The home directory is the location where you should place all FTP materials. Although there can be only one home directory, you can choose to add and create virtual directories. Virtual directories aren't visible to users, and can only be seen if the client machine knows the alias of the virtual directory. These directories are commonly used to distribute files that aren't open to the public, but still use anonymous names and passwords. With both home and virtual directories, you can designate the data storage area on another system. The input fields for a username and password in the Add or Edit dialog box are no longer grayed out if the directory is on an alternate system. Keep in mind that when you use the network, you must provide a valid ID and password for the server that you're attaching the FTP service to. Errors will be displayed and reported on each entry line on the directory sheet. The point at which you add directories (home or virtual), is also the point at which you'll designate read and write access. As with 3.5*x*, security will be limited according to the anonymous account's file permissions. Finally, due to limitations that some browsers impose—that the FTP listing be styled in UNIX for-mat—you may choose your directory listing system as UNIX or MS-DOS. This is a global setting for all directories. Some more cool and special function features are listed below:

Special Directories   can be used within the home directories to control the root directory displayed to FTP users. These directories must be physical subdirectories—they can't be specified by using virtual directories.

Username Directories   are directories within the home directory with names that match a particular username. If a user logs on with a username that has a matching directory in the home directory, that directory is used as the root. FTP username directories aren't created by default during setup.

Anonymous Directory   is also a directory within the home directory. If a user logs on using the password Anonymous, the directory name Anonymous is used as the root.

Annotated Directories   Each directory can contain a file that can be used to summarize the information that the directory contains and automatically provide access to remote browsers. This is done by creating a file called ~ftpsvc~.ckm in the FTP directory. Most of the time, you'll want to make this a hidden file so that directory listings don't display it. From an FTP client, you would type Site ckm at the command prompt, or use the Registry Editor to enable annotated directories by adding the following value:

```
HKEY_LOCAL_MACHINE\SYSTEM\CurrentControlSet\Services
    \MSFTPSVC\Parameters

AnnotateDirectories   REG_DWORD
Range: 0 or 1
Default = 0 (directory annotation is off).
```

This Registry entry doesn't appear by default in the Registry, so you must add an entry if you want to change its default value. If Directory Annotation is enabled on your FTP service, Web browsers may display error messages when browsing your FTP directories. You can eliminate such errors by limiting each annotation file to one line, or by disabling Directory Annotation.

Logging   This sheet allows you to enable FTP service logging. It can be enabled by checking the Enable logging box. You may either send the logs to file or to an *SQL/ODBC database.* If you elect to send it to file, you may specify the location where you'd like the log files placed. Also, you have the option to open a new log daily (Inyymmdd.log), weekly (Inyymmww.log), monthly (Inyymm.log), or when the file reaches a designated size (INETSRVn.log). The filenames for the log vary according to the trigger you use, as shown in each set of parentheses ending with a .log extension. If you decide to send the information to an SQL/ODBC database, you must provide an ODBC data source name, the Table, a username and password along with it.

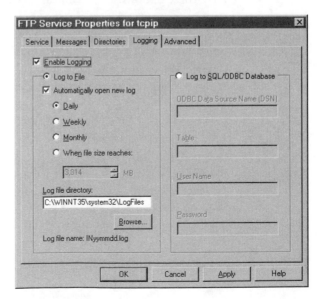

Advanced This sheet limits access to the FTP server in two ways: source systems and network utilization.

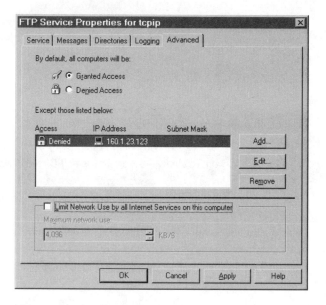

The functions presented here were offered in a limited manner, at best, in Windows NT 3.5x.

By default, all systems are granted access. If you want to limit access, you have three options. First, you can grant access to all computers with the exclusion of those you add as single computers, or a certain group of computers. Second, you can deny access to all computers, with the exception of those you add as single computers or a group of computers. When adding a single computer, use the button with the three dots to look up a host name from DNS (if registered) to get that system's IP address. When adding a group of computers, this option (host name lookup) isn't available, however you now have the option to specify a subnet mask. The last way the Advanced sheet allows you to limit access to the FTP server is by setting a maximum network utilization in terms of kilobytes per second. This is done by clicking on the box next to the Limit Network Use by all Internet Services on this computer dialog box. As you have probably figured out, this option effects all Internet services, WWW, FTP, and Gopher.

Gopher

W E TALKED ABOUT Gopher in Chapter 2, and although it's not shiny and new to TCP/IP, support for it is a new feature to Windows NT 4.0. To refresh your memory, a Gopher service is a function you can use to create links to other computers or services, annotate your files and directories, and create custom menus. The implementation that is included with Windows NT is full-featured, including something called Gopher Plus Selector Strings. This allows the server to return additional information to the client, like administrator name, modification date, and MIME type. From the Internet Service Manager, all configuration functions are the same as those for FTP, with the exception that there isn't an option to specify messages, or an option to specify read/write access from the directory sheet.

All Gopher files should be placed in the gopher home directory: (\Inetsrv\ Gophroot), by default. This makes browsing the gopher directories a breeze for clients. Tag files can be created to enable links to other computers or services, to annotate your files and directories, and to create custom menus. The gopher service will make the following available under a specified directory tree:

- Tags and how they are to be stored

- Indexes to speed up searches

- Activity log records

To enable Wide Area Information Search (WAIS) index searching, you must change the following entry in the Windows NT Registry from 0 (disabled) to 1(enabled):

HKEY_LOCAL_MACHINE\SYSTEM\CurrentControlSet\Services\GopherSVC\ CheckForWAISDB

Tag files allow you to jazz up the standard gopher display sent to clients with additional material, and also to provide links to other systems. Tag files are responsible for all the information about a file that's sent to a client. This information must include the name of the file to be displayed for the client. Typically, tag files contain a display name, host name, and port number. If you're utilizing Gopher Plus, you can add more information to each tag file, such as the server administrator's name and e-mail address, the file's creation date, and last modification date. In order to use these features, you must first create the file, and then store it on the gopher server. The tags for your gopher site can be created with the gdsset utility. For information syntax on this utility, type **gdsset** by itself on a command line. You'll then be presented with the following information:

```
Usage: gdsset [-crl] [-g<GopherItemType>] [-f <FriendlyName>]
        [-s <Selector>] [-h<HostName>] [-p<PortNumber>]
        -D<Directory> -d <filename>
         [-a <AdminName>]  [-e <AdminEmail>]
        -c change (edit/create) the existing tag information
        (Default is to create a new tag information)
        -r  read and dump the tag information on console
        -d  specifies that given file is actually a directory
        -g  specifies gopher object type.
```

The Gopher Object Type is a single character—usually a digit number from 0 to 9. The default type is 9 for binary. See the following Gopher type codes for complete details (valid when -r not used):

-f <FriendlyName>   specifies Friendly Name for object (valid when -r not used).

-l   specifies that link information is to be set for write (valid when -r not used).

-s <Selector>   specifies the selector for link (valid when -l is used).

-h<HostName>   specifies the Host for link (valid when -l is used).

-p<PortNumber>   specifies the Port number for link (valid when -l is used).

-a <AdminName>   specifies the Administrator Name, defaults to the service administrator's name in the Service dialog box of the Microsoft Internet Service Manager.

-e <AdminEmail>   specifies the Administrator Email, defaults to the service administrator's e-mail name in the Service dialog box of the Microsoft Internet Service Manager.

Note that this command line automatically sets the hidden file attribute on the tag files you create. Typical use of the command is as follows:

```
gdsset -c -g# -f description of file -a administrator's name
   -e e-mail
```

The remainder of the command options are typically for supporting advanced features such as providing links to other hosts. Also, this command can be used in *batch mode*, or *nested batch* with the for command. Refer to online help for more details on performing this action. After the information's been set for a file, you can quickly determine its accuracy by using the gdsset -r file-name command.

Gopher Type Codes

The following is a list of all the possible type codes for Gopher. Again, if not specified, the default is 9 for binary. These codes are used following -g in the gdsset command.

0   A file, usually a flat text file

1   A gopher directory

2   A CSO phone-book server

3   An error

4   A Macintosh file in Binhex format

5   An MS-DOS binary archive

6   A UNIX Uuencoded file

7   An index-search server

8   A Telnet session

9   A binary file

c   A calendar or calendar of events

g   A graphic interchange file (GIF) graphic

h   An HTML World Wide Web hypertext page

i   An in-line text that is not an item

I   Another kind of image file

m   A BSD format mbox file

P   A PDF document

T   A TN3270 mainframe session

:   A bitmap image (use Gopher plus information for type of image)

Tag files are hidden files. Use the ATTRIB command, Explorer, or File Manager to set the hidden attribute for tag files. On drives formatted with a FAT file system, the tag filename uses the same name as the file it describes, with .gtg as the file extension appended to the 8.3 name. The name then becomes 8.3.3. For example, if the content filename is Sample.txt, the tag filename would be Sample.txt.gtg. The tag files on FAT can be edited with most ASCII text editors. On drives formatted using NTFS, :gtg is appended to the filename instead of .gtg. In this case, if the content filename is Sample.txt, then the tag filename would be Sample.txt:gtg. Unlike FAT files, NTFS tag files can't be edited by most text editors because they're stored in an alternate data stream. If a tag file is stored on an NTFS volume, you must first manually move the tag file before you move the corresponding data files. When you move the tag file you'll have to modify the hidden attribute both before and after the move. Again, hiding and unhiding files is done through the ATTRIB command, File Manager, and Explorer.

World Wide Web Service

B EFORE WE GET caught up in the Web, it's important to understand the terminology involved. Here's a list of key terms and their definitions:

Internet: A global network of computers

Intranet: Refers to any TCP/IP network that is not connected to the Internet

World Wide Web (WWW): A graphical, easy-to-navigate interface for looking at documents on the Internet

Hyperlinks: Shortcuts on WWW documents to aid in connecting to other pages, downloading files, etc.

Uniform Resource Locator (URL): The standard naming convention on the Internet; for example, http://www.microsoft.com/home.html

Web Browser: A tool for navigating and accessing information on the Web (i.e. Internet Explorer, Mosaic and Netscape Navigator, etc.)

HyperText Transport protocol (HTTP): A protocol specification used to respond to browser requests. Your workstation can be configured to provide FTP and gopher services.

HTML: The document standard for Internet Web pages.

Windows NT 4.0 adds Web services to its suite of TCP/IP applications. Now you can create and design your own intranet or Internet Web page quickly and easily. Traditionally, this service has been performed by UNIX-based hosts or Windows NT systems utilizing third-party vendor software. The software is generally costly, and in many cases, more than just a bit of a challenge to configure.

In 4.0, the configuration method is the same whether you'll be using your system on the Internet or an intranet. The only major differences from one implementation to the next deal with how security is configured. With Windows NT workstation, just as sharing files doesn't make your workstation a dedicated file server, publishing Web pages doesn't make your workstation a dedicated Internet server. If you need a dedicated Internet server with advanced administration capabilities, and the ability to respond to a multitude of simultaneous connections, you should use Microsoft Internet Information Server. It's included with Windows NT Server Version 4.0.

Web pages are constructed in HTML (hypertext markup language), which includes both hypertext and hyperlinks. This is the standard document form Web browsers support. HTML enables a Web page to make connections and reference other Web pages both locally and on foreign hosts, even if they're part of an entirely different network. Although you can create these files in practically any text editor, it's generally a good idea to use a product such as Internet Assistant for Word (free from Microsoft), Netscape Navigator's Editor, or another HTML-specific editor. Doing so will ensure proper formatting and reduce debugging time, and allow you to link to any SQL/ODBC database. This support can be added by setting up the ODBC drivers and data sources using the ODBC applet in the Windows NT Control Panel. During installation, if you have an application running that uses ODBC, you might receive an error message telling you that one or more components are in use. If this happens, before continuing, close all applications and services that use ODBC. When setting up peer Web services, you'll find that most Internet browsers, such as Internet Explorer (ships with NT 4.0), structures its addressing sequence in URL format. URL syntax is a specific sequence of protocol, domain name, and path to the requested information. Configuring the Web Service sheets can be achieved through the Internet Service Manager. Most configuration functions are the same as FTP's, with some exceptions. First, there's no option to specify messages, since it's done by the HTML Web page. The other configuration differences are discussed below:

Service The configuration is the same as FTP's with the exception that password authentication is done at 3 levels:

- Allow Anonymous

- Basic (Clear Text)

- Windows NT Challenge/Response

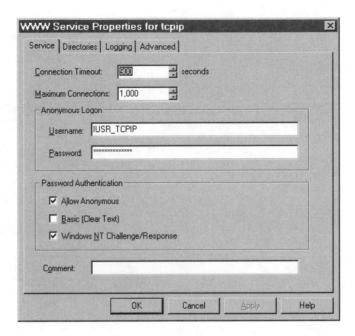

The anonymous configuration is the most common on the Internet, and is generally used to allow the public to see your Web page. When this is the only configured password authentication option, the user will be logged in as the anonymous account regardless of name or password. Basic, or clear text, is a simple level of password protection. As with FTP, passwords are sent unencrypted and therefore may be viewed with a packet analyzer. Depending on your needs, this can be a drag. By Default, the basic option isn't enabled, but basic authentication can be encoded when used in conjunction with *Secure Sockets Layer (SSL),* which ensures usernames and passwords are encrypted before transmission. All browsers support basic authentication. *Windows NT Challenge/Response* is a system by which the service will honor requests by clients to send user account information using the Windows NT Challenge/Response authentication protocol. This protocol uses a one-way algorithm—a mathematical formula that can't be reversed—to prevent passwords from being transmitted. The Windows NT Challenge/Response authentication process is started automatically when an access denied error is encountered on an anonymous client request.

Directories   This sheet is primarily the same in concept as FTP's configuration, however there's a few distinct differences. First, notice that by default, this sheet lists both a home directory and a virtual directory named scripts. This provides a secure place to locate your scripts files, as well as creates a public Web home directory. Next, you can select the enable default document to select a specific Web page, in HTML, to be delivered to your Web browser when it's not even specified to do so. Simply type the name of the default document in the designated dialog box. You can also enable directory browsing on the directory sheet. Directory browsing allows a user to be presented with a hypertext listing of directories and files so they can navigate freely through your directory structure.

You can choose Edit Properties to add or modify directory entries. You have the same Virtual Directory options as with FTP. This allows you to add directories outside the home directory, including those that reside on other hosts. See the FTP Directory sheet for complete details on doing this. Also, as with FTP, virtual directories won't appear in WWW directory listings; you must create explicit links in HTML files for the user, or the user must know the URL in order to access virtual directories. You can also virtualize a server by clicking on the box next to Virtual Server. This will allow you to specify an IP address for the entry. Finally, as with FTP, the Web service uses access control. It must match any existing NTFS rights to work. These rights include

Read, Execute, and Require Secure SSL Channel. Read should be selected for information directories, but it's not a good idea to use this option for directories containing programs. Execute allows clients to run any programs in a given directory. This box is selected by default for the directory created for programs. Put all your scripts and executable files into this directory. Do not select this box for directories containing static content. Select the Require secure SSL channel (Not Installed) box if using Secure Sockets Layer (SSL) security to encrypt data transmissions. This must be installed with the key manager in order work.

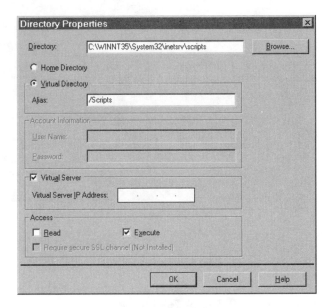

Key Manager

THE KEY MANAGER is used to create a Secure Socket Layer security encryption implementation. The key manager may be launched by selecting Start ➢ Programs ➢ Microsoft Internet Server (Common). Key manager is a central tool that can be used to manage all security keys on any NT-based system with Microsoft's Peer Web Services. You can connect to a remote system by choosing the Servers pull-down menu, or by using the tool bar.

To create a new key, select Create New Key in the Key pull-down. Fill in the information in this dialog box, then click OK to create two files. The first file is a key file containing a key pair. The second file is a certificate request file. When your request is processed, the provider will return a certificate to you.

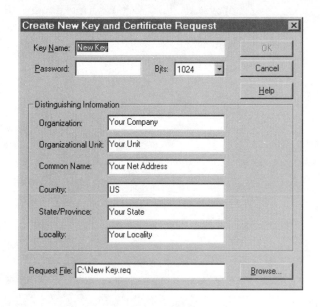

Key Name   A descriptive name for the key you are creating

Password   Specifies a password to encrypt the private key

Bits   Generates a key pair—by default 1024 bits long. Options are 1024, 512 or 768 bits

Organization   Your company name

Organizational Unit   The division or department within your company; for example, Sales

Common Name   The domain name of the server; for example, www.company.com

Country   Two-letter ISO Country designation; for example, US, FR, AU, UK, and so on

State/Province   The full, nonabbreviated name of your state or province

Locality   The full name of the city where your company is located

Request File   The name of the request file that'll be created or accepted by default. Accepting default automatically copies the Key Name you have designated, and attaches a .req extension to it to create the request filename. For example, if you have typed security in the Key Name box, the default request filename will become security.req.

Do not use commas in any field. Commas are interpreted as the end of that field and will generate an invalid request without even giving you so much as a warning!

When you've filled in all the information, click OK. Retype your password when prompted, and click OK again. Your key will appear in the Key Manager window under the computer name. Once completed, you'll need to contact VeriSign's Web Site at www.verisign.com to get details on how to get a certificate to activate your key. The key generated by Key Manager isn't valid for use on the Internet until you obtain a valid key certificate for it from the proper key authorities. Until you do so, the key can't be used, and will lie dormant on its host computer.

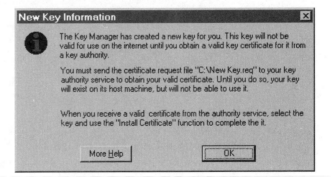

Once you have your key, you should then select the Key Graphic, and use the Key pull-down to select Install Certificate. This will validate the key and give you a date range during which the key is usable. A summary for the key appears in the lower-right corner of the screen, and reflects the information that you gave when you created the key. When installing the key, you'll be prompted to select or type in the IP address of the server to which you want to apply the Secure Sockets Layer key. Your choices are none, default, or to specify or select an address.

Applying Your Certificate to Your Server

After you complete your certificate request, you will receive a signed certificate from the certification authority. Consult your certification authority for complete details. It'll look something like the following example:

```
-----BEGIN CERTIFICATE-----

JIEBSDSCEXoCHQEwLQMJSoZILvoNVQECSQAwcSETMRkOAMUTBhMuVrM

mIoAnBdNVBAoTF1JTQSBEYXRhIFN1Y3VyaXR5LCBJbmMuMRwwGgYDVQ

QLExNQZXJzb25hIEN1cnRpZm1jYXR1MSQwIgYDVQQDExtPcGVuIE1hc

mt1dCBUZXN0IFN1cnZ1ciAxMTAwHhcNOTUwNzE5MjAyNzMwWhcNOTYw

NTE0MjAyOTEwWjBzMQswCQYDVQQGEwJVUzEgMB4GA1UEChMXU1NBIER

hdGEgU2VjdXJpdHksIE1uYy4xHDAaBgNVBAsTE1B1cnNvbmEgQ2VydG

lmaWNhdGUxJDAiBgNVBAMTG09wZW4gTWFya2V0IFR1c3QgU2VydmVyI

DExMDBcMA0GCSqGSIb3DQEBAQUAA0sAMEgCQQDU/71rgR6vkVNX40BA

q1poGdSmGkD1iN3sEPfSTGxNJXY58XH3JoZ4nrF7mIfvpghNi1taYim

vhbBPNqYe4yLPAgMBAAEwDQYJKoZIhvcNAQECBQADQQBqyCpws9EaAj

KKAefuNP+z+8NY8khckgyHN2LLpfhv+iP8m+bF66HNDU1Fz8ZrVOu3W

QapgLPV90kIskNKXX3a

------END CERTIFICATE-----
```

Beautiful, isn't it?! Copy and save the text to a file, using a tool such as Notepad, and give it a name you can remember—something like Certif.txt. Then use Key Manager to install your signed certificate onto the server. Exercise 14.12 will lead you through the steps.

EXERCISE 14.12

Installing a Certificate

1. Select Programs ➤ Microsoft Internet Server (Common) ➤ Key Manager.

2. Next choose Key ➤ Create New Key.

3. Fill in your information in the dialog box, then choose OK.

If you don't specify an IP address while installing your certificate, the same certificate will be applied to all virtual servers created on the system. If you're hosting multiple sites on a single server, you can specify that the certificate only be used for a given IP address by adding the specific IP address, for example: `160.191.82.54`.

Your final step to completing the setup is to commit to the changes. You may do this by either exiting the program, or using the pull-down menu.

Summing Things Up

THIS CHAPTER'S SUMMARY is gonna be a little different from the previous ones. This chapter is about an upgrade, so its whole reason for being is to discuss what's up with the changes. Instead of running the risk of boring you with a bunch of material we've already discussed in earlier chapters, we'll provide a list of what's shiny, new, and different in 4.0, along with a brief description of these changes that you can use as a handy, quick reference guide. Here you go:

- Windows NT 4.0 Windows 95-like interface is much easier to use, so navigating and customizing NT is a snap.

- A Network Monitor for analyzing and capturing network traffic is now included, along with an enhanced Task Manager that provides memory and processor utilization at a glance.

- The existing Diagnostics tool has been improved, and now displays the information about device drivers, network usage, and system resources in a more straightforward manner.

- Administrative wizards automate the most common management tasks such as adding user accounts. There are also wizards for adding or removing programs, modems, and printers.

- TCP/IP addresses can be configured though the Network icon inside the Control Panel, which is accessed by selecting Start ➤ Setting.

- The following is a list of tab screens found under the Network icon:

  - The Identification tab screen appears whenever you double-click the Network icon in the Control Panel. Windows uses the information in the Identification tab screen to identify a particular computer on the network.

  - The Services tab lists the network services installed on your computer. Clicking on a service allows you to view or change its properties, or to remove or update it.

  - The Protocols tab lists the protocols installed on your computer. Clicking on one of them allows you to view or change its properties, or to remove or update it.

  - The IP Address tab page offers additional options that are opened by selecting the Advanced button. You can assign additional IP addresses, gateways, and enable a special type of filtering called PPTP. Through the advanced button, you can perform some of the security tasks typically handled at a firewall, or router.

  - The Adapter tab lists the adapters installed on your computer. Click an adapter to view or change its properties, or remove or update the card.

  - The Bindings tab lists the Network bindings (connections between network cards, protocols and the services) that are installed on your computer. You can use this page to disable network bindings or to arrange the order in which the computer finds information on the network.

  - The WINS address tab handily allows you to pick a primary WINS Server and a secondary WINS Server.

  - The Traps tab allows you to configure the trap destination on a Windows NT 4.0-based computer. Use the Microsoft SNMP Properties page to enter the host name, IP address, or the IPX address of the computer(s) running an SNMP manager program.

- The Point-to-Point Tunneling Protocol (PPTP) is a recently developed tool that supports multiprotocol Virtual Private Networks (VPN). It works by enabling users to both remotely and securely access corporate networks via the Internet. By selecting Enable Security, then choosing the configure button, you'll have access to the Advanced Security configuration button, which presents you with a set of three lists—TCP Ports, UDP Ports, and IP Protocols. Each of these lists have the option available to "permit all," or "permit only" permitting you to specify the TCP, UDP, and IP protocol entries to be passed.

- Just adding the appropriate LAN/WAN card or cards to a Windows NT Server allows you to configure it as a router. The Windows NT Multi-Protocol Routing service provides flexible and economical routing solutions that answer the call for costly, dedicated routers.

- Windows NT Server Version 4.0 has expanded support for DNS by implementing a DNS server, and includes a snazzy graphical interface from which the database files can be managed.

- Clients running the Windows NT Server DHCP service now have the ability to use the BootP relay service. This enables clients on one subnet to access a DHCP server on another subnet, and means a Windows NT server will forward BootP and DHCP requests across an IP router.

- The Windows NT 4.0 Microsoft Internet Information Server is both a network file and application server that supports three protocols: HTTP, FTP, and Gopher.

- The Internet Services Manager, located in the Microsoft Internet Server (Common), is designed to assist you in the configuration and enhancement of your internetwork services. By using a single program to manage Internet services, you're able to manage all Internet services running on any Windows NT system in your network in a streamlined manner. The main reason behind changing views is to refine and assist the management process. There are three control view formats, found in Microsoft Internet Service Manager's View menu:

    Report view This selection provides an alphabetical listing of all selected computers.

Servers view This view is ideal for larger installations of the Internet Information Server. It's the computer name of all systems running any of the Peer Web services. This display is an easy to view tree which displays the services as traffic lights—Red (stopped), Yellow (paused), and Green (running).

Services view This is the most efficient way to determine where a particular service is running. All systems running a service such as FTP will be listed under that grouping.

There are three functions performed in the Internet Services Manager: connecting to a server, services control, and service configuration:

Connect to Server Enabled through either the connect button or the Properties pull-down menu, this function is used to attach you to the server you wish to manage.

Services Control Provides the ability to stop, start, or pause a service.

Service Configuration Accessed by double clicking on the leaf item in the displayed tree. When you double click the desired item, you'll access a setup page.

- In NT 4.0, services are configured with a new anonymous account created by setup, rather than defaulting to the guest account. The new account name is called IUSR_computername. It uses randomly generated passwords and privileges to log on locally.

- The Directories sheet offers the configuration of directories—a feature not fully offered by Windows 3.5x. By default, all files and subdirectories will be available, if placed in the home directory. The home directory is the location where you should place all FTP materials.

Special Directories can be used within the home directories to control the root directory displayed to FTP users.

Username directories are directories within the home directory with names that match a particular username.

Anonymous Directory is also a directory within the home directory. If a user logs on using the password Anonymous, the directory name Anonymous is used as the root.

Annotated Directories can each contain a file that can be used to summarize the information that the directory contains and automatically provide access to remote browsers.

Logging Sheet allows you to enable FTP service logging.

Advanced Sheet limits access to the FTP server in two ways: source systems and network utilization.

- The support for Gopher included with Windows NT is full-featured, including something called Gopher Plus Selector Strings, which allows the server to return additional information to the client, like administrator name, modification date, and MIME type.

- Tag files are hidden files created to enable links to other computers or services, and to annotate your files and directories, and create custom menus. Use the ATTRIB command, Explorer, or File Manager to set the hidden attribute for tag files. On drives formatted with a FAT file system, the tag filename uses the same name as the file it describes, with .gtg as the file extension appended to the 8.3 name.

- The gopher service will make the following available under a specified directory tree:

  - Tags and how they are to be stored

  - Indexes to speed up searches

  - Activity log records

- Windows NT 4.0 adds Web Services to its suite of TCP/IP applications. Now you can create and design your own intranet or Internet Web page quickly and easily.

- Microsoft Internet Information Server is useful if you need a dedicated Internet server with advanced administration capabilities, and the ability to respond to a multitude of simultaneous connections.

- The Key Manager is used to create a Secure Socket Layer security encryption implementation, and is a central tool which can be used to manage all security keys on any NT-based system with Microsoft's Peer Web Services.

Exercise
Answers

APPENDIX

A

Chapter 1

Exercise Answers

1. What is TCP/IP?

Answer: A suit of protocols that provide routing addressing in wide-area networks, and connectivity to a variety of hosts, including hosts on the worldwide Internet.

2. What are the layers in the four-layer model used by TCP/IP?

Answer: Application, Transport, Internet, and Network Interface.

3. What core TCP/IP protocols are provided with Microsoft TCP/IP?

Answer: TCP, UDP, ICMP, IP and ARP.

4. What parameters are required for a TCP/IP host to communicate in a wide-area network?

Answer: IP address, Subnet mask, and Default Gateway.

Scenario Solutions

SCENARIO #1 It's Monday morning. Just as you arrive at your desk, your boss calls you into his office, and says he read about TCP/IP in a Microsoft magazine over the weekend. Because he now knows that all Microsoft products are fabulous, he's set on someone implementing MS TCP/IP at all twelve branch office sites. He says that because of your quality work over the past few months, you're his first choice. However, before he names you the project's leader, he wants you to give him a complete explanation of TCP/IP, and how it will meet his networking needs. Can you? Try it.

Answer: The acronym *TCP/IP* stands for *Transmission Control Protocol/Internet Protocol*. Essentially, it's a set of two communication protocols that an application can use to package its information for sending across a network, or networks.

TCP/IP also refers to an entire collection of protocols, called a *protocol suite*. This collection includes application protocols for performing tasks like e-mail, file transfers, and terminal emulation.

SCENARIO #2 To get a jump on the competition, you need to find some information on a new, highly efficient protocol being developed. Where would you find this information? How would you access it, and through which server? If you have access to the Internet, try this as an exercise on your computer.

> **Answer:** FTP to DS.INTERNIC.NIC or e-mail to rfc-info@ISI.EDU, including the message: help: ways_to_get_rfcs.

SCENARIO #3 Your boss tells you she spent lunch at the gym, where she overheard a great way to look up information on the Internet. She tells you that it organizes subjects into a menu system, and allows you to access the information on each topic listed. She's frustrated because she can't remember what its called—can you?

> **Answer:** Gopher organizes topics into a menu system and allows you to access the information on each topic listed.

SCENARIO #4 You are the Senior Communication Technician for a small computer store. The sales staff is complaining that they cannot deliver or receive mail on their TCP/IP computers. All other applications on the network seem to work OK. The location of the problem is likely to be on *which layer* of the DOD model?

> **Answer:** The Application/Process layer of the DOD is responsible for sending and receiving mail using the Simple Mail Transfer Protocol.

SCENARIO #5 The IS department is planning on implementing TCP/IP. Your manager, who knows and understands the OSI reference model, asks you "What are the layers in the four-layer model used by the DOD for TCP/IP and how does each layer relate to the OSI reference model?" What do you tell him?

> **Answer:** The four layers of the DOD model and how they relate to the OSI model is shown below:

DOD	OSI
Process/Application layer	Application, Presentation, and Session
Host-to-Host or Transport	Transport
Internet	Network
Network Access	Data Link and Physical

SCENARIO #6 You are the network administrator for a large accounting office. They have seven offices, all connected. You get a complaint call from a remote office about how their workstations cannot connect to the network. After talking with them for a few minutes, it appears that network connectivity is down at all seven offices. What layer of the DOD model is likely at fault?

Answer: The Network Access layer is responsible for network connectivity.

SCENARIO #7 The accounting department calls you about two problem workstations in their department, complaining that "they're taking turns like twins, with only one being able to log in to the network at a time." All the other workstations in the department are fine. What's the problem, and how do you fix it?

Answer: Two workstations with the same hardware address (MAC address) can only work one at a time. Change out the network card.

SCENARIO #8 You're the network manager for a large aircraft company. The reservationists have been griping for two weeks about the slow response of their computers. You've narrowed the problem down to noise on the thinnet coax cabling. Which layer of the DOD model is responsible?

Answer: The Network Access layer is responsible for the physical specifications of the cabling. Make sure the specifications of the cable are correct, such as length and terminators.

SCENARIO #9 Your co-worker calls you because she is confused about the differences between the OSI reference model and the DOD model. She can't figure out where packets are framed with the hardware address and a cyclic redundancy check. What do you tell her?

Answer: The Data Link layer of the OSI model is responsible for framing and hardware addressing, while the Network Access layer is responsible for the DOD model.

SCENARIO #10 You're in an interview for an important position at a good company. You've studied hard, and know your TCP/IP. The interviewer asks you, "What is the connectionless protocol at the Internet layer of the DOD model, and what is its function?" Do you stare back blankly, with mouth agape, or answer confidently with....?

Answer: The Internet Protocol. The complex task of routing is performed at the Internet layer.

SCENARIO #11 After breezing through that last question, the interviewer then asks you, "At what layer are messages segmented, and what protocol is used for segmenting them?" What's your answer?

> **Answer:** TCP at the Host-to-Host layer. TCP takes large blocks of information from an application and breaks them down into segments, which it then numbers and sequences so that the destination's TCP protocol can order the segments back into the large block the application intended. After these segments have been sent, TCP waits for acknowledgment for each one from the receiving end's TCP, retransmitting the ones not acknowledged.

SCENARIO #12 Your pal just landed a job as a Help Desk operator, and is brushing up on her TCP/IP protocols to prepare for her first day. She calls you with this question: "Ones and zeros are extracted from the cable and formed into logical groups called frames. The hardware destination is then checked, and a cyclic redundancy checksum is performed. If the hardware address is correct, and the CRC matches its original mathematical algorithm, the packet is then sent to which protocol at which layer?" What do you tell her?

> **Answer:** Ones and zeros are extracted from the cable and formed into logical groups called frames. The hardware destination is then checked, and a cyclic redundancy checksum is performed. If the hardware address is correct, and the CRC matches its original mathematical algorithm, the packet is sent to IP at the Network layer to verify the IP address. If the IP address is valid, it is then sent to UDP or TCP at the Host-to-Host layer.

SCENARIO #13 You're a software developer who enjoys writing video games to play on the Internet with TCP/IP. You want to use the fastest protocol at the Transport layer of the OSI model to ensure no delay when blowing up all the Morphofreaks. What protocol do you use? Also, at what corresponding layer of the DOD model would this protocol run?

> **Answer:** UDP (User Datagram Protocol) at the Host-to-Host layer. UDP receives upper-layer blocks of information instead of streams of data like TCP, and breaks them into segments. Like TCP, it gives each segment a number for reassembly into the intended block at the destination. However, UDP does *not* sequence the segments.

SCENARIO #14 Your UNIX diskless workstations cannot logon to the host. After troubleshooting, you notice that when they boot up, the hardware address is sent to the host, but the host rejects them. Which protocol is asleep on the job?

Answer: BootP (Boot Program). When a diskless workstation is powered on, it broadcasts a BootP request on the network. A BootP server hears the request, and looks up the client's MAC address in its BootP file. If it finds a match, BootP assigns an IP address to the host.

SCENARIO #15 You need to install network management to keep track of network errors and to baseline for future growth. Which protocol do you use, and which layer of the DOD does it operate on?

Answer: The Simple Network Management Protocol can get information about your network and help you baseline. It runs at the Process/Application layer.

Chapter 2

Exercise Answers

1. In Class A, Class B and Class C, which octets represent the network ID and which represent the host ID?

   Answer:

   Class A: The network ID uses the first octet, the host ID uses the last three octets.

   Class B: The network ID uses the first two octets, the host ID uses the last two octets.

   Class C: The network ID uses the first three octets, the host ID uses the last octet.

2. Which numbers are invalid as a network ID and why? Which numbers are invalid as a host ID and why?

   Answer: As a network ID, 127 is reserved for loopback functions. As a network ID and a host ID, all ones (255) and all 0's are invalid. All 1's are used for broadcasts. All 0's indicate the local network or "this network only."

3. When is a unique network ID required?

   Answer: A unique network ID is required for each physical network and for connection between two routers on a wide-area network.

4. In a TCP/IP Internetwork, what components require a host ID besides computers?

Answer: Each TCP/IP-based host requires a host ID that is unique to the network ID, including routers.

5. What are two common addressing problems and their effects?

Answer:

Network IDs on a local network don't match. Local hosts cannot communicate.

Network IDs on a local network are duplicate. Windows NT hosts cannot initialize; other TCP/IP hosts may or may not be able to communicate or possibly hang.

6. What is the purpose of a subnet mask?

Answer: To mask a portion of the IP address so that IP can distinguish the network ID from the host ID.

7. What requires a subnet mask?

Answer: Each host on a TCP/IP network requires a subnet mask.

8. When is a default subnet mask used?

Answer: A default subnet mask is used when a TCP/IP host is not part of a subnetwork.

9. When is it necessary to define a custom subnet mask?

Answer: When you divide your network into subnets.

Multiple-Choice Answers

1. Problem: Your company has offices in Los Angeles, San Francisco, and Sacramento. Each office currently has around 100 users and will be on its own subnet. Within the year, you expect to open offices in San Jose and San Diego. Each office will never have more than 350 users. You are assigned the network address 146.85.0.0, and you need to assign a subnet mask to the computers on your network so you can support this configuration.

Solution: Specify the subnet mask 255.255.254.0

How well does this solution address the problem?

A. Meets the requirements and is an outstanding solution

B. Meets the requirements and is an adequate solution

C. Meets the requirements but is not a desirable solution

D. Does not meet the requirements, although it appears to work

E. Does not meet the requirements and does not work

Answer: A. The subnet 255.255.254.0 will provide 126 subnets and 510 hosts on each subnet. This is an excellent solution, as it will meet the customer requirements of 350 hosts per subnet.

2. **Problem:** Your company has offices in Los Angeles, San Francisco, and Sacramento. Each office currently has around 100 users and will be on it's own subnet. Within the year, you expect to open offices in San Jose and San Diego. Each office will never have more than 350 users. You are assigned the network address 146.85.0.0, and you need to assign a subnet mask to the computers on your network so you can support this configuration.

Solution: Specify the subnet mask 255.192.0.0

How well does this solution address the problem?

A. Meets the requirements and is an outstanding solution

B. Meets the requirements and is an adequate solution

C. Meets the requirements but is not a desirable solution

D. Does not meet the requirements, although it appears to work

E. Does not meet the requirements and does not work

Answer: E. Class B subnet mask must start with 255.255.—no exceptions!

3. **Problem:** Your company has 25 offices in the United States. Each office currently has around 100 users and will be on its own subnet. Within the year, you expect these numbers to double. You are assigned the network

address 146.85.0.0, and you need to assign a subnet mask to the computers on your network so you can support this configuration.

Solution: Specify the subnet mask 255.255.255.0

How well does this solution address the problem?

A. Meets the requirements and is an outstanding solution

B. Meets the requirements and is an adequate solution

C. Meets the requirements but is not a desirable solution

D. Does not meet the requirements, although it appears to work

E. Does not meet the requirements and does not work

Answer: A. With a subnet mask of 255.255.255.0, it will provide 254 subnets, each with 254 hosts—an excellent solution for this customer.

4. **Problem:** Your company has 25 offices in the United States. Each office currently has around 100 users and will be on its own subnet. Within the year, you expect these numbers to double. You are assigned the network address 146.85.0.0, and you need to assign a subnet mask to the computers on your network so you can support this configuration.

Solution: Specify the subnet mask 255.255.240.0

How well does this solution address the problem?

A. Meets the requirements and is an outstanding solution

B. Meets the requirements and is an adequate solution

C. Meets the requirements but is not a desirable solution

D. Does not meet the requirements, although it appears to work

E. Does not meet the requirements and does not work

Answer: E. With a subnet of 255.255.240.0, it will provide 14 subnets. The customer needs 25 now and up to 50 in the future. Does not meet the requirements.

5. **Problem:** Your company has been assigned a Class C address 196.43 .201.0. There are currently four subnets on your network and you expect the number of subnets to increase. Each subnet must

be able to support 60 hosts. You need to assign a subnet mask to the computers on your network so you can support this configuration.

Solution: Specify the subnet mask `255.255.255.224`

How well does this solution address the problem?

A. Meets the requirements and is an outstanding solution

B. Meets the requirements and is an adequate solution

C. Meets the requirements but is not a desirable solution

D. Does not meet the requirements, although it appears to work

E. Does not meet the requirements and does not work

Answer: E. The subnet mask `255.255.255.224` will provide 6 subnets with 30 hosts on each subnet. Does not work for the customer requirements.

6. You are designing a network and have been assigned the address `201.14.6.0`. You want to have six subnets and must be able to support 12 hosts. Which subnet masks meet your requirements?

A. `255.255.255.240`

B. `255.255.255.128`

C. `255.255.255.224`

D. `255.255.255.248`

Answers:

A. `255.255.255.240` provides 14 subnets each with 14 hosts. It meets the requirements.

B. `255.255.255.128` will give no subnets. This does not meet the requirements.

C. `255.255.255.224` will provide 6 subnets, each with 30 hosts. This meets the requirements.

D. `255.255.255.248` will provide 30 subnets, each with 6 hosts. This does not meet the requirements.

7. You have been assigned a Class A address and intend to have eight subnets on your network. Which subnet mask would you use to maximize the number of hosts on each subnet?

   A. `255.255.255.0`

   B. `255.0.0.0`

   C. `255.240.0.0`

   D. `255.255.240.0`

Answers:

   A. `255.255.255.0` will provide 65534 subnets with 254 hosts on each subnet. This will meet the requirements.

   B. `255.0.0.0` will provide no subnets. This will not meet the requirements.

   C. `55.240.0.0` will provide 14 subnets, each with 1,048,574 hosts. This will meet the requirements.

   D. `255.255.240.0` will provide 4094 subnets, each with 4094 hosts.

Multiple-Choice Exercise Group Answers

Exercise A Answers:

   1. Top to bottom: B, A, C, B, A

   2. A, B

   3. C

   4. D, E

Exercise B Answers:

   A. 256 is incorrect. The highest possible value in an octet is 255 (254 for a valid host).

   B. 255 is invalid for a host id.

   C. 231 is a class D address and is not supported as a host address.

   D. Zero is not valid for a host. Zero specifies This network only.

    E. Zero is not a valid host address.

    F. Zero is invalid.

    G. 127 is reserved for loopback.

    H. 255 is a broadcast address.

    I. All 1's (255.255.255.255) specifies a broadcast.

Exercise C Answers:

    I. Class A OR Class B

    2. B and D

    3A. Assign high numbers to all servers, for instance 200-250.

    3B. Assign low numbers to all UNIX workstations, for instance 150-200.

    3C. Assign numbers to the Windows NT Workstation computers using a different octet than used by the servers and UNIX workstations.

Exercise D Answers:

    I. 2 local networks (D and E) +3 wide-area networks (A, B, and C) = 5 total.

    2. 50 Windows NT Server computers +200 Windows NT Workstation computers +50 UNIX hosts +5 router interfaces = 305.

    3. The router interface D.

Exercise E Answers:

    I. 255.0.0.0

    2. 255.255.0.0

    3. 255.255.255.0

    4. 255.240.0.0

    5. 255.255.254.0

    6. Using 7 bits = 255.254.0.0. Using 8 bits = 255.255.0.0.

7. Using 7 bits will provide up to 126 subnets and 131,070 hosts per subnet.

   Using 8 bits will provide up to 254 subnets and 65,534 hosts per subnet.

8. Using 5 bits = 255.255.248.0.

9. Using 5 bits will provide up to 30 subnets and 2046 hosts per subnet.

Scenario Solutions

SCENARIO #1   You need to get an IP address assigned so you can broadcast your company on the Internet. Who do you contact?

   Answer: NIC (Network Information Center)

SCENARIO #2   You need to send a broadcast message on the network informing users that the server is going down. When you send the multicast transmission, which address will IP use to broadcast the message to all users?

   Answer: 255.255.255.255. or 1111111.11111111.11111111.11111111

SCENARIO #3   The NIC assigns you a Class B address for your company's network. How many octets define the network portion of the address?

   Answer: The first two octets (16 bits) in a Class B network are reserved for the network address.

SCENARIO #4   The NIC has assigned a Class C address for your new Internet Web server. How many bits can you use for the host address?

   Answer: In a Class C address, 8 bits are reserved for host addresses.

SCENARIO #5   You look in your workstation configuration and notice there's an IP address of 127.0.0.1. What does this mean?

   Answer: 127.0.0.1 is the loopback address for the local host, so you can test your workstation without loading up the network with a bunch of stuff unnecessarily.

SCENARIO #6   You decide you want to subnet your Class B network with an address of 255.240.0.0. When implemented it does not work. Why?

   Answer: A Class B subnet mask must start with 255.255 as the first two octets. No exceptions.

SCENARIO #7   Your boss read in a Microsoft magazine that creating subnets will help her network run more efficiently. She's decided to implement this, and wants you to lead the project. She wants you to outline what the advantages of subnetting the network are so she can justify the project to her superiors in a meeting this afternoon. What will you equip her with? Take a minute to create a list of the benefits of subnetting for her.

Answer:

- Reduced network traffic

- Optimized network performance

- Simplified management

- Facilitates spanning large geographic distances

SCENARIO #8   You have four offices and 25 nodes at each office. Which subnet mask would you assign to your Class C network address of `201.201.201.0`?

Answer: `255.255.255.224`. This subnet address would give you six subnets with thirty nodes per subnet.

SCENARIO #9   You have a Class B network address of `187.32.0.0`. Which subnet address would give you at least 200 subnets?

Answer: `255.255.255.0`. All bits in the third octet used for subnetting would give you 254 subnets, each with 254 nodes.

SCENARIO #10   Your network is not assigned an address for the NIC and you do not need to be on the Internet. You create a Class A address of `36.0.0.0` with a subnet mask of `255.255.0.0`. How many subnets can you use and how many hosts can be on each subnet?

Answer: 254 subnets each with 65,534 hosts. All bits in the second octet are used for subnets, which leave the second and third octet (16 bits) for hosts.

SCENARIO #11   Your IS manager asks you if their is some kind of computer that will map host names to IP addresses for groups of computers called domains. What do you tell him?

Answer: Network Information Services (NIS)

SCENARIO #12   You're called upon to help train a new network help-desk employee who is confused about the Domain Name System. How do you explain it to her?

Answer: The Domain Name System (DNS) is a mechanism that helps users to locate the name of a host and to map a name to an IP address on machines throughout the Internet.

SCENARIO #13   The CIO of your company is assessing the knowledge level of his network operating system staff. He calls to ask you the difference between NIS and DNS. What do you say?

Answer: The major difference between NIS and DNS is that an NIS server covers a smaller area. NIS servers relate only to a group of computers, not the entire Internet. DNS covers a large area and is on the Internet.

SCENARIO #14   The host table on your UNIX server needs to be updated. You need to add the recently acquired New York site with an IP address of 132.132.45.98. It also needs an alias of NY. Where is the host table file and in what order would you place the information in the table?

Answer: The file is located in /etc and named hosts. The format would be:

```
Ip address        Host name     Alias     Comment

132.132.45.87     New York      NY        #New York office
```

Chapter 3

Multiple-Choice Answers

1. What are the protocols that use dynamic routing?

   A. Routing Information Protocol

   B. Dynamic Information Protocol

   C. Open Shortest Path First

   D. Open Safest Path First

   Answers: A and C

2. When configuring multiple default gateways, which is true?

A. Although more than one default gateway can be configured, only the first one will be used for routing purposes. The others will be used only as backup should the primary one become unavailable for some reason.

B. Multiple default gateways cannot be configured with NT.

C. Although more than one default gateway can be configured, only the last one will be used for routing purposes. The others will be used only as backup should the primary one become unavailable for some reason.

D. More then one default gateway can be configured, and NT uses a round-robin approach when choosing the default gateway.

Answer: A

3. What is the TRACERT utility?

A. The TRACERT utility is essentially a verification tool. It's used to substantiate the route that's been taken to a local host.

B. The TRACERT utility erases any traces of viruses on Windows NT.

C. The TRACERT utility works with dynamic routing to help trace the shortest paths.

D. The TRACERT utility is essentially a verification tool. It's used to substantiate the route that's been taken to a destination host.

Answer: D

4. What is IP routing?

A. InterProcess routing is used for delivering e-mail.

B. IP routing works only on local networks.

C. IP routing is the process of sending data from a host on one network to a remote host on another network through a router, or routers.

D. IP routing, a function of the Network Access layer of the DOD reference model, routes packets between hosts.

Answer: C

Scenario Solutions

SCENARIO #1 Your boss frantically comes up to you and says he put two NIC cards in his NT server, but the workstations on each segment can't see each other. He knows that to route IP packets to other networks, each multi-homed computer (static router) must be configured two ways, but he can't remember what they are. What are the two things you need to set on the NT Server?

Answer:

1. A default gateway address of another router's local interface

2. An entry in each router's routing table for each network in the internetwork

SCENARIO #2 You get a call from a company who thinks they need some routers. They have a small network, and read in a magazine that they should use static routing. They want to know more about how static routing would meet their networking needs. What do you tell them?

Answer: Static routing is a function of IP. Static routers require that routing tables are built and updated manually. If a route changes, static routers do not inform each other of the event. Also, they do not exchange routes with dynamic routers.

SCENARIO #3 It's your first day on the job at Terrific Technology Teaching Center, and as a co-instructor you are asked to teach on the enabling of IP routers. Take a moment to explain the procedure now.

Answer: Add multiple network adapter cards to a computer, and select the Enable IP Routing check box.

SCENARIO #4 Later, a student comes up to you confused and asks if he needs to add a routing table to a computer running as a multihomed computer, and connecting two subnet segments. What do you tell her, and why?

Answer: No, because the computer already has an interface to both segments

SCENARIO #5 You have two NT servers and a router to the Internet. Should you build a static router between the NT servers, or will the dynamic router to the Internet be sufficient?

Answer: Build a static route between the NT servers and then use the dynamic router as a default gateway.

SCENARIO #6: What information would you put into the static routing table?

Answer: Destination network name or network ID, the IP address or host name, and a subnet mask of the router

Chapter 4

Multiple-Choice Answers

1. What is IP address resolution?

A. Resolving duplicate IP addresses

B. The successful mapping of an IP address to its hardware address

C. Resolving invalid subnet masks

D. Resolving errors when IP tries to resolve an IP address to a hardware address

Answer: B

2. How do you resolve IP addresses locally?

A. By typing `Resolve IP address ip-address`

B. By typing `ARP -s ip-address`

C. With an ARP request and an ARP reply

D. With a RARP request and a RARP reply

Answer: C

3. How does your computer resolve IP addresses remotely?

A. It sends an ARP to the destination machine.

B. It sends a RARP to the destination machine.

C. It sends a RARP to the default gateway.

D. It sends an ARP to the default gateway.

Answer: D

4. What is true about the ARP cache?

  A. It's cleared out every time the computer is rebooted.

  B. The ARP cache stores only dynamic IP and hardware addresses.

  C. The ARP cache stores only static IP and hardware addresses.

  D. It's permanent.

  Answer: A

5. What's the maximum lifetime of an entry in the ARP cache?

  A. 2 minutes

  B. As specified by the system administrator

  C. 10 minutes

  D. ARP entries are permanent and can only be removed by typing `ARP -d`.

  Answer: C

6. Aside from the initial entry into the cache, if the destination system isn't contacted again, how long will the entry remain in the cache?

  A. 10 minutes

  B. 2 minutes

  C. 5 minutes

  D. Until deleted

  Answer: B

7. Under Windows NT, if the cache fills up, what happens to old and new entries?

  A. If their lifetime expires, old entries are deleted, and new ones added.

  B. Regardless of whether or not an old entry's lifetime has expired, it is deleted in favor of adding the new one.

  C. Old entries are cached for future use, and new ones added to the ARP table.

Answer: B

Scenario Solutions

SCENARIO #1 You're a computer science professor at a major university. One of your students wants to know why an IP address needs to be resolved. She asks why it's necessary to know both the software and hardware addresses—why isn't knowing the hardware address enough? Explain.

Answer: An IP address must be resolved to determine which host owns it. IP addresses are easier to work with in that they follow a logical system. Hardware addresses tend to be a lot less friendly and difficult to manage. Knowing both also reduces the risk of error.

SCENARIO #2 You're being interviewed for a network specialist position. Your potential employer asks, "In what way could an incorrect subnet mask cause problems? When would this problem occur, and who, if anyone, would notice?" How would you answer?

Answer: Incorrect subnet masks cause problems when a host is attempting to determine if an address is local or remote, because during this process, a host will examine the subnet mask to determine which portions of the address are network-based and which are node-based. If a remote machine is discovered on the local network, a broadcast storm can result, causing systems to time-out, and hang. It would affect the entire network, and therefore, many would notice.

Chapter 5

Multiple-Choice Answers

1. What is a domain name?

    A. The Microsoft implementation of a NetBIOS name server

    B. A text file in the same format as the 4.3 BSD UNIX file

    C. A hierarchical name that is implemented using a Domain Name Server (DNS)

    D. A flat name that is implemented using a Domain Name Server (DNS)

    Answer: C

2. What is Host name resolution?

   A. A b-node broadcast on the local network for the IP address of the destination NetBIOS name

   B. The process of mapping a host name to an IP address

   C. A hierarchical name that is implemented using a Domain Name Server (DNS)

   D. A local text file that maps IP addresses to the NetBIOS computer names

Answer: B

3. What is true of a host name? Choose all the correct answers.

   A. The NAMEHOST utility will display the host name assigned to your system.

   B. It is an alias assigned to a computer by an administrator to identify a TCP/IP host.

   C. A host name never corresponds to an IP address that is stored in a HOSTS file or in a database on a DNS or WINS server.

   D. Host names are not used in Windows NT commands.

   E. A host name cannot be used in place of an IP address when using ping or other TCP/IP utilities.

   Answer: B

4. Which are common problems associated with host name resolution?

   A. Multiple entries for the same host on different lines

   B. Host name is misspelled

   C. Case-sensitivity

   D. IP address is invalid

   Answers: A, B, and D

Scenario Solutions

SCENARIO #1 You have enabled all Windows NT name resolving techniques: WINS, b-node broadcast, and LMHOSTS, in addition to the HOSTS file and DNS. But none of these methods resolves a host name. What is the only way to communicate with this host?

Answer: If none of the methods work to solve the hosts name, the only way to communicate with the host is to specify the IP address.

SCENARIO #2 When resolving names with a HOSTS file, the local names are being resolved while none of the remote host names are being resolved. What would stop the remote host names from being resolved?

Answer: The default gateway is not defined or incorrect.

SCENARIO #3 When resolving names with a HOSTS file, you notice that a host name is being resolved incorrectly. When checking the HOSTS file, you don't see a problem, as the name is spelled correctly and the IP address is correct. What else could be wrong?

Answer: There are multiple entries for the same host on different lines.

SCENARIO #4 Your company needs to resolve names on the Internet for its customers trying to look up information on the state of the company. What service will you use to resolve names?

Answer: Domain Name System

Chapter 6

Multiple-Choice Answers

1. What is NetBIOS naming?

    A. A b-node broadcast on a local network

    B. A local text file used for addressing

    C. Computer names used to communicate with other hosts

    D. Entries in the LMHOSTS file

    Answer: C

2. Which of the following are NetBIOS over TCP/IP node types?

A. NBNS

B. P-node

C. L-node

D. M-node

Answer: B and D

3. What is the NetBIOS Name Resolution?

A. The local cache containing locally registered computer names

B. A server configured with the DNS daemon

C. The process of successfully mapping a computer's NetBIOS name to an IP address

D. A broadcast used for registration and resolution

Answer: C

4. What is the NetBIOS Name Resolution via LMHOST method?

A. A local text file in the same format as the 4.3BSD UNIX/etc/hosts file

B. A static file used to resolve NetBIOS names to IP addresses

C. Stored in the registry, and used in Windows NT commands

D. A computer name assigned during Windows NT installation

Answer: B

Scenario Solutions

SCENARIO #1 You are trying to connect to an NT server with the NET USE \\server_name command. That works OK, but when you try NET USE \\ IP _address, it gets a bad command or filename. You checked the IP address and it is correct. What could the problem be?

Answer: The NET USE command requires a NetBIOS name. For example, to connect to a server with an IP address of 192.123.45.67, you could not say NET USE F: \\192.123.45.67\share. The actual name is required, and therefore, the system must still resolve the name.

SCENARIO #2 You get calls from users complaining that NetBIOS names are not being resolved all the time. "It's flaky," as one user puts it. You open the LMHOSTS file and find some errors: a misspelled name, some old IP addresses, and a couple of misplaced comments. What effect can these erroneous entries have on the LMHOSTS file?

Answer:

1. A misspelled name will keep the LMHOSTS file from resolving the name.

2. An old IP address will cause the resolved name to be misdirected. (This is worse than one being resolved, since you will be directed to the wrong system, if one at all.)

3. A misplaced comment will generally have no effect so long as it does not disrupt the standard format of the LMHOSTS file.

SCENARIO #3 When cleaning out the LMHOSTS file, you found entries that started with #PRE. Where should you locate the LMHOSTS entries with the #PRE identifier? Why?

Answer: Entries should be placed at the END of the LMHOST file. These entries are only read when TCP//IP initializes, and are not read again.

SCENARIO #4 You have been promoted to network manager. Your first job is to make sure you are using all of the company's bandwidth properly. Which node modes should you use? Which mode will be the most efficient for your network?

Answer: If all of the destination hosts you need to resolve NetBIOS names are on the same subnet then Microsoft's Enhanced b-mode is most efficient. However, since this is hardly the case, the best overall efficiency tends to come from h-node, m-node, and p-node systems. This is largely due to the fact that they have little waste in finding their target system. H-node and M-node systems are equally reliable, however the H-node is more desirable because it is less chatty. In the purest sense, Microsoft's Enhanced b-node can generate the least traffic if all required systems are preloaded into memory. As this is not commonly the case, usually p-node systems are regarded as the most silent. Given a choice, use an H-node system.

SCENARIO #5 Someone in your office deleted the # signs in the LMHOSTS file because they thought they were comments. After you replaced the # signs, and the phones stopped ringing (two hours later!), this staff member wants to know what the # identifiers that are used in the LMHOSTS file are used for. What do you tell them?

Answer:

1. #PRE (for loading resolution names into memory)

2. #DOM (discussed later, for domain validation)

3. #INCLUDE (for including remote system's LMHOSTS files)

4. #BEGIN_ALTERNATE (beginning of alternate block inclusion search)

5. #END_ALTERNATE (end of alternate block inclusion search)

6. # (comments and text)

Chapter 7

Multiple-Choice Answers

1. What are the four steps in the DHCP lease process?

   A. Contact, Offer, Selection, Acknowledgment

   B. Request, Offer, Election, Acceptance

   C. Request, Offer, Selection, Acceptance

   D. Petition, Offer, Election, Acknowledgment

   E. Request, Offer, Selection, Acknowledgment

   Answer: E

2. Why are initial broadcasts used, and what uses them?

A. Routers use them to update the routing tables of all DHCP servers on the network.

B. Client machines use them to secure leases and notify all DHCP servers that they now have one, so the servers won't send out more DHCPACK's, and thus create duplicate addresses.

C. DHCP servers use them to secure client leases, and release them if they're not renewed when 50% of the lease has expired.

D. Client machines use them to locate a DHCP server in order to acquire an IP address for a specific period of time.

Answer: D

3. What is the default period of time a DHCP lease is extended to a client?

A. 24 hours

B. 48 hours

C. 72 hours

D. 3¼ days

E. Unlimited

Answer: C

4. How often should the Jetpack utility be used?

A. An administrator should use it when the leases of the client machines on the network have expired.

B. Depending on the size of the network, and how many changes typically occur on it, the requirement varies from every few days, to every couple of months.

C. As often as possible. Changes that aren't recorded and updated can go into error, causing chaos on the network.

D. Because space in the DHCP.MDB file is valuable and fills up fast, the Jetpack utility should be run every 72 hours to remove obsolete IP address entries.

Answer: B

5. How many DHCP servers are required for a network that possesses three subnets, each with DHCP clients on it, and whose routers are supportive of the BootP protocol?

A. One DHCP server is all that's required.

B. Since there are three subnets on the network, three DHCP servers would be required in order to ensure fault tolerance.

C. Two servers are required in order to ensure the network's fault tolerance.

Answer: A

6. Does Microsoft support DHCP server options that Microsoft clients will not support? Explain.

A. Yes. The additional DHCP server options are there for other IP based platforms, such as UNIX, which utilize different information.

B. Yes. Additional server options exist in order to enable communication on the Internet.

C. No. DHCP servers are for DHCP clients only. Machines operating under different platforms, like UNIX, utilize servers that correspond to theirs—never DHCP servers.

D. Yes, but only if Power PCs, which support all types of software platforms, exist as client machines on that network.

Answer: A

7. Once configured, what are the administrative functions performed on a DHCP server?

A. Backup, renew, release

B. Backup, restore, delete

C. Backup, restore, compact

D. Backup, renew, compact

Answer: C

Scenario Solutions

SCENARIO #1 It's late—almost time to go home. You've only got one more DHCP client to get a lease for, and that's almost done. Just as you kick back and throw your tired dogs up onto the desk, DHCPNACK appears on your screen. What does this mean, and what are the possible reasons for it appearing on your screen?

> **Answer:** DHCPNACK is a negative lease acknowledgment message. It means that your selection has been rejected. This most often occurs when a client is attempting to re-lease its old IP address, which has since been reassigned elsewhere. It can also mean that the requesting client has an inaccurate IP address—perhaps as a result of being moved to a different subnet, or, because there are no available IP addresses for this subnet.

SCENARIO #2 As Network Manager, you find yourself needing to bring down one of your DHCP servers—the one that just happens to serve the CEO's client machine. You've checked, and sure enough, that client's lease will most certainly expire, causing all the Big Cheese's TCP/IP functions to come to a grinding halt before you could possibly complete your work on the troubled server. To complicate things, if you don't bring down and repair that server, all the clients using it—including the CEO—will be in big trouble. Are you about to become unemployed, or are there solutions to this dilemma? Explain.

> **Answer:** Yes—you will still find yourself employed if you use the trusty IPCONFIG/RENEW command to schedule a time for the server you're working on to come up and meet all of your user's lease renewal needs.

Chapter 8

Multiple-Choice Answers

1. How many WINS servers are recommended for a network of 10,000 clients?

   A. 1000

   B. 50

C. 1

D. 2

E. 10

Answer: D

2. What are two benefits to a WINS server?

    A. IP addressing to multiple clients

    B. Reduces traffic

    C. Can only be updated statically, so it's very secure

    D. Internetwork and Inter-domain browsing capabilities without configuring and maintaining an LMHOSTS file at each computer

    Answers: B and D

3. How can WINS support a nonWINS client?

    A. Using DHCP

    B. Using a proxy agent

    C. Using an LMHOSTS file

    D. Using a push partner

    E. Using a pull partner

    Answer: B

4. How must WINS be configured to support an environment of multiple non-WINS clients spread across a wide area network at two different sites?

    A. One WINS server should be configured for both locations.

    B. Two WINS servers should be configured, one per location. The WINS servers should be set as pull partners with static entries for the non-WINS clients. A proxy agent should also be configured on each subnet that has nonWINS clients.

C. Three WINS servers should be configured: two servers in one location, and one server in another, running as pull partners with static entries for the nonWINS clients. A proxy agent should also be configured on each subnet that has nonWINS clients.

D. Two WINS servers should be configured, one per location. The WINS servers should be set as push partners with static entries for the nonWINS clients. A proxy agent should also be configured on each subnet that has nonWINS clients.

Answer: A

Scenario Solutions

SCENARIO #1 You work at a large retail computer shop. A customer asks if a 386DX-25MHZ system with 12MB of memory would be enough to run the WINS service process. Is it? What should you ask of your customer before answering his question (besides his credit card number)? What suggestions should you make?

Answer: Although this configuration would work in the strictest sense of meeting the minimal requirements, in most cases, there will not be adequate power for it to run smoothly. However, before you can answer this question, you should ask how many clients will be using this service, how often is it cleared (of extinct systems), how many replication partners exist, would the system be a primary or secondary system, and so forth. In most situations, it would be worth exploring the feasibility of upgrading, however, if you have a small network and the WINS server was just a token to the operating function, the issues presented in the answer really would not matter.

SCENARIO #2 You are a network administrator for a computer manufacturer. They have a large network and need to install WINS on it to help keep traffic down. They have a few O/S2 and UNIX computers, and need to register them in the WINS database. How do you do this?

Answer: By using a WINS proxy agent. A WINS proxy agent extends the name resolution capabilities of the WINS server to nonWINS clients by listening for broadcast name registrations and broadcast resolution requests, and then forwarding them to a WINS server.

SCENARIO #3 You are installing two NT computers at your home office. After installing an NT Server running DHCP and WINS, you want to backup the WINS database. What are the steps to do this?

Answer:

1. From the WINS Manager Mapping menu, choose Backup Database.

2. Specify the location for saving backup files.

3. If you want to backup only the changes that have occurred since the last backup, select Perform Incremental Backup.

4. Choose OK.

The WINS database is backed up automatically every 24 hours after you specify the backup directory.

Chapter 9

Multiple-Choice Answers

1. Which Windows NT service provides browsing capabilities requiring no extra configuration?

    A. The Windows 95 Computer Browser service

    B. The Windows NT Computer Browser service

    C. The Windows NT Computer LMHOSTS service

    D. The Windows NT Computer WINS service

    Answer: B

2. What's the function of the Master browser?

    A. The Master browser collects information and puts it in the LMHOSTS file.

    B. The Master browser collects and maintains the LMHOSTS list of available network resources. It also distributes this list to Backup browsers.

C. The Master browser collects and maintains the master list of available network resources. It also distributes this list to Backup browsers.

D. The Master browser collects and maintains the backup list of available network resources. It also distributes this list to Master browsers.

Answer: C

3. What's required in the LMHOSTS file for a nonWINS client to browse resources on another subnet, and to ensure interdomain activity?

A. The following entry for each domain controller located on a different subnet:

```
master_browser ip_address #PRE #DOM:domain_name
```

B. The following entry for each domain controller located on a different subnet:

```
ip_address master_browser #DOM:domain_name #PRE
```

C. The following entry for each domain controller located on the same subnet:

```
ip_address master_browser #PRE #DOM:domain_name
```

D. The following entry for each domain controller located on a different subnet:

```
ip_address master_browser #PRE #DOM:domain_name
```

Answer: D

4. What's required on domain controllers to ensure account synchronization can be accomplished in an internetwork?

A. Each domain controller requires an LMHOSTS file with the following entry:

```
ip_address master_browser #PRE #DOM:domain_name
```

B. Each domain controller requires a HOSTS file with the following entry:

```
ip_address master_browser #PRE #DOM:domain_name
```

C. Each domain controller requires an LMHOSTS file with the following entry:

```
master_browser ip_address #PRE #DOM:domain_name
```

D. Each domain controller requires a HOSTS file with the following entry:

```
ip_address master_browser #DOM:domain_name #PRE
```

Answer: A

5. A user calls and says that she can see that the server she wants to connect to is listed, but she is unable to connect to it. How could a server appear in the browse list but not be available?

A. She can connect. It's user error.

B. The server could be down. It is possible that the server has shut down but has not yet been removed from the list.

C. The administrator has not yet purged the browser list.

D. The user needs to reboot her workstation.

Answer: B

Scenario Solutions

SCENARIO #1 You have three networks tied together with a router. The router has a capacity for NetBIOS name broadcasts. For optimum performance, should you use the LMHOSTS files and WINS, or simply let the router pass NetBIOS name broadcasts?

Answer: Good question! Depends on your network. It would be easier to just let the broadcasts fly across the network. You wouldn't have to worry about creating or updating the LMHOSTS file and WINS. However, this would be at the cost of network bandwidth—a big expense! If you have a small to medium size Ethernet network, and the bandwidth usage is around 2 to 3 percent, you should be OK with letting those broadcasts fly. On the other hand, if the bandwidth usage is 5 percent or higher, think about creating LMHOSTS files and installing WINS servers. Another solution is to try it and see what the user's response time is when allowing broadcasts to go through the router, or routers. If they don't seem to notice any delay, give 'em all the time they need. It's a good idea to plan for the future by having your LMHOSTS and WINS servers ready to go when needed.

SCENARIO #2 Unclear on the issue of browsers, Management invites you into a meeting to clear up the matter. They want to know what types of browsers can systems that are running Windows NT Workstation or NT Server become. What do you tell them?

Answer:

- Master browser

- Preferred Master browser

- Backup browser

- Potential browser

- Non-browser

SCENARIO #3 A student of yours knows that Microsoft has added a pair of tags to the LMHOSTS file: #PRE and #DOM, and remembers that these tags enable the nonWINS client to communicate with a domain controller to accomplish three very important things. However, this student is unable to recall exactly which three things, and asks you. What would you answer?

Answer:

- Registration

- Verification of a user account

- Changing of passwords

Chapter 10

Multiple-Choice Answers

1. What are some common machines that use TCP/IP to interoperate for file and print services?

    A. Apple Macintosh

    B. DEC VAX systems

    C. DOS systems with TCP/IP

  D. TCP/IP-based printers

  E. Windows 95

  Answer: All of the above.

2. What does the RCP command do?

  A. Request for Copy (a client requesting a file)

  B. Remote Compression

  C. Remote Copy (similar to FTP, except doesn't require a user validation)

  D. Request for Copy Protocol (a file transfer protocol)

  Answer: C

3. What are the three basic functions to Windows NT FTP Management?

  A. Session

  B. Security

  C. Logging

  D. Fragmentation

  Answers: A, B, and C

Scenario Solutions

SCENARIO #1 Your company has just purchased a communications server which has been installed with an IP address of 160.1.8.8. Although the communications unit has NASI (a network specification for a networked pool of modems) support, you do not have any NT-based software to support this function. All that you really want to do is just get to any dumb terminal that can dial a BBS so you can get the latest instructions on how to install a software package that was shipped without an addendum. You call the software company and ask them to fax it to you, but the tech tells you they only have it on their BBS. You then decide to call the communication server manufacturer to find out if it can be accessed by anything else aside from the NASI compliant software. They tell you that you can Telnet to the communications server's IP address on ports 232 to 248 (16 ports), and access it as a dumb terminal using "AT" Modem commands. Using Microsoft's Telnet program, how do you Telnet to that server on port 232?

Answer: From the command line, type TELNET 160.1.8.8 232. This will connect you to the dumb terminal in your Telnet session. You can then issue your "AT" modem commands, such as ATDT, just as if you were directly in front of a dumb terminal with a modem.

SCENARIO #2 Suppose that you have full Internet access, and wish to get some compressed executable files from Microsoft's FTP site, which is running on Windows NT. Given proper access, would you be able to retrieve the files and if so, how?

Answer: Assuming that you have the proper access, you could get (download) the files with no problem. You would simply locate the files. Type binary to set the file transfer type and either use the mget or get commands.

SCENARIO #3 Suppose that you have full Internet access, and wish to get some compressed text files from Novell's FTP site, which is running on a UNIX-based system. Given proper access, would you be able to retrieve the files, and if so, how?

Answer: FTP is a standard protocol that is platform-independent. It does not matter what operating system the host is running. The only problem you may encouter is getting support for long filenames. However, this is not an issue in Windows NT. The process for retrieving the files is identical to the question above. You would simply locate the files, type binary to set the file transfer type, and either use the mget or get commands. It doesn't matter if the content is ASCII if the file is compressed. Until the file is decompressed, the file itself is still binary.

SCENARIO #4 A Windows FTP server is configured so that only an anonymous user (defined as Administrator instead of Guest) can access the server. The default access has been cleared from the home directory partition, and no other access has been assigned. What can the user see as an anonymous administrator?

Answer: Nothing. Despite the fact that the user is the equivalent of the administrator, the user is still blocked , and limited to the combined limits of both the FTP server security as well as system security. In this case, the FTP server is creating the limitation.

Chapter 11

Multiple-Choice Answers

1. Which MIBs are supported by Microsoft Windows NT?

A. Internet MIB II

B. Lan Manager MIB II

C. Microsoft WINS MIB

D. Microsoft LMHOSTS MIB

E. Microsoft DHCP MIB

Answers: A, B, C, and E

2. What does the Microsoft SNMP service use to resolve a host name to an IP address?

A. LMHOSTS

B. HOST

C. DNS

D. p-node broadcast

E. b-node broadcast

F. WINS

Answers: A, B, C, E, and F

3. What is the default community name?

A. Public1

B. Public

C. community

D. send agent

E. GetRequest

Answer: B

4. What is an MIB?

    A. An information base of errors

    B. An information base of packets sent to the default gateway

    C. A set of manageable objects representing device data

    D. A set of manageable objects representing network data

Answer: C

Scenario Solutions

SCENARIO #1 You want to add SNMP to your NT workstation, but you don't want just anybody getting in and changing your MIBs. What security option should you put in place to stop SNMP packets from being tweaked by unwanted visitors?

Answer: To specify security settings, choose the Security button to open the SNMP Security Configuration dialog box: Choose Only Accept SNMP Packets from These Hosts. If checked, this computer should accept packets only from hosts that have specific IP or IPX addresses, and the host name is in the associated box.

SCENARIO #2 You've decided to install TCP/IP on your NT server. You also want to add SNMP for monitoring purposes. How do you do this?

Answer: Select Control Panel ➢ Network ➢ Add software ➢ TCP/IP ➢ SNMP ➢ OK.

SCENARIO #3 The network manager has set up your NT workstation to respond to SNMP requests coming from an SNMP management system. While doing so, she told you all about the sort of stuff the management system will be requesting. What are the operations she told you will be requested by the SNMP management system?

Answer: The primary function of an SNMP agent is to perform the Get-Request, GetNextRequest, and SetRequest operations requested by a management system. An agent is any computer running SNMP agent software, typically a server or router.

Chapter 12

Multiple-Choice Answers

1. What TCP parameter do you set to control the size of the sliding window?

   A. DefaultTTL

   B. ForwardBufferMemory

   C. NumForwardPackets

   D. TcpWindowSize

   E. SizeWindowTcp

   Answer: D

2. What happens to your host if you set the window too small?

   A. It can cause delays in transmission and create a higher number of ACKs.

   B. It will cause improvement in transmission rates.

   C. It will cause a smaller number of ACKs.

   D. It can cause improvement in transmission and create a smaller number of ACKs.

   Answer: A

3. What happens to your host if you set the window too large?

   A. It can find packets that are lost.

   B. It can lose packets if routers become congested from too much data being transmitted.

   C. Your workstation will work faster from more data being received.

   D. Your workstation will work more slowly from more data being received.

   Answer: B

4. In what hive do you set the TcpWindowSize?

A. HKEY_LOCAL_MACHINE\SYSTEM\CurrentControlSet\Tcpip\Services\Parameters

B. HKEY_LOCAL_MACHINE\SYSTEM\SetControlCurrent\Services\Tcpip\Parameters

C. HKEY_LOCAL_MACHINE\SYSTEM\CurrentControlSet\Services\Tcpip\Parameters

D. HKEY_LOCAL_MACHINE\SYSTEM\CurrentControlSet\Parameters \Services\Tcpip

Answer: C

Scenario Solutions

SCENARIO # 1 Your workstation on the Microsoft TCP network seems to be working more slowly than when you first added TCP/IP onto it. After putting a network probe on the network, you see a lot of ACKs coming from your workstation. What could the problem be, and how can you fix it?

Answer: A sliding window that's too small can cause delays in transmission and create a higher frequency of ACK's. You can fix this by going to the hive and changing the TcpWindowSize parameter to a larger size.

SCENARIO #2 Your Microsoft NT workstation with TCP/IP has been running fine for the last couple of weeks. However, this morning you notice sluggish response time from the server, and people around you are complaining. When looking at the router you notice the utilization is over 80 percent of average. What could the problem be, and how can you fix it?

Answer: A window that is too large can result in lost packets because routers can become too congested when too much data is transmitted. You can fix this by going to the hive and changing the TcpWindowSize parameter to a smaller size.

Chapter 13

Multiple-Choice Answers

1. Which utility in TCP/IP communications is used to check connectivity between the Network Interface layer and the Internet Layer?

   A. ARP

   B. NETSTAT

   C. PING

   D. NBTSTAT

   Answer: C

2. What are two popular ways to troubleshoot a TCP/IP host problem?

   A. PING

   B. NETSTAT /a

   C. Establish a session

   D. NBSTAT /r

   Answers: A and C

3. What does NBTSTAT do?

   A. Verify that TCP/IP is configured correctly and that another host is available.

   B. Check the state of current NetBIOS over TCP/IP connections.

   C. Browse and edit the parameter configurations.

   D. View the ARP cache to detect invalid entries.

   Answer: B

Scenario Solutions

SCENARIO #1 Your Windows NT workstation cannot talk to a host in another building, but it works locally. Your co-workers' workstations are working fine. What is the troubleshooting step you should take?

Answer: Check your configuration. Either your subnet mask is incorrect or your default gateway is entered incorrectly.

SCENARIO #2 Your Windows NT workstation cannot talk on the network either locally or remotely. What are the troubleshooting steps you should take?

Answer: First ping your localhost address of 127.0.0.1. If you're successful, then ping your IP address. If that works, take a look at your configuration and check your subnet mask and default gateway.

SCENARIO #3 You have just installed TCP/IP and cannot ping hosts by their NetBIOS name on your network. Your IP address, subnet mask and default gateway are correct. What is the problem?

Answer: Either your resolution methods are not working (i.e. HOSTS file, LMHOSTS, WINS or DNS), or the remote host either doesn't have a NetBIOS name or is not functioning correctly.

SCENARIO #4 When pinging any host on your network you get a `request timed out` message. You check your configuration in the local host and your IP address is 201.89.57.37. Your subnet mask is 255.255.0.0 and your default gateway is 201.89.57.1. What is the problem?

Answer: The subnet mask is a Class B mask. Change the mask to 255.255.255.x.

SCENARIO #5 When starting your Windows NT hosts, the following message appears:

```
At least one service or driver failed during system
startup. Use Event Viewer to examine the event log for
details.
```

What could the problem be?

Answer: The TCP/IP protocol could be disabled. Check the bindings for TCP/IP, and the Event Viewer for more details.

SCENARIO #6 When attempting to connect to a server by its host name, you get the following message:

```
network path was not found
```

What could the problem be?

　Answer: The LMHOSTS file could contain incorrect entries. Change the LMHOSTS file, then use `nbstat -R` to clear the NetBIOS Name Cache.

SCENARIO #7 When trying to connect to a host on another network, you receive the following error message:

```
The network path was not found.
```

You can connect to all hosts on your local network. What is the problem?

　Answer: The default gateway is incorrectly configured on your host, or the router is down.

SCENARIO #8 You are copying large files from a server to your workstation and it is extremely slow. All other hosts are fine. What is the problem?

　Answer: Increase the size of the TcpWindowSize parameter. The TcpWindowSize is located in HKEY_LOCAL_MACHINE\System\CurrentControlSet\Services\Tcpip\Parameters.

Glossary

Abstract Syntax Representation, Revision #1 (ASN.1) A description of a data structure that is independent of machine-oriented structures and encodings.

Address In TCP/IP, an IP address is a 32-bit numeric identifier assigned to a node. The address has two parts, one for the network identifier and the other for the node identifier. All nodes on the same network must share the network address and have a unique node address. For networks connected to the Internet, network addresses are assigned by the Internet Activities Board (IAB).

Addresses also include IPX addresses—the internal network number and external network number—and the MAC address (Media Access Control) assigned to each network card or device.

Agents In the client-server model, the part of the system that performs information preparation and exchange on behalf of a client or server application.

ANSI (American National Standards Institute) A non-profit organization responsible for the ASCII (American Standard Code for Information Interchange) code set, as well as numerous other voluntary standards.

API (Application Program Interface) A set of routines that an application program uses to request and carry out lower-layer services performed by the operating system.

Application Layer The layer of the OSI model that interfaces with User mode applications by providing high-level network services based upon lower-level network layers. Network file systems like named pipes are an example of Application layer software. See *Named Pipes, Open Systems Interconnect Model, Application.*

Archie A program that helps Internet users find files. Participating Internet host computers download a listing of their files to Archie servers, which index these files. Users can then search this index and transfer these files using FTP. Archie functions as an Archive search utility, hence its name.

ARP (Address Resolution Protocol) IP address to hardware address translation protocol.

ARPANET (Advanced Research Projects Agency Network) A packet switched network developed in the early 1970s. The "grandfather" of today's Internet, ARPANET was decommissioned in June, 1990.

Asynchronous Data Transmission   A type of communication that sends data using flow control rather than a clock to synchronize data between the source and destination.

Autonomous System   Internet TCP/IP terminology for a collection of gateways (routers) that fall under one administrative entity and cooperate using common Interior Gateway Protocol (IGP).

Bandwidth   In network communications, the amount of data that can be sent across a wire in a given time. Each communication that passes along the wire decreases the amount of available bandwidth.

Batch Program   An ASCII file that contains one or more Windows NT commands. A batch program's filename has a BAT or CMD extension. When you type the filename at the command prompt, the commands are processed sequentially.

Binary   The numbering system used in computer memory and in digital communication. All characters are represented as a series of 1s and 0s. For example, the letter A might be represented as 01000001.

Binding   A process that establishes the initial communication channel between the protocol driver and the network adapter card driver.

Bits   In binary data, each unit of data is a bit. Each bit is represented by either 0 or 1, and is stored in memory as an ON or OFF state.

Boot Partition   The volume, formatted for either an NTFS, FAT, or HPFS file system, that contains the Windows NT operating system's files. Windows NT automatically creates the correct configuration and checks this information whenever you start your system.

Bridge   A device that connects two segments of a network and sends data to one or the other based on a set of criteria.

Browser   A computer on a Microsoft network that maintains a list of computers and services available on the network.

Browsing   The process of requesting the list of computers and services on a network from a browser.

Buffers   A reserved portion of memory in which data is temporarily held pending the opportunity to complete its transfer to or from a storage device or another location in memory.

CCITT (Consultative Committee on International Telegraphy and Telephony)   A committee, sponsored by the United Nations, that defines network standards, including X.400 and X.500. This committee has been recently renamed to International Telecommunications Union/Telecommunications Standardization Sector (ITU/TSS).

Checksum   A number that is calculated based on the values of a block of data. Checksums are used in communication to ensure that the correct data was received.

Circuit Switching   A type of communication system that establishes a connection, or circuit, between the two devices before communicating and does not disconnect until all data is sent.

Client   Any device that attaches to the network server. A workstation is the most common type of client. Clients run *client software* to provide network access. A piece of software that accesses data on a server can also be called a client.

Client/Server Network   A server-centric network in which some network resources are stored on a file server, while processing power is distributed among workstations and the file server.

Coaxial Cable   One of the types of cable used in network wiring. Typical coaxial types include RG-58 and RG-62. The 10base2 system of Ethernet networking uses coaxial cable. Coaxial cable is usually shielded. The Thicknet system uses a thicker coaxial cable.

Communication Protocol   For computers engaged in telecommunications, the protocol (i.e. the settings and standards) must be the same for both devices when receiving and transmitting information. A communications program can be used to ensure the baud rate, duplex, parity, data bits, and stop bits are correctly set.

Connectionless   The model of interconnection in which communication takes place without first establishing a connection. Sometimes called datagram. Examples: LANS, Internet IP and OSI CLNP, UDP, and ordinary postcards.

Connection-Oriented   The model of interconnection in which communication proceeds through three well-defined phases: connection establishment, data transfer, and connection releases. Examples: X.25, Internet TCP and OSI TP4, and registered letters.

Control Panel   Windows family utility containing management tools.

CRC (Cyclic Redundancy Checksum)   A redundancy check in which the check key is generated by a cyclic algorithm. Also, a system checking or error checking performed at both the sending and receiving station after a block check character has been accumulated.

CSMA/CD (Carrier Sense, Multiple Access with Collision Detect)   Different devices on a network may try to communicate at any one time, so access methods need to be established. Using the CSMA/CD access method, a device first checks that the cable is free from other carriers and then transmits, while continuing to monitor the presence of another carrier. If a collision is detected, the device stops transmitting and tries later. In a CSMA network with collision detection, all stations have the ability to sense traffic on the network.

CSNET   Computer+Science Network. A large computer network, mostly in the U.S. but with international connections. CSNET sites include universities, research labs, and some commercial companies. Now merged with BITNET to form CREN.

Daemon Program   A utility program that runs on a TCP/IP server. Daemon programs run in the background, performing services such as file transfers, printing, calculations, searches for information, and many other tasks. This is similar to a TSR program in DOS. Daemons are fully supported by UNIX, however.

DARPA (Defense Advanced Research Projects Agency)   The U.S. government agency that funded the ARPANET.

Data Frames   Logical, structured packets in which data can be placed. The Data Link layer packages raw bits from the Physical layer into data frames. The exact format of the frame used by the network depends on the topology.

Data Link Layer   The OSI layer that is responsible for data transfer across a single physical connection, or series of bridged connections, between two Network entities.

Data Packet   A unit of data being sent over a network. A packet includes a header, addressing information, and the data itself. A packet is treated as a single unit as it is sent from device to device.

Data Transfer Rate   The data transfer rate determines how fast a drive or other peripheral can transfer data with its controller. The data transfer rate is a key measurement in drive performance.

Datagram   A packet of information and associated delivery information, such as the destination address, that is routed through a packet-switching network.

Dedicated Line   A transmission medium that is used exclusively between two locations. Dedicated lines are also known as leased lines or private lines.

Default Gateway   IP uses the default gateway address when it cannot find the destination host on the local subnet. This is usually the router interface.

Device Driver   A piece of software that allows a workstation or server to communicate with a hardware device. For example, disk drivers are used to control disk drives, and network drivers are used to communicate with network boards.

DHCP   is a method of automatically assigning IP addresses to client computers on a network.

DOD Networking Model   A four layer conceptual model describing how communications should take place between computer systems. The four layers are Process/Application, Host-to-Host, Internet, and Network Access. DOD is the acronym for Department of Defense, the government agency that provided the original funding for the development of the TCP/IP protocol suite.

Domain   A logical grouping for file servers within a network, managed as an integrated whole.

Domain Controller   Primary server within a domain and primary storage point for domain-wide security information.

Domain Names   The name by which a domain is know to the network.

DNS (Domain Name System)   is the distributed name/address mechanism used in the Internet.

Dumb Terminal   A workstation consisting of a keyboard and a monitor used to put data into the computer or receive information from the computer. Dumb terminals were originally developed to be connected to computers running a multiuser operating system so that users could communicate directly with them. All processing is done at and by the computer, not the dumb terminal. In contrast, a smart terminal contains processing circuits that can receive data from the host computer and later carry out independent processing operations.

Error Control   An arrangement that combines error detection and error correction.

Error Correction   A method used to correct erroneous data produced during data transmission, transfer, or storage.

Ethernet   The most popular Data Link layer standard for local area networking. Ethernet implements the Carrier Sense Multiple Access with Collision Detection (CSMA/CD) method of arbitrating multiple computer access to the same network. This standard supports the use of Ethernet over any type of media including wireless broadcast. Standard Ethernet operates at 10Mbps per second. Fast Ethernet operates at 100Mbps. See *Data Link Layer*.

EGP   Exterior Gateway Protocol is a reachability routing protocol used by gateways in a two-level Iinternet. EGP is used in the Internet core system.

FDDI   A network specification that transmits information packets using light produced by a laser or light-emitting diode (LED). FDDI uses fiber-optic cable and equipment to transmit data packets. It has a data rate of up to 100Mbps and allows very long cable distances.

Frame   A data structure that network hardware devices use to transmit data between computers. Frames consist of the addresses of the sending and receiving computers, size information, and a check sum. Frames are envelopes around packets of data that allow them to be addressed to specific computers on a shared media network. See *Ethernet, Fiber Distributed Data Interface, Token Ring*.

FTP (File Transfer Protocol)   A TCP/IP protocol that permits the transferring of files between computer systems. Because FTP has been implemented on numerous types of computer systems, file transfers can be done between different computer systems (e.g., a personal computer and a minicomputer).

Full-Duplex   A method of transmitting information over an asynchronous communications channel, in which signals may be sent in both directions simultaneously. This technique makes the best use of line time but substantially increases the amount of logic required in the primary and secondary stations.

Gateway   In e-mail systems, a system used to send and receive e-mail from a different e-mail system, such as a mainframe or the Internet. Gateways are supported by Message Handling Services (MHS).

Gopher   An Internet tool that organizes topics into a menu system that users can employ to find information. Gopher also transparently connects users with the Internet server on which the information resides.

GOSIP   Government OSI Profile. A U.S Government procurement specification for OSI protocols.

Half-Duplex   A method of transmitting information over a communication channel, in which signals may be sent in both directions, but only one way at a time. This is sometimes referred to as local echo.

Handshaking   In network communication, a process used to verify that a connection has been established correctly. Devices send signals back and forth to establish parameters for communication.

Hardware Address   See *Mac Address*.

Hop   In routing, a server or router that is counted in a hop count.

Hop Count   The number of routers a message must pass through to reach its destination. A hop count is used to determine the most efficient network route.

Host   An addressable computer system on a TCP/IP network. Examples would include endpoint systems such as workstations, servers, minicomputers, mainframes, and immediate systems such as routers. A host is typically a system that offers resources to network nodes.

Host Name   A TCP/IP command that returns the local workstation's host name used for authentication by TCP/IP utilities. This value is the workstation's computer name by default, but it can be changed by using the Network icon in Control Panel.

Host Table   The HOSTS or LMHOSTS file that contains lists of known IP addresses.

Host-to-Host Layer   The DOD model layer that references to the Transport layer of the OSI model.

Hub   An Ethernet Data Link layer device that connects point-to-point Physical layer links, such as twisted pair or fiber optic cables, into a single shared media network. See *Data Link Layer, Ethernet*.

ICMP   Internet Control Message Protocol. A protocol at the Internet layer of the DOD model that sends messages between routers and other devices to let them know of congested routes.

IAB (Internet Activities Board)   The technical body that oversees the development of the Internet suite of protocols commonly referred to as TCP/IP. It has two task forces, the IRTF and the IETF, each charged with investigating a particular area.

IEEE (Institute of Electrical and Electronics Engineers)   A professional ANSI-accredited body of scientists and engineers based in the U.S. IEEE promotes standardization, and consults for the American National Standards Institute on matters relating to electrical and electronic development. the IEEE 802 Standards Committee is the leading official standard organization for LANs.

IESG (Internet Engineering Steering Group)   The executive committee of the IEFT.

IEFT (Internet Engineering Task force)   One of the task forces of the IAB. The IEFT is responsible for solving short-term engineering needs of the Internet. It has over 40 Working Groups.

IGP (Interior Gateway Protocol)   The protocol used to exchange routing information between collaborating routers on the Internet. RIP and OSPF are examples of IGPs.

Internet   A global network made up of a large number of individual networks interconnected through the use of TCP/IP protocols. The individual networks comprising the Internet are from colleges, universities, businesses, research organizations, government agencies, individuals, and other bodies. The governing body of this global network is the Internet Activities Board (IAB). When the term Internet is used with an upper-case "I," it refers to the global network, but with a lower-case "i," it simply means a group of interconnected networks.

Internet Address   A 32-bit value displayed in numbers that specifies a particular network and a particular node on that network.

Internet Layer   The layer in the DOD model that relates to the Network layer of the OSI model.

Internetwork Packet eXchange   The Network and Transport layer protocol developed by Novell for its NetWare product. IPX is a routable, connection-oriented protocol similar to TCP/IP but much easier to manage and with lower communication overhead. See *Internet Protocol, NetWare, Net-Ware Link*.

Internetworking   The process of connecting multiple local-area networks to form a wide-area network (WAN). Internetworking between different types of networks is handled by a *router*.

IP (Internet Protocol)   The Network layer protocol upon which the Internet is based. IP provides a simple connectionless packet exchange. Other protocols such as UDP or TCP use IP to perform their connection-oriented or guaranteed delivery services. See *Transmission Control Protocol/Internet Protocol, Internet*.

IP Address   A four-byte number that uniquely identifies a computer on an IP internetwork. InterNIC assigns the first bytes of Internet IP addresses and administers them in hierarchies. Huge organizations like the government or top-level ISPs have class A addresses, large organizations and most ISPs have class B addresses, and small companies have class C addresses. In a class A address, InterNIC assigns the first byte, and the owning organization assigns the remaining three bytes. In a class B address, InterNIC or the higher level ISP assigns the first two bytes, and the organization assigns the remaining two bytes. In a class C address, InterNIC or the higher level ISP assigns the first three bytes, and the organization assigns the remaining byte. Organizations not attached to the Internet can assign IP addresses as they please. See *Internet Protocol, Internet*.

IPTUNNEL   A software driver that permits the encapsulation of IPX packets inside of IP packets for transmission over an IP network. This allows NetWare servers to communicate through links that support only TCP/IP, such as UNIX machines.

IPX External Network Number   A number that is used to represent an entire network. All servers on the network must use the same external network number.

IPX Internal Network Number   A number that uniquely identifies a server to the network. Each server must have a different internal network number.

IRTF (Internet Research Task Force)   One of the task forces of the IAB. The group responsible for research and development of the Internet protocol suite.

ISDN (Integrated Services Digital Network)   A new network standard that allows high-speed communication over ordinary category 3 or 5 copper cabling. It may someday replace conventional phone systems with high-speed, digital lines.

ISO (International Standards Organization)   A world-wide federation of national standards bodies whose objective is to promote the development of standardization and related activities in over 90 countries, with a view to facilitating international exchange of goods and services.

LAN (Local Area Network)   A network that is restricted to a local area—a single building, group of buildings, or even a single room. A LAN often has only one server, but can have many if desired.

LPC (Local Procedure Call)   A mechanism that loops remote procedure calls without the presence of a network so that the client and server portion of an application can reside on the same machine. Local procedure calls look like remote procedure calls (RPCs) to the client and server sides of a distributed application. See *Remote Procedure Calls*.

MAC (Media Access Control) Address   The Hardware address burned into the Network Interface Cards. The MAC address is six bytes long, three given to the manufacturer from the IEEE, and three bytes designated by the manufacturer.

Mailslots   A connectionless messaging IPC mechanism that Windows NT uses for browse request and logon authentication. See *Interprocess Communications*.

MAN (Metropolitan Area Network)   A network spanning a single city or metropolitan area. A MAN is larger than local area networks (LANs), which are normally restricted to a single building or neighboring buildings, but smaller than wide area networks (WANs), which can span the entire globe. The term MAN is rarely actually used outside of Novell education.

Maps   To translate one value into another.

Master Browser   The computer on a network that maintains a list of computers and services available on the network and distributes the list to other browsers. The Master Browser may also promote potential browsers to be browsers. See *Browser, Browsing, Potential Browser, Backup Browser*.

Message Switching   A type of network communication that sends an entire *message*, or block of data, rather than a simple packet.

MIB (Management Information Base)   The entire set of objects that any service or protocol uses in SNMP. Because different network-management services are used for different types of devices or for different network-management protocols, each service has its own set of objects.

MILNET (MILitary NETwork)   Originally part of the ARPANET, MILNET was partitioned in 1984 to make it possible for military installations to have reliable network service, while the ARPANET continued to be used for research.

Modem   A device used to convert the digital signals produced by a computer into the analog signals required by analog telephone lines, and vice-versa. This process of conversion allows computers to communicate across telephone lines.

Multihomed Host   A computer connected to more than one physical data link. The data links may or may not be attached to the same network.

Multilink   A capability of RAS to combine multiple data streams into one network connection for the purpose of using more than one modem or ISDN channel in a single connection. This feature is new to Windows NT 4.0. See *Remote Access Service*.

Named Pipes   An interprocess communication mechanism that is implemented as a file system service, allowing programs to be modified to run on it without using a proprietary application programming interface. Named pipes were developed to support more robust client/server communications than those allowed by the simpler NetBIOS. See *OS/2, File Systems, Interprocess Communications*.

NetBEUI (Network Basic Input/Output System Extended User Interface)   The primary local area network transport protocol in Windows NT. A simple Network layer transport developed to support NetBIOS installations. NetBEUI is not routable, and so it is not appropriate for larger networks. NetBEUI is the fastest transport protocol available for Windows NT.

NetBIOS   A client/server interprocess communication service developed by IBM in the early 1980s. NetBIOS presents a relatively primitive mechanism for communication in client server/applications, but its widespread acceptance and availability across most operating systems makes it a logical choice for simple network applications. Many Windows NT network IPC mechanisms are implemented over NetBIOS.

NetBT (NetBIOS over TCP/IP)   A network service that implements the NetBIOS IPC over the TCP/IP protocol stack. See *Network Basic Input/ Output System, Interprocess Communications, Transmission Control Protocol/Internet Protocol.*

Network Address   A unique address that identifies each node, or device, on the network. The network address is generally hard-coded into the network card on both the workstation and server. Some network cards allow you to change this address, but there is seldom a reason to do so.

Network Layer   The layer of the OSI model that creates a communication path between two computers via routed packets. Transport protocols implement both the Network layer and the Transport layer of the OSI stack. IP is a Network layer service.

NFS (Network File System)   A distributed file system developed by Sun Microsystems which allows a set of computers to cooperatively access each other's files in a transparent manner.

NIC (Network Information Center)   Originally there was only one, located at SRI International and tasked to serve the ARPANET (and later DDN) community. Today, there are many NICs operated by local, regional, and national networks all over the world. Such centers provide user assistance, document service, training and much more.

NIC (Network Interface Card)   Physical devices that connect computers and other network equipment to the transmission medium used. When installed in a computer's expansion bus slot, an NIC allows the computer to become a workstation on the network.

Node   In TCP/IP, an IP-addressable computer system, such as workstations, servers, minicomputers, mainframes, and routers. In IPX networks, the term is usually applied to nonserver devices: workstations and printers.

NOS (Network Operating System)   The software that runs on a file server and offers file, print, and other servers to client workstations. Windows NT Server 4.0 is a NOS. Other examples include NetWare, Banyan VINES, and IBM LAN Server.

Octets   A set of 8 bits or 1 byte.

OSI (Open System Interconnection)   A model defined by the ISO to conceptually organize the process of communication between computers in terms of seven layers, called protocol stacks. The seven layers of the OSI model provide a way for you to understand how communication across various protocols takes place.

OSPF (Open Shortest Path First)   A proposed standard, IGP for the Internet.

Packet   The basic division of data sent over a network. Each packet contains a set amount of data along with a header, containing information about the type of packet and the network address to which it is being sent. The size and format of packets depends on the *protocol* and frame types used.

Packet Switching   A type of data transmission in which data is divided into packets, each of which has a destination address. Each packet is then routed across a network in an optimal fashion. An addressed packet may travel a different route than packets related to it. Packet sequence numbers are used at the destination node to reassemble related packets.

Packets   A unit of information transmitted as a whole from one device to another on a network.

PDC (Primary Domain Controller)   The domain server that contains the master copy of the security, computer, and user accounts databases and that can authenticate workstations. The primary domain controller can replicate its databases to one or more backup domain controllers and is usually also the Master browser for the domain.

Peer-to-Peer Communication   A networked computer that both shares resources with other computers and accesses the shared resources of other computers.

Peer-to-Peer Network   A local area network in which network resources are shared among workstations, without a file server.

Physical Layer   The cables, connectors, and connection ports of a network. The passive physical components required to create a network.

Ping (Packet Internet Groper)   A packet used to test reachability of destinations by sending them an ACMP echo request and waiting for a reply. The term is used as a verb: "Ping host A to see if it is up."

Polling   The process by which a computer periodically asks each terminal or device on a LAN if it has a message to send, and then allows each to send data in turn. One multipoint connection or a point-to-point connection, polling is the process whereby data stations are invited one at a time to transmit.

Potential Browser   A computer on a network that may maintain a list of other computers and services on the network if requested to do so by a Master browser.

PPP (Point-to-Point Protocol)   This protocol allows the sending of IP packets on a dial-up (serial) connection. Supports compression and IP address negotiation.

Presentation Layer   The layer of the OSI model that converts and translates, if necessary, information between the Session and Application layers.

Process/Application Layer   The upper layer in the DOD model that refers to the Application, Presentation, and Session layers of the OSI model.

Protocol Suite   A collection of protocols that are associated with and that implement a particular communication model (such as the DOD Networking Model, or the OSI Reference Model).

PSTN (Public Switched Telephone Network)   A global network of interconnected digital and analog communication links originally designed to support voice communication between any two points in the world but quickly adapted to handle digital data traffic when the computer revolution occurred. In addition to its traditional voice support role, the PSTN now functions as the Physical layer of the Internet by providing dial-up and leased lines for private, exclusive use.

RARP   The TCP/IP protocol that allows a computer that has a Physical layer address (such as an Ethernet address) but does not have an IP address to request a numeric IP address from another computer on the network.

Registry   Windows NT combined configuration database.

Request for Comments   The set of standards defining the Internet protocols as determined by the Internet Engineering Task Force and available in the public domain on the Internet. RFCs define the functions and services provided by each of the many Internet protocols. Compliance with the RFCs guarantees cross-vendor compatibility.

RIP (Routing Information Protocol)   A distance-vector routing protocol used on many TCP/IP internetworks and IPX networks. The distance vector algorithm uses a "fewest-hops" routing calculation method.

Router   a) A device that connects two dissimilar networks, and allows packets to be transmitted and received between them. b) A connection between two networks that specifies message paths and may perform other functions, such as data compression.

Serial   A method of communication that transfers data across a medium one bit at a time, usually adding stop, start, and check bits to ensure quality transfer.

Session Layer   The layer of the OSI model dedicated to maintaining a bidirectional communication connection between two computers. The Session layer uses the services of the Transport layer to provide this service.

Simple Network Management Protocol (SNMP)   A management protocol used on many networks, particularly TCP/IP. It defines the type, format, and retrieval of management information of nodes.

Simplex   Data transmission in one direction only.

SLIP (Serial Line Internet Protocol)   An implementation of the IP protocol over serial lines. SLIP has been obviated by PPP.

SMTP (Simple Mail Transport Protocol)   The Internet electronic mail protocol. Defined in RFC 821, with associated message format description in RFC 822.

Start Bit   A bit that is sent as part of a serial communication stream to signal the beginning of a byte or packet.

Stop Bit   A bit that is sent as part of a serial communication stream to signal the end of a byte or packet.

Subnet Mask   Under TCP/IP, 32-bit values that allow the recipient of IP packets to distinguish the network ID portion of the IP address from the network ID portion of the IP address from the host ID.

Switched Line   A communications link for which the physical path may vary with each usage, such as the public telephone network.

Synchronous   Pertaining to two or more processes that depend upon the occurrence of a specific event such as a common timing signal.

TCP   A Transport layer protocol that implements guaranteed packet delivery using the Internet Protocol (IP).

TCP/IP (Transmission Control Protocol /Internet Protocol)   Generally used as shorthand for the phrase "TCP/IP protocol suite."

Telnet   A TCP/IP terminal emulation protocol that permits a node, called the Telnet client, to login to a remote node, called the Telnet server. The client simply acts as a dumb terminal, displaying output from the server. The processing is done at the server.

Terminal Emulation   The process of emulating a terminal, or allowing a PC to act as a terminal for a mainframe or UNIX system.

Token-Passing   see *Token Ring*.

Token Ring   The second most popular Data Link layer standard for local area networking. Token Ring implements the token passing method of arbitrating multiple-computer access to the same network. Token Ring operates at either 4 or 16Mbps. FDDI is similar to Token Ring and operates at 100Mbps. See *Data Link Layer*.

Transport Layer   The OSI model layer responsible for the guaranteed serial delivery of packets between two computers over an internetwork. TCP is the Transport layer protocol for the TCP/IP transport protocol.

Transport Protocol   A service that delivers discrete packets of information between any two computers in a network. Higher level connection-oriented services are built upon transport protocols.

UDP (User Datagram Protocol)   UDP uses a connectionless, unguaranteed packet delivery method. It resides at the Host-to-Host layer of the DOD Networking Model, and is used in IP networking. It is far faster than TCP because it doesn't have flow-control overhead. UDP can be implemented as a reliable transport when some higher level protocol (such as NetBIOS) exists to make sure that required data will eventually be retransmitted in local area environments.

UNC (Universal Naming Convention)   A multivendor, multiplatform convention for identifying shared resources on a network.

UNIX   A multitasking operating system, created by AT&T's Bell Labs, that is used on a wide variety of computers including Internet servers.

UseNet   A massive distributed database of news feeds and special interest groups maintained on the Internet and accessible through most Web browsers.

WAN (Wide Area Network)   A network that extends across multiple locations. Each location typically has a local area network (LAN), and the LANs are connected together in a WAN. Typically used for enterprise networking.

WINS (Windows Internet Name Service)   A network service for Microsoft networks that provides Windows computers with Internet numbers for specified NetBIOS names, facilitating browsing and intercommunication over TCP/IP networks.

WWW (World Wide Web)   A term used for the collection of computers on the Internet running HTTP (hypertext transfer protocol) servers. The WWW allows for text and graphics to have hyperlinks connecting users to other servers. Using a Web "browser" such as Netscape or Mosaic, a user can crosslink from one server to another at the click of a button.

Index

C

X

Z

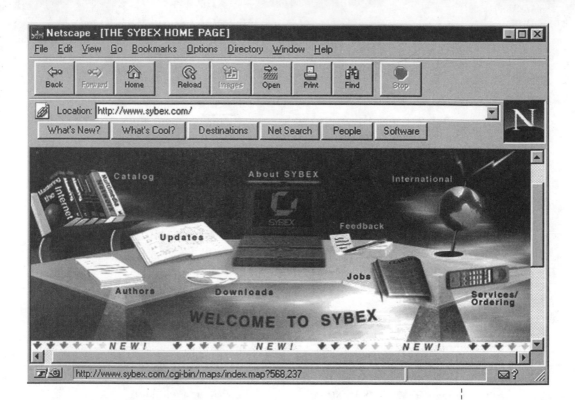